RELIGION AND PUBLIC EDUCATION

Edited by
Theodore R. Sizer

UNIVERSITY
PRESS OF
AMERICA

University Press of America, Inc.

P.O. Box 19101, Washington, D.C. 20036

ISBN: 0-8191-2001-4 (Perfect)

ISBN: 0-8191-2000-6 (Cloth)

Printed in the United States of America

Reprinted by arrangement with Houghton Mifflin Company

Library of Congress Catalog Card Number: 80-6223

CONTRIBUTORS

Nicholas Wolterstorff

George R. La Noue

Arthur Gilbert

Frederick A. Olafson

Harvey G. Cox

Samuel H. Miller

William D. Geer, Jr.

Theodore Powell

William B. Ball

Lawrence Kohlberg

Fred M. Newmann

Donald W. Oliver

Neil G. McCluskey, S.J.

Talcott Parsons

Eugene B. Borowitz

Max L. Stackhouse

William Lynch, S.J.

Paul H. Hirst

Contents

PART TWO

Challenges to Our Educational System

PART THREE

Secularism, Pluralism, and Religion in Our Society

PART FOUR

Theological Perspectives on Public Education

PART FIVE

The Concept of the Religiously Neutral School

About the Authors

NICHOLAS WOLTERSTORFF, Professor of Philosophy at Calvin College, Grand Rapids, Michigan, has also taught at Yale University, Haverford College, and the University of Chicago. He is the author of *Religion and the Schools*, has contributed to *The Encyclopedia of Philosophy*, and has published articles in various anthologies, periodicals, and professional journals.

GEORGE R. LA NOUE, Assistant Professor of Government and Education, Teachers College, Columbia University, is a member of the national church-state committee of the American Civil Liberties Union and a member of the Commission on Religious Liberty of the National Council of Churches. He is the author of *The Politics of Church and State*.

RABBI ARTHUR GILBERT has served since 1965 as Director, National Department of Religious Curriculum Research, Anti-Defamation League of B'nai B'rith. From 1960 to 1965 he was Director, Project Religious Freedom and Public Affairs, National Conference of Christians and Jews. He is the author of *A Jew in Christian America* and co-author with a priest and minister of an inter-faith Bible commentary and reader. Rabbi Gilbert is a member of the editorial boards of the *Journal of Ecumenical Studies* (Duquesne University Press), Villanova Law School's *Religion and the Public Order*, and the Jewish publication *The Reconstructionist*. He is Vice-President of the New York Chapter of the Religious Education Association.

FREDERICK A. OLAFSON, Professor of Education and Philosophy at Harvard University since 1964, has taught previously at Princeton, Johns Hopkins, and Vassar. His principal interests are in ethics and social philosophy and in the history of modern philosophy. His published works include *Society, Law and Morality* and *Principles and Persons: An Ethical Interpretation of Existentialism*. He has also contributed many articles to philosophical journals and other types of periodicals.

HARVEY G. COX, Associate Professor of Church and Society at Harvard Divinity School, is an ordained minister of the Baptist Church and has served as Director of Religious Activities at Oberlin College, Program Associate for the American Baptist Home Mission Society, worker for the Gossner Mission in West Berlin, and Assistant Professor of Theology and Culture at Andover Newton Theological School, Newton Centre, Massachusetts. He is a member of many organizations and is Chairman of the Board of the Blue Hill Christian Center, Vice-President of the Massachusetts Chapter of the Americans for Democratic Action, and co-director of the Center for the Study of Religion and Social Issues at Woods Hole, Massachusetts. Dr. Cox is the author of *The Secular City* and of articles in *Commonweal, Christianity and Crisis, Harper's, Redbook, The Christian Century, Motive, Christian Scholar,* and *Junge Kirche.*

SAMUEL H. MILLER, Dean of the Harvard Divinity School and John Lord O'Brian Professor of Divinity since 1959, formerly taught at Andover Newton Theological School, Newton Centre, Massachusetts, and was pastor of Old Cambridge Baptist Church, Cambridge, Massachusetts, from 1935 to 1959. A trustee of the Northfield (Massachusetts) Schools, he has also served on the boards of directors of the Academy of Religion and Mental Health and the Institute of Pastoral Care. He is the author of a number of books, including *The Life of the Soul, The Great Realities,* and *The Dilemma of Modern Belief.*

WILLIAM D. GEER, JR., Principal of Newton South High School, Newton Centre, Massachusetts, since 1965, came to that position from the Lawrenceville School, Lawrenceville, New Jersey, where he was an English teacher and house master. While at Lawrenceville he worked in the Lawrenceville-Rutgers Summer School and created a cooperative program involving Lawrenceville, the Trenton School system, Rutgers University, and a Trenton high school.

THEODORE POWELL, Executive Secretary, Connecticut State Board for Regional Community Colleges since 1965, was formerly staff consultant to the Connecticut Study Commission on Higher Education. He has taught history at the University of Hartford evening college and has lectured at various institutions, including Notre Dame, Princeton, and the University of Michigan. He has served as consultant to the National Conference of Christians and Jews, the American Jewish Committee, and the National Council of Churches of Christ. For the NCCJ, he produced, wrote, and narrated the film *Buses and Ballots.* His many writings include contributions to the "Education Supplement" of the *Saturday Review,* the *NEA Journal, PTA Magazine, Religious Education,* and *Religion and the Public Order.* His books include *The School Bus Law, The Long Rescue,* and *Democracy in Action.*

WILLIAM B. BALL, General Counsel, Pennsylvania Catholic Conference, was formerly a professor of constitutional law (Villanova University Law School) and a corporation attorney. A member of the bars of New York, Pennsylvania, and of the U.S. Supreme Court, he has represented clients in litigation in the church-state, civil liberties, and civil rights areas. He has written extensively on constitutional law problems for legal periodicals and has contributed articles to *Saturday Review, Commonweal, Teachers College Record, Catholic World,* and *America.* In 1961 he was the principal author of the National Catholic Welfare Conference's legal study on federal aid to education. A member of the American Law Institute, he serves on the boards of directors of the National Catholic Social Action Conference, the St. Thomas More Institute for Legal Research, and Our Lady of Angels College. He has received honorary degrees from the Catholic University of America and St. Francis College.

LAWRENCE KOHLBERG, Associate Professor of Psychology and Human Development, University of Chicago, was previously Assistant Professor of Child Psychology at Yale University and a fellow at the Center for Advanced Study in the Behavioral Sciences, Palo Alto, California. He is currently writing a book summarizing the results of a ten-year longitudinal study on the development of moral ideology and character, a topic on which he has also written three articles and three book chapters. Another area of Dr. Kohlberg's interest and research is psychosexual and cognitive development in children.

FRED M. NEWMANN, Assistant Professor of Education at Harvard University, specializes in curriculum development and research in secondary-school social studies. Former positions of his include those of high-school teacher, supervisor of practice teaching, and writer of programmed instruction. Dr. Newmann has conducted research on adolescent attitudes toward political authority, and he is currently co-director, with Donald W. Oliver, of the Harvard Social Studies Project and editor of a series of case material on the analysis of public controversy (forthcoming). He is the author of several articles in professional journals.

DONALD W. OLIVER, Professor of Education at Harvard, has done his major work in the area of social studies curriculum development and evaluation. He has conducted research on methods of evaluating social studies through the analysis of oral dialogue, and, with Fred M. Newmann, is now directing the Harvard Social Studies Project and editing a forthcoming series of case materials on the analysis of public controversy. Dr. Oliver is co-author (with James P. Shaver) of *Teaching Public Issues in the High School.*

NEIL G. McCLUSKEY, S.J., Visiting Professor of Education at the University of Notre Dame, had the same title in 1966 at Columbia University Teachers College and has also taught at Seattle University and Gonzaga University, Spokane. At the latter institution he was successively Dean of the School of Education, Director of the Honors Program, and Academic Vice-President. For the past ten years he has served on the Editorial Committee of *Religious Education,* and he is also a member of the Board of Directors of the Religious Education Association. Between 1955 and 1961 he was Education Editor of the Jesuit weekly, *America.* Father McCluskey is the author of two books, *Public Schools and Moral Education* and *Catholic Viewpoint on Education,* and editor of *Catholic Education in America: A Documentary Study.* He has also contributed chapters to eleven books on education, and his published articles are to be found in some thirty journals, magazines, and encyclopedias here and abroad.

TALCOTT PARSONS is Professor of Sociology at Harvard University where he has taught for many years, serving as Chairman of the Department of Social Relations for its first decade, 1946–1956. He is best known for his authorship of numerous articles in academic journals and symposia and for authorship or co-authorship of a number of books, including *Structure of Social Action; The Social System; Toward a General Theory of Action; Essays in Sociological Theory; Family, Socialization and Interaction Process; Economy and Society; Theories of Society;* and, most recently, *Societies: Comparative and Evolutionary Perspectives.*

RABBI EUGENE BOROWITZ, Professor of Education and Jewish Religious Thought at the New York School of the Hebrew Union College–Jewish Institute of Religion, also serves as Visiting Professor of Religion at Princeton University. He has held similar appointments at Columbia University Teachers College and Temple University and was formerly National Director of Education for Reform Judaism. Rabbi Borowitz has contributed a column on current theological literature to the quarterly *Judaism* and annually summarizes recent books on religious philosophy for the Central Conference of American Rabbis' *Journal.* He is author of *A Layman's Introduction to Religious Existentialism* and numerous articles on theology and education.

MAX L. STACKHOUSE, Assistant Professor of Christian Ethics at Andover Newton Theological School, Newton Centre, Massachusetts, graduated from Harvard in 1965. He was Lecturer in Ethics at Harvard Divinity School and a fellow of the Harvard-M.I.T. Joint Center for Urban Studies before accepting his present post. Dr. Stackhouse is active in several church, ecumenical, and social action groups. His essays have appeared in *The Secular City Debate, Voluntary Associations, New Theology No. 4,* and in professional and church journals.

WILLIAM F. LYNCH, S.J., writer in residence at St. Peter's College, Jersey City, since 1962, was director of the honors program at Georgetown University from 1958 to 1962 and editor of the national quarterly *Thought* from 1950 to 1956. He is the author of *Christ and Apollo, The Image Industries, The Integrating Mind, Images of Hope, An Approach to the Metaphysics of Plato through the Parmenides,* and co-editor of *The*

Idea of Catholicism. Father Lynch is particularly interested in the relation of theology to the secular world and is currently writing a book on the relation between the religious imagination and the secular imagination.

PAUL H. HIRST, Professor of Education at King's College, University of London, since 1965, where he teaches philosophy of education, has previously held appointments at Oxford University and the University of London Institute of Education. Before turning his primary interest to philosophy, he spent seven years teaching mathematics. He has published papers on moral and religious education in the *British Journal of Educational Studies* and the *Hibbert Journal* and has contributed to several volumes of essays on the philosophy of education, including *Philosophy and Education,* edited by Israel Scheffler; *Philosophical Analysis and Education,* edited by R. D. Archambault; and *The Concept of Education,* edited by R. S. Peters. He is secretary of the newly formed Philosophy of Education Society of Great Britain.

Introduction

Few issues in American society have been argued more irrelevantly and more misleadingly than that of the place of religion in public schooling. Few issues have been argued for so long or so passionately. And few issues have come to so little resolution.

The reasons for this are not hard to find, as the issue is really a tangle of threads which cross the traditional lines of inquiry — legal or constitutional, philosophical, theological, historical, psychological, social. Students of the problem have often looked at it in only one way — the constitutional, for example — and have all too quickly reached conclusions from that vantage point alone. The results, not surprisingly, have been uneven.

This volume is an attempt to improve these results and thus our understanding of the significant contemporary relationship of religion and schooling. The essays and the Conference on the Role of Religion in Public Education at which they were discussed were the idea of Herold Hunt, Arthur Gilbert, and Theodore Powell, who, serving together on committees of the National Conference of Christians and Jews, had long been dissatisfied with the level of discussion of the issue. They suggested a broadly defined review of the problem. The National Conference allocated the principal funds for the conference and book and representatives of the Harvard Graduate School of Education, the Harvard Divinity School, and Houghton Mifflin Company joined in the planning. Roland Barth served ably as executive officer for the group.

All the papers save those by Paul Hirst and Max Stackhouse were prepared before the conference held at Cambridge in May of 1966 and were the subjects of discussion by the eighty participants (whose names appear on pp. 347–350). The papers were then revised by their authors and appear in this present final form. In no true sense am I their "editor": the conference served as such. My role has been solely as convener and provoker.

In the context of the public schools, what *is* "religion"? In the legal sense, it has most often meant sectarian teaching, the presentation to children of positions drawn from particular sectarian traditions which they are expected to accept on faith. This latter part of the definition is crucial, as most public schools, particularly in history and literature classes, present religious information, that is, ideas and forms that are a part of our culture and other cultures. However, these are not sets of ideas that children are asked to believe, to accept, but rather ones they are expected to understand in the context of the study of a culture. (Rarely, though, do teachers systematically make this distinction for children; rarely do schools consider teaching children criteria for making decisions of understanding, on one hand, and belief, on the other; and rarely do they consider the impact on children's beliefs of the teaching of religious forms for an understanding of a culture, and, more importantly, the impact of this teaching on their attitudes toward belief.) In some contexts, then, "religion" in schools has meant teaching for belief, for inculcation, for conversion — if that is not too strong a word these days. The teaching of religion so defined and in its most extreme forms has been constitutionally prohibited in this country. It has been tolerated in its less extreme forms and in special ways for most of our history, a point I shall take up separately later.

"Religion" defined as information about people's differing beliefs is frequently taught in public schools, though almost always with as little public notice as possible and as part of another subject. Such teaching tends to be sloppy and incomplete, for few social studies and English teachers are properly prepared to teach it and the different religious traditions come to students' attention only if they have a place in some larger topic. The formal study of Roman Catholicism for more than a few Protestant and Jewish children may be limited, for example, to the Church at the time of the Reformation. Or Protestantism may appear only as a study of sects such as the Shakers. Or Jewish traditions may be seen only in the context of the early twentieth-century East European immigration to the United States.

Those who see "religion" in public schooling as the giving of information *about* religion would have thorough courses in comparative religion offered. Although the legality of such courses has not, to my knowledge, been tested, I doubt whether they would run afoul of the courts. The problems with them are that their organizers often fail to recognize that many children do "believe," and thus have more than intellectual feelings about the material, and that their teachers rarely face up to the issue of how one acquires criteria for selecting among them (or discarding them all). Most children, after all, are far less interested in religions as cultural phenomena than as explanations and directions for their own lives. If one talks with students who have taken, usually in independent schools, apparently "successful" courses, one finds these courses most often to have dealt primarily with the students themselves and with religion as belief and not with the doctrines of sects. They have not been as narrowly taught as was described above in my first definition of religion as belief; but they are surely concerned with criteria for choice of a religious way of life. In this sense they raise again a possible constitutional objection. They also raise another intriguing possibility: What if the study of criteria leads some youngster to disavow the dominant tradition of his family? A properly taught course would surely cause this to happen in more than a few cases. Is it the function of the school so to do?

There are those who would protest at this point that a distinction must be made between "religion" and "philosophy" and that the search for "criteria" just mentioned is really a philosophical journey calling upon the discourse of logic and metaphysics. Religion, they argue, has its own discourse and must be so taught. Too, this is a different formulation from the first definition above, in which religion was construed as inculcation. It is rather the development of a sensitivity to religious problems, a sensitivity more than the purely intellectual of the philosophical realm. Krister Stendahl has called it "sophistication and sensibility," which presumably comes from both a knowledge of traditional religious forms and the humility derived from groping toward unseen and unseeable absolutes. In my first construal, the child is directly taught a belief, and in my second, he is taught a variety of beliefs and some means of perhaps choosing among them, but here the student is readied, made aware of the religious dimension of life, which, so the argument goes, is a significant aspect of being human.

How such teaching is to be done in a public school baffles the imagination; indeed, perhaps the public school — or, rather, any institution of "formal" education — is a poor place to attempt it. (The constitutional issue might arise here, too.) Further, the shape of such "awareness" is hard to define and accordingly is difficult to teach. However, it provokes a final definition of "religion" as something having a psychological dimension. One can construe "religion" as a person's *Weltanschauung*, the way he sees reality and his place in it. Every man tries to explain his presence, his birth and the question of his death; in this explanation, the argument runs, is his religion found. When groups of men evolve similar explanations, these are called formal "religions." Presumably schoolmen wish to help children find their places in life; accordingly we should make sure they ask the right questions of reality and unreality ("Who am I? Where am I going? Why does what happens happen?") and counsel them to find explanations that put them at peace with themselves and with the world. The child fits his religion to himself; he is not fitted to the religion. The school raises issues and supports the child in his search for answers. It does not give answers, and if the child remains baffled, the school lives with the situation and does not interfere with a scheme based on the first conception of religion presented above.

This construal of "religion" is probably the most commonly accepted and practiced. The child's first brush with philosophical issues often comes in the public school, and the school helps the child to recognize them as issues. Much of the so-called guidance movement is based on this notion of "help": in spite of the authoritarian label "guidance," counselors are trained at least to assist children to make their own decisions — if less about the choice of a college, more about conduct and their place in the world. For some, then, religious teaching in public school should be primarily "helping" and in virtually no sense the giving of information or the explicit development of a religious sensitivity.

I have deliberately sketched out four extreme positions less to shed light on the broad question than to show the varied ways in which religion in schooling is construed. One must consider them all in some form or one will miss the point — as most of the legal church-state decisions in education have done.

Two questions remain: Why teach "religion" — however construed — at all? And why do we worry so much about the matter today? The former is easily answered: Religion as sect, or as metaphysics, or as a kind of sensitivity, or as psychological adjustment, or all bundled confusedly together is in the mind of every man and of his child. No one can teach anything and stay away from it because it touches all that man has done (and that, of course, is what schools, arrogantly I suppose, exclusively teach about). To be honest with ourselves, we should examine the "religion" we do teach and that which we might and should teach.

The present concern is also relatively easy to explain. Nineteenth-century Americans, when they went to school, attended supposedly secular common schools, which can be more accurately described as liberal Protestant schools. Scuffle though educators and churchmen might, there was a vague consensus on the part of the majority of Americans of how doctrinaire the schools should be; and the Roman Catholic Baltimore decrees in the 1880's suggest the extent of Protestant domination. But nineteenth-century America *was* Protestant, and its Jeffersonian definition of church-state divisions was a Protestant definition. Further, most nineteenth-century Americans, the religious enthusiasms of the age notwithstanding, really didn't care.

Twentieth-century immigration and the rapid growth of Catholic parochial schools (and, more recently, of Jewish day schools) changed this state of affairs. Catholics, drawing from the economically poorer sectors of society, looked longingly at tax monies for their schools. From the 1920's on, the debate over aid to education was constantly divided by the Catholic demand — which was increasingly insistent as the low quality of parochial schools became more apparent. When by the 1950's about 15 per cent of American school children were in financially unstable Catholic schools, the national necessity for some resolution was obvious. The Elementary and Secondary Education Act of 1965 was an adroit political and religious compromise (though there had been other minor ones earlier) and came at a time of general ecumenical spirit. The debate about the Act and now the debate in local communities raises sharply and in a somewhat altered form the question of "why religion" and "what religion" in the public — as well as the private — schools. Clearly this is a time of important turning for religion and education in the United States.

The essays in this book are devoted to explaining this turning in useful ways. They deliberately take different approaches and perspectives and run a broad ideological spectrum. There is a significant distance, for example, between the Borowitz and Powell essays, or between those of Newmann and Oliver and of Geer. What emerges is a variety of points of view, and such common emphases as evolve are collected in Paul Hirst's concluding essay. The three sponsoring groups — the Faculties of Education and of Divinity at Harvard and the National Conference of Christians and Jews — hope only that the volume will both spark and deepen the present debate on religion in public education.

THEODORE R. SIZER

Dean of the Faculty of Education
Harvard University

Preface to the Second Edition

The fifteen years that intervene between the conference at which the following papers were presented and the present moment have reflected no diminution of the importance of the topic of "religion and public education": The uneasy fault line between religion and public life in America still shifts and persists with its old and familiar dangers.

Unhappily, however, the optimism of the mid-'60s, well reflected in the following chapters, with its ecumenism and belief in the power of schools, has today thinned out. The hoped-for new sensibleness and sensibility about religion in the public schools have not been achieved. While there have been new court decisions on where the division between "religion" and "public education" must be drawn, none of these has broken really new ground. There have been new efforts at revising or creating religiously-oriented private schools, most notably the so-called Christian academies that appeared in some numbers in the late '70s, but the percentage of school-aged children served in the non-public sector has nonetheless hovered consistently at the 10-15% mark. No significant new public school curricular or publishing efforts in the area of religion have been seen. In a word, conditions today are remarkably similar to those perceived in 1966. Religion then and now was a talked-about issue in public education, but—when all was said and done—*not* a pivotal one, an issue with the political or Constitutional momentum of, say, racial segregation or school finance.

It is with this sobering conclusion that these essays must today be read. Their continued currency is ironic testament to the lesser importance placed on religion within the public schools than many of us fifteen years ago believed to be the case or had hoped for. However, the fact that this issue is not on center stage does not mean either that it has disappeared or that it is not intrinsically important. Religion continues to be mis-defined or sloppily-defined by school authorities; the law and customary practice ill serve the institutions of religion and public schooling. Americans deserve better—and it is with this belief that the essays were first written and are now republished.

Theodore R. Sizer
Phillips Academy, Andover
June 1981

❧ Religion and
Public Education

PART ONE

Teaching *About* Religion

I

Neutrality and Impartiality

Nicholas Wolterstorff

What is it that the public school is supposed to aim at with respect to religion? What is the broad principle against which we must test whether a certain way of treating religion is or is not permissible in the public school? What is the general directive laid down to the public school with respect to its treatment of religion? And why? Why must this be the aim? Why must this be the broad principle? Why must this be the general directive?

Unless we have clarity and agreement on the proper answers to these fundamental questions, we are not going to arrive at any very firm conclusions as to whether this or that treatment of religion is proper in the public school. It is my own feeling that we do not yet have such clarity and agreement. So I should like to devote the major part of my discussion to answering the question: What is the general directive which the public school is obliged to follow with respect to its treatment of religion?

This question has, of course, not lacked for attention. Ringing in the ears of all of us are many popular phrases: "separation of church and state," "strict and lofty neutrality as to religion," "a high wall of separation between church and state," "no expression of creed or practice of worship, nor any indication of hostility thereto," "no restriction on the free exercise of religion," "equal protection of all segments of society, whatever their beliefs or lack of belief," "no preferment to any religion," "to insure religious freedom for all," "religion and government to remain each within its respective sphere," "nothing that aids one religion, aids all religions, or prefers one religion over another," "neither support for religion nor hostility to religion," "to foster neither religious belief nor disbelief, neither to encourage nor discourage patterns of behavior dependent upon religious convictions," "a public education devoid of any practice that contradicts, inhibits, or disagrees in any way with any particular belief." The list can be doubled or tripled with small effort. But do all these phrases, and the many others used in the same context, have the same force? If not, which are acceptable and which are not acceptable as a characterization of the public school's proper treatment of religion? This is what I wish to explore.

Constitutional Restrictions on Governmental Treatment of Religion

The question of the proper treatment of religion in the public school is, in our country, inseparable from the question of what the government may do with respect to religion. Our Constitution lays down two restrictions in this area. It says, for one thing, that there shall be no law prohibiting the free exercise of religion, by which is presumably meant that the government, *whether in its legislative, its executive, or its judicial function*, shall not prohibit the free exercise of religion.

In our country the word "religion" is frequently, perhaps *most* frequently, used in such a way that some people have a religion and some do not; and a not unnatural interpretation of the words of this constitutional prescription is that, though the government must not prohibit those who have a religion from exercising it, nothing enjoins the government regarding its treatment of those who lack religion. Many people have in fact drawn this conclusion. The United States Supreme Court has clearly and decisively declared, however, that this interpretation is mistaken, and that the freedom which this prescription was designed to secure extends equally to those who lack religion. Thus it must be understood as demanding that the government not prohibit the exercise of either religion or irreligion. No matter what a man's *Weltanschauung*, no matter what his world and life view, whether it is religious or irreligious, the state is not to act so as to prevent him from implementing or exercising it. The state is not to do anything, the purpose or avoidable effect of which is to put restraint, constraint, coercion, or compulsion on some man's attempt to implement his way and view of life as he sees fit. It is not coercively to discriminate among men on account of their religions or irreligions.

Our Constitution also declares that there shall be no law respecting an establishment of religion — by which is also presumably meant that the government, whether in its legislative, executive, or judicial function, shall not establish religion. This at least means that the government shall not in any way show preference for any religion(s) or for any irreligion(s); nor, contrariwise, shall it in any way express hostility toward any religion(s) or any irreligion(s). It shall neither do anything, the purpose or avoidable effect of which is to aid some religion(s), or some irreligion(s), nor do anything, the purpose or avoidable effect of which is to inhibit some religion(s), or some irreligion(s).

When we put this idea together with that of the other prescription, we see that what the two together demand is that, with respect to their religions and irreligions, all men shall stand before the government as equals. Or, to put it from the side of government, what they demand is that the government shall treat all men impartially with respect to their religions and irreligions. The government is neither to prohibit the free exercise of any religion or irreligion nor to express favor or disfavor of any. Not only is it not *coercively* to discriminate against anyone on account of his religion or irreligion; it is not to *discriminate* against anyone on account of his religion or irreligion.

The Supreme Court, at least as I read its opinions, has interpreted the prescription against the establishment of religion as demanding still more. It has, in effect, interpreted the word "establishment" so that, logically, *all* the religions and irreligions in a society can be established. The establishment clause, it has said, does not merely forbid *preferential* or *discriminatory* treatment of any religions or irreligions. It even forbids that the government do anything which has the purpose or avoidable effect of giving aid or support to all religions and irreligions *impartially*. Thus, as I understand it, our government would not be allowed to do what some European governments did after the last war, namely, to extend subsidies or loans to the various religious and irreligious bodies for the rebuilding of their ruined churches, synagogues, mosques, meeting halls, etc. The words most frequently used to express this relation of government to religion are words which do not in fact occur in the First Amendment: "separation" and "indifference." Our government must be not only *impartial* with respect to all religions and irreligions — that is, it must not only avoid both *prohibiting the free exercise of* any religion or irreligion and *preferring* any religion or irreligion over any others. It must also be indifferent to (the welfare of) all religions and irreligions collectively. There must be a wall of separation.

WHAT THE PUBLIC SCHOOL IS

How does the public school fit into a state which operates under these regulations? Two preliminary remarks are in order. First, we must keep sharply in focus what the public school is. It is that one elementary and secondary educational system in each community which is supported by public tax funds. Its officers and personnel are not, in any very strict sense, officials or employees of the state. But the important fact is that it and it alone — among all the elementary and secondary educational systems in a given community — receives public tax money. It is not because the state itself does the educating in public schools, but rather because the state allows only one educational system, the public school system, to receive tax support, that the treatment of religion is a different sort of problem for the public schools from what it is for all others. The public schools and their officials are also, of course, *regulated* by the state. But regulation does not distinguish them; the same holds true, almost universally, for non-public schools.

WHAT THE PUBLIC SCHOOL MAY DO

Second, in all that follows I shall be talking about what public *schools* may do, not about what public school *teachers* may do. The distinction is crucial. The First Amendment speaks to what the government and governmentally sponsored institutions and agencies may and may not do; it does not speak to what individuals may and may not do, except insofar as in the doing of something by some individual, the government does something. The President of the United States may profess his belief in God, may go to church, may attend prayer breakfasts, may urge the importance of belief in God. He may, in short, be avowedly and openly partial. But the *federal government* may not be. Similarly, the teacher in a public school system may profess his belief in God, may go to church, may attend prayer breakfasts, may urge the importance of belief in God. He too may be avowedly and openly partial. But the school system in which he teaches may not be. The impartiality and indifference with respect to all religions and irreligions which is legally demanded of a school is not demanded of its personnel — except inasmuch as in the doing of something by the personnel, the school does something. The Constitution does not demand impartiality and indifference with respect to all religions and irreligions on the part of its citizens. Not only would there be no possibility of such a demand's being satisfied; it would also constitute an intolerable infringement on the free exercise of men's religions and irreligions. The Constitution only demands impartiality on the part of government and governmentally sponsored institutions and agencies.

Though the distinction between what an institution may do and what its personnel may do is clear enough in concept, it is likely to be difficult to apply, especially, it seems to me, in the schools. It is often difficult or impossible to decide whether, in a teacher's doing something, the school is also doing something. Thus it is unclear, in many cases, how the legal prescription of impartiality and indifference is to be applied to what teachers do. The school may not indicate a preference for Protestant Christianity. May a teacher, during school hours, do so — to his class? By "may," here, I mean *legally*. There might be considerations of prudence and morality which would lead a teacher to conclude that he *should* not do this. But may he legally? What the Supreme Court has said thus far, I feel, gives no guidance on this matter whatsoever. It is perhaps apropos to observe that in our state colleges and universities the individual teacher is given a great deal of freedom to express his own views. So far as I know, there have never been any legal protests against this.

So I find this distinction between what a school may do and what its personnel may do not only important to make but hard to apply. Yet the distinction and its applications have, so far as I know, never been explored in any depth. In fact, in almost all discussions on the place of religion in the public schools the distinction is overlooked and confused. But since I myself do not now see through the issues involved, I shall speak only about schools, leaving it to some other person to discuss how all this pertains to the work of teachers.

Formulating a General Directive for the School

What general directive, then, ought the public schools to follow with respect to religions and irreligions? The answer which comes first to mind is that the public schools must maintain exactly the same stance toward religions and irreligions that the state must. The general directive would be this:

> *1. The public school shall be impartial and indifferent with respect to the religions and irreligions in society.*

IMPARTIALITY

The attempt to carry out this directive in contemporary American society at once raises an interesting and important dilemma. In our society there is a large group of people who believe that the education their children receive should *not* be set in the context of any religious or irreligious *Weltanschauung* and should *not* incorporate religious practices. In fact, some of these people regard their religion or irreligion as *obligating* them to provide such an education for their children; it is, for them, a matter of conscience, not a matter of casual preference. But there are also, in our society, large groups of people who believe that the education their children receive *should* be set in the context of some religious or irreligious *Weltanschauung* or *should* include religious practices. Most of these groups regard their religion or irreligion as *obligating* them to provide such an education for their children; it is, for them also, a matter of conscience, not a matter of casual preference.

So suppose that the public school, to avoid going contrary to the conscientious convictions of the latter group of people, adopts the policy and practice of providing an education which is explicitly set in the context of some religion and includes the practices of that religion. The school will then be doing something contrary to the religion or irreligion of some members of the former group. It will also be doing something contrary to the religion or irreligion of those members of the latter group who, though they are convinced that their children should receive an education set in the context of some religion or irreligion, including its practices, think it should be a different one from the one the school happens to have picked. Thus, given the makeup of our society, the public school, if it followed such a policy and practice, would of necessity be giving preferential treatment to some one religion from among all the religions and irreligions that exist in our society, and would also of necessity be discriminating against some others. Worse, its discrimination would be *coercive* discrimination; the public school would be infringing on the free exercise of the religions and irreligions of those people whose conscience forbids them to allow their children to have an education of the sort indicated. For these people would have to start their own schools and thereby forego the benefit of state funds. Therefore, if the public school is to be impartial with respect to all religions and irreligions, it cannot have as its policy or practice the providing of an education which is set in the context of some religious or irreligious *Weltanschauung* or which includes religious practices.

Now suppose that the public school takes the opposite course, i.e., to avoid going contrary to the convictions of the members of the former group — those who feel in conscience obligated to give their children an education which does *not* include religious practices and is *not* set in the context of some religion or irreligion — adopts the policy and practice of providing an education of just such a pattern as they desire. The school will then be going contrary to the convictions of the latter group — those who believe that the education their children receive *should* be set in the context of some religion or irreligion or *should* include religious practices. Thus, given the makeup of our society, the public school, if it followed such a policy and practice, would still be giving preferential treatment to some from among all the religions and irreligions in society and would still be discriminating against some others. And worse, it would still be *coercively* discriminating; it would be infringing on the free exercise of the religions and irreligions of those people whose conscience forbids them to allow their children to have an education of the sort indicated. For now these people would have to start their own schools and thereby forego the benefit of state funds. Therefore, if the public school is to be impartial with respect to all religions and irreligions it cannot have as its policy and practice the providing of an education which is *not* set in the context of any religion or irreligion, and which does *not* include any religious practices.

It is not true, of course, that the public school must adopt one or the other of the policies and practices discussed above. There is a third course: it may adopt no policy and practice on the matter, in which case determining the course to be followed would presumably be at the pleasure of the individual teacher. But that would be offensive to *all* parties concerned. In a society as diverse as ours, therefore, it is impossible for the public school to be impartial and indifferent with respect to all religions and irreligions in society. It *cannot* give full freedom to all. It *cannot* avoid discriminating against some and preferring others. It *cannot* act in full accord with the Constitution.

The question then becomes — to put it in perhaps overly pejorative terms — Whose freedom is to be infringed, and who is to be discriminated against? And notice that it is not relevant here to argue that one or the other party to the dilemma is religiously misguided; the only thing relevant is that there are people with such convictions in our society.

AFFIRMATIVE IMPARTIALITY

To begin the answer, let us note that bias may be indicated, and produced, not only by what one says but also by what one does not say. In the dilemma just explored, we saw that some people are offended when religious exercises *are* conducted in the schools, and when the whole education *is* set in the context of some religion, whereas others are offended when these things are *not* done. We can then distinguish between what I shall call *affirmative* impartiality and *full* impartiality. A man will display affirmative impartiality with respect to the religion or irreligion of two men if nothing he says or does manifests preference for the religion or irreligion of the one over that of the other. He will display full impartiality if, in addition, there is nothing such that his not doing or saying it manifests preference for the religion or irrelgion of the one over that of the other.

The Supreme Court has clearly enjoined the public schools to practice affirmative impartiality with respect to all religions and irreligions in society. Unfortunately, however, it has tended to regard this as insuring *full* impartiality, and has thus regarded the injunction to affirmative impartiality as grounded directly and solidly on the Constitution. If I am right in what has preceded, the Constitution cannot be used to justify demanding affirmative impartiality of the public schools. Rather, it is tradition that seems to me to justify the policy of affirmative impartiality on the part of the public schools. The public school has traditionally been conceived as the place where we muffle our differences and deal only with that which we agree on. Each of us may then believe that what we wind up with is woefully incomplete for the full education of a child. But the teaching of religious or irreligious views, we have said, is the task of the home and/or the church. We have talked in terms of the unabridged right of each parent not to have alternative religious views forced on his child, rather than in terms of the unabridged right of each parent to educate his child in full accord with his own religious convictions. Thus affirmative impartiality with respect to the religions and irreligions in society is the traditional ideology of the public schools; it ought to remain such unless there are cogent reasons for changing it and thereby radically restructuring one of our fundamental institutions.

I acknowledge that this argument is not a strong one. For one thing, not everyone subscribes to the view that we ought to preserve our traditions unless there is good reason for changing them. But more important, to my mind, is the fact that affirmative impartiality has by no means been *uniformly* the traditional ideology of the public school. There is no shortage of cases in which the public schools have not even tried to achieve affirmative impartiality with respect to the religions and irreligions in society. Protestants have used the schools to do and say things offensive to Catholics, Christians have used them to do and say things offensive to Jews, theists have used them to do and say things offensive to atheists, atheists and liberal Christians have used them to do and say things offensive to evangelical Christians, and so on and on. There is ground for suspecting, then, that Americans have not always been sincere when they have said that religious differences should not be allowed to enter the public schools. Furthermore, not all spokesmen have said that the schools should aim at what I have called affirmative impartiality. Some have sounded a countertheme — namely, that the public schools should take it on themselves to inculcate students with our American religious heritage.

So the weakness of my argument must be granted. But the few other arguments of which I am aware seem even weaker. It is sometimes said, for example, that the practice of anything other than affirmative impartiality in the public schools will incite religious hostility. But when many people in our society are offended by an affirmatively impartial education for their children, to enjoin affirmative impartiality in the public schools is certainly not to get rid of religious hostility; and it is totally unclear to me whether there is *more* occasion for religious hostility when prayers are allowed, so that those who are offended must start their own schools, than when prayers are forbidden, so that those who are *then* offended must start their own schools.

In short, I think there is a case, though not a very strong one, for the rightness of affirmative impartiality in the public schools. But even if the case is worthless, the course to be followed is plain, for the Supreme Court has spoken.

Therefore, the general directive for the public schools must be this:

2. *The public school shall be affirmatively impartial, and indifferent, with respect to the religions and irreligions in society.*

But what, more specifically now, will such affirmative impartiality come to? Frequently a statement of the following sort is offered as an explanation of what is intended:

2a. The school shall neither manifest agreement or disagreement with the religious beliefs of any citizens, nor shall it manifest its approval or disapproval of their engaging in any of their religious practices.

Essential to an understanding of this general directive is an understanding of the term "religious beliefs." I do not wish to assign special and peculiar meaning to these words. When most Americans use the phrase "religious beliefs," I think that they have in mind belief in the existence, and beliefs concerning the nature, of some deity — and perhaps also, though less frequently, belief in the existence of man or man's soul beyond his physical death. God and immortality seem to be the chief focus of what people mean by "religious beliefs." Such beliefs are also usually thought to be beliefs concerning what transcends spatiotemporal reality and lies beyond our bourne of space and time. Hence the frequent use of the religious-secular contrast.

So if 2a is to be carried out, the schools cannot require or recommend praying and devotional reading of sacred scriptures by students or teachers, or anyone else, nor can they in any way indicate disapproval of praying and devotional reading of sacred scriptures. They cannot require or recommend the recitation of theistic creeds by students or teachers, or anyone else, nor can they in any way indicate disapproval of the recitation of such creeds. They can neither teach that God exists nor teach that He does not, neither teach that people should believe that He does nor teach that people should believe that He does not. They cannot teach that God is love, or that He is vengeance, or that He is all-mighty, or that His capacities are limited. They cannot teach anything at all, one way or another, about the character of God, nor can they recommend that men believe, or disbelieve, anything about the character of God. They can teach nothing one way or the other as to the immortality of man, or as to the nature of immortality, nor can they recommend either belief or disbelief in these matters.

Agreement or disagreement with religious beliefs, and approval or disapproval of religious practices, can also be expressed implicitly, by indirection, by presupposition. This too is forbidden by 2a. The public schools cannot teach that all men ought to worship God. They cannot teach that man's greatest satisfaction lies in the contemplation of God. They cannot teach that all men ought to love one another because we are all sons of God. They cannot teach that we ought to tell the truth because God wills it. They cannot teach that we ought so to live that we will have no fear of facing our Maker. Equally, they cannot teach anything which implies disagreement with any of these beliefs. They cannot teach that we ought to eat, drink, and be merry because tomorrow we die and are gone forever.

No doubt it will be difficult to decide, in many cases, whether a certain belief is or is not a religious belief. For example, is Tillich's belief in the

Ground of Being an example of a religious belief? But there seems to me to be no point in trying to reach greater precision and clarity on this matter, for a more serious problem confronts us.

Suppose, for example, that a school proposes to teach the importance of concern for others in human relationships. Not only *ought* we, it teaches, to show concern for each other, but in addition, there is no richer satisfaction to be found in human life than that which is to be found in showing concern for other human beings. Suppose that the school further proposes to teach its students to steer clear of materialism. We ought, it teaches, always to put physical things in our service, never to be enslaved to them. We ought to be free men, rid of material cares, open to the future, ready to accept what comes our way. We should not structure our lives so that we are cast into despair if the car we have bought turns out to be worthless, the house we live in to leak, the riches we have struggled for to be lost.

Is it legitimate for the school to engage in this sort of moral education? Notice that religious beliefs are neither expressed nor implied, nor is hostility to them expressed or implied. The pattern of life here recommended does not depend on religious, or anti-religious, beliefs. And the reasons offered, insofar as any are, presuppose neither religious nor anti-religious beliefs. I have, of course, chosen this example with some forethought. Biblical scholars have stressed two things, among others, as characterizing the pattern of action which Jesus recommended to his followers: concern and freedom. So the sort of moral education I have sketched out is very much in accord with Christianity. But it does not seem inconsistent or incoherent to try to exercise concern and freedom without having religious beliefs. This is not to say, of course, that the character of a Christian's concern and freedom will be exactly the same as that of an atheist's concern and freedom. The background motivations, attitudes, beliefs, reasons, etc., will differ vastly. But still, the patterns of action may very well be the same. Furthermore, though the reasons Jesus gave for urging these patterns of action obviously presuppose religious beliefs, other reasons, not presupposing religious beliefs, can be offered for the same patterns of action. Jesus said, "If God so clothes the grass of the field, which today is alive and tomorrow is thrown into the oven, will he not much more clothe you, O men of little faith? Therefore, do not be anxious." But there are other reasons which can be put forward for not being anxious, for being free, than that we have a heavenly Father who cares for us.

Yet it is a serious question whether a school which engages in this sort of program of moral education is affirmatively impartial with respect to all religions and irreligions. For although its teaching neither presupposes any religious beliefs nor manifests hostility to them, what it teaches is *incompatible* with the tenets of some religions and irreligions. Not everyone thinks that concern is important and worthwhile in human relationships; not everyone thinks that we ought not to be materialistic. And though for some people these may be flitting, unattached convictions, for others they constitute fundamental tenets in their religion or irreligion. It would seem, then, that a school is scarcely being affirmatively impartial with respect to their religion or irreligion if it teaches that we ought to show concern for one another and ought not to be materialists.

The Religious and the Secular.   Perhaps we ought to bring more sharply into focus what is going on here. We Americans have tended to suppose that a man adopts or exercises a certain religion by virtue of assenting to certain propositions about the supernatural, and by virtue of engaging in certain religious practices — acts of worship and devotion. Thus our literature on freedom of religion is rife with the assumption that the free exercise of religion is guaranteed by guaranteeing freedom of conscience and freedom to worship as one sees fit. But this way of regarding religion, common as it has been since the eighteenth century, profoundly distorts all great religions. The tenets of these religions are far more comprehensive than the religious beliefs of these religions, and to adopt such a religion is to do far more than follow its religious practices. Religions are secular as well as religious. The prophets of the Old Testament, who found their fellow Jews regularly offering sacrifices in the Temple and punctiliously following the ritual laws, while at the same time oppressing the unfortunates of their society, never once allowed that such men were genuine servants of God. They were, they said, impostors. And St. James in the New Testament says that the man who professes to have the true religion but has never committed himself to improving the lot of the needy is a liar. The point scarcely needs further development. Christianity and Judaism — and in this they are not peculiar — incorporate tenets much more comprehensive than their religious beliefs, and they demand for their exercise a far wider range of acts than their religious practices.

Indeed, some recent theologians have argued that the Christian religion need not be viewed as including any religious beliefs at all, and need not be thought to demand of its devotees any religious practices. Christianity, they say, is not a secular *as well as* a religious gospel. It is *exclusively* a secular gospel. Yet it is, they say, a gospel, good news concerning how man should live and think and act and feel and see things, a gospel which presupposes neither the existence nor the non-existence of God, yet which differs radically from the other world and life views of mankind. Christianity, under this interpretation, begins to resemble various oriental religions, for in some of these, too, it is difficult or impossible to find any religious beliefs or practices. Perhaps here is the place to remind ourselves that the Supreme Court has recently alluded to Ethical Culture, Secular Humanism, etc., as religions.

So 2a is evidently unsatisfactory. It reflects an outmoded and inadequate eighteenth-century understanding of religion and its bearing on human life. We can no longer work with that old dichotomy between the religious and the secular and assume that the schools are impartial if they confine themselves to the secular. The religious-secular distinction has become useless.

The Teaching of Moral Principles.   Let us then consider the following adaptation of 2a as the general directive which the public schools ought to follow:

> 2b. *Nothing that the public school says or does shall manifest either agreement or disagreement with a tenet of some citizen's religion or irreligion.*

This seems to me almost grossly unsatisfactory. For example, one of the tenets of Judaism and Christianity is that murder is wrong. But surely the public schools can manifest their agreement with this principle. In fact, there is probably no sane person at all in our society who has a religion or irreligion containing tenets that conflict with this principle. It may be that a good many moral principles cannot be taught by the schools because they conflict with one or another religion or irreligion; perhaps most of the so-called "higher principles" fall into this category. But some moral principles are compatible with all religions and irreligions in our society, and the fact that they are among the tenets of one or another religion or irreligion cannot be allowed to have the consequence that they cannot be taught by the schools.

The Purpose and Effects of Impartiality.   So let us also discard 2b, and replace it with this:

> 2c. *Nothing that the public school says or does shall manifest disagreement with a tenet of some citizen's religion or irreligion.*

This seems to me still unsatisfactory. Suppose, for example, that one of the tenets of someone's religion is that there are no irrational numbers. Is the public school then proscribed from teaching irrational numbers? Suppose that one of the tenets of someone's religion is that there are no germs. Is the public school then proscribed from teaching the germ theory? Suppose that one of the tenets of someone's religion is that the earth is flat and has four corners. Is the public school then proscribed from teaching that the earth is a slightly flattened sphere?

It will be helpful, at this point, to glance back at the more comprehensive problem of the relation between religion and the state. Various religions in our land hold to pacifism. Yet our country violates this tenet of theirs and goes to war. A few of the religions in our land consider it wrong to pay taxes to the state. Yet our country violates this tenet of theirs and assesses taxes. From these and countless other examples of the same sort it is clear that one can surely not interpret the demand that the state be impartial as meaning that the state may do nothing in violation of the tenets of any citizen's religion or irreligion. Let us here distinguish between *impartiality* and *neutrality* by saying that a state is neutral with respect to the religions and irreligions of its citizens just in case it does nothing which in fact aids or hinders, expresses agreement or disagreement with, one religion or irreligion over another. Obviously, in our religiously diverse society, the state cannot be neutral.

How, then, are we to interpret the demand that the state be impartial? We must distinguish between the *purpose* of what the state does and the *effects* of what it does. If the state is to be impartial with respect to the religions and irreligions of its citizenry, it must not have as its *aim* or *purpose* to aid or hinder, manifest agreement or disagreement with, any one religion or irreligion over any other. In the aims and purposes of its actions, the state must be "religion blind." What it aims to accomplish may well be in accord with, or in violation of, the tenets of one or another religion or irreligion. But *that* it is thus in accord or violation may not be the state's reason for adopting its aim.

The means it uses to achieve its aims are quite a different matter, however. If the state has two means of accomplishing a given aim, both legal, one of which has the effect of imposing a burden on or manifesting disagreement with some religion or irreligion over some other, the other of which does not have such a discriminatory effect, then surely, to be impartial, it must select the latter. Correspondingly if the state has two means of achieving a given aim, both legal, one of which has the effect of aiding or manifesting agreement with some religion or irreligion as against some other, the other of which does not have such a preferential effect, then, to be impartial, it must select the latter.

It is not difficult to apply these points to the schools. If there is to be a public school at all in our diverse society, one cannot hold that it must be neutral with respect to the religions and irreligions of our citizens; that is, one cannot hold that nothing the school says or does shall manifest agreement or disagreement with a tenet of some citizen's religion or irreligion. Rather, in what it says and does the school must not have as its aim or purpose the expression of agreement or disagreement with some citizen's religion or irreligion. Further, if the school has the choice of two means of achieving its ends, one of which expresses agreement or disagreement with a tenet of some citizen's religion or irreligion and the other of which does not, it must select the latter. If these two conditions are met, then one may justly say that the school is (affirmatively) impartial, even though it may, indeed, not be neutral in the sense we have given to the word "neutral."

Thus the school may not teach the germ theory in order to express disagreement with some religion. It is, however, entitled to have as one of its aims the acquainting of its students with contemporary scientific hygiene, and how it could do so without introducing the germ theory is difficult to see. And it could also, when introducing the theory, mention that certain religions dispute the theory.

Difficulties with Affirmative Impartiality. Let us, then, state the following as the general directive which the public school ought to follow:

> 2d. *Nothing that the public school says or does shall have as its purpose, or as an avoidable feature or effect of its manner of achieving its purpose, the manifesting of approval or disapproval of any citizen's religion or irreligion.*

Before we conclude that this, finally, is satisfactory, we ought to consider, briefly, what scope is to be given to the application of the words "any citizen's." May the school take into account just the convictions of its own constituents, or must its concern be broader in scope?

If each school maintained affirmative impartiality with respect only to the religions and irreligions in its own constituency, the freedom of all would be protected; there would be no coercive discrimination. This would apparently not, however, be enough to avoid the establishment of religion or to avoid non-coercive discrimination. If a state government provides tax money to a school, it would seem that the school must then, strictly, be affirmatively impartial with respect to all the religions and irreligions in that state. And if the federal government provides tax money to a school, it would seem that that school must, strictly, be impartial with respect to all religions and irreligions in American society. I come to this conclusion hesitantly, since it places a staggering responsibility on the school. It is hard enough for a school to achieve affirmative impartiality with respect to all the religions and irreligions represented in its own constituency. If it must now aim at affirmative impartiality with respect to all religions and irreligions represented in American society, its chances of success appear slim. Yet, *strictly*, sensitivity to the religious makeup of American society generally seems to be what is demanded.

With this clarification, it seems to me that the policy the public school must follow is that stated in 2d. Adherence to this policy — and nothing short of adherence to it, as far as I can see — will secure affirmative impartiality.

The difficulties involved in trying to carry out such a directive are immense. We have already seen that the school must be sensitive to the religious makeup of our entire society. In addition, the possibility of manifesting disapproval of some religion is not confined to any particular part of the curriculum. In the consideration of the theory of evolution in a biology course, of various facets of the nature of man in a psychology course, of the character of political authority in a social studies course, of the background causes of the Reformation in a history course — in all these cases, and in many other less obvious ones, the school can easily go contrary to the tenets of some religion or irreligion in what it says. On many significant issues, the public school, in our religiously diverse society, may either have to be silent or shift from teaching that such and such is the case to teaching that certain people *believe* that such and such is the case.

Possibilities Open Under the General Directive

In conclusion, let us consider whether some of the ways in which it is commonly said that the public school ought to treat religion in its curriculum can, with any likelihood, be made to fit within this general directive, and, further, whether it is *desirable* that religion be so treated in the curriculum.

Following certain hints of the Supreme Court, many people are saying today that, though the public schools cannot engage in the teaching *of* religion, they can teach *about* religion. What sorts of things might be regarded as cases of teaching *about* religion? And is the public school permitted to do all these things?

RELIGION IN SOCIETY

It is often said that one cannot understand history without understanding the role of religion in the changing cultural currents of mankind; that one cannot get a balanced picture of contemporary American society without understanding the place and role of the various religions in our society; that one cannot understand the arts without understanding the impact of the various religions on the work of artists; etc. More generally, it is often said that one cannot understand the acts and cultural products of human beings without understanding the role of man's religions and the sacred writings of these religions. And since the schools surely must concern themselves with the acts and cultural products of human beings, one may conclude that the schools must deal with religions and irreligions insofar as they have affected what men do and make.

With all these points I agree. I very much doubt whether a school can, in treating such matters, achieve *neutrality* with respect to all religions and irreligions in society; certainly a teacher cannot. But perhaps there is some hope that schools can achieve affirmative *impartiality*.

The study of sacred writings as cultural products

It is often said of late that we should allow the Bible, and presumably other sacred scriptures, to be studied in our schools, not just as something which has had an influence in political history, in art, in language, etc., but also as a cultural product in its own right, having certain literary and linguistic qualities, providing us with information about the social, political, intellectual, and economic conditions of the times, reflecting the psychological makeup of its writers, and so on. In other words, the Bible, like any other important document, should, whenever relevant, be studied for historical purposes, literary purposes, linguistic purposes, etc. It is said that to forbid it to be thus studied places an intolerable and unwarranted restriction on the work of the historian, the literary scholar, the linguist, etc.

With these points I also agree. But caution seems in order. For a great many of us in our society consider the Bible the presentation of God's Word to man. And a good many of those who so regard it argue, if I understand them, that unless it is presented as such, it is bound to be misunderstood. What seems to me to be a correct answer to this argument is as follows: To treat the Bible as a cultural phenomenon is not to deny, any more than it is to assert, that it is the presentation of God's Word to man. It may very well be, of course, that to treat the Bible without explicitly regarding it as the presentation of God's Word to man is, from the standpoint of some, to introduce bias and distortion. But then, it must be remembered, the basic directive assigned to the public school is that it be *affirmatively* impartial. It cannot be faulted for what it does not do and say, only for what it *does* do and say. Therefore, I think that the objections to treating the Bible as a cultural phenomenon are generally misguided. But I feel sure that many people will never be persuaded on this score.

The study of comparative religion

It is sometimes said that we ought to study the various religions, not only as a part of and an essential to some other study, but rather in their own right. Therefore, it is said, we ought to introduce the study of comparative religion and the study of the history of religion into our schools.

I think it is clear, in terms of the general directive which I have suggested, that this *may* be done. The question is whether it *should* be done. The fact that the various religions are there to be studied is not reason enough. The schools cannot undertake to offer courses in everything that can be studied, not even everything important. And the education of men is not, after all, limited to what they learn in schools. Two reasons are customarily adduced in justification for such study: (1) It will develop in the student an understanding of the religions and irreligions of other men. (2) It is the proper business of the school to help the student choose some religion or irreligion, whichever one he wishes, for the living of his life, and to that end the school should set before him the various options.

What Is Religion? We are treading on extraordinarily porous and dangerous ground. If the schools are going to put the study of religion qua religion into their curricula, they will, I think, have to arrive at some understanding of what religion is, some interpretation of this fundamental phenomenon in human affairs. Are the religions of mankind an attempt to understand mysterious and wonderful happenings? An attempt to explain why there is any life at all? An attempt to give man a sense of security as he faces the unknown? An attempt to assuage his feelings of guilt? An attempt to find a pattern by which man shall live his life? An attempt to find solace in the face of evils and disasters? An attempt to account for marvelous and mysterious feelings and experiences? The response to a sense of dependence? A way of seeing things? The projection of unsatisfied economic or psychological needs? The outcome of an innate idea? The development of an in-created sense of divinity? Man's response to God? In what is included for consideration and in what is excluded from consideration in a study of religion, in what is emphasized and in what is de-emphasized, in the way various phenomena are linked together, some more or less coherent principles of interpretation will be used, implicitly or explicitly. But such principles of interpretation are not at all likely to be acceptable to all religions and irreligions in our society. Some of them will indeed be acceptable to a larger range of religions and irreligions than others. But suppose, to take a rather gross example of the problem, that there were both Marxists and Christians in the community. How would both ever be satisfied with the same treatment of religion? I do not even think it likely that evangelical and liberal Christians are going to be satisfied with the same treatment. In short, it seems virtually certain that courses in religion in the public schools will always produce sharp dissatisfaction in the community.

Aims of the Study. In spite of this distasteful consequence, the reasons for including the study of religion qua religion in the public school curriculum may still be sound and persuasive. As already mentioned, the aims usually proposed for such courses are those of presenting the student with various options, so that he can make his own choice, and of developing an understanding of the religions and irreligions of others. Let us look briefly at the first aim. Parents of many religious persuasions hold that it is their duty as parents to train their children in the ways of their fathers, to inculcate in the child the parental religion. They do not feel that they should present the options in a take-it-or-leave-it fashion but that it is clearly their calling as parents to "train the child in the way he should go." To me it seems not unreasonable for a parent who takes this task with high seriousness to disapprove of presenting his young child with all sorts of options, on the ground that this will confuse the child and make of no effect his own attempts at bringing up the child in the parental religion. The pivotal question here, I suppose, is the empirical one of whether parents really can as effectively inculcate in their children the parental religion when the school is confronting them with options. If they cannot, and I am myself inclined to think that they cannot, then for the schools to present options is to do something which frustrates one of the obligations of the parent's religion — namely, that he should do his best to have the child adopt the parental religion.

The other aim mentioned, that of developing understanding of others and their religions, appears to me a far more weighty one. This is, surely, an important aim, and a course in religion might well help to achieve it.

We find ourselves, then, in the curious situation in which courses in religion qua religion are likely to produce sharp dissatisfactions in society and an overall gain in mutual understanding. Accordingly, I find it not at all clear, one way or the other, whether such courses are desirable.

THE STUDY OF SACRED WRITINGS AS RELIGIOUS DOCUMENTS

Finally, to make a point closely connected with the foregoing, it is sometimes said that the public schools can and should deal with the sacred scriptures of the various religions as religious documents, that is, as documents expounding or expressing a certain religion. It is agreed, of course, that the schools must not teach what these sacred scriptures teach; they must rather teach *that* the sacred writings teach this and that. The reasons are usually the same as those offered for teaching religion as religion: the result will be a better understanding of the religions and irreligions of other men, and the student will have various options for his own belief.

Many of the objections raised to teaching religion qua religion are also relevant here. For example, as far as I can see there is no hope in the near future of finding an interpretation of the message of the Bible which is satisfactory to all versions of Christianity. Furthermore, many parents would be dismayed at having their young children presented with various alternative interpretations of the writings they hold sacred, and with various alternative sacred writings; I, for one, would find their dismay understandable. Thus the school which has a course treating sacred scriptures as such must expect vociferous objection. Whether the likely overall gain in mutual understanding is worth the price of such hostility I do not know. So in this case too, whether such courses are desirable is much less clear than whether they are permissible. Of course, vast numbers of things written by human beings, other than sacred scriptures, expound or express a religion; to ignore them in the schools would be impossible, and to ignore their message would be equally impossible. But these are not *sacred, authoritative* writings. It is when we try to interpret the message of the sacred, authoritative writings of the great religions that there seems to me no hope of avoiding serious objection. Perhaps elective rather than required courses would mute most of the objections and still secure significant advantages.

In summary, the study of the role of religion in culture and society, the study of sacred writings as cultural products, the study of comparative religion, and the study of sacred writings as religious documents all seem to be permissible studies for the public school. They can all, in principle, be made to fit within the general directive of affirmative impartiality. Further, the school cannot avoid studying the role of religion in culture and society. The other forms of teaching about religion can, however, be avoided. Whether, in spite of this, the school should step into these areas is unclear to me. For, as far as I can see, in doing so the school will inevitably stir up dissatisfaction among one or another religious group in the community.

2

The Conditions of Public School Neutrality

George R. La Noue

Toward the end of the Supreme Court's opinion in *Abington School District v. Schempp*, Justice Clark took special note of one of the most common arguments against the removal of prayer and Bible reading from the public schools:

> It is insisted that, unless these religious exercises are permitted, a "religion of secularism" is established in the schools. We agree, of course, that the State may not establish a "religion of secularism" in the sense of affirmatively opposing or showing hostility to religion, thus "preferring those who believe in no religion over those who do believe." *Zorach v. Clauson* supra, at 314. We do not agree, however, that this decision in any sense has that effect. . . . [Prayer and Bible reading] are religious exercises, required by the States in violation of the command of the First Amendment that the Government maintain strict neutrality, neither aiding nor opposing religion.[1]

Two of the concurring opinions in *Abington* also utilize the concept of neutrality between religion and irreligion as the decisive principle, but they warn of the difficulty in applying the concept. Justice Goldberg, joined by Justice Harlan, wrote:

It is said, and I agree, that the attitude of the state toward religion must be one of neutrality. But untutored devotion to the concept of neutrality can lead to invocation or approval of results which partake not simply of that noninterference and noninvolvement with the religious which the Constitution commands, but of a brooding and pervasive devotion to the secular and a passive, or even active, hostility to the religious. Such results are not only not compelled by the Constitution, but, it seems to me, are prohibited by it.[2]

Justice Brennan, in his seventy-six page concurring opinion, added,

Inevitably, insistence upon neutrality, vital as it surely is for untrammelled religious liberty, may appear to border upon religious hostility. But in the long view the independence of both church and state in their respective spheres will be better served by close adherence to the neutrality principle. If the choice is often difficult, the difficulty is endemic to issues implicating the religious guarantees of the First Amendment. Freedom of religion will be seriously jeopardized if we admit exceptions for no better reason than the difficulty of delineating hostility from neutrality in the closest cases.[3]

The Court's affirmation in *Abington* of the constitutional requirement that the public schools be religiously neutral was hardly a novel position.[4] In 1943 the Court accepted the concept of neutrality when it considered the issue of compulsory flag salutes, a secular ritual with religious overtones for some. Justice Jackson, speaking for the Court in *West Virginia State Board of Education v. Barnette,* insisted:

Free public education, if faithful to the ideal of secular instruction and political neutrality, will not be the partisan or enemy of any class, creed, party or faction. If it is to impose any ideological discipline, however, each party or denomination must seek to control or, failing that, to weaken the influence of the educational system.[5]

Later in Jackson's opinion the neutrality concept was reiterated in a famous passage, the relevance of which to American life is as great today as it was in 1943:

If there is any fixed star in our constitutional constellation, it is that no official, high or petty, can prescribe what shall be orthodox in politics, nationalism, religion, or other matters of opinion, or force citizens to confess by word or act their faith therein.[6]

Four years later Justice Jackson again took up the theme of public school neutrality but this time coupled with some tantalizing questions. In *Everson v. Board of Education* he noted in passing,

[The public school] is organized on the premise that secular education can be isolated from all religious teaching so that the school can inculcate all needed temporal knowledge and also maintain a strict and lofty neutrality as to religion. The assumption is that after the individual has been instructed in worldly wisdom, he will be better fitted to choose his religion. Whether such a disjunction is possible, and if possible whether it is wise, are questions I need not try to answer.[7]

Since Jackson was dissenting on entirely different points in *Everson*, he probably did not have to answer his own questions. But the questions will not go away. They are woven into the two great church-state questions of our time: religion in the public schools and tax aid for parochial schools. Can public educational policy be truly neutral toward religion?

The Challenge to Public School Neutrality

In 1961 the National Catholic Welfare Conference (NCWC) prepared a lengthy legal brief in rebuttal to the Department of Health, Education and Welfare's (HEW) "Memorandum on the Impact of the First Amendment to the Constitution upon Federal Aid to Education."[8] The HEW memorandum, written largely by Attorney General Robert Kennedy's staff in the Justice Department, predictably agreed with President John Kennedy that general aid to parochial schools was unconstitutional, while the NCWC brief not very surprisingly reached the opposite conclusion. What is significant here is that one of the NCWC's principal arguments for public support of parochial schools was that public schools were not really neutral. The brief notes that

> . . . an "orthodoxy" is expressed — inescapably so — even in a curriculum from which religious "orthodoxies" are absent . . . . there is little guarantee that the public schools can, in actuality, maintain a completely non-"value"-inculcating program. Since life itself, humanity, history, and the social sciences are all involved in the daily life of any educational institution, "values" inevitably creep in.[9]

Furthermore, public educators have often claimed a deep concern for moral and spiritual values, although, as the Educational Policies Commission of the National Education Association and the American Association of School Administrators has stated, "as public institutions, the public schools of this nation must be non-denominational. The public schools can have no part in securing acceptance of any one of the numerous systems of belief regarding a supernatural power and the relation of mankind thereto."[10] The NCWC brief points out, however, that withdrawing the public schools from promotion of "any one of the numerous systems of belief regarding a supernatural power" hardly solves the problem.[11] Citing Leo Pfeffer[12] (doubtless tongue in cheek) and *Torcaso v. Watkins*[13] as evidence, the brief notes that modern legal theory accepts the fact that there are religions or substitutes for religion that are non-supernatural —

secular humanism, for example. Consequently, the NCWC brief concludes that, if no constitutionally valid line can be drawn between supporting supernatural religions and non-supernatural religions and that if all schools teach values, the only solution is to provide public support for all schools.[14]

Recently the challenge to public school neutrality has been motivated by opposition to the Supreme Court's decision banning public school prayer and Bible-reading.[15] The coalition that has been formed to amend the First Amendment in order to reintroduce these rituals into the schools includes such unlikely theological bedfellows as Bishop James A. Pike and Bishop Fulton J. Sheen, but the movement has been mainly generated by pressure from right-wing Protestantism. The fundamentalists (of whatever denomination) argue that the Court decisions took God out of the schools. They intend to put Him back in. They want neither public schools nor a government that is neutral toward religion. Citing as evidence a long list of public documents from the Declaration of Independence to the revised pledge of allegiance, the fundamentalists are determined to restore their version of the nation's religious heritage through constitutional amendment. They will not be satisfied until both the government and its schools are committed to, at the very least, Judeo-Christian theism. Public school neutrality toward religion, even if possible, is as abhorrent to the fundamentalist as personal religious indifferentism.

Whether the challenge to public school religious neutrality has come from those with financial or theological axes to grind or from those genuinely concerned for academic freedom and cultural pluralism, their contentions must be taken seriously.[16] Until some system can be worked out that defines and guarantees such neutrality, proposals to strengthen the role of religion in the public schools will be educationally and constitutionally unstable and the public schools themselves subject to continued attack.

The Legal Concept of Religious Neutrality

Philosophers may doubt that any position is really neutral, for there are value judgments in every commitment. The concept of legal neutrality, however, is simple and easier to define, since it must prove practicable when implemented in the daily affairs of the state. Legal neutrality is not value-free, nor does it require that the state's policy be balanced precisely at the midpoint of the claims of all the contending interest groups. Either of those requirements would be impossible to fulfill in the real world of political life. Legal neutrality toward religion is, instead, a state policy of refraining from weighting the scales of religious choice by refusing to commit the state's prestige or resources to either help or hinder religion. To use the classic phrase, neutrality requires that the state not intervene in the marketplace of ideas on behalf of any of the forces of religion or irreligion contending there. Since the public school is the central market-place of ideas in our democracy, particular care must be taken to see that the scales of religious choice are not weighted in the classroom.

The basis of the legal concept of religious neutrality is, of course, the First Amendment of the federal Constitution ("Congress shall make no law respecting an establishment of religion, or prohibiting the free exer-cise thereof") and also Article VI ("no religious Test shall ever be re-quired as a Qualification to any Office or public Trust under the United States"). It is important to note that philosophically neither provision is neutral or value-free. Doubtless in 1789 these constitutional principles were more acceptable to religious dissenters and non-believers than they were to the established Congregationalists in Massachusetts or to the Anglicans in Virginia. Nevertheless, non-discrimination, non-establish-ment, and religious liberty are neutral principles since they forbid the state from coercing belief or disbelief. The process of interpreting these principles is a continuous one, however. The Supreme Court's ruling that Bible-reading and prayer violate the neutrality of the public schools by no means exhausts the question of what full religious neutrality requires.

The Implementation of Legal Neutrality

THE PROHIBITION OF RELIGIOUS DISCRIMINATION IN PERSONNEL POLICY

The Constitution initiates its policy of religious neutrality in Article VI with a prohibition against religious discrimination in the hiring of public personnel, and that is the point at which public school neutrality must begin. Any school that attempts to screen out candidates on the basis of their particular religious affiliations or beliefs would obviously not be neutral. Attempts to enforce sectarian codes of morality or discrimination against those who voluntarily follow such codes would also be unneutral. They would, in Justice Jackson's words, permit a public official (in this case a petty one) to prescribe what is orthodox in religion.[17]

There is an alternative approach to religious neutrality. One might try to strike a religious balance by seeking out candidates who represent the various religious traditions. This is often the pattern followed in staffing departments of religion in state universities. A less satisfactory example is the New York City Board of Education, whose membership has tradi-tionally and rigidly been three Protestants, three Catholics, and three Jews.[18] This pattern has often been reflected in top administrative posi-tions in the public school system and is reinforced by the three religious associations for school personnel.

Whatever the merits of attempting to represent the various religious traditions in university departments of religion, this approach has some obvious disadvantages for public schools. In the first place, when the religious balance concept is utilized, promotion within the system often requires continued acceptability to the religious leadership in the community. It can lead to a conflict of interest when public school officials must defend the school's academic freedom or conduct negotiations with parochial school officials about participation in public programs. More important, the religious balance concept tends to discriminate against non-believers, for they belong to a less definable and less organized group. Furthermore, since talented personnel is scarce in almost every educational field, the introduction of a restrictive religious factor in hiring impedes educational progress.

In short, the only educationally and constitutionally sound policy for the public schools to follow is to bar all questions about religious affiliation, practice, or belief from the hiring process. In general, state policy does forbid formal questions of this kind although informal probing still occurs illegally in some parts of the country. Where such inquiry does occur, it is most often directed toward ferreting out religious skeptics rather than the religiously orthodox.

Even though all the evidence on public school personnel policies is to the contrary, there are still those who claim that the public schools are citadels of godlessness or secular humanism. This caricature is sometimes supported by a few selected quotations on religion from John Dewey or William Torrey Harris, as though their credos were somehow binding on all public school personnel; but any sociological examination of the almost 27,000 public school districts in this country would quickly dispel this notion.[19] To be sure, there are those (some influential) in the system who support Dewey in matters of religion, but there are many more who look to Buddha, Moses, or Christ for their principles. Actually public school teachers tend to be theistic, just as the general American public tends to be theistic. If one were to compare the various professions, public school teachers would probably turn out to be among the most theologically orthodox. Their religious backgrounds will reflect regional variations, of course. One would expect to find more Catholics teaching in Massachusetts than in Mississippi and more atheists in New York than in New Hampshire. Overall, however, the public schools' staffs are educated in various types of institutions, secular and religious, and hold as many different theological viewpoints as there are in America.

In addition to distorting the reality of the religious attitudes in the public schools, the creators of the caricature have failed to distinguish between the legal neutrality of the public school system as a system and the personal values of the people who staff it. A public school staffed by people who are mainly secular humanists does not necessarily create an "establishment of secularism" any more than a school staffed by people who happen to be Christians creates an "establishment of religion." Legal establishment requires some *systematic state action* to benefit or hinder religion. A discriminatory hiring policy would be that kind of state action, but if there is no discrimination, the personal views of public officials are not a criterion of establishment.

A personnel system based on merit rather than on religious affiliation is a major condition for legal neutrality. In most cases, if teachers are then left free to teach, and students to learn, the school will be legally neutral. At some points, however, the school must make official policy on the treatment of religion, and these points will require careful consideration if neutrality is to be preserved.

THE PROHIBITION OF A "RELIGION OF SECULARISM"

In the passages cited earlier, Justice Jackson, for one, seemed to equate a secular education with a religiously neutral education. Such an equation without further examination begs the question. "Secular," of course, is a word with many meanings; and it bears different, even antithetical, connotations. Although in works like Harvey Cox's *The Secular City*[20] the concept carries with it no threat to true religion, nevertheless, "secularism" or "secularist" commonly refers to a rejection of religion. Even if the term "secular" is confined to meaning not touching on or dealing with religion, a secular education may still not meet the constitutional test of neutrality. In other words, must a public school accept some responsibility for providing opportunities for religious education (however defined) if the school is to be fully neutral?

In *Abington*, after Justice Clark ruled out any establishment of a "religion of secularism" in the public schools, he suggested,

> In addition, it might well be said that one's education is not complete without a study of comparative religion or the history of religion and its relationship to the advancement of civilization. It certainly may be said that the Bible is worthy of study for its literary and historic qualities. Nothing we have said here indicates that such study of the Bible or of religion, when presented objectively as part of a secular program of education, may not be effected consistent with the First Amendment.[21]

There are two important aspects of Clark's statement. First, the treatment of religion the Justice suggests is objective and empirical (comparative religion, history of religion) rather than doctrinal and normative. Since the *McCollum*[22] decision, the objective-empirical approach seems to be constitutionally required when religion is taught *in* the public schools. Second, the role of "objective" religion in the public schools is considered an educational problem — "one's education is not complete" — rather than a constitutional problem. The Court's language regarding the inclusion of "objective" religion is permissive, but are there instances in which constitutional neutrality requires that the public school accede to demands for opportunities for religious education?

APPROACHES TO RELIGIOUS EDUCATION

Several solutions to the problem of religious education and the public schools are currently being widely discussed. There is the "objective" approach, by which religion is taught as a part of other subjects or as a separate subject in the public schools, and the "sectarian" approach, by which religion is taught through released-time or shared-time arrangements by the churches themselves. The public schools' constitutional obligation, if any, for each of these methods of religious education requires separate consideration. All answers in this area must be regarded as highly tentative, based as they are on only fragments of judicial pronouncements.

The Objective Approach. Of all the approaches to the teaching of religion, the one probably receiving the most support among educators is that the religious aspects of history, literature, art, music, drama, etc., ought to receive fair (academically justified) attention in the teaching of those subjects. The educational merit in this approach is obvious, but is such an arrangement also constitutionally required? Suppose the program of a particular public school were challenged on the grounds that it purposely and systematically excluded information about religion from its curriculum. The Anti-Defamation League and the NAACP have made similar kinds of charges regarding the treatment of minority groups in certain public school textbooks. If the allegations about the omission of either religious or racial information were true,[23] would this school practice violate the equal protection clause of the Fourteenth Amendment or (in the case of religion) the establishment clause of the First Amendment? If purposeful exclusion of information were proved, it would seem to be evidence that the public schools had illegally become, in Justice Jackson's words, "a partisan or enemy of [a] class, creed, party or faction"[24] and that there ought to be some judicial remedy.

The courts would, of course, be very reluctant to enter into the matter of curriculum design or textbook selection. Nevertheless, after two decades of church-state cases, integration cases, and academic freedom cases, it is apparent that the Supreme Court is, in Edward S. Corwin's phrase, functionally a national school board. Although the courts would properly place a heavy burden of proof on allegations of discriminatory exclusion of racial or religious information, this kind of issue is within the courts' responsibility to preserve a neutral school. Finally, it should be said that, although neutrality may require proper consideration of religion throughout the curriculum, there is no constitutional protection from academic analysis or criticism of religion.[25]

Some would contend, however, that teaching about religion through other subjects is not enough. There are no more intellectual grounds, they would argue, for teaching religion as a part of history or literature than vice versa. Consequently, they insist that comparative religion or some other form of objective teaching about religion should take its place as a separate subject alongside the other disciplines in public schools. This contention has a certain logic, but it has met with resistance from public educators. Assuming it were possible to design a satisfactory comparative religion course, the enormous shortage of qualified teachers in this field remains a serious problem. To begin programs in religion without trained teachers would be to open the schools to the possibility of overt religious proselytizing. Furthermore, in most public schools, initiating a program in religion would mean hiring one or perhaps two new teachers. These teachers would be in such a sensitive position that their personal beliefs might become the subject of intense community interest. Generally the teacher and the course would have to reflect the religious attitudes of the dominant segment of the public school's constituency to a much greater degree than when religion is integrated throughout the curriculum. One can imagine a Jew or an agnostic teaching about religion in public school literature or history classes in most parts of the country, but it seems unlikely that persons of those persuasions would be hired to teach public school comparative religion classes, no matter how competent they were. Regardless of who taught the course, friendly examination of non-Western religions or rigorous scrutiny of local "established" sects would be discouraged. In short, the very visibility of the courses creates so many problems that relatively few courses in comparative religion can be found in the public schools. There are a growing number of "Biblical literature" courses, particularly in the Midwest, but they are often neither comparative nor objective. They are, instead, a defensive response of cultural Protestantism to the Court decisions barring prayer and Bible-reading.

Assuming that an objective course in religion could be designed and, avoiding questions about the proper procedure for instituting it, do parents and students have a constitutional right to demand such a course in the public school curriculum? Such a contention seems extremely dubious to me. If the right exists, it would have to rest on the free exercise clause of the First Amendment. I can find no language or inference in the Supreme Court's opinions to support this right, nor can I logically construct a case for it. There seems to be no more of a religious *right* to a course in comparative religion than to one in comparative government or comparative literature. The existence of such a course appears to me to be primarily a matter of educational rather than of constitutional considerations.

The Sectarian Approach. In general, the public seems to concur in the administrators' lack of enthusiasm for comparative religion courses. What most of the parents interested in religious education really want is to have their children trained in the traditional faith of their fathers. This "sectarian" approach cannot, of course, take place legally within the public schools; but the schools may cooperate with either released time (students primarily enrolled in public schools who take their religious instruction in religious schools) or shared time (students primarily enrolled in parochial schools who take some courses in the public schools). Both programs can create formidable administrative problems, but, on the plus side, they turn over the sticky issues of how religion should be taught and who should teach it to the religious groups themselves. Although the responses have been mixed, requests for released time and shared time have sometimes met resistance by public school authorities. When this happens, can a parent constitutionally demand such an arrangement?

Two court cases provide some insight, though they are far from conclusive. The state of Oregon has had for many years a law which states: "Any child attending the public school, on application of his guardian or either of his parents, may be excused from such school for a period or periods not exceeding 120 minutes in any week to attend weekday schools giving religious instruction in religion."[26] The critical words are "may be excused." When the superintendent of School District 24 refused a parental request, the case went all the way to the Oregon Supreme Court. *Dilger v. School District 24* is not a classic document of religious liberty; the Court split four to three, and the majority opinion is timidly written. The justices appeared to be more concerned with Oregon's traditions of statutory construction than with questions of conscience. Nevertheless, the majority decided that "may be excused" had to be interpreted "must be excused." The Court found that school officials could determine the time of the release, but that giving them discretion over an individual's right to be released for religious instruction would be "illegal." No interpretation of the Oregon State Constitution or of the First Amendment was made, nor were any precedents on discretionary power involving religion cited, so the case provides little help regarding the overall problem.

The shared-time case is even more obscure. The eastern public high school developed generally from college preparatory academies. Training in manual and vocational arts was added later, usually in separate departments or schools, but under public auspices. The Pennsylvania law of 1911 governing such training stated that "no pupil shall be refused admission to the courses in these special schools or departments by reason of the fact that his elementary education is being, or has been received in a school other than a public school."[27] Despite the statute, when a seventh-grade pupil from a parochial school applied to a manual training program in one of the Altoona public schools, he was refused on the grounds that such admission would illegally aid the parochial school. The student's guardian then sought a writ of mandamus from a state district court and was successful. After pointing out that the parochial school would receive no public funds from the arrangement, the district court declared:

> It must be borne in mind that the entire common school system in Pennsylvania was created and devised for the elevation of our citizenship as a whole. It is often termed a public or free school system, thereby meaning it is supported by the public, and to be open to all of lawful age who will avail themselves of its advantage, subject only to necessary regulations and limitations essential to its efficiency.[28]

On appeal, the state Supreme Court affirmed the district court's ruling but confined itself to a narrow, statutory interpretation without utilizing the dicta or the logic of the lower court opinion.[29]

Since the Pennsylvania case, there have been various administrative rulings in several states on the question of whether shared time illegally aids parochial schools, but no court has faced that issue or the question of whether a request for shared-time attendance must be honored if the program is legal in a particular state. Assuming that the constitutionality of shared time will be upheld on a national level and in most states (as I assume), is there a constitutional right to such an arrangement?

I believe the answer to the question of a constitutional right is the same for both released time and shared time. If some legal programs exist in a state on the basis of a permissive state statute or unchallenged custom, then public officials may not arbitrarily deny a request to participate in them in the parts of the state where they exist or *to initiate them in other parts of the state.* Public school officials should be permitted a reasonable amount of time and flexibility in working out the arrangements, but they should not be given unregulated discretion over an educational opportunity that involves an act of conscience. To arbitrarily give such an opportunity to some in a state but not to others might violate the equal protection clause. If, however, there is no provision or practice in a state for released time or shared time, then there seems to be only a moral, not a constitutional, mandate on state legislatures to permit such arrangements.

In *Zorach v. Clauson,* Justice Douglas, speaking for the Court, suggested that

> When the state encourages religious instruction or cooperates with religious authorities by adjusting the schedule of public events to sectarian needs, it follows the best of our traditions. For it then respects the religious nature of our people and accommodates the public service to their spiritual needs.[30]

The Justice, however, did not indicate that the free exercise clause requires the creation of released-time programs.[31] If such a right exists, it would probably be sustained on an equal-protection-clause argument in a case involving a permissive statute like Oregon's.

A public school's formal arrangements for the teaching of religion can certainly affect its legal neutrality. It has been suggested here that fair treatment of the religious aspects of other subjects may be constitutionally required while separate courses in religion are optional. Although provision for released time or shared time is not in itself constitutionally mandatory for every state, once it exists the state must extend equal protection of the law to every child wishing to participate. Furthermore, if such an arrangement "follows the best of our traditions" because it "respects the religious nature of our people," then the tone of neutrality in the public schools would be enhanced by provisions for this kind of opportunity.

OTHER ISSUES BEARING ON RELIGIOUS NEUTRALITY

In addition to the formal arrangements for religious education in or out of the public school, there are some other issues that will affect the quality of religious neutrality in every school. For example, what should be the school policy on the teacher's freedom to respond to questions about religious truth? Public school students are a captive audience and teachers should not be permitted to proselytize, but the First Amendment does not bar either an honest question or an answer. There are, of course, professional considerations regarding the maturity of students and explanation of opposing points of view, but within these canons of good teaching (applicable to any subject) religious questions may be discussed vigorously and faculty opinions stated. If the teachers are chosen on a non-discriminatory basis, the pattern of their responses, if given freely, will meet the legal test of religious neutrality.

Another question that has troubled many communities is whether baccalaureate services and the celebration of Christmas should be permitted in the public schools. The nature of baccalaureate ceremonies varies among communities, but, in general, the baccalaureate is the religious counterpart to graduation and, as such, should not continue as a school-organized or school-sanctioned event. There is no reason, however, why baccalaureate services cannot be held in local churches separately or, if local conditions permit, cooperatively, with attendance by school officials if they wish.

Christmas and the celebration of other primarily religious holidays present a more complex problem. The failure of the public schools to recognize that in December, for one reason or another, Christmas is being celebrated may lead to a certain artificiality in education at that time of the year. Still, it is quite clear that public schools may not participate in the religious aspects of the holiday without violating the establishment clause. On the other hand, for the Christian the true meaning of Christmas is profoundly religious and any public school emphasis or promotion of the secular aspects of the holiday is, if not actually hostile to religion, at least degrading to the occasion. Therefore, the conditions of neutrality are probably best met when the public school avoids involvement in religious holidays except to the extent of permitting students and teachers released time for their personal celebrations.

Public School Neutrality as a Compromise

One may object to the considerations outlined here on the grounds that, despite its pretensions to neutrality, the public school system would, nevertheless, still be more acceptable to religious liberals and agnostics than to religious fundamentalists and militant atheists. The same argument, however, could be made against the First Amendment itself. It was not satisfactory to all groups in 1789, and it is not today. A government that remains uncommitted for or against religion and refuses to coerce religious belief or disbelief is still a comparative rarity even in the modern world. When put to the test, not all Americans believe in such a government; and they, of course, have the right to amend the Constitution. Those who would change our constitutional policy have rightly concluded that the decisive struggle is for control of the public schools and of public educational funds.

For these reasons, the religiously neutral public school system must be preserved. Whether the challenge comes from fundamentalists, who want "cultural Protestantism" taught in the schools, or from militant atheists, who want every trace of the role of religion in our culture excised from the schools, the attack must be resisted. Both sides would substitute indoctrination for education. Nor can we afford to accept the idea that the public schools are inherently godless or secularistic and that consequently the only fair solution is to publicly finance separate religious schools. Acceptance of such a theory would not only undermine the public school system but radically alter our traditional standards of justice. Educationally, the theory would have the ugly consequence of providing a rationale for overt religious hostility in public schools. Legally, it would be comparable to a decision in race relations to give up attempting to provide equal treatment for Negroes and to concede that the Black Muslims were right all along by financing a separate "black state." Finally, financing separate private schools would hardly be neutral since 95 per cent of them are religious schools and 90 per cent of them belong to one church.

The neutral public school is a compromise. It provides perfect satisfaction for neither the believer nor the non-believer. Alternatives to the public school should be permitted, and the public schools themselves should be as flexible as is constitutionally possible in providing opportunities for religious studies. If the public school is a compromise, so is the First Amendment; and that fundamental compromise requires that public educational policy (schools and funds) remain neutral toward religion.

Public school neutrality is not an easy ideal to achieve. After exhausting administrative alternatives, litigation may be necessary. Should a public school discriminate against religion, the same judicial remedy exists as was available when the public school attempted to promote religious rituals. The claim that the public school cannot be legally neutral must be rejected. If the public schools cannot be neutral, the government itself cannot be neutral, and our 176-year-old experiment in religious liberty will have become a hollow pretense.

NOTES

1. *Abington School District v. Schempp*, 374 U.S. 203, 224–225 (1963).

2. *Ibid.*, at 306.

3. *Ibid.*, at 246.

4. See Justice Brennan's history of the neutrality concept, *ibid.*, at 294–304.

5. 319 U.S. 624, 637 (1943).

6. *Ibid.*, at 642.

7. 330 U.S. 1, 23, 24 (1947). Justice Jackson also noted that, in his opinion, the public school was more consistent with Protestant values than with Catholic traditions. The legal significance of the compatibility of a public policy with denominational viewpoints is explored in the following pages.

8. Both the HEW memorandum and the NCWC brief are reprinted in *Georgetown Law Review*, 50:351 (1961).

9. *Ibid.*, at 438–439.

10. *Ibid.*, at 440.

11. This criticism seems a little unfair. The EPC's language is clumsy and reflects the kind of phrasing that inadvertently results from committee consensus. Furthermore, it antedates both *Torcaso* and *Abington*. The EPC's language is clearly too narrow, but one cannot assume therefore that the EPC would support, then or now, a public school role "in securing the acceptance" of a non-supernatural religion.

12. Leo Pfeffer has been for many years counsel to the American Jewish Congress. Both he and his organization have been opponents of federal aid to parochial schools.

13. *Torcaso v. Watkins*, 367 U.S. 488 (1961).

14. For a similar argument at the higher education level by a liberal Protestant see Harold Stahmer, "Defining Religion: Federal Aid and Academic Freedom," in *Religion and the Public Order* (University of Chicago Press, 1964), pp. 116–146.

15. See U.S. Congress, House Committee on the Judiciary, *Hearings on School Prayer*, Vols. I, II, III, 88th Congress, 2nd Session, 1964.

16. I recognize that these groups are overlapping.

17. *West Virginia State Board of Education v. Barnette*, 319 U.S. 624, 642 (1943).

18. For a discussion of this arrangement see Susan Doyle, "Religion and the New York City Board of Education," unpublished manuscript, Teachers College, Columbia University, 1965.

19. According to a National Education Association nationwide survey (as reported in *Education Digest*, May, 1957, p. 3), 87 per cent of male public school teachers and 93 per cent of female public school teachers were "active church members." This is significantly above the national average of 60 per cent church membership. For a description of public school personnel patterns in one New England city (New Haven) and their relationship to community groups see Robert A. Dahl, *Who Governs?* (Yale University Press, 1961), pp. 143–152.

20. Macmillan, 1965.

21. *Abington School District v. Schempp*, 374 U.S. 203, 225 (1963).

22. *McCollum v. Board of Education*, 333 U.S. 203 (1948).

23. It may be objected that it is a very different thing to exclude information about Negroes since they are a definite group. Exclusion of information about religion, however, may be considered a discrimination against believers in favor of non-believers.

24. *West Virginia State Board of Education v. Barnette*, 319 U.S. 624, 637 (1944).

25. For example, assuming educational appropriateness, if the school may put on the play *A Man for All Seasons*, they may also do *The Devils of Loudun*. If the students are assigned Aquinas and Luther, they may also read Voltaire and Paine. Establishment of religion or irreligion would only occur if there were a systematic attempt to promote or hinder religion.

26. As cited in *Dilger v. School District 24*, 352 P. 2d 564 (1960).

27. As cited in *Commonwealth ex rel. Wehrle v. Plummer*, 21 Pa. Dist. R. 182 (1911).

28. *Ibid.*, at 184.

29. *Commonwealth ex rel. Wehrle v. School District of Altoona*, 241 Pa. 224 (1912).

30. 343 U.S. 306, 314 (1952).

31. Justice Douglas said flatly, "It takes obtuse reasoning to inject any issue of free exercise of religion into the present case," at 311, but he was not thinking about the kind of claim presented here.

3

Reactions and Resources

Arthur Gilbert

The material in this chapter falls naturally into two divisions. The first contains *reactions* to the problem of teaching about religion in the public schools; the second offers a subjective, critical evaluation of the *resources* in preparation or now available for teaching about the Bible and religion as a secular subject in public education.

In the first section, under the general heading of *Reactions*, information on the following topics will be presented:

1. Rulings of the Supreme Court on the issue of teaching about religion in the public schools, and legal decisions or rulings subsequently rendered at the state level.
2. Policy statements of national Protestant, Catholic, and Jewish organizations and leading religious spokesmen.
3. Official positions by national educational associations.
4. Surveys into the extent and nature of religious material in the public school's social studies curriculum and courses in English literature.
5. A listing of recently organized non-profit, tax-exempt foundations or associations to foster "the proper" teaching of religion in the public schools.

No effort has been made to be all-inconclusive or exhaustive. These are representative studies and reactions, knowledge of which will be helpful to those who want to know what is now taking place with regard to this complex issue.

The second section, entitled *Resources*, will include the following:

1. A discussion of sectarian Bible classes now conducted under public school auspices in North Carolina, Tennessee, Texas, and Indiana, and a review of a new course for teaching the Bible as literature prepared by the Indiana University English Curriculum Study Center.
2. Examples of community conflict (in Texas, Arizona, and Massachusetts) over the way religion is presented in social studies textbooks now used in public schools.
3. A review of some widely publicized efforts to develop new approaches to the teaching of the Bible or religion, notably the efforts of Thayer Warshaw of Newton, Massachusetts, to develop a course on the Bible as a resource book for studies in the humanities; a discussion of religious themes in the experimental English curriculum being developed at the University of Nebraska; and a review of religion in the new social studies unit developed by the Pennsylvania State Department of Education.
4. Finally, the recounting of some successful and unsuccessful efforts by inter-religious committees in cooperation with public school superintendents (in the cities of Omaha and Pittsburgh and in the state of Florida) to deal with this question in a constructive way.

This report is intended to indicate the complexity of this issue and to serve as a caveat: much more consultation across faith lines and the involvement of religious scholars along with professional educators in the development of materials seems an absolute necessity.

I. Reactions

1. THE DOOR IS OPENED — THE LEGAL SITUATION

In its historic June 17, 1963, decision prohibiting the recitation of prayers and the devotional use of the Bible in the public school, the Supreme Court observed,

> . . . it might well be said that one's education is not complete without a study of comparative religion or the history of religion and its relationship to the advancement of civilization. It certainly may be said that the Bible is worthy of study for its literary and historic qualities. Nothing we have said here indicates that such study of the Bible or of religion, when presented objectively as part of a secular program of education, may not be effected consistent with the First Amendment.[1]

Justices Brennan and Goldberg concurred in this recognition of the importance of a factual study of religion. Justice Brennan stated, "Indeed, whether or not the Bible is involved, it would be impossible to teach meaningfully many subjects in the social sciences or the humanities without some mention of religion." Justice Goldberg added, "Neither the State nor the Court can or should ignore the significance of the fact that a vast portion of our people believe in and worship God and that many of our legal, political and personal values derive historically from religious teachings." And he advocated that "the teaching *about* religion" be "distinguished from the teaching *of* religion in the public schools."

It was not the first time the justices of the Supreme Court had encountered this problem. In the 1948 *McCollum* decision, which ruled unconstitutional the released-time program as practiced in Champaign, Illinois, Justice Jackson opined,

> I think it remains to be demonstrated whether it is possible . . . to isolate and cast out of secular education all that some people may reasonably regard as religious instruction. . . . I should suppose it is a proper, if not indispensable, part of preparation for a worldly life to know the roles that religion and religions have played in the tragic story of mankind. The fact is, that for good or ill, nearly everything in our culture worth transmitting, everything which gives meaning to life, is saturated with religious influences, derived from paganism, Judaism, Christianity — both Catholic and Protestant — and other faiths accepted by a large part of the world's population. One can hardly respect a system of education that would leave the student wholly ignorant of the currents of religious thought that move the world society for a part in which he is being prepared.[2]

In the *McCollum* case, as in the more recent *Schempp-Murray* case, the Supreme Court recognized that the ability to distinguish in education between that which is secular and that which is religious is a problem of "magnitude, intricacy, and delicacy." Justice Jackson, in 1948, rejected for the Court any role as "a super Board of Education for every school district in the nation." In 1963 Justice Brennan reiterated, "To what extent and at what point in the curriculum religious materials should be cited are matters which the Courts ought to trust largely to the experienced officials who superintend our nation's public schools."

On the face of it, then, the Court seemed to say the following:

It is proper in public education to demonstrate the connection many Americans believe to exist between the values of American society and the historic religions.

It is proper to teach about religions, the role of religious institutions, and the meaning of faith in the lives of important individuals, as such facts are relevant to an understanding of history.

It is proper to underscore those religious issues or provide that information about religious beliefs that are relevant for a profounder understanding of the arts and literature of Western civilization.

It is proper to read the Bible and study it for its literary significance and its historic importance.

But all of this information must be presented "objectively" as a "secular program of education."

The Court made no effort to explain what the word "objective" and "secular" mean. They left it to educators to provide the answer. With a surprising degree of confidence, some leaped to the challenge. Archibald Shaw, then Associate Secretary of the American Association of School Administrators, wrote, "If we school people are up to its implied challenge, the Supreme Court's decisions may well turn out to have done more for both education and religion than all the legislative hearings and church pressure together. Now at last we can work on building a curriculum that will lead our young people to a steadily broadening understanding of the role religion plays in the affairs of mankind."[3]

Since the Court's decision (1963–1966), the issue of the use of the Bible for instructional purposes has become the subject of legislation, litigation, and legal rulings in at least twelve states.

Legislation.   On May 14, 1963, Governor Edmund C. Brown of California signed a bill adding a specific section to the state's Education Code which made it clear that nothing in the Code should be interpreted as precluding references to religion or to the Bible where they are intrinsic to the curriculum. The bill said,

> Nothing in this Code shall be construed to prevent or exclude from the public schools' reference to religion or references to or the use of religious literature. art or music . . . when such references or uses do not constitute instruction in religious principles or add to any religious sect, church or sectarian purpose and when such references or uses are incidental or illustrative of matters properly included in the course of study.

In July, 1963, the Florida legislature passed a law authorizing but not requiring "secular courses in religion." The Pennsylvania legislature authorized its State Department of Public Instruction to prepare a course in the Bible as literature for non-mandatory use by senior high schools in the state. Later I shall describe the efforts in both states to implement these legislative instructions.

Litigation.   The Washington State Court on June 14, 1966, dismissed a suit brought by two fundamentalist Protestant pastors to enjoin the teaching of a course, "The Bible as Literature," at the University of Washington. The plaintiffs claimed that the Bible is an nfallible revelation from

God to man and not the proper subject of scholarly study, that the course promoted a secular view of religion, and that the professor taught the documentary theory of the writing of scripture as fact and offered no understanding of fundamentalist views of Holy Writ. In the plaintiffs' view such a course, supported by tax funds, violated the state constitution. However, the Court upheld the right of the state university, as part of its educational responsibility, to offer courses in the Bible as literature. The jurist noted also that the course is an elective and is not required for graduation.[4]

Attorney General Rulings. The attorney generals of Delaware, Georgia, Maine, and West Virginia, in letters to their respective state commissioners of education, affirmed the state's right to allow study of religion for educational purposes.

The attorney general of Delaware, for example, ruled in 1964 that public school funds could be used to purchase Bibles for use in the school curriculum. He defined the "secular purposes" for which religion might be studied in a public school as a source of "moral and intellectual teachings, respect for law, brotherhood, honorable thought and action, and knowledge of our actual heritage."[5]

The attorney general of Georgia, however, suggested a restriction. A course limited to "Bible Study" or "Bible History" might be a propagation of religion and was forbidden; but reading or discussing the Bible as part of a broader course in comparative religion or the history of religion was permissible.[6]

State Boards of Education. The superintendent of public instruction in Illinois advised local school authorities — without qualification or reservation — that the United States Constitution "does not prohibit the teaching of factual information on the history and tenets of religious bodies in the regular curriculum."[7]

The Indiana Board of Education in 1965 authorized an elective course, "The Bible as Literature," for high school seniors.[8]

In 1964, the State Board of Education in Maine authorized public schools to use the Bible in literature and history classes.[9]

The legal counsellor to the Texas Education Agency in 1965 ruled, "A Bible course offered as an elective and presented as a study of the Bible for its literary or historic qualities, i.e., as part of the secular program for education in the public school, is legally permissible."[10]

2. THE RESPONSE OF CHURCHMEN

Some zealous churchmen, educators, and politicians saw in a program to study about the Bible a device by which to circumvent the Court's decision banning the reading of the Bible in a devotional exercise. Thus, all one had to do was to develop a course consisting of Bible readings which all students may be required or permitted to take; such proposals were heard in a number of state legislatures and local boards of education. At the urging of Governor Wallace, for example, the Alabama State Board of Education, on August 6, 1963, made Bible reading part of the "required curriculum" of its public schools. The resolution affirming this new regulation also denounced the Court's decision as a "calculated effort to take God out of the public affairs of the nation." [11]

Many Protestants believe that a particularly uplifting experience may be encountered through the reading of God's Word; in fact, they hold that the moral well-being of our country depends on a program of public school Bible reading. As Dr. Robert A. Cook, representing the National Association of Evangelicals in testimony supporting the Becker Amendment to the Constitution, put it, "While the good that has come from the practice [Bible reading in the public school] cannot be measured, we believe that it has been considerable and provided a stabilizing influence greater than many realize."[12] In his sermon "Christian Philosophy of Education," Billy Graham, the noted evangelist, asserted, "Separation of church and state was never meant to separate school children from God! The trend to extricate God and moral teaching from the school is a diabolic scheme and is bearing its fruit in the deluge of juvenile delinquency that is overwhelming our nation." [13]

Since churchmen and educators who share this view are eager to have as many children as possible find God in scriptures, they have zealously pursued proposals to institute courses to teach about religion. They believe they are keeping faith with a widely held traditional conviction that religious instruction must be an essential part of true education. They are not concerned merely to develop programs limited to providing students with knowledge *about* religion. Rather, they favor such education as would challenge children to live lives informed by Christian ideals. They recognize in the fulfillment of that purpose no conflict for the public school as a secular agency in a pluralistic society. They hold still with A. P. Peabody, once United States Commissioner of Education, who long ago said, "We are by profession a Christian people. We recognize the great principles of religion in the devotional services in our legislatures and our courts of justice. Shall our children be trained as citizens without the inculcation of these fundamental religious ideas which will impress upon them the significance of prayer and the dread solemnity of an oath?" [14]

Other Protestants, however, acknowledge a serious problem that has resulted from the emergence in the United States of a complex religious pluralism. The Supreme Court's prayer and Bible-reading decisions, they realize, have brought to an end an era when the church could presume that through devotional rites public education was allowed to inculcate Christian ideals, or orient children's minds Godward, or instruct them in reverence, or confront them with God. If there is to be any teaching about religion in the public schools, it will have to be planned carefully and take into account all points of view; and most importantly, churchmen will have to accept the public schools' limited responsibility, by virtue of its secular character.

The National Council of Churches. Denominational officials at a church-state Study Conference called by the National Council of Churches in Columbus, Ohio, February 4–7, 1964, acknowledged that the Court's decision prohibiting devotional exercises forced Christians to "look beneath the veneer of religious observance to the real content of public education. Far too many Christians had unconsciously assumed that the deeper question of the moral and religious dimension of public education had been settled by the formal recognition of religion."

Participants at the study conference then affirmed their "full support to the endeavor" of public schools to engage in "objective teaching about the influence of religion in history and in contemporary society." Education which omits effective, objective dealing with the moral and religious dimensions of our culture and heritage, they said, is "truncated and incomplete."

The workshop dealing with this issue at the National Council of Churches conference made three specific proposals:

1. It called for "full and objective cognizance of the place of religion in the many courses which deal with the history of Western World civilization, American history, social studies, literature, music, art, etc."

2. It urged the development of programs to challenge children to "make value choices that will lead them to develop their moral integrity" and it acknowledged the "value of courses on the subject of ethics and moral action."

3. It encouraged "elective courses on the history of religion." In this regard, the consultation recommended research and fact-finding as to syllabi, experimental programs, etc., and support for the publication and use of more broadly inclusive textbooks and other supplementary educational material.

Recognizing that there is much distrust among religious groups concerning the objectivity of the religion to be taught in the public schools and the motives of those who press for such programs, the Conference urged its churches "to convene inter-faith and inter-church consultations . . . so that mutual understanding rather than rivalry or suspicion may prevail. . . . It may be that 'secular' groups and individuals should also be brought into such discussions." [15]

The Presbyterian Church in the U.S.A. Of interest, too, is the policy statement adopted by the 169th General Assembly of the Presbyterian Church in the U.S.A., in that this denomination's position was determined only after a thoroughgoing discussion in every church and synod in the country over a period of several years. On the issue of "Religious Sources and References Found in the Traditional Curriculum Material of the Public School," the Presbyterian statement declared:

> We hold that religious illiteracy is not congenial to the philosophy of general education nor in keeping with guidance practices that take into account the total needs of the child. We, therefore, join with responsible educators in their search for new and improved means of recognizing the importance of religion within regular academic subjects. We believe it reasonable and a part of honesty that teachers interpret points of view other than their own with fairness, at the same time that their own points of view are acknowledged. Such teaching would thereby give recognition to the place of religion in American culture as imparted through knowledge in such school subjects as art, the earth sciences, literature, music and the social sciences as well as the general counselling practices. The school should properly acquaint the student with general religious differences and contemporary beliefs, while at the same time guaranteeing that no attempt be made at indoctrination or for the calculated purpose of achieving a specific commitment. . . .
>
> We insist that the political guarantees of religious freedom and the principle of separation of church and state do not require the elimination of the religious backgrounds of our heritage. It is our conviction that the literacy and understanding that are required to support a free society demand an educational philosophy that frees instruction from controlled censorship and that requires the explanation of all points of view. . . . We hold that sound and objective scholarship equal or superior to those characteristic of other teaching areas must accompany any attempt to introduce a religious dimension into any teaching fields.[16]

Roman Catholic Opinion.   Catholic opinion with regard to the specific issue of teaching about religion builds upon two earlier resolutions adopted by the American hierarchy. These touch upon religion and education in general terms.

At the close of their annual meeting, November 16, 1952, the Roman Catholic bishops of the United States issued their first statement on "Secularism and the Schools." The bishops argued the importance of religion in education on the grounds that man cannot properly live without religion. "Without the hope that religion alone can give," they said, "he cannot rise above that pessimism, that sense of despair, which threatens to engulf the whole of civilization." Society, too, argued the bishops, draws its unity, its stability, and its holiness from religion: "When religion remains strong, it stands as a protective armor, safeguarding both individual and family. . . . In the last analysis, there is no society of free men without the creative and sustaining force of religion."

Then, directing their attention to the growth of secularism and the "divorce of religion from education," they declared:

To teach moral and spiritual values divorced from religion and based solely on social convention . . . is not enough. Unless man's conscience is enlightened by the knowledge of principles that express God's law, there can be no firm and lasting morality. Without religion, morality becomes simply a matter of individual taste, of public opinion or majority vote. Without religious education, moral education is impossible.

The bishops were quick to point out that in criticizing this secularist trend in education they did not intend to cast themselves as enemies of public education. They recognized that "the state has a legitimate and even necessary concern with education," but "if religion is important to good citizenship — and that is the burden of our national tradition — then the state must give recognition to its importance in public education." [17]

In 1961 the annual message of the Catholic hierarchy re-emphasized their conviction that religion in the public school is a necessity:

Popular education also bears a measure of responsibility for the decline and rejection of moral principles. At first there was no intention of excluding either religion or morality from the common tax-supported school. But the diversity of our religious pattern and the rising pressure of secularism have produced the school without religion and it is idle to suppose that this school could long inculcate in American youth moral convictions which would be firmly held.[18]

No official statement has since been made with particular regard for efforts to teach about religion in public education. Individual Catholic leaders, however, have urged American public school educators to give the proposal their serious consideration. Joseph Cardinal Ritter, Archbishop of St. Louis, was specific in his call upon the public school to initiate programs to teach about religion. Addressing more than 3,500 religious and lay teachers in his archdiocesan school system, Cardinal Ritter said the "new spirit of cooperation among churches" and recent U.S. Supreme Court decisions "should open the way for the public school systems to review their attitude toward religion in the schools." When schools remain "silent" on the subject of religion, "such silence speaks for itself, for it tells the student that here is a field that cannot be very important because it is not even mentioned in the school." "Rather," Cardinal Ritter said, "there should be a conscious, deliberate attempt on the part of the schools to encourage each student to follow his conscience in matters of religion and even have the courage of his religious convictions in the face of hostility and opposition." Recent Supreme Court decisions "uphold the right and obligation of the schools to teach about religion but not to teach religion itself," he stressed.[19]

In similar vein Daniel Callahan, Associate Editor of the Catholic magazine *Commonweal*, called upon American public schools to develop significant course offerings on religion: "Now there is a chance to give religion some intellectual and academic significance. That chance should not be thrown away." [20]

Rev. Robert F. Drinan, S.J., Dean of the Boston College Law School, addressing the Annual Convention of the American Association of School Administrators in Atlantic City, February 15, 1965, pointed to the value of such education for the development of better intergroup relations:

> Community understanding of religious differences cannot be advanced by silence and suppression of these religious differences in the greatest molder of future American opinion — the public school. Children cannot learn to understand, appreciate and respect religious differences if there is a blackout of discussion and even of recognition of these differences in the schools they attend for the first seventeen years of their life. . . . No one, of course, desires to permit any teacher to indoctrinate or any minority or majority group of religiously minded students to be able to use the public school for religious worship or sectarian instruction. What is suggested is that the enlarging religious and academic freedom now being extended to college professors and students in state-related institutions of higher education be made available with appropriate modifications to schools of less than collegiate rank.[21]

A Catholic response, insisting on interfaith agreement before any new courses were offered in the public school, was made by Rev. James R. Deneen, Superintendent of the Catholic Diocesan Schools, Evansville, Indiana, at an Institute on Religion and Public Education sponsored by the Board of Education of Hinsdale, Illinois. Father Deneen expressed his conviction that courses in specific religious doctrine are too advanced to be taught in an "academically defensible manner below the level of the junior year in high school." Such courses, if developed, he insisted, would require the creation of new materials and adequate guidelines. Furthermore, "No school district should attempt to teach religion or teach about religion until representative religious leaders in that community have reached a stage of easy communication and mutual trust." [22]

State Support for Religious Schools Urged.   Rev. Richard Regan, S.J., in his authoritative book *American Pluralism and the Catholic Conscience,* added yet another view, one that is held by many Catholics. Suggesting that the secular public school system obviously could not teach religion as adequately as Catholics and most religiously affiliated Americans would desire, he urged state support for religious instruction in sectarian schools. Father Regan insisted that it would be difficult, if not impossible, to create a public school curriculum providing "objective non-sectarian religious instruction," adding

The limits in the role which religion can play in public education derive from the nature of a common school in a pluralistic society. Of necessity, neither religionist nor secularist can be completely satisfied with the deference which each must make to the other in public education. This is precisely why Catholics and other religious groups have made sacrifices to support parochial school systems in which religious instruction and religious orientation can be freely imparted. If considerations of the democratic processes, by and large, favor the secularist's contentions against public sponsorship of religious instruction or exercises in common schools, no like factor argues against public support of private religiously-oriented, but secularly competent, education when parents choose such for their own children. The secularist cannot have his cake and eat it too; he cannot exclude government-sponsored religious instruction in the common schools and simultaneously deny the propriety of government support of religiously oriented education for those who wish it.[23]

Jewish Positions. Jewish reactions to the proposals to teach about religion in the public school have been more restrained than those of Protestants or Catholics. From bitter memory, Jews fear that the religion to be taught in government-sponsored schools, in a Christian-influenced environment, will short-change Judaism as a relevant and vital contemporary faith.

Rabbi Robert Gordis fully articulated many of the Jewish concerns in his book *The Root and the Branch.* Acknowledging that arguments for objective teaching about religion in public education were "incontrovertible," he immediately added,

> The history of recent events gives ground for feeling that here the danger of the "camel's head in the tent" is not imaginary. It cannot be denied that there are those who would regard teaching about religion merely as the opening wedge for the teaching *of* religion. . . . The study materials thus far produced in this area leave much to be desired from the standpoint of objectivity and content and raise the serious question whether adequate material can be prepared to meet the need.

Rabbi Gordis also raised questions concerning the adequacy of the training of teachers and the possible restrictions that parents might impose upon their children when it came to visiting other churches or learning about religion from ministers of other faiths. Finally, he suggested that even if teachers could attain to an attitude of objectivity, this in itself might become harmful. Many parents might consider public school courses in religion as "an adequate substitute for religious education in church schools." Or people might translate the public school teacher's position of objectivity "into an attitude of indifference to all genuine religious commitment." [24]

The major Jewish community relations agencies and religious bodies cooperating through the National Community Relations Advisory Council (NCRAC) jointly issued a statement that distinguished between the public school's function to teach about religion where relevant and intrinsic to the secular subject and the effort of the public school to develop separate, systematic courses in comparative religion or on the doctrines of religion.

> We believe that the public schools must and should teach, with full objectivity, the role that religion has played in the life of mankind and in the development of our society when such teaching is intrinsic to the regular subject matter being studied. Beyond this, we believe that the public school is not equipped to teach the doctrines of religion in a factual, objective and impartial manner. While such factual, objective and impartial study of religious beliefs may not be inconsistent with the principle of the separation of Church and State, we believe there is reason for concern lest the introduction of such teaching in the public school engender pressures upon school personnel from sectarian groups, compromise the impartiality of teaching and the integrity of the public education system to other grave consequences.[25]

A statement issued by the Anti-Defamation League of B'nai B'rith is characterized by some as a "softer view." Yet the ADL also distinguishes between teaching about religion where it is intrinsic to the curriculum and the development of separate courses in comparative religion.

> It is inherent to the teaching of history, literature, social studies, intercultural education, human relations, art and music to include what various religions and religious movements have contributed in these areas. The role that religion has played in the history and development of human society can be taught with substantial objectivity and when so taught is a desirable practice. But the teacher must not use such teaching as an instrument for religious indoctrination.
>
> Proposals have also been made that the public schools establish separate courses which would teach about different religious practices and beliefs. The ADL believes that the study of comparative religion is best undertaken only when students have achieved a degree of maturity. Otherwise in the minds of the immature, such teaching would tend to substitute questioning for faith. Whether expertly prepared teachers in elementary and high schools can utilize objectively a proper curriculum in this field remains to be seen. ADL stands ready to cooperate toward this end.[26]

3. EDUCATORS' DEFINITIONS OF THEIR ROLE
   IN TEACHING ABOUT RELIGION

The Educational Policies Commission. The Educational Policies Commission of the National Education Association, and the American Association of School Administrators have devoted specific attention to this issue over an extended period. In a historic policy statement issued in 1951, the Commission affirmed that the "public school can teach objectively about religion without advocating or teaching any religious creed. To omit from the classroom all references to religion and the institutions of religion is to neglect an important part of American life. Knowledge about religion is essential for a full understanding of our culture, literature and history and current affairs." Acknowledging "that religion is controversial," the Commission added, "this is not an adequate reason for excluding teaching about religion from the public schools . . . general guides on the teaching of all controversial issues may be helpful. If need be, teachers should be provided with special help and information to equip them to teach objectively in this area." [27]

Superintendents of Large City Schools. In 1958 an Educational Platform for Public Schools was adopted by sixty superintendents of schools in cities of 100,000 to 200,000 population. According to this platform, religion "as a separate subject" tends to become sectarian and ought to be taught in the home and church, not by the public school. To the extent that information about religion "permeates most school subjects . . . it is an essential element of general education." [28]

The Teacher Education and Religion Project. Between 1953 and 1958 the American Association of Colleges for Teacher Education (AACTE) conducted an exploratory study of ways and means to teach the reciprocal relations between religion and other elements of human culture. Supported by a substantial grant from the Danforth Foundation, the five-year study involved fifteen colleges and universities in various sections of the country. The project was concerned particularly with the problem of teaching about religion within the specific field of professional education, the humanities, the social studies, and the natural sciences. In the summary report, the AACTE study was said to be "an academic enterprise, one which was limited in scope to curricular affairs; one which was concerned with where religion was intrinsic to the various disciplines taught by college and university teachers in teacher education institutions."

The project was posited on the assumption of a lack of religious enlightenment in teacher education. According to the report,

> There is little doubt that our teachers' knowledge of the religious beliefs and practices of the children they face in the classroom is seriously limited. Most departments of education, like the colleges and universities that house them, make relatively little provision for the religious enlightenment of their students. A prospective teacher may enter many of our major universities and colleges with an essentially innocent and folklore understanding of the role of religion in western culture. He may also be essentially ignorant . . . of his own religious tradition and lamentably misinformed about others.

The AACTE report also observed that there was a tendency, particularly in history courses, to give much more attention to religion in remote times than in recent times and to place emphasis upon unusual and colorful events rather than upon the most important and representative items. Certain supplementary resources were suggested for use in the social studies. Among these were the occasional use of clergymen as sources of information, explorations by students of periodical literature published by various religious groups, and visits to churches and synagogues for the purpose of promoting understanding.

One of the direct outcomes of this five-year study was that several of the teacher education institutions added courses to their college curricula, and in one case a college established a department of philosophy and religion.

In his summary statement, A. L. Sebaly, national coordinator of the project, asserted, "To attack problems of this size and complexity requires imagination, boldness and courage. More than these individual qualities it requires cooperative effort by scholars from many backgrounds and patient attention to the constructive accommodations of diversity. The AACTE project was a mere beginning." [29]

The National Council for the Social Studies. In 1957, following three years of deliberation, a committee on concepts and values of the National Council for the Social Studies issued a statement defining fourteen "central principles and values" or societal goals of American democracy and the relation of social studies curricula to them.

Principle 8, "The Effective Development of Moral and Spiritual Values," asserted,

> Democracy in the long run will rise or fall according to the extent that individual citizens live by accepted ethical, moral and spiritual values. In our interdependent society the individual rights guaranteed in our Constitution become meaningless unless they are exercised in a manner harmonious with the moral and ethical principles that are the foundations of Western democracy.
>
> Responsibility for helping young people develop moral and spiritual values is shared by the three great institutions, home, church and school. Working within the context of freedom of religion and separation of church and state, our public schools cannot become involved in theological teachings. However, the school can and must carry its share of responsibility for developing moral and spiritual values. It can focus directly on problems of social ethics. And by teaching about the institutions of religion the school can help young people appreciate the great part that organized religion has played and does play in the growth of an individual's moral and spiritual values.[30]

The American Association of School Administrators. On June 30, 1964, a Commission on Religion in the Public Schools of the American

Association of School Administrators repeated the educators' conviction
that the history of Western civilization cannot be understood without
some knowledge of the great religious and church influences reaching
back to earliest recorded times. "The real rub, however," confessed this
Commission, is the present "meagerness of the material available that is
truly objective, balanced and educationally sound."

> There is a good deal of local improvisation of materials. There are some
> statewide efforts. But what is needed is a heavily supported project led by
> educators calling on scholars in the humanities and religions and using the
> best programming and presentation skills available. The Commission
> strongly favors the production of material of the highest educational and
> technical excellence in the history of religion and comparative religions.

Commenting on various approaches for the teaching of religion in the
public schools, the Commission said,

> The desirable policy in the schools is to deal directly and objectively with
> religion whenever and wherever it is intrinsic to learning experience in the
> various fields of study and to seek other appropriate ways to teach what has
> been aptly called "the reciprocal relations" between religion and other ele-
> ments in human culture. The implementation of that policy calls for much
> more than an added course either for teachers or for the high school cur-
> riculum itself. It requires topic by topic analysis of the separate courses and
> cooperative efforts by the teachers to give appropriate attention to these
> relationships.[31]

In March, 1965, the AASA convened a group of thirty denominational
leaders representing the Jewish, Protestant, and Catholic faiths, to advise
it whether "it ought undertake to direct the development for public
secondary schools of materials in the field of religion in history and of
the world's religions." In a summary report on their two-day meeting
the chairman, then AASA associate secretary Archibald B. Shaw, noted,
"In substantially every aspect of the discussion where religion and public
education were joined there was a wide range of disagreement among the
participants." One assumes, he added, "that it would be greater still in a
larger and less well-informed group."

Despite disagreement on philosophic issues, the participants agreed that
the AASA should "take the lead with teachers of art, music and literature
— the humanities as they are found in secondary schools — to make a
topic-by-topic analysis of the separate courses in order to seek out the
appropriate ways to teach the reciprocal relationship between religion
and other elements in human culture."

Agreement substantially unanimous, but significantly hedged by individual interpretations, was also expressed on the need for material of the
highest educational and technical excellence on religion in history (rather

than the history of religion) and on understanding of the world's religions and ideologies (rather than comparative religion).

> It was unanimously agreed that however self-sufficient and self-teaching any materials might be (and there was some disagreement as to whether these qualities were desirable) the teacher has a crucial role. No plans are worthwhile that do not take this into account. Even those who would emphasize the value of self-sufficient material agree that in-service involvement and education of teachers is a *sine qua non* to any progress in this field.
>
> The group was divided as to whether separate units or supplementary material was desirable or whether an elective course could be added to the curriculum. They were in substantial agreement, however, that history, problems of democracy and social studies need an infusion of materials recognizing the importance of religious institutions, religions, ideologies and religiously motivated men in human affairs past and present.

A number of other significant suggestions emerged: No single best course or set of materials can be prepared. Choices must be made available, therefore, for local district decisions. As materials are developed, continuous reference should be made to organizational representatives from churches, synagogues, and societies, and the materials should represent the cooperative efforts of scholars in religion, in history, in various subject fields, and in education generally.[32]

Surveys of School Administrators. A national survey of high school administrators conducted in September, 1960, by *The Nation's Schools* revealed sharp division in the ranks. Asked what they thought about the public school's responsibility to teach about religion, 52 per cent of the superintendents who responded said they favored such instruction. A Michigan school administrator commented, "I believe knowledge of the various religions — their basic beliefs and objectives — can be of significant value in helping to further national and world understanding." Most of the 45 per cent who were against teaching about religion anticipated that such an effort would create difficulties. An Ohio official predicted "the word 'about' would soon be lost and there would be trouble." [33]

A more recent study by the Associated Press[34] similarly revealed that while some public schools were offering courses in religion or the Bible, or both, a majority of school authorities display "a lack of enthusiasm for the whole idea." "Frankly, most teachers are scared to death to do anything with religion," said W. W. Dick, Arizona State Superintendent of Education. "People have strong feelings about religion," said Dr. F. Melvin Lawson, Superintendent of City Schools in Sacramento, California, and added, "Persons who try to teach such a course would be under severe scrutiny, to say the least. The teacher would have to be a genius to handle it without getting into hot water." Donald E. Kitch, acting Chief of Instruction for the California Department of Education, said that a course in comparative religion might be a valuable elective for high school students but "we just do not have the time. There are so many other things that are already required." Many of the school superintendents also reported that the introduction of such courses would be considered a violation of the separation of church and state in their communities; others suggested that there was really no indication of public interest in such courses. The view of Dr. James E. Allen, New York State Superintendent of Schools, on the other hand, was representative of the outlook of those who favored some effort to teach about religion — especially about its role in shaping America's heritage. "By bringing young people to an understanding of what a vital force religion has been, is and will continue to be," he said, "schools can create interest in, and respect for religion." (Superintendent Allen's emphasis on the benefits of such instruction *for religion* as against its importance for the integrity of the secular curriculum is exactly one of the crucial philosophic issues that need yet to be resolved.)

4. REFERENCE TO RELIGION IN CONTEMPORARY TEXTBOOKS

Several studies undertaken in recent years suggest strongly that American educators have resolved by *avoidance* the problem of what information to provide about religion in the public school curriculum.

Religion in the Social Studies and History Curriculum. The most authoritative survey of the treatment of religion in elementary school social studies textbooks is the three-year study undertaken by Dr. Judah J. Harris, a New York Educator. Analyzing 120 leading social studies textbooks used in elementary schools, Dr. Harris disclosed that they are "biased in favor of Protestantism over Catholicism and of Christianity over Judaism. Definitely sectarian, they ignore the pluralistic character of American life."

Dr. Harris notes that

. . . the Reformation is generally described from the point of view of Protestant reformers, the Catholic Church often depicted as evil, cruel and arbitrary. . . . Similarly, Martin Luther is treated in a wholly favorable light as a champion of freedom and enlightenment; no hint is given of what he advocated and practiced towards those whom *he* considered heretics. Nor is much space given to such movements as the Counter-Reformation; the fact that the religious intolerance of the seventeenth and eighteenth centuries was by no means a Catholic monopoly is virtually ignored.

All of Jewish history and Judaism after the Biblical period was also ignored by the textbooks. . . . [There was] no mention of the contributions of Jews to the development of the United States and their current role in

American life. . . . Only eleven of the 120 textbooks discussed Hitler and Nazism and only five mention the persecution of Jews; and one of these texts offered no indication of the immorality of Hitler's policies.

In general, the treatment of religious persecutions is either simplified or ignored to such a degree that young Americans never have a chance to learn about the need for improving interreligious attitudes.

The study concludes, "If textbooks are meant to help us reinforce democratic attitudes, they must be considerably more objective than they are now. They must tell the bad as well as the good for a real appreciation of the role of religion in the development of history."[35]

Mary Catherine Howley's study of history textbooks for Grades 7 and 8 from 1783 to 1956 concludes, "Twentieth-century American history textbooks contain so little data about religion that in their present form they are an inadequate source of information about America's religious heritage and hence are not a satisfactory basis for instruction about religion in the social studies."[36]

Since 1945, at least six unpublished master's or doctor's theses have examined the religious content of public school textbooks.[37] In each case, the author reports that references to religion drop sharply as recent history is dealt with. "American histories give substantially more attention to art, science, business and especially war. In the world histories, less attention is given to Christian beliefs than to beliefs of other religions."[38]

It must be acknowledged, of course, that reference to religion was once a predominant feature of many history and social studies textbooks and English readers. As several of these researchers point out, however, such material was often consciously intended to inculcate an emotional attitude favorable to religion. Noah Webster, for example, in his *History of the United States*, written in 1832, told his readers that "among the first and most important truths which you are to learn are those which relate to God and religion." Elaborating on this theme he advised students, "Let your first care through life be directed to support and extend the influence of the Christian religion and observance of the Sabbath."[39] Similarly, Charles Goodrich, in his *History of the United States*, written in 1823, said, "History displays the dealings of God with mankind. It calls upon us often to regard with awe His darker judgments and, again, it awakens the liveliest emotions of gratitude for His kind and benign dispensations. It cultivates a sense of dependence on Him, strengthens our confidence in His benevolence and impresses us with a conviction of His justice."[40]

The religious references in these books were Protestant in substance and form, for the earliest history texts were written from the vantage point and with the bias of New England Protestantism. Only later, grudgingly, were other Protestant denominations and then other religions recognized. Judaism, if treated sympathetically at all, was considered the precursor to Christianity. Very few references to Jews and Judaism following the year

70 A.D. were to be found. Most recent textbooks, therefore, with their omission of religion are freed at least of material with a blatant sectarian bias or proselytizing overtone.

The researchers also point out that a spiritual verve once communicated by reference to "God," "church," and "religion" now subsists in accounts of patriotic devotion and idealism. "Democracy," "America," the "welfare of mankind" — these are the secular ideals that have become the sanction and purpose of the moral sense encouraged in public school texts. The spirituality of religion has become secularized; yet, one can ask, is there not something religious in these secular ideals?

Suggestions for enriching the history curriculum with material on religion must be seen also in the perspective of the findings of some history scholars that "high school history teachers today do not seem to know very much about the subject they teach and do not do much to improve their qualifications for teaching it." Such were the conclusions of three Indiana University history professors who spent three years surveying the teaching of American history in the high schools of Indiana. The findings of these historians, Maurice G. Baxter, Robert H. Ferrell, and John E. Wiltz, who were aided by a Lilly Endowment grant, are published in *The Teaching of American History in High Schools*. Having contacted most of Indiana's teachers of American history by interview and questionnaire, the authors confessed that they found almost everywhere "apathy, if not plain hostility, towards history courses among high school students and often among parents." They disclosed that 66 per cent of the state's teachers of American history had earned their bachelor's degree in fields other than history; that 30 per cent had taken no graduate work in history; that over half had read no book on American history during the past year. In most Indiana high schools, the authors report, the typical high school history course is "a narrow, shallow review of sacred political items drawn almost exclusively from the textbooks failing to come closer to the present than a generation ago."[41]

The Bible in Literature Courses. Several studies have dealt with the use of the Bible in courses in English literature. A summary of offerings and enrollment in high school subjects in 1960–1961 published in June, 1964, by the United States Office of Education revealed that the total enrollment in English and language arts courses in secondary schools across the country was 12,972,236. Of this total, 4,473 were enrolled in courses in the Bible and Bible history. In addition, 1,533 were enrolled in humanities courses which may or may not have included instruction in the Bible. Enrollment in Bible courses was less than that in debating courses. These enrollments were found in sixty-eight schools in seventeen states.[42]

A nationwide study of four thousand communities by R. B. Dierenfield reported that 4.5 per cent of responding schools in 1961 conducted regular classes in the Bible. Over 50 per cent, however, reported units on the Bible in world history courses, and 32 per cent reported such units in literature courses; schools in the South reported a much higher percentage of such units than those in the Far West.[43]

The Cooperative Test Division of the Educational Testing Service sampled and surveyed public, private, and parochial schools in May, 1963, to determine the literary works most commonly taught in Grades 7 through 12 across the country. No one book of the Bible was taught in more than two schools of the 547 surveyed, with the exception of the Book of Job, which was studied in four schools.[44]

In April, 1964, the National Council of Teachers of English polled the editors-in-chief of the selected major publishing firms of literature texts for secondary schools and found that "in the standard literature anthology, the students will generally read up to a maximum of four Biblical selections including at times one or two psalms, a parable, perhaps a passage from St. Paul's Epistles and one Old Testament story. Most, if not all, will be included in the twelfth-grade books as part of English literature."[45]

Robert F. Hogan, Associate Executive Secretary of the National Council of Teachers of English in Champaign, Illinois, commented on these statistics: "Apart from those programs which openly flout or covertly circumvent the law, few schools provide students with an opportunity to learn about the Bible as literature. . . . Schools wishing to teach biblical selections as literature will find scant material in traditional texts. Literature programs based heavily on anthologies provide too few selections and these too late to give either a substantial or a well-timed body of reservoir literature."

Dealing with the controversial aspects of Bible study, Dr. Hogan added,

> It seems reasonable that while the question of Christ's divinity may be precluded from public education, the matter of his humanitarianism is not. If presenting the Bible as divine revelation is excluded, teaching it as humane letters is not. To study Job as a classic treatment of the theme of undeserved human suffering, to trace the shepherd image in the twenty-third Psalm, to explore how sentence rhythms and structures support the development of ideas in St. Paul's statement on charity (I Corinthians 1:13) is to study the Bible in an objective and secular fashion. . . . Schools wanting to avoid the strange situation in which the Bible falls before the censors will take the same steps that they would take when teaching any potentially censorable material. With the support of administrators and board of education, they will frame a clear philosophy of why they are teaching selections from the Bible, which selections and how these will be presented.[46]

Proposals for enriching English curricula by including study about the Bible, of course, ought to be seen in the context of recent studies which indicate that "English instruction in American schools is generally deficient." Reporting on a survey of the best public schools in forty-five states by fifteen University of Illinois faculty members, Professor James R. Squire, Executive Secretary of the National Council of Teachers of English, asserted, "The best that can be found in American high school English teaching is simply not good enough." More than 300 teachers in 168 schools were studied. "Our quarrel," said Professor Squire, "is with the incessant superficiality of much classroom study of literature — with, if you will, the evasion of literature." The report revealed that "Teachers continue to teach dates and places as if they were the essence of the subject; there is an over-reliance on geography, a preoccupation with the lives of the poets, a fascination with the Elizabethan stage, a concern with definitions and memory work."[47]

5. ORGANIZATIONS CREATED TO PROMOTE TEACHING ABOUT RELIGION

The decision of the Supreme Court, opening the door to the teaching of religion as part of secular education, stimulated the creation throughout the United States of several foundations and associations designed specifically to promote such "proper" teaching and to prepare materials that would guide and help teachers. Each intended also to serve as a clearing house for the sharing of experiences in this effort.

The Religious Instruction Association. The best known of these new associations, in that it has received the widest national publicity, is the Religious Instruction Association of Fort Wayne, Indiana. It was organized by Mr. James V. Panoch, an apartment building manager and former Illinois school teacher who had gained a reputation as a popular public school assembly lecturer on the Bible. Mr. Panoch, in fact, claims to have given assembly and classroom programs on the Bible in 80 per cent of the public schools in Indiana. Reared as a Baptist and at present a Methodist Sunday School teacher, Mr. Panoch started a course on "The Bible as Literature" for Fort Wayne's South Side High School students in the spring of 1964.

Although the King James translation serves as the basic text in his course, Mr. Panoch uses supplementary material. As he has explained, "The Bible is not sufficient for understanding. It talks of the Pharisees, for example, but it never explains who the Pharisees are." On the other hand, he has reported that his "objective presentation" of the Bible has raised criticism from religious fundamentalists. He rejects their criticism with this assertion: "The Gospel can come through in an objective presentation. The Bible is a very weak book if it needs my interpretation to be meaningful."

The Educational Council to Preserve the Nation's Religious Heritage. A non-profit organization, the Educational Council to Preserve the Nation's Religious Heritage, Inc., was organized in Fayetteville, North

Carolina, by a group of concerned Fayetteville businessmen. This group, too, aims "to encourage the reintroduction into public schools of objective courses of study about the Bible and the subject of religion."

The Fourth R Foundation. The most recent of these grass-roots organizations is the Fourth R Foundation, launched in March, 1966, in Lincoln, Nebraska. Its director is Mr. Stephen Cree, an Ed.D. candidate at the University of Nebraska and an ordained Methodist minister. Mr. Cree explains,

> The purpose of the Fourth R Foundation is the advancement of instruction about religion in the public schools. . . . One of our chief aims is to help the public schools to scrupulously avoid favoring any religious or anti-religious position no matter how worthy we as individuals may consider it to be. . . . The religious commitment of the students is none of the business of the Fourth R educator. He is concerned with what they know, not with what they believe or in whom they trust.

The Religious Heritage of America. A Religious Heritage of America Organization in existence since 1951 decided at its August 22, 1966, executive committee meeting at its headquarters in St. Louis to initiate a three-point program showing how religion can be taught effectively in public schools within the framework of constitutional rulings:

> In its three steps, RHA said it will: (1) contact the leaders of the eighty-six major religious groups in the U.S. asking them to use all available communication tools to inform their constituents that teaching *about* religion in the schools has not been banned, that there is nothing to prevent a teacher from setting aside a period each day for silent prayer created by each child and that the Court has not infringed upon anyone's freedom to pray; (2) seek the cooperation of writers on religion in reemphasizing the facts about the ruling of the Supreme Court on religion in public schools and (3) urge the presidents of the three major television networks to produce television documentaries on the public school and religion.

SUMMARY

This review of studies, policy positions, and court decisions reveals the following:

1. The degree to which any information about religion is now communicated within the public schools' social studies or literature curriculum is minimal.

2. The Supreme Court's recent decisions have stimulated churchmen and educators to reconsider the religious content of public school education.

3. There is no clear consensus, however, on what should be taught or how. Most religious groups are eager that the curriculum be enriched somehow, and educators are inclined to agree. In several states significant efforts have already been initiated to achieve that purpose.

4. Jewish religious groups are the most apprehensive about the religion that will be taught in the public school; educators, too, have warned the nation that any program to teach about religion needs to be undertaken carefully. The best scholarship and the cooperation of all religious groups should be marshaled toward that end.

5. More agreement can be obtained for the development of units to be incorporated into ongoing courses in history, social studies, or literature than for full courses in comparative religion or the history of religion. The implication appears to be that, where religion properly belongs to the subject matter, its inclusion is seen merely as an effort to teach English or history better; but where it is proposed that a separate course be developed there is fear that the purpose will be proselytizing and the content sectarian.

II. Resources

Despite the fact that the Supreme Court has ruled unconstitutional released-time classes when conducted on school property, the fact remains that in some states such Bible classes are conducted in public schools for credit toward graduation. In many other communities these classes are conducted off school property but public school authorities are involved in the authorization of textbooks and in setting standards for the awarding of credit. These Bible classes are frequently sectarian in content and proselytizing in purpose. From time to time, therefore, they have occasioned serious community dissension.

Responsible educational authorities have recenty initiated efforts to develop new courses for the study of the Bible or units for the study of religion as part of elective social studies or literature course offerings. These materials are a decided improvement. Nevertheless, inasmuch as they have often been developed without the consultation of religious scholars of all major faiths, they remain, in many ways, faulty or inadequate.

It is evident that a variety of approaches to the study of religion are under consideration: a unit on the Bible as literature; a study of the Bible as a source book for the study of humanities; the development of religious themes as they appear intrinsically to a thematic study of English literature; a study of the sacred writings of all religions in order to ascertain how men throughout the world define their relationship to God. Interreligious cooperation is required if such units are to be written with objectivity and in fairness to all faiths. In some communities, therefore, efforts have been undertaken to develop communication on this issue between educational authorities and clergymen.

1. SECTARIAN BIBLE CLASSES

A small percentage of public school systems in several states throughout the United States permit courses on the Bible to be conducted on school property for credit toward graduation. These are frequently released-time-type classes that were never withdrawn from the public school system despite the Supreme Court's 1948 *McCollum* decision. The biblical instruction is usually fundamentalist Protestant.

Controversy in North Carolina. Controversy over a Bible class in Reidsville, North Carolina, erupted in November, 1965, when the Rev. Raymond Petrea, pastor of Holy Trinity Lutheran Church, removed his daughter, a fourth-grade student, from the program and branded it unconstitutional. The classes are sponsored and financed by a private group — the Committee for Instruction of Bible in the Public Schools — and a special teacher is employed and paid by the Committee to teach each class one hour a week. A number of churches of several denominations support the program.

In withdrawing his daughter from the Bible class, the Lutheran pastor said, "I am not a crusader, but this kind of teaching reduces the Bible to the level of the fundamentalist or literal interpretation and I have conscientious objections to that." He also called unjust a system which results in his child's being singled out and "at least psychologically discriminated against because she was removed from the class."

The local Catholic priest, Rev. Thomas B. Clements, supported Mr. Petrea in his objections. Father Clements pointed out that the practice, to begin with, was a violation of state law. The North Carolina State Superintendent of Public Instruction had, in the past, made it clear that "Public school facilities may not be used for the purpose of giving religious instruction in schools even though the salaries of teachers are paid by religious organizations." In addition, Father Clements argued that the present system of teaching the Bible in Reidsville, if extended, "could mean that every faith which differs from another could ask and would have equal right to receive school time and school facilities for their teaching."[48]

In contrast, the official publication of the North Carolina Synod of the Lutheran Church of America supported such study of the Bible "for its historical, literary and ethical values as part of the public school curriculum." It agreed, however, that the classes should be voluntary and should be offered only on the high school level: "Lower grades, where a grade section studies different subjects throughout the day as a unit, make it impractical to inject a subject for voluntary study; when the unit is broken, a minority is created and becomes the victim of religious discrimination."[49]

Love Offerings in Chattanooga.   The National Conference of Christians and Jews found itself embroiled in controversy in 1963, when the Education Study Committee of the Chattanooga, Tennessee, Round Table called for inquiry concerning the constitutional character of the Bible classes conducted in the local schools. The NCCJ Committee charged that "the school time set aside by law for secular education was being usurped by the teaching of sectarian religion." For many years the Chattanooga school system has maintained a program by which selected teachers from outside the school system bring Bible instruction to the children *within* their classroom. "Although this practice is allegedly voluntary," the Education Committee asserted, "serious question exists in our mind as to the validity of its voluntary nature. The initiative must be taken to escape this teaching and not by those wishing to receive it."

When this report was published in the local papers, the chairman of the NCCJ Committee, Mrs. Arthur Cozza, received crank calls. "Some of the calls even threatened my life," she said. "I have been told I am a Communist and that I will be taken care of." She continued, "I cannot understand a person who supports Bible teaching in the schools who would threaten to take a life."

The following day editorial comments appeared in the local newspapers. *The Chattanooga News-Free Press* argued, "The teaching of Bible in the public schools here has been carried on for many years. It has been widely accepted and approved by the majority, while not taking advantage of any minority." Labeling the approach of the National Conference of Christians and Jews "intolerant," the editorial pointed out that the NCCJ Committee had cited the Supreme Court decision, "which has not been applied here and which is not in tune with what the Constitution itself declares."

The NCCJ Round Table then called a meeting at which the study report was to be discussed by its Executive Board. That meeting, however, was interrupted by a phoned bomb threat. At this time, Bible classes still take place in the Chattanooga public schools.[50]

Upon inquiry, the director of social studies instruction for the Tennessee Department of Education informed the author of this chapter that sixty to sixty-five sections of Bible are given at fifteen to twenty secondary schools throughout the state as part of the social studies curriculum.[51] The Public School Bible Study Committee of Chattanooga and Hamilton County, Tennessee, however, has reported that in 1964–1965 there were forty-five Bible teachers in seventy-eight schools with Bible classes in

Chattanooga and Hamilton County alone. Twenty-four thousand pupils took the year-long Bible course, and "love offerings" toward the financial support of this effort were made by parents and children in the amount of $22,368.[52]

The chairman of the committee responsible for the development of the Chattanooga program, Dr. J. Parks McCallie, explained that the Bible is in the public school curriculum not only for its value as a book of literature, or history, but "beyond all this because the Bible tells us of a God who so loved us that He gave His only Son to take the penalty of our sins on Himself and die on the cross that we might be forgiven all our evil deeds, just by trusting this wonderful Savior." He added,

> The religious education that is denominational teaching, such as the Supreme Court prevented in public schools of Champaign, Illinois, is not Bible teaching as conducted in Chattanooga, Tennessee, and elsewhere. No sectarian doctrines, or church rituals, or creeds are taught, but the language of the Bible is adhered to and teachers do not under any circumstances try to give a slant towards any denomination. Criticism is not made of anyone's faith or religion, but the Bible alone is given as the inspired Word of God, the basis of our American republic and guide of our Founding Fathers.[53]

Examination of the text material reveals, of course, that what may appear to be "non-denominational" to Dr. McCallie would not be so considered by all elements in the community. The announced general objective in the elementary grades, for example, is "to present the Bible in such a way as to make it live and to make Jesus Christ known." The specific objective for each pupil is "to lead them to reverence the Bible as the Word of God, to read the Bible every day, to become familiar with its contents, and to pray, to evaluate actions by Bible standards, and to love and trust the Lord Jesus Christ."[54]

The objectives of the very first unit introducing Old Testament material include the following: "to know that God provided salvation for all, but that only those who believe and trust Him have eternal life; to understand that without faith it is impossible to please God."

The specific objectives listed for lessons dealing with the New Testament include the following: "to recognize that Jesus Christ proved He was the Son of God by His works and by His words; to know that Christ's power alone can change lives and make eternal life possible; to see that it is the privilege and responsibility for every Christian to make Jesus Christ known; to realize the necessity of being born again; to believe that by His death and resurrection, Jesus provided the only way of salvation from sin."

Crude stick-line drawings illustrate the pupils' workbooks. In one of these, for example, human beings are seen rushing toward an open gate. Underneath is the slogan "Repent Now." Next to this is a drawing of the

gate closed, with the unhappy individuals outside beseeching the opportunity to enter. The slogan underneath is, "Someday, it will be too
late." Another stick drawing depicts a happy person sitting on the lap
of Abraham in heaven. Beside it are depicted sinners burning in the
fires of hell.[55]

Dallas Bible Plan. Another Bible-study plan, widely accepted throughout the South, is the course authorized and approved by the Dallas, Texas,
Independent School District for use by high school students. In 1964
Dallas claimed 186 Bible classes with 1,461 students.[56] These classes, however, are conducted off school property and the lesson guides are much
less crude in their sectarian purpose.

The plan for accrediting Bible study in the Dallas high schools for work
done out of school is an outgrowth of a movement begun in Dallas in
1927 by the Volunteer Bible Study Association for High School Credit.
In 1939 the community decided to provide separate courses in the Old
and New Testaments, each course counting one-half unit of credit toward high school graduation. With the cooperation of teachers of the
Bible credit work, a Bible study course was published in 1928 and revised and reprinted several times. The most recent edition in my posses-
sion is dated September, 1961. The course is authorized by the board of
education.

Classes may be organized by any Sunday School or church or any other
religious organization for the purpose of studying the Bible. While all
responsibility for instruction is assumed by the sponsoring organization,
the Dallas Independent School District provides the text at cost, conducts
a final examination, grades the papers, transmits the grades to the respective
high schools, and establishes credit for students who pass the examination.
There must be a minimum of forty class periods of ninety minutes net
teaching time, and the teacher must have a minimum preparation of at
least a high school education and sufficient teaching experience or training in Bible "to warrant success in teaching a Bible course."

While Christian denominations may have no quarrel with this course
as currently authorized, it is conceivable that Jews would be offended.
Among the minimum requirements listed for the Old Testament section
of the course, for example, is one that obliges the children to memorize
quotations from the New Testament. The introductory section addressed
to the students explaining the purpose of the course says,

> You should study this volume with eagerness for it holds within its sacred
> covers the historical facts and the religious development of that race of
> people whom God chose to weave the pattern of life for the Christian world
> to follow throughout the ages. . . . It will be easy for you to span the years
> between [the Old Testament and the contemporary day] and realize that
> the Jews have given us, through the Old Testament, an infallible proof of

the personal God and a *living Christ*. While there are sixty-six books in this one volume, they are unified in the person of Christ whose coming was prophesied in the first book of the Old Testament. As you study the lives of these Hebrew people, you will be conscious of the feeling of expectancy which existed throughout the Old Testament period and which *had its fulfillment in Jesus Christ*.[57]

Obviously, this is not how the Old Testament would be taught by Jews; Jewish scholars claim that any reading of the Old Testament through a New Testament perspective does violence to the very intent and meaning of the text itself.

Throughout the text, sectarian judgments are to be found. A discussion of the Temple and the Synagogue is climaxed with this assertion: "The Church is the highest step upward in man's desire to worship."[58] An analysis of the significance of Bible history in the Old Testament reader defines Jewish biblical history as preparing the way "for the coming of Christ in whom alone was and is the ultimate fulfillment of God's promises to Abraham. . . ."[59]

The bibliography includes no reference works that provide an understanding of Jewish perspectives on the Bible and the background essay on "Language and Manuscripts of the Bible" makes no reference to the important contribution of Jewish scholars to English translators of the Bible. Nor does it even mention the fact that there is an authorized Jewish translation.

The God of the Hebrews is mistakenly called "Jehovah," the Jews are called a "race," and other similar errors abound.

When I presented these criticisms to School Superintendent W. T. White for his comment and reaction, he dismissed the issue by insisting that "We make no effort to interpret the Bible for the various religions. All the classes are held in the churches under the direction of teachers selected by the particular church concerned. With that in mind I have no suggestions to make. . . ."[60] The sectarian nature of the officially approved and sanctioned course book is overlooked or purposely ignored.

Sectarian Religion in Indiana High Schools. Several high schools in Muncie, Indiana, provide a course of study on biblical literature based on manuals developed by W. Carl Rarick, who has taught biblical literature in the high schools of Delaware County, Indiana, for over twenty-five years. The sectarian bias of these texts is demonstrated by Mr. Rarick's own description of the purpose of his work: "The United States is by culture, ideals and tradition, a Christian nation and we dare not allow it to be otherwise. Our well-being, security and destiny depend on these essentials. It is indeed a great thrill to see high school classes of up to forty pupils reading their Bibles at least one hour every day trying to find what is stated therein."[61]

Another standard guide for pupils and teachers for use in the Bible classes in Indiana schools is the *Guide to the Study of the Old and New Testaments* by J. A. Huffman, first published in 1926 and revised in 1949.[62] It is, in fact, recommended by the state Department of Public Instruction. The book was originally copyrighted by John W. Kendall, then Secretary of the Indiana Board of Control for High School Bible Study for Credit. Its sectarian approach is evidenced immediately by its characterization of the Old Testament: "It is not a history of the Hebrew people as such; but deals principally with the Hebrews because it was through them that Christ was to come."[63]

The prophecies in Jewish scripture, presumed by Christians to refer to Jesus, are underscored at every point, reflecting an evaluation and an understanding of the Old Testament material solely from the Christian perspective. No contrary opinion is mentioned or allowed for. So consistent is this approach that when the Song of Solomon is discussed, its allegorical and typical interpretations are seen solely as representing reference to Christ and his church. There is no hint at all of the meaning of this text in the Jewish tradition. Similarly, Chapters 49–55 of Isaiah are interpreted as "prophecies that dwell upon the salvation which is to come through God's servant, meaning Christ."[64] The teacher is instructed here also to take "special note" of the several messianic passages: (1) a child of virgin birth, 7:14; (2) a child with divine names, 9:6, 7; (3) the vicariously suffering servant, 52:13–53:12.

The Bible in English Literature — The Indiana University Material. In an effort to replace such sectarian material and provide a more sophisticated approach to the Bible as literature for use in Indiana public schools, a project was undertaken at Indiana University. In May, 1965, it was announced that more than 350 teachers in 49 junior and senior high schools in Indiana were experimenting with new courses of study being prepared in the University's English Curriculum Study Center. In light of the crudely sectarian nature of the older material used in Indiana, this was a most welcome announcement. School teachers will use the trial programs in their classes for three years and will make suggestions for revision. The final courses of study will be printed and distributed by the Indiana State Department of Public Instruction in 1967. The work of these teachers is being channeled through the English Curriculum Study Center, which was funded by the United States Office of Education in September, 1963, with a grant of $250,000. General chairman for this program and editor of the courses of study is Dr. Edward Jenkinson, also coordinator for School English Language Arts at Indiana University.

One of the more than forty units prepared by the English Curriculum Study Center is an experimental unit on the Bible as literature for Grade 7. The introductory explanation to this unit, as originally devised, pointed out that

The Bible has been a constant source of reflection and allusion in the literature of Western cultures. The narrative literature of the Old Testament can be recommended to seventh-grade students, therefore, both for its intrinsic interests and for its continuing importance as part of the literary background of more recent works. The Bible provides opportunity to discuss a number of literary forms — myths, myth/history, biography, parable and moral tale. One objective of this seventh grade program is to acquaint students with the sheer abundance and variety of literary works in the Old Testament.[65]

The unit outline and the recommended selections, however, showed that the emphasis was placed not on "the variety of literary works" but only on that literature which is chiefly narrative and historic, i.e., the account of great biblical heroes — Abraham and Isaac, Joseph, Moses, David, Samson, Ruth, Esther, Jonah, Daniel. The one exception to this pattern was the philosophic treatment given in Genesis to the accounts of creation and the "origins of evil." The outline itself did not make clear the specific purpose and intent of each selection, nor could one find, in the outline, an integrated approach or rationale for these particular selections. Further, there was a varied approach to the material. In the creation accounts, and in the story of Adam and Eve, for example, the structure of questions for discussion was such as to point to answers reflecting a given pattern of religious response — a pattern that is clearly Christian in orientation. There was no indication at all that conflicting points of view or diverse interpretations of this same material exist.

The authors of the outline operated with the documentary theory, but they offered no guidance for understanding the problems of authorship of each of the books. Also lacking was a list of bibliographical references, which is essential if the teacher is to deal with this material in historic perspective and background and be fair to all faiths. In its first draft, therefore, the outline was inadequate and subject to every kind of distortion and misuse.

In response to my criticism and to others', the authorities of the English Curriculum Study Center decided to prepare a completely new outline. Professor James S. Ackerman of the Department of Religion at Connecticut College was engaged to write the new course in cooperation with Miss Jane Stouder of the English Curriculum Study Center staff. The material was sent to religious readers, scholars, and educators for their criticism in the fall of 1966.

Unfortunately, I found the course in its revised form inadequate and objectionable. In a critique to the English Curriculum Study Center I explained:

A central problem in teaching about the Bible is that it is not just literature. For many people it is the Word of God and the source of strongly held ideals and religious practices. A secular school system has every right to study the Bible as a literary document and to find in it the source for many allusions in the history of the literature of western civilization; it seems to me, however, that it would be absolutely imperative for teachers to know what traditions and understandings each religious group has brought to the Bible and how they interpret and use the various selections. Teachers need to know this: (1) so as not to offend needlessly the sensibilities of children nor shake them in their faith; (2) so as to enrich children's knowledge with an appreciation of each other's commitments.

The present unit is *inadequate* in that no such information is provided the public school teacher. Throughout the unit not only are cherished Jewish interpretations, understandings and practices ignored but at many, many points in this unit they are violated — and the teacher is not even made aware of the fact that if she teaches according to this outline she will be doing manifest harm and may stimulate outraged protest by infuriated parents.

The present unit is also *objectionable* on two grounds:

1. It views Hebrew Scripture with a Christian sectarian bias, without acknowledging that bias or allowing for other interpretations; and

2. It accepts one view from among the many held by critical Bible scholars without informing teachers concerning the critical issues involved, the alternative views held, and the consequences of the scholarly judgment made. This unit is as objectionable as if in a junior high school history class a teacher were to teach history from a Marxian, economic deterministic point of view and not even grant that other interpretations are possible or are held in the academic community to explain the same set of events.

Some examples of *Christian bias:*

The unit does not recommend for teacher use any authorized Jewish Bible translation or Jewish scholarly works on the Bible.

The unit delimits biblical history as beginning with an "Amorite herdsman" and ending with "fervent evangelizers." This is not Hebrew Scripture which is being described. It is Christian Scripture.

The unit concludes "Israelite-Jewish history" with the destruction of the Temple by the Romans at A.D. 70. Jews would not so conclude that history.

Scholarly bias:

Nowhere is the teacher provided the answers given by fundamentalists to the documentary theory.

At no time is the teacher informed that there are multiple interpretations for events, for which the author gives only one interpretation. Example —

Are there no reasonable men who believe that the stories of Genesis 1–11 are more than legends?

Is the key story for understanding all others in Genesis the sin of Adam, as the unit insists, or is it the selection of Abraham as Jews hold? Is the "final purpose" of Genesis "to account for a man as a proud sinner and God as a righteous judge"; or are other views possible?

Is Abraham a henotheist or monotheist? And do all scholars agree on but one answer?

Was the Egyptian pharaoh a monotheist? And do all scholars agree?

Did Moses receive his knowledge of Yahweh from the Midianites? And do all scholars agree?

Was God's selection of Israel completely unmerited? What do Jews say about this?

In the conquest of Canaan did Joshua precede Moses or follow him?

Did the book of Deuteronomy lie unnoticed in a storage room for a century as the unit contends; or was it written centuries before; or was it written just prior to Josiah's Reform?

I could go on and on. The point I wish to make is that there are several respectable theories to account for all of these events. Why should the unit choose but one answer above the others? Why not give information about the other options? Why not provide the children with an awareness of interpretations brought to these events in the long history of our developing religious traditions rather than these scholarly hypotheses which may shake their faith?

This unit suggests to me that the author's real intent is to teach biblical archaeology and history with a large dose of ancient Near Eastern theology rather than the Hebrew epic or narrative as literature. Such a course is much too sophisticated for the junior high school level.

I am not sure what the Indiana Curriculum Center will do now with the course on the Hebrew narrative. But I certainly hope they will not publish this second draft of their curriculum. It is worth another try. Their experience demonstrates, however, the need for a team of scholars in the development of such material.

2. COMMUNITY CONFLICT OVER RELIGION
   IN TEXTBOOKS CURRENTLY IN USE

The potentially explosive nature of any effort to teach about religion in the public school is evident in the interreligious tension that even now arises over material, minimal as it may be, that is currently included in standard public school textbooks. In recent years, for example, the official publication of the Texas Southern Baptist Convention campaigned against a widely used tenth-grade history book, *Men and Nations, a World History*, by Mazour and Peoples on the grounds that "certain portions about the history of Christianity are not true. . . . They are the traditions of the Roman Catholic Church." The editor of *The Baptist Standard*, E. S. James, concluded that this book "is pure religious propaganda that has no place in a public school."[66]

In Phoenix, Arizona, a controversy erupted in May, 1963, over the use by the public school system of the 1961 edition of *The Story of Nations*. Baptist minister Rev. Aubrey L. Moore, of the West Van Buren Southern Baptist Church, raised questions concerning portions of the book which, he contended, interpreted world history events from a Roman Catholic viewpoint. As a result of such Protestant objections the Phoenix Board of Education decided to remove four pages from the 1961 edition and replace them with a roughly similar section of the 1955 edition.[67]

In Worcester, Massachusetts, on the other hand, a thirty-page chapter on the history of Christianity was deleted from a history book used by ninth-grade students at the suggestion of Catholic clergy. The text, *A History of Civilization,* by Brinton, Wolff, and Christopher, was intended to supplement the regular ninth-grade history. The principal of the Forest Grove School explained that he had deleted the chapter on the ground that "teaching religion to ninth-graders is the job of churches, not the schools." Officials of the American Civil Liberties Union thereupon criticized "the opportunity apparently provided by school authorities to religious officials to exert influence in the selection of teaching materials to be used in the public schools."[68]

3. SOME NEW EXPERIMENTAL MATERIALS ON THE BIBLE AS LITERATURE

Thayer Warshaw — The Bible as a Source Book for the Humanities. In February, 1964, Thayer S. Warshaw, an English teacher at a Newton, Massachusetts, high school, attracted national attention through an article written for *The English Journal* describing his efforts to teach about the Bible to his eleventh- and twelfth-graders. The purpose of the course was to prepare them to understand the literary selections assigned within the high school English curriculum. As Warshaw explained, his approach to the Bible was to study it "not as a religious book, nor even as a literary work but as a source book for the humanities."[69]

Mr. Warshaw shocked the community by his revelation of the results of a test he had given to five classes of college-bound juniors and seniors. Of 112 rather sensible questions designed to discover whether these pupils were familiar with at least the most commonly known biblical names, stories, and quotations, more than 70 per cent were incorrectly answered. Students thought that Sodom and Gomorrah were lovers, that Jesus was baptized by Moses, that Jezebel was Ahab's donkey, and that the stories told by Jesus in his teachings were called parodies. Ninety per cent of the students could not define the word "parable."

Mr. Warshaw claims that not only were these ideas corrected by his course but students brought a new understanding to such classics as Melville's *Moby Dick* with its characters named Ishmael, and Ahab, and Elijah. In an address given before the Annual Meeting of the National Council of Churches, Division of Christian Education, Mr. Warshaw argued, "Is it important for the student to learn what it means when a man is called an Adonis or a Romeo, and yet unimportant for him to be able to tell a Jonah from a Judas? The Bible is indeed a religious book, but it is also part of our secular cultural heritage."

Mr. Warshaw has written an experimental text, *Teaching Aids for a Bible Unit,* intended to accompany the Anchor book *The Bible for Students of Literature and Art.* There is no doubt that his approach enhances a student's general knowledge of the Bible, particularly with regard to its role as a source for literary allusions and its richness as a source for quotations, song titles, movie titles, book titles, and the like. I am not certain, however, that there is a meaningful follow-through from the emphasis on memory work, which characterizes Warshaw's educational method, to an understanding of the profound religious, spiritual, or even literary significance of the biblical material under study, or that there is an adequate recall of allusions when one is confronted by another piece of literature.

Mr. Warshaw's pupils are given a five-minute quiz three times a week to test their knowledge on what they had been assigned in the Bible. The quiz consists of quotations to complete, names to identify, and incidents to remember, and it is corrected, graded, returned, and used for brief instructional sessions. In these sessions Warshaw frequently links as many passages as he can with literature, music, and art. Clearly the emphasis in such instruction is placed on memory work rather than on the conceptual challenge of the literary allusions and ideas being presented. Furthermore, by forcing the allusions uncritically upon a wide range of literature, art, folk music, place names in the United States, etc., Mr. Warshaw invokes material about which the student may have little knowledge and little feeling. In my judgment, he is using a sort of surface-scratching memory work, long ago abandoned by religious educators themselves. It is not how I would want the Bible to be taught.

Another example of Mr. Warshaw's unsophisticated approach to the biblical material is the essay on Bible translation that he provides teachers who purchase his booklet of background material. The essay deals chiefly with the King James Version of the Bible since this is the version he recommends. The essay avoids any mention of the drama, even the cost in human life, that was involved in the making of the various English translations of the Bible. It does not mention the polemic and theological content carried in translation. It makes no reference to the reasons for continued translations by scholars. In fact, Mr. Warshaw himself reports that when some of his students, contrasting translations in more recent revisons, challenged the "correctness" of the King James Version, he replied that he was not interested in correctness. He was interested in teaching the words that have influenced literature. The class had to learn the quotation as it appeared in the King James Version and leave questions of accuracy to theologians. Such an approach to the Bible, it appears to me, so denudes it of its intrinsic worth on its own merit as to raise objections to the validity of the study of the Bible in this form.

I accept the propriety of a public school English teacher's sending his students back to the Bible to read those stories, for example, that will shed light on who Ahab or Ishmael was, as background for a better understanding of the symbolic significance in Melville's use of these names in *Moby Dick*. But to make a whole course of Bible study for the alleged purpose of answering such questions, when and if they appear, seems to me a misuse of the time. To make a course out of the Bible solely as a *source book* for the humanities is to short-change the Bible, both as literature in its own right and as a vital source for great concepts and ideas held in significant regard in Western culture.

The University of Nebraska Curriculum Development Center — The Bible as a Source of Ideas. Perhaps the most sophisticated and exciting effort to deal with religious themes as they emerge naturally within the context of English literature is to be seen in the experimental material now being produced at the University of Nebraska's Curriculum Development Center. Operating under a grant from the Office of Education, the Center has produced a completely new curriculum for English for Grades 7 through 12. The reading selections are geared to thematic principles that enable the student not only to experience and learn about the varied forms of literature developed in the course of Western civilization but to recognize in a systematic way how literature has both reflected and shaped each generation's attitudes regarding the meaning of life and man's relation to nature and to other men. The curriculum explores the views reflected in literature regarding sin and loneliness, the leader and the group, the role of the hero, the nature of tragedy, etc. At many points in the curriculum, students are directed back to the Bible to find there the source of literary allusions. They are required to comprehend the significance for world literature of contrasting religious views of man's duty to God and community, sin and salvation.

Throughout most of the units, the religious material is objective; there is no effort to impose a sectarian viewpoint or to proselytize.[70] The Jewish student, nevertheless, will be confronted with a serious problem for which the material offers no help. Frequently, the most moving of the religious arguments are Christian in formulation. To be sure, this is an accurate reflection of how our literature in Western civilization developed. The Christological interpretations of Old Testament material, however, are given so forcefully that a Jewish student who does not believe that the doctrine of original sin, for example, is the proper interpretation of the Adam and Eve story will be confused and troubled unless a teacher indicates with sensitivity and care that the concept as articulated in the literature is a distinctly Christian interpretation. There are other Christian interpretations, and, of course, there are conflicting Jewish interpretations that may legitimately be given for the same passage in scripture. Unfortunately such information is not now included in the background material for children or teacher.

The largest portion of Old Testament material comes in the unit prepared for Grade 7, entitled "The Hebraic Historic Narratives." These are contrasted with selected Greek narratives and thus allow the student to recognize both the Hebraic and the Greco-Roman roots of our civilization. The differences between Greek and Hebrew pictures of God, the moral law, the nature of the hero, the meaning of the family, tribe, and nation, the relationship between Greeks and barbarians, Jews and Gentiles, and the attitude toward war are elicited. I note as a major lack, however, that the teacher's packet in this case provides no appreciative essay or instruction that makes exactly clear the answers to such an inquiry. In contrast, the essays explaining and analyzing the various elements in the literature selected for the unit on "The Christian Epic" for Grade 12 leaves nothing to chance or imagination.

In this case, again, Jewish children may be quite uncomfortable if it is not made explicit that biblical concepts in Judaism undergo a progressive development. Post-biblical Judaism — the religion Jewish children will know — differs sharply in many ways from the religion practiced by ancient Hebrews. Opportunities for interreligious understanding of a contemporaneous significance are missed throughout the unit. Thus, the exodus theme is followed by the Negro spiritual "Go Down, Moses," but no reference is made to the Passover Seder.

I was unsettled also by the failure to recognize in these historic narratives the theological purpose as seen in Jewish perspective. "The things important to the early Hebrew mind" were presented in the unit in the order of importance and with an emphasis that reflects what Christians think Jews find in their scripture: "Obedience, the Law, and the Covenant." This is not how the Jew would define the significance of the stories. If I might make such an effort: In the Jewish view, the Patriarchal narratives demonstrate how God chose out one man, one family, one nation from among all peoples in order to be His elect. He protected and preserved this people in a miraculous way so that He might reveal to them His law; and He ordained that by their faithfulness to the law they would become a blessing to the nations. By virtue of God's Covenant with Abraham and Moses, Israel is obliged to seek justice and to pursue peace; by the ethical qualities of their lives they are commanded to serve as a witness to the Living God who rules over men and nations. The "things important" to the Jewish mind are God, Torah, Israel.

The sophistication and sensitivity brought to the theological dimensions of "The Christian Epic" are missing in this unit's treatment of Old Testament narratives.

There are other notable omissions in the unit: Jewish bibliographic recommendations are scarce. The essay on the Bible and its versions treats, however inadequately, the significance of the Hebrew Canon and the role of Jewish scholars in influencing Christian biblical commentators and translators but ignores the existence of Jewish translations. The importance of translation in carrying theological argumentation is also omitted.

Finally, the unit ends with literary selections that suggest that Jesus is the fulfillment of Old Testament history.

Responsive to the criticisms of this author and others, the Nebraska Curriculum Development Center has agreed to rewrite the unit on Hebrew narrative and to enrich other parts of its curriculum with material from the treasure-house of Jewish literature. In order to assist its writers in developing this new material the Center will call a series of conferences with religious scholars of all faiths. I therefore await with eager anticipation the final publication of the Nebraska material.

"Man's Relation to God" — One of Six Themes in a Social Studies Unit in Pennsylvania. The Department of Public Instruction of the Pennsylvania Board of Education has developed and experimented with a unit entitled "Man's Relation to God" as part of a new program of studies in the humanities called "Universal Issues in Human Life."[71] The introductory explanatory statement makes it clear that "the unit is a study about religions and it is not a study of religion." Students are asked to understand the relation to God found in each man's great religions, the uniqueness of man's relation to God found in each religion, and the similarities between religions.

According to Dr. Richard A. Gibboney, then chairman of the Pennsylvania Humanities Commission, which is composed of outstanding teachers and scholars, the unit is intended to "incorporate a non-sectarian moral element into the curriculum and to provide a thread for the proper integrating of the separate subjects." Recognizing the "great additional burdens" imposed on any teacher who attempts to teach this unit, the Department of Public Instruction has advised superintendents and principals that they will permit it to be taught on an experimental basis only, with departmental approval required. Approval will be given only after the department has reviewed the school district's plan outlining the manner in which the unit will be presented, including the academic background of the teacher, plans for general supervision, library books available, and other pertinent educational factors.

The introductory statement also observes that, while knowledge of key terms and basic concepts, including the dates and names of the important leaders of religions, can be tested and used for academic evaluation, two important objectives cannot and *should not* be tested. These are (1) evidence in class discussion of the desire and ability of students to relate their own religious or philosophic viewpoints to the content of the course and (2) evidence in class discussion of the students' sympathetic appreciation of the religious experiences of non-Western civilizations and of the various denominations represented in the school.

Students are directed to readings in the religions of Hinduism and Buddhism, Confucianism and Taoism, Judaism, Christianity, and Islam. Each section of the unit includes references to selections in the holy writings of each religion and questions for discussion based upon the information and viewpoints contained in these writings. A series of related activities is offered, and books for reading and reporting on are included.

A Jewish critic might observe that the unit on Judaism is inadequate in its treatment of the Jewish faith. It bases its entire study upon biblical materials whereas the contemporary Jew's conception of his relation to God rests particularly upon the religious writings and historic developments of the Jewish people in the crucial *post-biblical* period. Furthermore, the aims of the subunit "The Biblical Foundation of Judaism" are so broad that it would be very difficult within the framework of a single course to do justice to all of them if any one were to be treated in depth. The aims include the following: to show the biblical foundation of the Jewish faith in God; to enable students to know the principal narratives and personalities in the Bible in their historical and social settings; to lead the student to understand and assimilate the thought and to feel the literary beauty of the masterpieces; to give the student an opportunity to study primarily in the Bible itself, rather than in secondary sources.

I am convinced that the biblical selections ought to be arranged differently in order to meet each of these purposes. It is impossible to meet them all by the usual chronologically developed reading in the biblical text or by reading the biblical text in accordance with the given canonical order of the books, which is the order followed in this particular unit. A thematic presentation of biblical material is far different from a historic order of material or a review of biblical books in their canonical sequence. And each arrangement fulfills a different purpose. The authors of the Pennsylvania program have not resolved this issue. Nor have they taken into account the more important developments of Jewish thought in post-biblical writings.

The bibliographic selections are sparse and do not represent all points of view in Judaism.

It is good to know that a revision of the units based on teachers' experience and evaluation is planned. In a letter I received on August 17, 1966, the new Curriculum Development specialist agreed that the criticisms offered were "generally in line with those that I have heard since assuming responsibility for this guide. . . ."

In an effort to develop a more sophisticated interdisciplinary approach to this material, the Neshaminy School District in Langhorne, Pennsylvania, applied in 1966 for an ESEA Title III humanities grant of $220,000. The school district has already started preparation for the engagement of consultants from various religions and academic disciplines and the in-service training of teachers. Should the grant be given, this school district may provide a pilot program in the use of religious materials in the humanities and social studies curriculum of the public high school.

Religion in the American Cultural Heritage — San Mateo, California. Crestmoor High School of San Mateo, California, Union High School District initiated a new program for sixty high school juniors in the fall semester of 1966. It combined into one complete program courses in

United States history and American literature. The methodology of the classwork — including use of films and filmstrips, field trips, guest speakers, art-display work, and individual projects — excited its own interest. The program received national attention, however, when it was announced that local clergy had agreed to lecture students on the Judaic-Christian heritage as part of the introductory unit on America's "Cultural and Intellectual Heritage." A priest, a minister, and a rabbi conducted sessions on the history of their religious communities in America. Although the program was well received, there are problems built into it that make it of questionable value for all school districts. Not every high school can command the cooperation of scholarly clergy across faith lines who are capable of fitting into the secular requirements of public education. In addition, this approach tends to separate the religious material for particular attention; some educators would prefer that the experience of religious groups in American history be considered along the way wherever relevant to the discussion.

Course Offerings for Teachers in Newton, Massachusetts. An effort to provide secondary school teachers with the background to enable them "to present the Bible in a truly objective way, in an educationally sound manner to their students, and to relate religion as a phase of the culture to such subjects as history, literature, art and music" has been undertaken in Newton, Massachusetts, where courses in religion have been prepared by an Institute of Religious Studies in cooperation with the Andover Newton Theological School. An interfaith faculty representing Jewish, Catholic, and Protestant scholarship gives the courses for school teachers and administrators residing in the Greater Boston area. Dr. Charles E. Brown, superintendent of the Newton schools, commented, "Such an offering certainly fills a need" and indicated that the Newton school system will give teachers credit for this course and will do everything it can to publicize it.

4. RECENT INTERFAITH EFFORTS TO DEVELOP RELIGIOUS MATERIALS

Failure in Omaha. In February, 1965, Paul A. Miller, Superintendent of Omaha schools, called upon a committee of religious leaders and educators, meeting under the auspices of the NCCJ, to help his school system prepare material on "the religious heritage in our American heritage." Dr. Miller envisioned a resource unit which teachers could use to supplement teaching in several subjects rather than a specific course about religion. The attempt to develop such material foundered, however, when it became evident almost immediately that there would be little agreement among the clergy concerning its purpose and content.

An initial presentation made by Dr. E. W. Stimson, pastor of the Dundee Presbyterian Church, was so sectarian in tone that further efforts seemed inadvisable. Dr. Stimson argued that it would be impossible for the public schools to train children in "the basic moral principles and the moral discipline of good citizenship were they stopped from *inculcating* a certain amount of religion basic to our nation's institutions and culture and common to all major religions." He charged that it was "a dangerous departure" from the American tradition to speak of the neutrality of government on religion as though it meant "the neutrality of our government between all religion and atheism rather than neutrality between religious bodies, all of which can be trusted to aid our democracy by teaching belief in God and the basic moral law." He added, "Our government cannot be neutral between its own doctrine of moral theism and the atheistic materialism of Communism if it is to exist in the present world conflict. From the beginning of our history, our government and its schools have never been neutral regarding the basic common core of religious and moral truth shared by all religious faith as over against atheism and moral license, but only neutral between the sectarian differences of different religious organizations."

Dr. Stimson argued that if schools do not teach belief in God and moral law we are sunk. "Talk of leaving all such training to church and home is nonsense," he declared, "because the only place many Omaha children can get moral instruction is in school. About half never attended a Sunday school."

After several meetings, when the NCCJ dialogue group realized how sharp the disagreement and how complex the issue, this effort was abandoned.[72]

An Interfaith Study of Religion in the High School Social Studies Curriculum, Pittsburgh, Pennsylvania. A more carefully planned effort in Pittsburgh, Pennsylvania, was undertaken under the auspices of the project, "Religious Freedom and Public Affairs," of the National Conference of Christians and Jews. With the cooperation of the Pittsburgh public school system the NCCJ brought together a small group of religious scholars across faith lines, professors of education, and the appropriate supervisory personnel of the Pittsburgh school system in order to consider the role of religion in the social studies curriculum of the Pittsburgh high schools. The group met regularly over a year and a half under the direction of Professor Lawrence Little, Chairman, Department of Religious Education, University of Pittsburgh. They evaluated textbook material currently used in Pittsburgh schools, interviewed teachers and supervisory personnel, and deliberated among themselves on how curricula could be enriched and on the problems that might be confronted were religion to be introduced into the public school curriculum. The findings have been published in a booklet entitled *Religion in the Social*

Studies.[73] It has been made available to the administrative personnel of the Pittsburgh school system for their use in developing a further program in this area.

There was general agreement that the material concerning religion now communicated through the textbooks used in the Pittsburgh senior high schools is inadequate. For example, Dr. Richard K. Seckinger, Associate Professor of Foundations of Education at the University of Pittsburgh and a member of the committee, reported on two basic reference books used in the eighth-grade course in United States history. He concluded,

> Because of the superficial attention this text gives to the role religion has played in the shaping of American civilization there is little reason to hope that a pupil would get from his study of this history much of an understanding of our basic religious heritage. . . . The deeper meanings of the great religious events of the past are unexplained and the wider place of religion in the history of the United States remains unidentified and, therefore, obscure.

Over half of the references to religion, Dr. Seckinger points out, are to be found in the colonial period, while the entire study of religion in nineteenth-century America is told in just eight selections, only one of them of paragraph length. "For all practical purposes," he says, "the subject is totally ignored in the author's story of America in the first half of the twentieth century."[74]

Other committee members evaluating textbooks used in the tenth, eleventh, and twelfth grades made similar observations. Dr. Leonard A. Swidler, then Professor of History at Duquesne University, notes that the text used for the tenth-grade course in world history provides much fuller coverage to the Greco-Roman than to the Hebraic-Christian pillar of Western civilization.[75]

Dr. Elwyn A. Smith, then Professor of Church History at Pittsburgh Theological Seminary, in his appraisal of the textbooks for the eleventh grade, observes that since the books "reveal a deficient grasp of what history itself is" they are obviously inadequate in their treatment of religion. "Religion is not extraneous to history and should not be thrust into texts as an extraneous element." [76]

Dr. Aharon Kessler, Dean of the College of Jewish Studies, in his criticism of the text used in the twelfth grade, noted particularly that the presentation of ancient Jewish history, archaeology, and biblical exegesis was distorted, inaccurate, and "steeped in ignorance."

In a summary statement the committee urged better textbooks and the development of elective courses in the history of religion, called for expanded library facilities, counseled more adequate preparation of teachers for dealing with religion in public school situations, and recommended some means of continuing communication between public school personnel and religious leaders when controversy arises at points of mutual concern.

The committee agreed also that

> . . . the function of the public school is to provide the basis for good general education . . . it is not to indoctrinate in any particular form of religious belief nor to secure commitment to any sectarian expression of religion. It cannot properly impose any particular form of religious ritual. By its very nature the public school must be secular in the sense that it must be free from ecclesiastical control. Inculcation of religious beliefs, stress upon sectarian history and values and habituation in sectarian rituals are properly the responsibility of the churches.

The committee warned that public school officials and teachers "must be left free to provide instruction about religion as they may deem it necessary as an element of any program of general education; neither the type nor the content of the instruction must be dictated by religious groups." The committee charged, on the other hand, that some writers of textbooks seemed to lack adequate information regarding particular religious groups and institutions. "Greater accuracy might be assured," they suggested, "by inviting competent scholars in relevant fields to review and criticize the materials before publication."

The committee also felt that teachers might be greatly helped if the materials were prepared specifically to aid in dealing with religion in certain controversial periods of history, as at the time of "the Crusades, the Reformation, the colonization of America, the secularization of education and the spread of sectarianism among religious groups in modern society."

There is no movement evident at the present time indicating that the Pittsburgh school system will act upon any of these suggestions — but it is still too early to make a judgment. The committee, although it included public school personnel, was unofficial. The religious scholars were chosen by the NCCJ and do not represent the officialdom in their community. If the NCCJ report wields an influence, it will do so only by the excellence of its study, the relevance of its suggestions, and the interfaith dialogic nature of its process. Time will tell.

An Officially Appointed Committee of Scholars and Educators in Florida. In 1964 Florida State Superintendent of Education Bailey and Attorney General Kynes issued a statement entitled "Bible Reading and Prayer in the Public School." It called upon the State Courses of Study Commission "to consider the feasibility of including as part of the instructional program of the public schools instruction in comparative religion or the history of religion and instruction in [the] literature and historic qualities of the Bible." The Florida Department of Education thereupon appointed a twelve-member State Committee on Comparative Religions and the Bible. Working in cooperation with the Department of Religion at Florida State University at Tallahassee, this Committee is considering the development of several approaches for teaching about the Bible and religion, including (1) an elective course on comparative religion, (2) cross-disciplinary materials involving teachers at all grade levels, and (3) a unit on the history of religion in the Bible to be included in humanities or social studies courses.

It is now legal in Florida for courses in the Bible to be taught for credit in English literature. However, Professor Robert Spivey, Chairman, Department of Religion, Florida State University, reports that in 1964–1965 only ten such courses were given for credit in the state, by six teachers, involving 231 pupils.

The twelve-man Committee has listed the following objectives in its program to develop "literacy in religion":

1. To help students gain knowledge of the historical developments of the major religions.
2. To help students gain a knowledge of the basic concepts and the important leaders in each religion.
3. To relate the history of religions to the advancement of civilization.
4. To help students see relationships, similarities, and differences of religions.
5. To help students gain the ability to apply generalizations and principles to new situations as they developed in modern times.
6. To help students gain an understanding of the Bible as a force in literature, culture, and Western civilization.

In an address delivered December 10, 1965, at a statewide Institute on Religion and Public Education, Professor Spivey described this program and then articulated his own convictions regarding its limitations:

> A fitting and proper way for the study of religion is instruction rather than indoctrination. What is required is teaching not preaching. . . . The study about religion is not a panacea for those who would like to shore up the values of our society. The study about religion does not necessarily make a person more religious. . . . Inculcation of moral and spiritual values is not the direct product of teaching about religion although the possibility exists of such results as a by-product.[77]

The Committee is at present developing guidelines for teachers and has co-opted religious scholars to serve as consultants in the review of curricular materials. It offers a pilot program, therefore, in a responsible, across-the-faith-lines effort to prepare properly for teaching about religion in public education.

ᴌMARY

1. In light of the sectarian nature of Bible guides now used in public schools and the unsatisfactory quality of much of the new material being created, there is good reason to question the wisdom of hasty or massive efforts to teach about religion in the public school.

2. New ways need to be found to bring together religious leaders, scholars, and educators in order to develop new teaching materials. The efforts in Florida and in Pittsburgh are in the right direction.

3. There is good reason to believe that, given the proper funds and auspices, our academic institutions in cooperation with textbook publishers could develop acceptable materials. Despite the criticisms I have raised, the efforts at the University of Nebraska and by the Pennsylvania Department of Education are certainly worth encouragement.

4. It is important, too, that we continue to pursue many approaches to this subject so that our communities may have multiple choices of materials. However, we should abandon some of the sentimental notions for the study of religion in the public school. Within the limitations of a secular school system, in a religiously pluralistic society, we can hope only to inform the students concerning the role, good and bad, of religions in our culture. Such study cannot be undertaken to win commitment to God. Knowledge about the Bible will create a more informed and literate student. It will not necessarily produce a more moral person.

5. Despite these limitations, efforts to enrich the curriculum ought to be encouraged, for the present status of public education with regard to providing knowledge about religion is scandalous, either by virtue of what is not taught or because of the blatantly sectarian nature of what is taught. American educators can do better.

NOTES

1. *Abington School District v. Schempp* and *William J. Murray III v. Curlett*, 374 U.S. 203 (1963).

2. *McCollum v. Board of Education*, 333 U.S. 203 (1948).

3. *Reader's Digest*, February, 1965, p. 54.

4. *Calvary Bible Presbyterian Church v. University of Washington*, Supreme Court Kings County #657, 671 (1966).

5. Letter to State Superintendent of Public Instruction, September 4, 1964, cited in "A Survey of Developments Since the Supreme Court Prayer Decisions of 1962 and 1963," prepared by Sol Rabkin for the National Community Relations Advisory Council, New York, 1966 (mimeographed).

6. Letter to State Superintendent of Schools, September 4, 1964, cited by Rabkin, *op. cit.*

7. Circular Series A #150, 1963, p. 5, cited by Rabkin, *op. cit.*

8. Rabkin, *op. cit.*

9. *Ibid.*

10. *Ibid.*

11. Religious News Service, August 6, 1963.

12. *New York Times,* May 2, 1964.

13. Quoted by W. Carl Rarick, "Biblical Literature as a Regular Course in High School," Muncie, Ind., undated.

14. A. P. Peabody, Report of the U.S. Commissioner of Education for the year 1897–1898, pp. 1563–1564.

15. Department of Religious Liberty, National Council of Churches, Report of the National Study Conference on Church and State held at Columbus, Ohio, February 4–7, 1964 (mimeographed). See pp. 17–24.

16. Board of Christian Education, Presbyterian Church in the U.S.A., "The Church and the Public Schools," June, 1957.

17. National Catholic Welfare Conference, News Service, Washington, D.C. November 16, 1952.

18. *Denver Catholic Register,* November 26, 1961.

19. Religious News Service, October 7, 1966.

20. *Religious Education* (New York), November–December, 1964, pp. 463–465.

21. "Can the Public Schools Deal Adequately with the Role of Religion in History and Life?" address delivered by Rev. Robert F. Drinan, S.J., at the Annual Convention of the American Association of School Administrators, Atlantic City, N.J., February 15, 1965.

22. "The Role of Our Public School Teachers in the Religious Development of Youth," address delivered by Rev. James R. Deneen at a teachers institute, Downers Grove, Ill., March 15, 1965.

23. Rev. Richard J. Regan, S.J., *American Pluralism and the Catholic's Conscience* (Macmillan, 1963).

24. Rabbi Robert Gordis, *The Root and the Branch* (University of Chicago Press, 1962).

25. Synagogue Council of America and National Community Relations Advisory Council, "Safeguarding Religious Liberty," October, 1962.

26. From the ADL Policy Statement issued by the National Commission Meeting in New York, January, 1963.

27. Educational Policies Commission, "Moral and Spiritual Values in the Public Schools," 1951, pp. 77–80.

28. George H. Reavis, "An Educational Platform for the Public Schools," reprinted in *International Journal of Religious Education* (National Council of Churches, New York), May, 1958, pp. 23–25.

29. American Association of Colleges for Teacher Education, Final Report, Teacher Education and Religion Project, 1953–1958.

30. National Council for the Social Studies, Committee on Concepts and Values, *A Guide to Content in the Social Studies,* 1957.

31. American Association of School Administrators, "Religion in the Public Schools," 1964, pp. 56–61.

32. Report prepared by Dr. Archibald Shaw, Associate Secretary, American Association of School Administrators, April 5, 1965.

33. *The Nation's Schools,* September, 1960.

34. Reported in the *New York Times,* September 26, 1965.

35. Judah J. Harris, *The Treatment of Religion in Elementary School Social Studies Textbooks* (Anti-Defamation League, 1963); see also Lloyd A. Marcus, *The Treatment of Minorities in Secondary School Textbooks* (Anti-Defamation League, 1961).

36. Mary Catherine Howley, "The Treatment of Religion in American History Textbooks for Grades Seven and Eight from 1783–1956," doctoral thesis, Columbia University, 1959, p. 229.

37. James H. McCausland, "Religious Content of the Basic Social Science Textbooks in the Secondary Schools of Three Pennsylvania School Districts," M.A. thesis, University of Pittsburgh, 1948. Harold A. Pflug, "Theistic Religion in Missouri Public School Textbooks," Ph.D. dissertation, Yale University, 1950. Harold C. Warren, "Changing Conceptions in the Religious Element in Early American School Readers," Ph.D. dissertation, University of Pittsburgh, 1951. Karl K. Wilson, "Historical Survey of Religious Content in American Geography Textbooks, 1784–1895," Ph.D. dissertation, University of Pittsburgh, 1951. John H. Dawson, "A Survey of the Religious Content of American World History Textbooks Written Prior to 1900," Ph.D. dissertation, University of Pittsburgh, 1954. William K. Dunn, "The Decline of the Teaching of Religion in the American Public Elementary Schools in the States Originally in the Thirteen Colonies 1776–1861," Ph.D. dissertation, Johns Hopkins University, 1956.

38. Howley, *op. cit.,* p. 6.

39. Noah Webster, *History of the United States* (Durrie and Perle, 1832), p. 6.

40. Charles Goodrich, *A History of the United States of America* (Barbert & Robinson, 1823), p. 6.

41. Indiana University Press, 1965.

42. Gladys S. Wright, "Summary of Offerings and Enrollments in High School Subjects, 1960–1961," U.S. Office of Education, Catalogue OE–24010, June, 1964, p. 4.

43. *Religious Education* (New York), May–June, 1961.

44. Cooperative Test Division of Educational Testing Service, Washington, D.C., Scarvia B. Anderson (ed.), May, 1963.

45. National Council of Teachers of English, Champaign, Ill., Robert F. Hogan, Associate Executive Secretary, April, 1964.

46. *English Journal,* September, 1965.

47. *New York Times,* December 29, 1965.

48. Religious News Service, November 24, 1965.

49. *Ibid.,* January 13, 1966.

50. Full report contained in Annual Report, Project Religious Freedom and Public Affairs, National Conference of Christians and Jews, New York, 1962–1963.

51. Correspondence from Supervisor of Social Studies Instruction, State Department of Education, dated May 3, 1965.

52. Report issued by J. P. McCallie, Chairman, Public School Bible Study Committee, Chattanooga and Hamilton County, Tenn.

53. J. P. McCallie, "Why Have the Bible in the School's Curriculum?" one-page flyer, undated.

54. *Bible Teaching in the Public Schools of Chattanooga, Tenn., Basic Teachers' Guide for Grades 4, 5, 6,* revised and edited by Miriam Kinne and published by the Bible Study Committee.

55. Luella Loewan, *The Son of Man, Studies in Luke* (Bible Study Committee, second printing [rev.], 1962).

56. Communication providing statistical data received from superintendent's office, dated March 19, 1965.

57. *The Bible Study Course — Old Testament*, Dallas Independent School District, Dallas, Texas, Bulletin 150, reprinted by authorization of the Board of Education September 14, 1961, p. 3.

58. *Ibid.*, p. 33.

59. *Ibid.*, p. 70.

60. Letter to the author, July 12, 1966.

61. Rarick, *op. cit.*

62. J. A. Huffman, *Guide to the Study of the Old and New Testaments* (Standard Press [Winona Lake, Ind.], rev. 1949; reissued by Wesley Press [Marion, Ind.]). Recommended for use in Indiana public schools. See *Digest of Courses of Study for the Secondary Schools of Indiana*, Department of Public Instruction Bulletin 232, pp. 58–59.

63. Huffman, *op. cit.*, p. 18.

64. *Ibid.*, p. 96.

65. "The Bible as Literature," for Grade 7, English Curriculum Study Center, Indiana University, first draft prepared in 1965.

66. *Baptist Standard* (Dallas, Texas), 75:4–5 (1963).

67. Religious News Service, May 17, 1963.

68. *Evening Gazette*, October 4, 1962.

69. Thayer S. Warshaw, "Studying the Bible in Public School," *English Journal*, February, 1964.

70. "Experimental Materials," University of Nebraska Curriculum Development Center, 1965; see particularly "Religious Story: Part II, Hebrew Literature," for Grade 7, and "Christian Epic" for Grade 12.

71. "Universal Issues in Human Life," Pennsylvania Humanities Commission, Commonwealth of Pennsylvania, Department of Public Instruction, Harrisburg, 1965.

72. Edward W. Stimson, "How the Public School Can Teach More About Religion," paper prepared for discussion with Omaha Board of Education, February 26, 1965, printed in *Omaha World-Herald*, February 26, 1965.

73. Lawrence C. Little (ed.), *Religion in the Social Studies, The Pittsburgh Report*, (National Conference of Christians and Jews, 1966).

74. *Ibid.*, p. 56.

75. *Ibid.*, p. 58.

76. *Ibid.*, p. 60.

77. Address available in mimeographed form through the National Conference of Christians and Jews.

4

Teaching About *Religion: Some Reservations*

Frederick A. Olafson

In this essay I will assume that the teaching of religion in the public schools is unconstitutional, and with this premise I want to consider in what ways, other than the straightforward indoctrination that is thus excluded, religion might figure in the instructional programs of the public schools. Specifically, I wish to make a number of points that have a bearing on the desirability and feasibility of two somewhat different kinds of academic work concerned with religion. One of these would consist of courses devoted, either partly or wholly, to the imparting of information about the major world religions; and I am assuming that both the doctrinal content and the history and sociology of these religions would be taken up in such courses. The other would be primarily designed to enable students to develop a measure of understanding of what might be called the religious aspect of human life, i.e., the features of our situation as human beings that perennially inspire one form or another of religious affirmation. Such an understanding would presumably be gained by analyses of typical expressions of religious thought and feeling which might be drawn from a variety of sources, among them imaginative literature, biography, and the literature of devotion.

The premise noted above is one which seems to me to be justified both on the ground that it accurately reflects the effective legal situation in which we find ourselves and on the further ground that such a limitation is in keeping with the general spirit and principles of a pluralistic and democratic society as I understand them. With respect to the two proposed methods of introducing a consideration of religion into the academic work of the public schools, my general feeling is that there can be no objection of principle to either one and that in certain circumstances there might be a good prospect that the introduction of work along the lines just described would prove both successful and beneficial. At the same time, however, I am strongly convinced that teaching *about* religion can be successful only if certain prior conditions are satisfied and if our expectations as to the kinds of benefits it would yield are realistic. Because I do not feel at all sure, on the basis of such public discussions of this matter as I have followed, that these qualifications are either widely understood or accepted, I propose to devote my essay to a statement of them. Thus, while I may appear at the outset to be giving a general endorsement to proposals for teaching about religion that are currently being advanced, it will become clear, I think, in the course of my discussion that I do not share either the motives or the expectations of their most vocal sponsors. Whether a program of teaching about religion to which the reservations I will propose are attached would be of any interest to the latter is a question I will leave until the end.

Standards for Courses About Religion

Let me begin by considering the proposal for academic work that would give young people some basic and accurate information about the major religious communions and their traditions. Quite clearly, this is an application to the elementary and secondary levels of an idea — that of courses in comparative religion — which has enjoyed considerable success in colleges and universities for some years. It will be useful, therefore, to remind ourselves that the historical and sociological study of religion treats religion simply as one aspect of human culture without any presuppositions as to the validity of the epistemic claims it typically makes. No doubt such studies have on occasion been pursued in an atmosphere of enthusiastic religious affirmation; and no doubt, in order to seem worthwhile at all, they must rest on some assumptions as to the importance of religious beliefs and practices within human life itself and for the purposes of a comprehensive understanding of human history and society. Nevertheless, I think it would be widely agreed that these studies really prosper only when they are pursued in rigorous isolation from all forms of religious partionship and with a high degree of that scholarly objectivity that cleaves unflinchingly to the truth, even when the interests of piety and edification might seem to suggest in its place a certain saving vagueness.

I make this observation only because I am strongly convinced that we must ask ourselves whether, in transferring this kind of teaching about religion to the lower schools, we are also prepared to have religion discussed there with the same degree of objectivity and freedom we expect and often achieve in our colleges. Are we prepared, for example, to have both St. Francis and Dr. Verwoerd recognized as men who believe they were acting in obedience to the will of God? I do not cite this example because I believe it must somehow shake the faith of persons with religious beliefs but because I fear there may be many who think that it would and who would therefore insist on having only certain approved and respectable examples of religiously inspired lives presented to young children. In order to avoid misunderstanding, let me say that I have no objection at all to the selectiveness and simplification that are characteristic of the stories told to children in the context of genuine religious instruction. What I *am* concerned to point out is the fact that teaching about religion is a quite different sort of undertaking, in which different standards must be applied. I feel very strongly that this distinction with all its implications must be faced before a decision is made to go ahead with a program of teaching about religion. Nothing could be more undesirable than that such teaching should turn out to be no more than a disguised and non-sectarian form of indoctrination in behalf of a diluted and nondescript theism. The history and present reality of religion as an aspect of human culture are just too variegated to lend themselves to any form of instruction premised on the simpleminded assumption that religion is somehow a "good thing." If the ethos that inspires programs of the kind we are considering is to be that of those unpaid television commercials which unctuously instruct us to attend the church of our choice next Sunday, it would be best that the whole project should be abandoned at the outset.

A SECULAR VIEW OF RELIGION

In raising this question I have implicitly posed the first condition which, in my view, must be satisfied before a program of teaching about religion is undertaken. This is simply that we must be ready to look at religion as a human and historical reality through secular glasses and without ulterior motives of prettification or edification. To many, the term "secular glasses" implies hostile eyes, and it is often argued that a treatment of religion that bypasses the ultimate issues of the truth or validity of the claims about man and the world made by religions inevitably expresses a skeptical attitude with respect to the possibility of any rational adjudication of these matters. It is not possible within the compass of this essay to deal adequately with the issues raised by this objection. Here I would only note that such issues need not impinge very directly on the kind of instruction I have in mind. What young people need and what can surely be given them without any great complications' arising is simply certain quite rudimentary, clear, and accurate elements of information about the beliefs, traditions, and practices of major religious groups in their own society and elsewhere. If they do not have this kind of information, they will be condemned to live in that extraordinary miasma of myth, fantasy, and downright malicious falsehood that still obscures from us the human reality of so many lives that are lived under different religious auspices from our own. Surely such information can be imparted in a direct and helpful way without any need for elaborate precautions on the part of the teacher to avoid the appearance of either endorsement or skepticism. The students themselves can of course be expected to try to push the teacher into all sorts of discussions bearing on the truth or morality of this or that tenet of a specific faith, but it does not seem to me to be beyond the powers of a reasonably good teacher to avoid such involvements without appearing — or being — either cowardly or dense. The point is that the story of the religious life and development of a people is deeply interesting simply in human terms without raising questions about the ultimate claim to truth of specific religious doctrines; and it seems perfectly feasible and legitimate for a teacher to limit his consideration of religion to the aspect of it that can be made intelligible in these terms.

There is, of course, no way of being absolutely sure that a given community is really prepared to accept a program of teaching about religion in which the limitations I have been describing are observed. The adoption of such a program will therefore present a necessary element of risk — a kind of bet made by the responsible persons within the schools on the good sense and civic maturity of the religious groups that compose the community. Unfortunately, the very situations in which some positive contribution to mutual understanding among differing religious groups is most needed are likely to be those in which the chance of success is smallest and the wisdom of initiating a program of instruction in the schools most dubious. Where a deep-seated mistrust of the intentions of the public school still prevails within particular religious communities, as it often does, and where ancient animosities still divide one religious group from another, any effort the schools make in this area will automatically be subject to the kind of hostile scrutiny that can quickly paralyze and discourage even the best-intentioned teacher. We are all unhappily familiar with the type of interest taken in the public school by the zealots of one persuasion or another whose chief satisfaction it is to detect some failure on the part of a teacher to show due deference to the idols of their special cults — secular or religious. We are familiar too with the stultifying effect upon *all* teaching of the kind of nervous caution that is the teacher's well-nigh inevitable response when he becomes aware of this disposition to "catch him out." My point, then, is simply that the public school should not be called upon to take responsibility for creating a degree of understanding and mutual respect among differing religious groups when it cannot count upon a large measure of support and sympathy for its program within the community itself. It already has enough responsibilities, over and above its specific academic function, without being asked to initiate programs in as sensitive an area of concern as religion typically is and in circumstances where the ground has not been prepared by the prior achievement of a large measure of understanding among the religious groups in the community in question.

COMPETENCE OF TEACHERS INVOLVED

Let me now lay down the second general condition which, as I see it, must be observed by a school undertaking a program of teaching about religion. This is, in fact, a double-barreled requirement to the effect that, first, the school must recruit the teachers for the instructional programs from its own staff rather than from extramural religious institutions or schools and, second, that these teachers must have a rather high level of training and competence if they are to be able to do this work successfully. I am not, of course, arguing that outside people — among them both clerical and lay representatives of various religious communities — should never be invited to speak to a class at some appropriate juncture in a program of teaching about religion. What I *am* saying is that the school must not even seem to accept the view that a given religious tradition can be fairly and accurately presented only by one of its adherents. This, it seems to me, is precisely what would be conveyed by a school's turning over its program of teaching about religion to an outside team composed of representatives of the major religions. Quite apart from the artificial and — to me, at least — distasteful aspects of such "equal-time" arrangements, it is not particularly likely that, to take just one example, local clergymen as a group would have any strong aptitude for teaching within such a program as I envisage. It is even less likely that a program dependent upon outside help would develop any real unity of style in its treatment of the materials presented. Indeed, since a satisfactory program would require that "religion" be set in the context of the wider life — economic, political, and technological — of a society, it would clearly have to be staffed by highly competent and experienced teachers who would be able to give the students some sense of the complex historical reality of which religion forms a part. This is the point of the second part of the general requirement stated above. It scarcely needs saying that such teachers do not grow on trees. As it is, they are usually fully occupied with the tasks already assigned to them by the school. It is particularly important to bear in mind at the start the limited human resources available to such programs, since any sudden or incautious commitment to a program of teaching about religion would quickly be crippled by the simple lack of competent staff. Unfortunately, as we all know, once programs are launched, they are very difficult to keep within the limits that a due regard to the availability of competent staff would impose. I am suggesting, therefore, that a realistic estimate of these human resources and a decision of principle as to the way they are to be allocated form a necessary preliminary to any move by a school into programs of teaching about religion.

Demands of special courses in an overloaded curriculum

The matter of priorities brings me to the third requirement which I wish to propose: New programs in this field should be adopted only if they are so designed as not to interfere with the integrity of the total instructional program of the school or to reverse the priorities on which we are disposed to base that program over the long run. I have in mind the fact that inadequate understanding on the part of so many young people of the major religious traditions is only one among the many deficiencies in their general culture for which the schools must seek some remedy. To mention just two such deficiencies, how many young people today have any real understanding of the workings of our economic system and how many acquire even the rudiments of scientific literacy? The answer, I am afraid, must be "Very few." But if this is the case, and if the need for imaginative new programs in social studies and science is as urgent as perhaps all of us might agree it is, what relative weight are we to assign to the need for programs in the teaching of religion and to the claims they would make on the limited resources of the school and on the already crowded academic schedules of most students? In my opinion that priority must be quite low, both by reason of these competing claims and because it seems wise for the school to commit its resources to programs in which it alrady has some established competence instead of venturing into fields in which its degree of capability and its likelihood of gaining acceptance from the community at large are very much smaller. Above all, it would seem to me to be a supreme folly to initiate special courses in religion instead of seeking to introduce more and better materials bearing on religion into the courses in history and social studies that are already being given. Special courses in religion, like the special courses in communism which the urgencies of our time have sometimes led us to establish, are all too likely to involve a violent dislocation of the corpus of studies through an essentially arbitrary isolation of a single aspect of a complex reality. To be sure, an intense conviction of the transcendent importance of the set of phenomena that is selected for special treatment may appcar, at least to the sponsors of such projects, to justify the monocular and obsessive vision of the social world which they unwittingly encourage. But if the considerations I have been putting forward have any weight, they must lead us to reject any perfervid, "crash program" approach to the study of religion in favor of one that is cooler and more balanced and stands a correspondingly better chance of outliving the hastily conceived projects of partisan enthusiasts.

The Senior Elective Course.   I have been arguing that the other urgent demands on the curriculum of the secondary school and a concern for the integrity of our understanding of human society cast serious doubt on the advisability of introducing new courses in religion into the, curriculum. To this conclusion I would propose one exception. In the proper circumstances, I think it would be legitimate to offer as an elective in the senior year a course in which students would have an opportunity to read and discuss a number of books and essays dealing in a relatively informal way with a broad range of the philosophical and quasi-philosophical questions that are beginning to concern some young people at that age. Among these, of course, are questions of a religious sort as well as others having to do with fundamental moral issues, with the nature and extent of political authority, and many others. Under the direction of a good teacher, a course of this kind might make a valuable contribution to the effort of young people to arrive at something that could be called a philosophy of life. There would always be a danger of its degenerating into a semester-long "bull session," however, unless precautions were taken, as, for example, by requiring that the students enrolled do a fair amount of writing. The fact that such a course would be offered as an elective for a presumably not very large group of qualified and interested students should help to assure it an intelligent reception and to obviate the other difficulties I have mentioned in connection with such programs. In any case, this is an idea that seems worth experimenting with where favorable conditions exist. While I envisage it more as a course in a rather informal kind of philosophy, religious questions would, as I have indicated, have their own important place in it, and discussion of them might be expected to benefit from the wider critical auspices under which it would proceed.

Work of the kind I have just been describing might go some distance toward achieving the objective of the second kind of teaching about religion distinguished at the beginning of this paper. As I noted there, this objective is a more sensitive appreciation of those aspects of human life that give relevance and plausibility to the promises of religious faith. Insofar as the objective is at all feasible, however, it is probably best achieved by indirection, and it is likely to depend, as does so much that is most precious in what we gain from our formal education, upon the genius of a particular teacher. It is as likely to be realized through the teaching of literature as in a program of instruction explicitly concerned with religion. Indeed, if any of the teaching about religion which I have been describing is done really well, *some* increase in understanding and sensitivity will very likely result, even though the primary aim of the instruction may have been to convey information. For these reasons, I cannot help thinking that it would be a mistake to try to devise procedures for nurturing what is evidently a quite elusive and not easily analyzable quality of mind. The wisest course would rather be the negative one of avoiding those approaches to the subject of religion which block and stultify such latent powers of sympathetic understanding as a young person may possess, and of allowing the final result to depend on the degree of care and intelligence which we bring to the task of teaching about religion — or, for that matter, about anything at all.

Expectations of Moral Impact of
Teaching About Religion

I turn now to a consideration of the benefits that might reasonably be expected to follow from a program of teaching about religion if undertaken in the favorable conditions which I have been trying to specify. I propose to disregard any purely intellectual benefits that would result from simply knowing more about different religions or religion in general and I will also pass over such collateral benefits in the form of increased harmony and mutual respect among religious groups as may accrue to our society as a result of the greater understanding produced by teaching about religion. I will concentrate instead on the widely held belief that teaching about religion might somehow have a beneficial effect on the moral character of our young people. Sometimes such teaching is even spoken of as instruction in values; but since, for me at least, the term "values" seems more naturally to apply to the contents of a stock portfolio, I shall avoid it and speak simply of moral education and character training. The question I wish to raise and will attempt to answer is whether there is any reason to think that teaching about religion in any of the forms which I have recognized as appropriate in the public schools could be expected to have a significant influence on the moral character and tendencies of young people.

In attempting to answer this question, it will be useful to bear in mind the sort of concern out of which a call for moral education in the schools typically issues. Many people are deeply worried about what they believe to be the failure of our society to transmit an understanding of the moral principles of a democratic society to our young people. They are understandably disturbed by the mindless character of a great deal of our popular culture as well as by the schedule of national priorities that is reflected in the way we spend our money, not to speak of the brutal impulses that set a crowd of young people to crying "Jump" to some poor distracted creature on a rooftop. At the same time, the weakness of the institutions that are traditionally supposed to assume responsibility for the moral formation of young people — the family and the churches — is only too visible. In these circumstances it becomes almost inevitable that an appeal should be made to the public schools to do something to reverse the trends. Somehow young people must be given a sense of the importance of simple decency and respect for other human beings, and since such notions form a part of our conception of "citizenship" it seems logical to ask the schools to make an effort to bring young people to a better understanding of what they involve. For the great majority of our population, all of these fundamental moral ideals have strong religious associations, so it is quite natural that moral education should be thought of as closely connected with some form of religious education. Since straightforward religious training cannot be carried on in the public schools, however, teaching about religion is often put forward as a kind of substitute which, it is hoped, will somehow accomplish the same purpose of character training.

Although I feel considerable sympathy with the concern felt by those who make this sort of case for programs of teaching about religion I am very much afraid that their hopes are doomed to disappointment. Indeed, I doubt very much whether such hopes would ever have been entertained if the conditions I have laid down for the programs had been understood and accepted. Certainly one can agree that to study the religious life of a people is to learn something — perhaps a great deal — about the moral code and the effective priorities by which that life is guided. These insights may in turn stimulate reflections on one's own way of life that prove fruitful and ultimately affect how one feels and acts. Still, it is quite evident that, if teaching about religion is to be subject to the limitations I have been proposing, its impact on personal moral reflection must inevitably remain secondary and to a large extent unpredictable. An understanding of the role of the sacraments in Roman Catholicism or of the social bases of Protestant denominationalism may have great value, but it would, to say the least, be unwise to claim that it will provide a sense of moral direction for our young people. While teaching about religion has its own important contribution to make to a soundly based philosophy of life, it cannot generate or revive our sense of what is worthwhile in life, nor can it by itself deliver any final evaluation of the religious ideals it reviews. If we try to make the study of religion as an aspect of human culture an instrument for conveying our own moral ideas, we will only succeed in distorting it and in rendering it incapable of making the contribution which may legitimately be expected of it.

There is another, deeper reason why expectations that teaching about religion would have a significant moral impact are bound to be disappointed, and it is one that has nothing to do with the special restrictions that are implied by the nature of the scholarly disciplines on which such teaching draws. Even if we were to permit ourselves the widest possible freedom to draw moral implications from such studies, the effect of our moralizing upon the minds and hearts of young people would never be very considerable. The fact is that no amount of talk — however lucid and inspiring and profound it may be — is going to change attitudes and lives unless it is associated with a mode of living and acting that makes it credible and "real." To some extent, the personality and general style of life of an individual teacher can provide this indispensable non-discursive counter-part to what might otherwise strike his students as just so much high-minded palaver. Very likely many people who call for programs of moral education in the schools have been much influenced by the example of remarkable teachers who are able to make their students believe in the relevance and the possibility of ideals and modes of life of which their environment otherwise gives no hint. Nevertheless, even such rare teachers as these will be hard put to reach many students unless their efforts are supported by the school as a whole and unless the school as a whole provides an environment in which the ideals of concern for other human beings and of fairness in one's dealings with them are reflected in day-to-day operating procedures. Here, I think, is the true locus of the moral education which, for better or worse, our schools continually provide; by comparison, the content of some special course or set of courses and even the personal influence exerted by individual teachers, important as they may be, pale into insignificance. What I am saying is that if the school can exert a beneficial moral influence on young people, it will do so by providing a setting within which they can see that things are being done for them and not just to them, and in which, perhaps for the first time in the experience of many of them, moral words become moral realities. But the corollary to this proposition is that a truly good school will provide sound moral experiences for its students and will not therefore need any special programs in moral education. On the other hand, a school which is unable or unwilling to do what would make it a good school cannot hope to offset the bad moral experiences its students necessarily have by any program of official uplift. If it is so misguided as to undertake one nevertheless, the young will fortunately be too shrewd to be taken in.

I am aware that by reinterpreting the problem of moral education as a problem that concerns the total relationship of the school as an institution to the individual child, I have not solved it or even suggested how it might be solved. I have simply been arguing that in a primary sense we educate children by the way we treat them, and not by what we tell them — or at any rate not by what we tell them outside some system of practice that can give a concrete sense to the moral notions we employ. It should be recognized, of course, that there are real limitations on the power of the school — particularly the public school — to set itself up as a kind of distinct moral community in which certain ideals of human intercourse are realized to a higher degree than they are in the surrounding society. The school, after all, is supported by the community it serves, and it draws its students and much of its staff from that community. In these circumstances it is bound to run into difficulties if it attempts to act as what Lionel Trilling in a somewhat different context has called an "adversary culture." We should remember, too, that if our young people are morally confused, so is the society from which they come. It is more than likely that people in the schools — salt of the earth though they may be — are in some measure affected by the same confusions. At any rate there is a danger that in attempting too confidently to point the way for young people we may simply fail to understand the problems they face or, worse still, we may fall into self-parody in the mistaken belief that the example of our own rocklike certitude will be enough to carry them through. Nevertheless, none of these caveats should deter the school from making the attempt, within the limits of prudence and practicality, to become in its everyday procedures and atmosphere the kind of community in which the ideals we ask our young people to emulate are effectively and visibly realized. If proposals for special programs of moral education in the schools distract our attention from that fundamental task, it will be a misfortune indeed.

The Danger of Religiosity

I come now to the question touched on at the beginning of this essay, which concerns the degree of interest that the conception of teaching about religion I have outlined might have for those persons who are currently urging the public schools to do something in this field. In discussing the contribution this teaching might make to moral education I have already dealt with one major motive behind such advocacy and I will confine myself here to considering the benefit to religion itself which might be expected from programs of teaching about religion. I am assuming that the expectation of such a benefit is another important reason in favor of these programs in the minds of many of their sponsors.

Essentially, I have just one point to make, and it is one that reflects a certain conception of religion which I happen to hold but which may not be widely shared. There is no need to dispute the claim that a well-conceived program of teaching about religion might dispose some young people more favorably toward a faith that they have come to know better or that it might make the faith of those who are already believers more discriminating and intelligent. This same teaching might, however, have a quite different effect. It might lead to a religious attitude in which any sense of a reference beyond human history and culture is lost and in which religion is finally and not just provisionally treated as a dimension of human existence. Sometimes when I hear religion spoken of as one of the "humanities" I wonder whether something of this kind has not already happened. One does not have to be a Barthian to feel that there is something deeply antithetical to the true religious spirit in any approach to religion which establishes too smooth a continuity between it and the other manifestations of human culture. It may indeed be difficult to imagine "Western culture" without Christianity, but to look favorably on Christianity because of its contribution to this prestigious development is something else again. In its more pernicious forms a religiosity motivated in this way amounts to little more than a worship of ourselves worshiping — a kind of complacent sense of wonder at what man has wrought in God. To be sure, these excesses can be avoided, but I fear that if an effort were made to encourage religious faith by means of an historical study of its role in human culture, the faith so nurtured would bear the marks of its origins. I would therefore question whether persons with religious convictions are wise to propose programs of teaching about religion with expectations of real benefit to the religious life of our young people.

PART TWO

Challenges to Our Educational System

5

The Relationship Between Religion and Education

Harvey G. Cox

The very fact that we can raise the question of the relationship between religion and education indicates something about the problematical character of both in our society. In many past societies religious systems have functioned as the symbolic anchorage and sacral legitimation of the values and institutions of the society, and any question of the *relation* between religion and education would not have made sense. Education was the preparation of the young for full participation in all aspects of the life of the society, including its institutions, its values, and its religious affirmations. Today, however, when we talk about the relationship between religion and education it is almost unanimously agreed that there is a problem if not a crisis. The problem exists not only in the relation between them but in the two entities themselves. Both education and religion are undergoing jarring transitions. We have been asking about the purpose and style of educating children since the progressivist era, and the questions remain unanswered. The whole issue of the aim of education is receiving radical reappraisal. At the same time, religion is facing a series of crises brought about by rapid social change, the increasing confrontation of the major world religions, the secularization of most societies, and the elimination by scientific inquiry of many of the areas of mystery once associated with religion.

In this essay I will deal with the theme of religion and public education on two levels. First, I will discuss some of the pedagogical and theological issues involved in teaching religion in the context of public education in America. Second, I will examine the relationship between religious and public educational institutions in American society. This is an arbitrary division, because the question of teaching religion can never be wholly separated from the question of the institutional *settings* within which such education occurs.

Theological and Pedagogical Issues

At the theological or the pedagogical level, the question of religious teaching in a pluralistic society is a thorny one. The dilemma might best be stated by listing two series of axioms. Each series reveals principles on which most people would find agreement but which, taken together, exhibit built-in contradictions.

PROBLEMS OF A PLURALISTIC SOCIETY

The first series of axioms has to do with the status of religious education in a religiously pluralistic society and goes as follows:

1. We live in a pluralistic society and affirm the value of this pluralism; therefore we oppose the imposition of any particularistic religious system on the society as a whole. The commitment to pluralism is shared by all major sectors of our society, including most religious groups.

2. We know that our kind of pluralistic society requires a consensus at its core and that the consensus involves a commitment to values which make such a society possible. These values include tolerance, respect for the person, equality before the law, the right of any individual to hold opinions differing from those of the majority and to be protected in the expression of his opinions, and the belief that in an open arena the truth will win out over error.

3. We know from our study of sociology that values ordinarily require some grounding in even more basic cultural affirmations about the character of human life, the worth of human personality, and the meaning of human enterprise itself. We recognize that these affirmations are often expressed symbolically as religious beliefs about man, the universe, and history.

We do not want to elevate values to a religious status, nor do we want to substitute for traditional religions some synthetic religion such as Americanism. Still, we realize that when we rely as a society on the values which safeguard pluralism but do not nurture the symbolic affirmations in which they are anchored we have no evidence that the values themselves will continue to flourish. Our commitments to pluralism and to secular education thus seem in some measure contradictory.

THE PLACE OF RELIGION IN EDUCATION

The second series of axioms has to do with the place of religion in the academic curriculum of a school.

1. Our belief could be summarized in this quotation from the Supreme Court decision.

> It might well be said that one's education is not complete without a study of comparative religion or the history of religion and its relationship to the advancement of civilization. It certainly may be said that the Bible is worthy of study for its literary and historic qualities. Nothing we have said here indicates that such study of the Bible or religion, when presented objectively as part of a secular program of education, may not be effected consistent with the First Amendment.

We recognize that quite apart from their claims to truth religions have played and continue to play undeniably important roles both in history and in the contemporary life of man.

2. We believe that children, in whatever sort of school they are attending, should be encouraged to experience the full range of ideas and options of life in all its richness and variety. Naturally this includes religious expressions unless they are arbitrarily excluded for some ideological reason.

3. We know that one can learn only a limited amount about religion by reading or hearing about it. All good teaching requires fidelity to the phenomenon being taught, and it is of the essence of the religious as such that one really learns about it only through some empathic identification with it. Religion, like chemistry or drama, is taught badly if people are not encouraged to act it out. In religion "acting out" would include the ritual of various religions, the disciplines they require, and the service they motivate. We would reject on educational grounds a chemistry course in which there was no opportunity for laboratory experience. Similarly, a course about religion which did not include some element of empathic identification would likewise be educationally spurious.

4. We also know, however, that practice of religious rituals and related activities in a classroom is of questionable constitutional validity. It can lead to confusion, discomfort, and insidious comparisons among young children. It can have a seriously damaging effect especially on the child who belongs to a religious tradition which is a minority in his own classroom. All of us would agree that this sort of damaging impact on children should be excluded.

5. We seem to have to choose, therefore, between (a) avoiding religion in education as much as possible and thus preventing pupils from exploring a range of human thought and activity which no one can deny is a part of the historical and contemporary world; (b) looking at religion entirely "objectively" and discouraging any sort of participation — and therefore falsifying the phenomenon of religion as such; and (c) involving pupils in

religious activities, rituals, and the expression of various kinds of religious beliefs, thereby running the risk of creating strife and division.

CONFRONTING THE DILEMMA

Inadequacy of the Functional Aspect of Religion. The first set of axioms reveals the paradox of what happens to religion when it is viewed from a functional perspective alone. It is my conviction that religious experience must transcend a merely functional definition even if it is to fulfill the function in question. The Zuñi rain dance contributed what is probably an indispensable factor to the integration of Zuñi society. But it was a latent function. The moment the dancers began to believe that the manifest function of the dance (to cause rain) was secondary or even spurious and the real reason for the dance was social integration, they would probably have stopped dancing.

The fact that religious beliefs legitimate values which the society finds useful or essential not only is an insufficient basis for perpetuating the religion but will not ultimately succeed in maintaining the religious system. This means that we cannot perpetuate religious practices or teach religious doctrines simply because they enshrine values we hold to be important quite apart from or even in opposition to the religious beliefs themselves. Religion cannot be sustained on this self-consciously functional basis alone, both for sociological reasons and for theological ones from the perspective of biblical religion. When a person does something because it pleases God, ethics and theology are in proper relation. But when he decides that a particular ethic is useful and then prescribes belief in God as a way to legitimate the ethic, God is automatically demoted to the status of an "idol." The society and its needs have become ultimate and God has become a means of assuring its stability. Rather than the people serving God, God becomes a helper to the people.

The desire to provide a symbolic focus for a set of previously selected values is not a proper basis for teaching religion in the schools. It both endangers the values and desecrates the religion. If we do believe that certain values (tolerance, right of dissent) are necessary for a pluralistic society, we should say so in our teaching. We should frankly admit that we respect these values because they make it possible for a variety of people to live together amicably. We should avoid trying to give them a religious luster. If we try to religionize these values, a crisis in the child's religious beliefs may at the same time threaten the values. Besides, he will learn something about religion (namely, that it is mainly good for sacralizing socially useful values) which many religious people would find repulsive to religion.

Dealing with Controversial Subjects. The second series of axioms raises the specter of divisiveness in the classroom if religion is dealt with vigorously and directly in all its contradictions. Here the main answer of most educationalists and religious educators has been a timid one. They have sought to avoid controversy, to exclude the possible acrimony of religious differences from the classroom. Like sex and politics, religion should be kept out or at best dealt with in a "neutral" manner that stresses commonalities rather than differences. Certainly avoiding a sectarian bias is a worthwhile objective, but the usual way of stating this objective seems to make dullness a virtue. A church document on the possibility of public funds for parochial schools says,

> Public school teaching, as is stated in the teacher manuals of any public system, must strive toward a balanced neutral presentation of religious questions. Descriptive or empirical teaching about religion is acceptable but teaching supported by public funds must avoid normative teaching or teaching for commitment.

As Robert Lynn comments in his *Protestant Strategies in Education*, this paragraph goes beyond a mere plea for integrity in teaching material and fairness in presentation, with which anyone would have to agree. The sharp emphasis on an absolute distinction between normative and objective teaching becomes, he argues, "a dubious contribution to good educational policy." [1] Dr. Lynn characterizes this as a "flatlander" approach to controversial subjects, one which studiously avoids the heights and depths of conflict and renders public education tepid and uninteresting. He suggests that the critical problem is not that we need strictures against "normative teaching" (whatever that may be). It is the lamentable absence of the freedom of intelligent dissent by both teacher and pupil which marks many if not most public schools today. Teachers hesitate to open up touchy issues. Parents and community groups complain. Principals try to keep the lid on. The result is monotony. But monotony is never educationally helpful. "The health and vitality of any school system," Lynn suggests, "depends upon its ability to deal with controversy without fear of reprisal." [2]

If recapturing controversy in the classroom is one of our main tasks today, then a central educational issue of religion and public education is how religion may increase the level of conflict in schools, thus making them more interesting and vital educational settings. Churchmen should not compromise and synthesize religious teaching into a pabulum of tedium that will offend no one. When and if religion is taught in American public schools, it should be taught in such a way that pupils may experience and deal with conflicts of opinion over very basic matters. Students should learn as early as possible that, although some people believe the various religions are merely different roads to the same celestial destination, many others think the differences between religious systems are of crucial significance. How all this can be taught is a difficult matter, but teachers cannot even begin to work at it until initial agreement is reached that the classroom is a place to *handle* the most explosive issues, not to *avoid* them. Teaching religion in public school classrooms may have many educational values. Here I only wish to argue that, since religion is something about which people have had and still have strong, conflicting ideas and feelings, this is no reason to *exclude* it but a very good reason to *include* it in the public school classroom.

Institutional Issues

One difficulty with discussion about "religion" and "public education" is that both words are abstractions. Religion can refer to the pedagogical and theological issues just discussed. It can also mean the religious institutions of the society and their relationship to the institutions of public education on the social institutional level. In the United States, religion is institutionalized in the form of churches, denominations, and inter-denominational agencies. At this level of analysis theological ideas function either as values which the institutions seek to implement or as ideologies which they use to defend institutional interests. It is on the point where religious institutions interact with the institutions responsible for public education that attention is now focused. I will consider how these institutions have operated in terms of certain issues bearing on public education and what might be hoped for in the future. As this discussion proceeds, it should become clear that one unresolved issue is what is really meant by a "public" school, whether the line between "public" and "private" or parochial education is becoming less clear, and what this could mean both for religion and for public education.

THE EDUCATION OF THE POOR

The center of attention for institutional relations between religion and public education today is the education of the poor. The test case for American public policy in the education field in the forthcoming decade will be how our society survives the crisis in urban education. No documentation is necessary here to argue the enormous seriousness of this crisis. The execrable condition of most urban school systems in America, especially those parts of school systems serving the poor and Negro ghettos, needs no elaboration. Survey after survey has documented it. It has been estimated that Americans spend roughly twice as much on the public education of the affluent child as they spend on the poor child. But we make up for this penny-wise policy a thousandfold even on the monetary level with soaring costs in welfare, unemployment compensation, police and prison expenses, and decreased productivity. This is to say nothing of the inestimable human cost involved in barring millions of human beings from effective participation in the polis. It is no exaggeration to say that the ugly problem of urban education confronts American society with a test of its seriousness about its confessed religious values. Certainly a failure in this area will doom not only the school system but the whole society to accelerated outbreaks of violence such as the one that occurred in Watts in the summer of 1965. What are the issues for urban education and how have religious institutions helped or hindered the search for viable solutions?

There are two underlying obstacles to the creation of a satisfactory urban school system in America. The first is inadequate political support for urban schools, reflecting no doubt various degrees of racism in the American public, ranging from the shrill fear of New York City's Parents and Taxpayers who picket integrated schools to the sophisticated disdain of suburbanites who vote down any proposal for sharing in the cost of neighboring core city schools while hypocritically contributing annually to the NAACP. The second obstacle is the staleness and introverted conservatism of urban school bureaucracies. A variety of factors has led to the appearance in most cities of a school system characterized, from top administrators down to classroom teachers, by an atmosphere of caution, uniformity, insecurity, and suspicion of change.

This combination of moneylessness and mindlessness throws up a roadblock whose removal is made all the more difficult by the reciprocal relation of the two. If the problem were money alone, sufficient enthusiasm might be engendered to pour endless dollars into the system until results began to appear. But given the present decrepitude in urban schools this sort of program would seem to many people like a useless waste of national resources. On the other hand, if the problem were simply finding the talent and ideas for changing city schools, many would volunteer if only the needed cash were on hand. But as it is, we are faced with both problems at the same time and the response is often paralysis.

The Withdrawal of the Churches from Urban Areas. How have the religious institutions related to this stalemate? Sadly enough, despite their unending preachments about the equality of races and the sacredness of the human person, and even despite their reiterated commitment to the cultivation of the mind as an important religious value, the religious institutions of America have been among the principal culprits in the ruination of urban education in America. The crime was in most cases not completely intentional. It was a sin of omission more than commission. Nevertheless, the tactics of the churches have contributed in no small measure to the catastrophe we now face. How did it happen?

First, it happened because of a religious flight from the poor, a wholesale abandonment by the churches of the core city with all its problems. For Protestants the postwar decades have been marked by the construction, at astronomical costs, of thousands of churches in suburban areas, and the callous discarding of church after church in the city. Denominations wrangled with one another over who should build churches in so-called "high-potential areas" (which, as Peter Berger once remarked, did *not* mean high potential for prayer). Inner-city church buildings were feverishly sold to Negro congregations; city mission societies retreated behind the ramparts of settlement houses, and the urban schools (along with every other major city institution) were left to deteriorate for lack of funds and attention.

The middle-class Protestant desertion of the urban schools had been anticipated by the Roman Catholic decision of a century before to construct, at enormous expense and effort, a parallel school system. In retrospect, the Catholic withdrawal had somewhat better theological grounds than the Protestant one. At least it was based on an effort to preserve the purity of the Catholic faith, whereas Protestants really had no religious basis for the removal to the suburbs. Still, the Catholic strategy has left its mark. The proportion of school children in our cities who attend Catholic schools varies from 42 per cent in Pittsburgh and 26 per cent in New York down to much smaller proportions in areas of the country with fewer Catholics. In the ten states with the largest concentrations of Catholics, however, Catholic schools now educate between 20 and 25 per cent of the total school enrollment.

The Catholic retreat from public education in the city has had many deleterious results. It has frequently divided public attention and concern so that neither system was adequately supported. Roman Catholics who felt doubly taxed have sometimes opposed fiscal measures designed to improve public schools. Often Catholics have viewed public schools as a place to send discipline problems from their own schools. Many people outside the Catholic Church and some within it have seen the parochial school system as a source of disunity within the body politic, and a number have suspected (usually without real evidence) that what was going on in Catholic schools was something closer to indoctrination than education. Nevertheless, Catholic schools do exist within the city and do provide a resource for urban education that we overlook at our peril. A discussion of the place of religion in educating the American public fails if it does not take this resource into consideration.

If middle-class Catholics, Protestants, and Jews fled with their religious institutions from the scene of their crime of negligence, and if middle- and lower-class Catholics abandoned the public school system for a parochial system, the only groups left in many cities were the poor — both black and white — and the rich. The rich, often of Protestant lineage, had long since switched from the public schools of the city to elite private schools and boarding schools. The poor soon became the main clientele for urban school systems. Left with no real attention from other groups, the urban school systems began to degenerate quickly into their present quasi-custodial roles. School politics was often controlled by teachers and administrators for their own ends, and school boards receded from public attention. Only the protests of Negro parents in the early 1960's brought the chaos and crisis of urban schools back into public view.

The Intransigence of Religious Groups Concerning Educational Legislation. But the negative role of religious institutions does not end with their withdrawal from urban education. They continued to use their institutional power to prevent the passage of the only kind of national legislation which could begin to eliminate the poverty of urban schools. It is no exaggeration to say that the main obstacle to federal aid to education in the past two decades has been the intransigence of religious groups and their power to veto needed legislation. For years Roman Catholic leaders with a dog-in-the-manger attitude opposed any legislation which did not include federal monies for Catholic schools as well. Responding in kind, Protestant leaders were willing to sacrifice millions of exploited urban youngsters on the high altar of separation of church and state by blocking any legislation that did include support for parochial schools. In this stand the Protestants were often abetted by Jewish groups with an ideological liberal commitment to a purist separation of church and state.

Under the American political system, in which single power groups can veto a given measure even if they do not have sufficient power to originate an alternative, the plight of the public schools grew steadily worse while the various religious groups congratulated themselves on their ability to maintain the purity of their principles.

It would be tempting here to try to uncover how much of the stubbornness of religious groups on this issue is the expression of authentically held religious values and how much is institutional and ideological self-defense. However, these facets are never easy to separate, and in any case the result is the same. Protestants who opposed federal aid which would include Catholic schools found themselves in alliance with those who opposed any increase in the society's financial commitment to education and with others who saw in federal aid a dire threat to local school autonomy. Thus the timeworn Protestant commitment to separation of church and state could easily serve as a cover for the conservatism which has long characterized middle-class Protestantism in America. Roman Catholics, having built up an institutional interest in their own schools and faced with rising costs on every hand, saw that federal aid which did not include them would result in a steady diminution of the number of families who would be able to send their children to Catholic schools. Some Catholics discerned in this process the incipient breakdown of the cohesiveness and social control which had made their church a power to be dealt with in the urban scene.

A New Era in Church-State Relations. Fortunately 1965 saw the beginning of a decisive change in the attitude of both Protestant and Catholic officials in the question of federal aid. It hinged on the growing recognition that aid to *pupils* in parochial schools need not be construed as aid to the schools themselves. Thus when Protestant leaders from the National Council of Churches testified in Washington on the Johnson administration's Elementary and Secondary Education Act in January, 1965, they were willing to go much further than ever before in accepting a wide range of federal aid for children in parochial schools. Also, although the 1965 legislation was not all they had hoped for and carefully avoided channeling money into Catholic schools as such, Catholic leaders did not oppose it. The bill was passed. It signaled a new era in church-state relations in the area of public education.

At the same time, the much honored wall of separation was being breached at dozens of other points. Federal grants and loans flowed out to church-related colleges. Poverty grants came from the Office of Economic Opportunity to churches and church-sponsored programs for tutoring, nursery schools, and manpower retraining. Low interest loans amounting to millions of dollars were used by church groups for constructing housing for the aged and middle-income projects. It seemed clear that the absolutist interpretation of separation of church and state was dead in America and that only a very few people were sorry to see it go.

It would be a mistake to assume, however, that religious institutions in America are completely converted on the issue of federal aid to public education. There is still a great deal of suspicion and wariness. Many churchmen will watch these novel elements of the new education act with great care in an effort to find abuses which will justify a return to previous positions. Still, the possibility is now present that religious groups can cooperate in finding ways to exploit the new fluidity in church-state relations, not to bolster their own positions but to concentrate massive new support in fund-starved urban systems. Catholic, private, and public schools might initiate joint programs of after-school activities, adult education, cultural enrichment, vocational training, etc. The possibilities are limitless, especially in view of the purposely vague wording of the section of the Education Act of 1965 on "supplementary education centers." There is no reason, for example, why urban churches, Catholic and Protestant, might not set up such centers in their own facilities using federal grants. For the Protestants this might help relieve justifiably guilty consciences about the Sunday School buildings and church parlors and kitchens which go unused for days at a time. City mission societies and church education agencies, often frustrated for ways to touch the urban crisis creatively, but sometimes with good facilities and trained staffs at their disposal, could help plan and coordinate such programs.

It is obvious that this plethora of new institutional settings makes possible the emergence of new types of education in religion. But it would be wrong for religious groups to view the fluidity of the current scene mainly from this perspective. Their first commitment should be to educate, and there are reasons to believe that they can help. Churches find themselves today with facilities, staffs, and buildings located on the very turf where the crisis of the urban poor has reached its flame point. With a new ecumenical openness coming from one side and new ways of understanding the separation of church and state on the other, all that is needed is the willingness to imagine and experiment, and to make sure that greedy institutional self-aggrandizement neither freezes the tender bud of ecumenicity before it can bloom nor cements over the fissures in the wall of church-state separation before they can be utilized as channels for vitalizing the education of urban children.

NEW EDUCATIONAL PATTERNS

Church-Run Schools. Within the next few years church groups may begin to run pilot schools in cities on contract arrangements with local school boards, analogous to the way they now contract with poverty boards. Thus would come into being a type of school which would be neither "public" nor "private" in the usual sense. Indeed, if the sponsoring agencies encouraged parents and other community groups to take an active hand in planning and conducting these schools, they would be "public" in a more authentic sense than many urban public schools today. Also, whole new types of heretofore untried schools will begin to appear directly under poverty programs. The "academies of transition" now operating in Harlem on a pilot basis are good examples. They help bridge the gap between the rhythm, life style, and daily schedules of school dropouts and the routine of ordinary schools. These are "public" schools, and if the Harlem experience is valid, the role of religion in motivating and rehabilitating such youngsters is considerable.

Educational Experimentation. But even if religious institutions end their conspiracy against federal help for urban schools, even if massive financial support somehow becomes politically possible, there remains the second problem, the gray pallor of bureaucratic mediocrity which hangs over our urban schools, smothering real creativity. Here the question is not how to get more money for the schools but how to change them so that the money is wisely spent.

Again this question must be answered, at least at first, on the political level. In order to change the schools, the present pattern of control of the schools must be changed, and groups with novel and untried approaches to education must be allowed to experiment. Admittedly some experimentation will fail and certain new ideas, after a trial period, will have to be discontinued. But even a failing educational experiment could not be much worse than the level of the average public school in an American city today. Even when the substance of an experiment does not fully succeed, those with whom the experiment has been carried out often profit simply by having been involved as the subjects of whatever was tried. This was proved at the Hawthorne General Electric plant where the workers with whom the experiment was being conducted showed markedly improved attitudes toward their work just because the experimenters were interested in them as people and in how they were responding to the conditions which were part of the experimental design.

The Responsibility of Religious Institutions. Most experimentation in education is now going on either in private schools or on a very limited level in public schools where experiments are usually isolated from the system in general. Most of those who now control urban education in America are reticent to see anything really new tried, since radical changes would result in a threat to their positions of power. If religious institutions wish to see extensive change in urban schools, they must be willing to help organize the political support needed to bring it about.

Though at first this may seem like a call for a vast change in the attitude of the churches toward the political process, such is not the case at all. The churches in America have been deeply involved in espousing and opposing political causes throughout the nation's history. Abolitionism, child labor legislation, civic reform measures, and more recently civil rights are only the most dramatic instances in which organized church participation in the political process has taken place. Prohibition is a somewhat more unfortunate example. If the energies expended by Protestant church groups to prevent public money from going to Catholics, and the energy expended by Catholics to prevent legislation which did not cut them in on the subsidy, could be combined and directed toward organizing support for a lively, heterogeneous, and humane educational system in our cities, it could make an epochal difference. As it is now, Protestant churches never blush to oppose specific candidates who, for example, advocate lotteries. They have been more reluctant, however, to oppose candidates who are indifferent or hostile to new approaches to urban education. Again the advent of the ecumenical era could make a marked difference in this regard. If Catholic educators heretofore wrapped up in the admittedly overwhelming problems of keeping the Catholic school system going could cooperate with Protestants in efforts to educate their constituencies on urban school issues, clarify policy options, and even, when the situation warranted, support candidates in diocesan newspapers and through other channels, who knows what could happen in American cities? It was not until after the re-election of Louise Hicks to the Boston School Committee that the Boston *Pilot*, the archdiocesan newspaper, openly declared its opposition to her by gently reprimanding its readers for electing her. The question which naturally comes to mind now is what the *Pilot* will do next time. Will it state its opinion unequivocally *before* the election? Or will it once again wait until it is too late and then merely settle for handwringing? There are some indications that the Catholic press here and there, even on the diocesan level, is willing to plump more consistently for issues transcending mere Catholic institutional self-interest.

As a matter of fact, the churches have demonstrated that on certain issues their voices, when well organized and articulate, can have a real effect on public opinion and on voting. Preliminary surveys have shown, for example, that in areas of California where a determined effort was made to explain the Rumford Act and its moral significance in church groups the anti-fair housing measure collected smaller majorities than in areas of similar ethnic and socioeconomic populations where no such effort was made. The question is not whether the churches have either the facilities or the right to engage in political activity in support of better schools, but whether they decide to do so.

There is evidence that in some cities the churches have begun to move toward more active engagement in the political struggle of the poor, not only for better schools, but for better cities in every regard. The decision of church groups, both Catholic and Protestant, to finance the organization of poor communities to apply political power is one of the most important events in recent church history. It has happened in various ways in, among other cities, Chicago, Rochester, Buffalo, Kansas City, and Cleveland.

On the institutional level, religious groups should enlarge their support for federal aid to urban schools, experiment boldly with new types of "public" schools, and help mobilize religious constituencies to demand creative change in urban education.

NOTES

1. Robert Lynn, *Protestant Strategies in Education* (Association Press, 1964), p. 78.
2. *Ibid.*, p. 79.

6

Oppositions Between Religion and Education

Samuel H. Miller

Religion and education have been married, divorced, and remarried so often in their long history that it is easy to say that they cannot get along with each other any better than they can do without each other. There has always been a tendency for one party to dominate the situation, and then the inevitable split has occurred, forcing a temporary and uncomfortable separation. In time, however, separation proved painful, and the couple has always come to a hopeful reconciliation, yet never altogether satisfactorily, or for long.

Somewhere behind this uneasy relationship there must be strains, inbuilt incompatibilities, basic realities too refractory to cohabit comfortably without loss of certain intrinsic integrities. There is something that "doesn't love a wall," but, on the other hand, something that does. Education does not resist the intrusion of religion just out of prejudice, and religion does not find the conditions imposed by education embarrassing merely out of a perverse arrogance. There are reasons, if we can disentangle them from the heated debate on the separation of church and state or the murky obscurities of sentimental tolerance. It is obvious that a place could be found in the organization of courses and classes for religion as one more subject, but clearly that does not suffice. Too many things are left unanswered for such a facile inclusion to help anybody. In the printed catalogue it looks good, but in the practical operation of teaching it is the beginning of trouble. The grinning devil of sectarianism haunts the effort from the start, and religion gets lost somewhere in the struggle to be neutral.

We tend to distort the problem when we think of religion only in its sectarian or ecclesiastical forms, however much these seem to be the operational realities. Until we search behind the institutional façade of diversity for a better understanding of the perennial strain between these two important aspects of man's personal and social consciousness, we shall be trying to play the game blind, pushing the figures around the chess-board without respecting the inherent rules of the game. In this essay I shall be concerned with two things: first, to locate the refractory material in religion which does not lend itself — at least not without great difficulty — to the educational process, and second, after recognizing the incompatibles, to ask how that fact itself can be introduced into the educational process, and how far we can go with it.

Let us begin with an attempt to define the essential function of religion, and hope that thus we may uncover the intrinsic source of its resistance.

Inclusiveness and Specialization

There are four ways to isolate the distinctive thrust of religion. The first is concerned with assembling the chaos of existence and history in such a way as to suggest or affirm the reality of a cosmos. Whether it be called Providence or the Kingdom of God, or *Heilsgeschichte*, religion presumes by faith that everything "works together for good to them that love God." Religion is the effort to bring together all the disparate and even contradictory fragments of life so as to articulate the mystery of their mutual dependence. Fundamentally, it is not an attempt to explain or even to reveal a unity, but only to point out and hold together, however loosely or precariously, the paradoxes, the opposites, the contrarieties, as Blake called them, of this world. Religion embraces and in an imaginative act of faith symbolizes the *coincidentia oppositorum* of life and death, of heaven and hell, of freedom and necessity, of sin and spirit, of goodness and evil, of suffering and salvation, of body and mind. In short, faith articulates a meaning hidden in mystery and makes no effort to explain it. Its concern is to be faithful to the whole, to believe in the affirmative significance, without subtracting the least thing or the most destructive from it.

This does not mean that religion is interested in abstract generalities. It is not interested in the extraction of truth from things or events, or in a mosaic of collected ideas from many philosophies. At its primary level it sees totality in concrete instances, the whole or the ultimate is revealed or reflected in the unique but common part, as in the rite of the Eucharist, or in the event of the crucifixion, or in the person of Jesus the Christ. Religion sees revelation taking place *in* history, not above it. The concrete fragment is a microcosm wherever it is adequately opened up and disclosed; the whole is in it. Reality is known in the totality of relationships.

Indeed, this is the significance of the primary act of religion in worship. The liturgy, from whatever tradition — the mystical Orthodox, or the redemptive Catholic, or the Quakers' use of silence, or the Protestant reliance on the Word — is a cultic act by which the worshiper recovers the reality that all things are in God, even the most uncanny, the terrible, like pain and death. Mortal man and holy God, this common world and the mystery of the future, the bread we break and the bread from heaven, all are in His hands. Worship is the affirmation that God is sufficient to bring all things together in meaning.

It is immediately evident that the patterns of attention in religion and in education are not the same. Contrary to the attempt of religion to include the total diversity of life in some kind of mysterious affirmation, despite all the ironies of conflict and confusion, education sorts everything out quite neatly and puts each thing in its own place with as much precision as possible. Education thus thrives on specialization, dividing and subdividing, multiplying categories and classes until the cosmos once again tends to resemble chaos, or at best the university disappears in the multiversity.[1] Common discourse then is compartmentalized in leakproof vocabularies as sectarian as anything that ever came out of the fanaticism of religion. There is no difficulty whatever in adding another "piece" to such an expanding picture puzzle of education, except at that point where the "piece" has some pretensions beyond itself, of reflecting on the nature of the whole, or perhaps illogically presuming that opposites can be yoked together for the sake of a truth more clarifying in its mystery than an explanation in its clarity.

ART AND EDUCATION

Something of the same problem is uncovered in the usual attempt to introduce art into the educational process. Almost always, and especially at the university level, such a venture becomes a course *about* art, *about* its history, its chronology, its styles, its authenticity, but not a course *in* art. Art is separated from the dangers of subjective response or reaction, delivered from the accidents of personal prejudice and amateur ignorance. And, to a large degree, it ceases to be what it was in the mind of the artist or to do what it is supposed to do in the life of the responsive observer. A similar situation is described by Northrop Frye, who says that "the difficulty often felt in 'teaching literature' arises from the fact that it cannot be done; the criticism of literature is all that can be directly taught."[2]

ART AND RELIGION

Art is like religion in that it reaches beyond the given surface of life for a hidden reality and affirms it in terms of the concrete world. It unites many things in a vision which might well be described by Cassirer's phrase, "intensive compressive." One of the best examples of this is a description in Jerome Bruner's work, *On Knowing*, of a Renaissance statue, once in the Toledo Cathedral, now in the Metropolitan, known as the Santa Maria Blanca:

> . . . a graceful half-smiling Virgin holding the Christ child who reaches up as if to chuck her under the chin. This White Virgin is all the faces of woman — mother, wife, flirt, daughter, sister, mistress, saint, and harlot. As one looks a bit, there are impulses-in-restraint to father her, to be mothered by her, to make love to her, and just to watch how the face will change when the Child finally pokes her under the chin. . . . here, if anywhere, one may speak of the experience of art as a mode of knowing . . . the energy of all one's discordant impulses creates a simple image connecting the varieties of experience in her extraordinary face.[3]

Art and religion have this in common: they are concerned with a surplus, with a compression of many things into one, with a promiscuous and dangerous imprecision, which passes far beyond the ideational and incites the feelings and mysterious associations, but does it in such a way as to focus all of them at one point, in a single image. This appeal to the creative labors of the whole psyche is what makes both art and religion discomforting adjuncts in which it is easier, and therefore tempting, to deal only with transmissible ideas.

Symbols and Ideas

The second distinctive aspect of religion can be seen in its vocabulary. The "part-whole" structure of religion is communicated not, in the first place, by ideas but by symbols. They may be simple symbols, as in a thing so charged with meaning that it means more than itself; or complex symbols, as in the rite, where things and persons, history and revelation, are related in a meaningful series of actions, reminding and recovering an elusive experience; or symbols embodied in myth, in which an event becomes transparent to the transcendent forces operating in human life and yet withal maintains the full mystery of the inexplicable action of God. These three — symbol, rite, and myth — are the constituent elements by which religion transmits its wisdom, witnesses to the revelation of what is beyond the "trance of ordinary experience," and celebrates what it cannot explain. They are "intensive compressions," and they stand over against the elaborated decompression of the ideological world.

Direct analysis provides no access to what is contained in the symbol or in the rite or in the myth. It can be elicited only by an interior route by which the self lends its own substance, its "insight," its own specific quality, its own peculiar circumstances, to the open-ended shell of the symbol, or the passion of the repeated gesture. Reality in this sense cannot be known except by participation. Perhaps this is what Yeats meant when he said, "Truth cannot be known, but it may be embodied." At any rate, one may say that what can be known objectively — even if it be the Bible itself, or the Christ, or God — is not essentially religious, though it may have been extracted from the field of religion.

In contrast to this peculiar vocabulary of religion, which may be characterized as "believing" in contrast to knowing, is the vocabulary of education. The latter vocabulary consists of ideas — ideas abstracted from everything, everywhere, even from religion, as is proper — and they are intended for storage, for classifying the world of happenstance, for exchange, and for communication. Lionel Trilling speaks of ideas as "pellets of intellection" and notes their passionate elaboration in the culture of the nineteenth and twentieth centuries. We live on ideas; we wring them out of everything; indeed, we find difficulty in thinking of anything until we have extracted the idea from it, spit out the substance, pinned down the beauty and classified it, and carefully sketched it in two dimensions!

Trying to introduce the complex dimensions of the symbolic — its burgeoning richness as well as its vague but highly individual connotation — into the ideological world is like trying to get a live camel flattened out into a blueprint. It is too thick, too intensive, too compressed. Once the camel is pared down, it is no longer alive; once the symbol is reduced to an idea, it loses its power and dynamic significance. This is the curse that has followed the Protestant Calvinistic tendency to iconoclasm. Symbols are not ideas; rites are not ideas made into ceremonies; myths are not ideas translated into an obese form of fiction. Each retains its existence in the concrete realities of time and space but is open to the rich overtones beyond any specific time or space. The ideological world, the world of ideas, is quite appropriately precise, objective, and discrete. It applies largely to one stratum of consciousness. On the other hand, religion tends to be extremely thick and unprecise, with much obscurity, for it deals with the whole, which is never attained, and it must transcend the nice limits of the subjective and the objective. The world must not be acknowledged at the expense of the person, nor must the person exceed his proper place in the world. Religion applies to all strata of consciousness, including the ideational, but it extends in every direction, embracing the subconscious and the emotional, and balks at no limits or contradictions.

This presents us with one of the crucial issues of the rapprochement between religion and education. Reinhold Niebuhr refers to it in an essay on "The Two Sources of Western Culture": "We cannot fruitfully reverse the process of the past centuries and give a new dignity to the Hebraic-Christian component of our culture which has been projected by the difference between religious and scientific symbols." That warfare between scientists and churchmen has left a heritage of intellectual and spiritual confusion of the worst sort, and with it a natural resistance to the traditional obscuration in the use of religious symbols.

But however difficult the problem may be, neither education nor religion can easily absolve itself of its appropriate responsibilities. As Suzanne Langer long ago pointed out, in this epoch where symbolic exercises have been all but lost, "relatively few people . . . are born to an environment which gives them spiritual support. . . . A mind that is oriented, no matter by what conscious or unconscious symbols, in material and social realities, can function freely and confidently even under great pressure of circumstance and in the face of hard problems. . . . Any miscarriage of the symbolic process is an abrogation of our human freedom."[4]

No one reading the literature of our time, with its universal agony of alienation, anxiety, and loss of identity, will need to be persuaded that ideas, however numerous, will not of themselves bring man to fulfillment. Indeed, they may lead only to that "immorality of knowledge" in which the "uncontaminated intellect delights in its own erudition." Ideas may be accumulated; symbols must be penetrated. But how we are to regain sufficient reflectiveness in this non-reflective age of discursive haste poses a severe problem. Academic pressures and the character of academic compulsion lead to a superficial sophistication, to more knowledge and less wisdom.

Learning and Salvation

The third of the recalcitrant oppositions between religion and education is the difference between the traditional terms "learning" and "salvation." That there has been a widespread, perhaps not explicit, assumption that salvation lies in learning cannot hide the general disillusionment with this mistaken kind of liberalism. There is no inevitable relationship between knowledge and wisdom; indeed, most of the staggering moral problems of our age have been instigated by our inability to handle wisely the advantages of our ascending intelligence, as in the case of atomic fission, or mass communication. On the other hand, I do not want to be led astray by mere verbal distinctions, when in actuality the two terms may refer to the same phenomenon.[5] However, education does seem to proceed on the ideological basis that a body of knowledge allows one to conform to the nature of the world satisfactorily and profitably, whereas in religion there is always the presumption that human consciousness must undergo a radical reorientation in reference to the world in order to fulfill its proper destiny, or in order to become itself. It begins in dependence, or, as we might say, in innocence, and proceeds by some sort of "agon" or "metanoia" in which it is separated from its illusions, shattering the pattern of conformity to nature and to society, before being ultimately restored to a creative relationship at a new level of freedom. Certainly the Greek heritage is no less insistent on this than the Jewish and Christian faiths. A shift from innocence to moral responsibility is required, from naïve knowing to paradoxical believing, from the simplicity of law to the subtlety of grace.

This introduces a new concern in the process of "teaching." Not only does one teach a subject, but one teaches a man — and teaches him in such a way that he not only knows the truth but can become it. As Professor Paul Holmer speaks of this Kierkegaardian element,

> To the ethical and religious man there is no need to weep if the cognitively delineated cannot properly be called reality. . . . Needless to say, this implies no derogation of science or gnosis — it means only that one does not apply intellectual criteria to all things human and that one states in a way that man is not only a subject for knowledge but is also a subject in the process of making his own existence. . . . He believes there is a kind of logos within subjectivity.

To be sure, in education there is an expectation of growth. Questions of maturity, poise, judgment are all included, but the human condition, the consciousness of man, is not so radically conceived. The educational process has its crises — and again, I do not want to underestimate them — but they are not directly related to being as much as to mind, to a change of consciousness as much as to the accumulation and organization of ideas. In religion, many levels of being are assumed, and the question is how to break into a higher consciousness, whereas in education the concern is less with levels of being as with circles of comprehension extending farther and farther on the surface of the same ideological sea. I do not deny a connection between these two fields, but there is certainly a distinction to be made in the major emphasis.

Mystery and Knowledge

The fourth of the grating incompatibilities is the difference between mystery, as the ultimate reference of religion, and knowledge, as the medium of understanding reality. Religion is intent on reaching beyond the world of phenomenal appearance to the ultimate mystery out of which all things come. Whatever else the terms may mean in this controversial age, God is the affirmation of that mystery which is never to be confused with the forms of function and temporality. Idolatry is always rejected because it compromises the essential mystery with things knowable, whether they be wooden objects or intellectual ideas or poetic metaphors.

Classical religion, both Jewish and Christian, is based firmly on the *deus absconditus*, as Pascal affirms it by saying that "any religion which does not teach the hiddenness of God is false." Whenever the mystery declines and the metaphors harden into ideas, religion loses its vitality. It moves back into the secondary line of ideological rigidity, where it may gain security and a certain kind of certainty but unfortunately loses its connection with the primal force of undifferentiated creativity from which it is always derived.

Education, on the other hand, is concerned with knowledge — knowledge as a way to reduce mystery. Here we may be diverted by a misunderstanding of the use of the same word for different things. The mystery in which religion is interested is not the result of ignorance or of any foggy self-mystification. It is not the kind of mystery which may be reduced in quantity by successive steps of more and more complete knowledge. Far from being lessened by knowledge, the mystery at the heart of religion is in a sense increased the more intimate and penetrating knowledge becomes.[6] It is the mystery of being itself, the very ground out of which things rise into their specific and discrete existences. It is the mystery never perceived directly, but only indirectly, through the refractory medium of the finite. It is a mystery not diminished by facts, or ideas, for such knowledge refers only to the existential structure and not to its intrinsic being.

I suppose the best quotation for this mystery I could manage is one taken from Plato: "Something there is which every soul seeketh, and for the sake of this doeth all her actions, having an inkling that it is, but what it is she cannot sufficiently discern, and she knoweth not her way, and concerning this she hath no constant assurance as she hath of other things."

Here then are the four aspects of a primary disjunction between the functions of education and religion. Because of them, whatever relationship is effected is subject to the stresses inherent in two different perspectives, two ways of handling the raw material of human experience. To presume that a reconciliation is possible by avoiding these conflicting emphases is to sidestep the very nature of the operational presuppositions and intentions.

Practical Issues

If we turn to the practical problems of introducing religion into the educational curriculum, we meet several serious questions beyond the primary ones already suggested. As long as a culture is religiously homogeneous, the issue is relatively dormant. Religion may form a rather large and acceptable climate of common opinion and value in which teaching takes on a certain associative or emotional coloration. But once there are several conflicting faiths, and these are splintered by self-conscious or fanatical traditions, the issue becomes explicit and severe. In the American situation of developed pluralism it is hard for most educators to think of the religious problem except in terms of the sectarian fragments, which are fairly exclusive. This approach has plenty of justification, for the sectarians themselves have been stubbornly and blindly attached to their specific tradition as if it inevitably led to the invalidity of all others. Indeed, religion in the West has largely derived its vitality from its passionate concern for differences and its pride in diversity as a ground of freedom.

Objectivity in teaching religion

It is probably this factor which leads us usually to teach religion, then, as facts, or as history, or even as a comparative study. We can thus objectify the data, treat all contenders impartially, and reduce religion to the status of another course. Such ideological reduction, however, is really no more religious than a course in mathematics or in economics. An undiscriminating array of factual phenomena, presented from a pseudo-neutral point of view, usually has a rather cynical result. In fact, teaching of this kind could be done with such a negative foundation that the whole superstructure would lack any sustaining sense of meaning or significance. And by "negative foundation" I do not mean intentional hostility or deliberate cynicism concerning religion, but merely a lack of understanding of the intrinsic and substantial functions which give any religion its proper and valid place in society.

Let there be no misunderstanding. The history, ideas, and structure of religion in their historic character are as necessary to religion as to any activity of man. But removed from the body of living functions, they are no longer living religion; and when the living functions are not articulated, when they are ignored as if they did not exist, nothing of value is left. In an earlier age one might not have worried about this, but in our day when the connections between religion and the healthy life of the individual or the dynamics of society have been largely lost, it is necessary to point them out and to give them special attention.

In short, then, the first step is a double one. The ideological reduction of religion in order to make it into a body of ideas or events for the educational process is the easiest way to fool ourselves. The teaching of religion must rest firmly on a base of a critical affirmation of religion's function. There is an ecology of faith, a total world of roots and skies, of weather and growth, an environment in which it takes its place and fulfills its responsibilities with many other things — art, science, industry, government. To teach it as if it were a "special" history or concerned only with the cultic mysteries within church or synagogue is not to teach religion at all. This is like appraising the body of a car without paying any attention to its engine.

If we really intend to teach religion, we must have some kind of interpretation of religion, some sense of the individual and society. Unless there is an honest way to respect its significance and to explicate its importance to the individual and to society, our cynicism will 'show through and cancel out every vestige of value.

Religion, after all, is a way of dealing with life, of organizing and evaluating the raw materials of existence, of weighing and measuring the meanings of human experience. It is concerned with eliciting the inner mystery, the hidden or obscure significance of events and things, no matter where or when they occur. It tries to get behind the surface, under the label, back to the core, where true integrity and the center of its being lie. Any subject taught suggestively enough may come quite close to being religious; any religious material taught blindly may end up being quite irreligious.

SUGGESTIVENESS

One of the essential factors in the teaching of religion is suggestiveness. It is the practical counterpart to the theoretical appreciation of reality articulated by the symbol. Facts, however true, without suggestiveness become at last factitious, and are as deadening as no learning at all.

One can observe suggestiveness in Thayer S. Warshaw's use of the Bible in a basically strictly non-interpretive manner. Warshaw linked the biblical events or personages with Melville's *Moby Dick*, or Mann's *Joseph and His Brothers*, or Michelangelo's "Moses," or Honegger's *Le Roi David*, or MacLeish's *J. B.* In short, the biblical material was reflected variously in literature and art in such a manner as to lend new perspectives to old patterns. This "suggestive" approach enhanced the primary material without actually getting involved in sectarian interpretation. Any movement toward a synthesis is in reality toward religion. It may not get very far, or it may not become explicit, but it is on the way, and to the degree that it connects a congeries of events at different levels, or reveals a web of implications in unsuspected areas, it comes near the vision of religious truth.

IDEOLOGY AND CULTIC ACTIVITY

Probably the most radical question to be asked about the relation of religion to education is simply whether religion can be transmitted except in its cultic acts. This does not refer to the liturgical activity of the religious group only, but also to the social culture as a whole. It is plain that we are now living in a technological culture the mores and dynamics of which have nothing in common with the religious heritage of Judaism or Christianity. Can religion maintain itself, validate its classic function in sustaining meaning for the individual and a structure for society? Technology does not have the equipment of reflective metaphor sufficiently broad or deep to support society. It may provide us with a collectivity but not a community.

A similar question must be asked of the transmission of religion: Can it be accomplished ideologically, or must the cultic act be incorporated in the process? Certainly our current embarrassment flows from the fact that the family, once the social structure in which all the overtones of religious reality reverberated, has been disintegrated by a series of destructive revolutions. It has been neutralized, purged of all those emotive powers by which religion itself was domesticated and handed down as an intrinsic part of life's most intimate relations. Under these circumstances schools are being forced to raise the question of assuming another family responsibility.

THE PERSONAL QUOTIENT

One of the significant phenomena of education in the contemporary situation may be illustrated by what happened to Lionel Trilling when he was persuaded to teach a course in the contemporary novel. Although he had misgivings about the educational propriety of dealing with anything as modern as the twentieth-century novel, he took on the task, only to find that it was impossible without some loss of privacy; he was forced to stand in the dock and give witness; the novels held him up to trial.

> No literature has ever been so shockingly personal as that of our time — it asks every question that is forbidden in polite society. It asks us if we are content with our marriages, with our family lives, with our professional lives, with our friends . . . the questions asked by our literature are not about our culture but about ourselves . . . if we are saved or damned — more than with anything else, our literature is concerned with salvation. No literature has ever been so intensely spiritual as ours. I do not venture to call it religious, but certainly it has the special intensity of concern with spiritual life which Hegel noted when he spoke of the great modern phenomenon of the secularization of spirituality.[7]

I use this as an example of what seems to be a rather typical and widespread phenomenon in the broad fields of education today.[8] Despite the vast academic factories, the research assembly lines, the factualizing machinery, the eruption of the personal quotient is increasingly evident and quite passionate in many areas. In a sense, this is the essential religious factor appearing in a new quarter without benefit of traditional forms and explicit identification. What it says, I believe, is that religion may be appearing within the educational field itself in an implicit mode rather than being merely added or inserted from the outside. Indeed, one might well say that we would not be discussing the question of how to include religion if the desire to know how had not already arisen within the educational process itself.

Is Education Educational?

Up to this point I have been talking about the primary differentiation of the functions of religion and education, the practical issues which arise from their cohabitation, and to what extent the two can be reconciled. But there is another aspect of religion in education which may ultimately prove to be of greater significance than the remarriage of the divorced couple. Is it possible to elicit from the current situation of human concern the personal implications of our present system and method? The term "personal" is in no sense intended to refer to the individualistic, but rather to human reality. Humanly speaking, are people getting from education the help toward a sane, satisfying existence they require and deserve? Is the system and its particular intentions somewhat unbalanced, the result of unexamined prejudices, inherited and superstitiously reinforced by habit? Are we really educing the full potential of persons or merely conforming to a pattern of expectation in a culture so given to hurry and haste and quantitative mass-mindedness that we have blindly exploited one aspect of the mind at the expense of the others?

This "human" question is, of course, at bottom both a moral and a religious question. It may be totally impossible to incorporate religion in the educational field because of its integral cultic nature, but there still exists the question of how educational education is, if it is unable to raise the issue of mutual meaning in the field of schizophrenic specialization. How do the fragments fit together in the human mind? How do they support one another, and what is it that supports their common validity? The responsibility of education for reaching toward these larger syntheses has been suggested by Robert Oppenheimer. In his address at the Bicentennial Celebration of Columbia University he spoke of surveying our time from a high altitude, whence the diversity and richness of our culture may be easily seen to be flourishing. But equally evident is what he calls an odd fact, that there are no paths from science to science, or from the sciences to the arts. This, he suggests, is not only dangerous but wasteful. To open up such paths in order to achieve some sense of order or unity is an urgent necessity. Larger syntheses in the world of thought must move beyond the stalemate of our present specialized securities. This, in substance, is the intent of the religious imagination, and everything which assists it helps to heal the wider and deeper fractures now extant in modern man's consciousness.

Certainly the hope of some kind of reconciliation becomes brighter when it is seen within the field of education itself that there are implications of a larger reality in the human sense, and equally in the larger allusiveness of all fields of knowledge which open a path of suggestiveness native to its own concerns. Without this, we shall be trying to mix oil and water. But once we catch a glimpse of Trilling's world of human seriousness and Oppenheimer's plea to be as deep as we are broad, we may be able to move toward the goal of what the ancients once called "the intellectual love of God."

NOTES

1. Karl Jaspers, in *The Idea of the University* (Beacon, 1959), pp. 46, 47, declares the necessary unity of knowledge in the following terms but scarcely describes the actual situation: "The doctor, the teacher, the administrator, the judge, the clergyman, the architect, are each in his own way professionally concerned with man as a whole, and the conditions of human life as a whole. Preparation for these professions is unthinking and inhuman if it fails to relate us to the whole. . . . The university deteriorates if it becomes an aggregate of specialized schools alongside of which it tolerates the so-called 'general education' as mere window dressing and vague talk in generalities. Scholarship depends on a relation to the whole. Individual disciplines are meaningless apart from their relation to the whole of knowledge. Therefore it is the intention of the university to impart to its students a sense of the unity both of his particular field of study and of all knowledge."

2. Northrop Frye, *Fables of Identity* (Harcourt, Brace & World, 1963), p. 7.

3. Jerome Bruner, *On Knowing* (Harvard University Press, 1962), p. 70.

4. Suzanne Langer, *Philosophy in a New Key* (Mentor, 1948), p. 234.

5. Lionel Trilling, in his *Beyond Culture* (Viking, 1960), p. xiii, asserts for education almost precisely the same purpose I have described as the distinctive function of religion. I doubt whether his statement is generally applicable: "It is a belief which is still pre-eminently honored that a primary function of art and thought is to liberate the individual from the tyranny of his culture in the environmental sense and to permit him to stand beyond it in an autonomy of perception and judgment."

6. "We wish our lives to be one continuous growth in knowledge; indeed, we expect them to be. Yet well over a hundred years ago Kierkegaard observed that maturity consists in the discovery that 'there comes a critical moment where everything is reversed, after which the point becomes to understand more and more that there is something which cannot be understood'" (Loren Eiseley, *The Firmament of Time* [Atheneum, 1966], p. 177).

7. Trilling, *op. cit.*, pp. 8, 9.

8. R. H. Super (ed.), *Matthew Arnold — Lectures and Essays in Criticism*, Vol. III in a ten-volume series (University of Michigan Press, 1963). "He foresaw that the 19th century's grim but necessary preoccupation with industrial growth would pass away, and a time would come 'when man has made himself perfectly comfortable and has . . . to determine what to do with himself.' "

7

Religion and the Uncertain Schools

William D. Geer, Jr.

One of the most curious aspects of the issue of the place of religion in the public schools is who raised the question in the first place and why. Certainly the churches and churchmen, who now seem on the verge of jettisoning their own Sunday school programs, are not the ones who have posed the questions that have led to the current reassessment of religion's place in education. The Supreme Court cannot be held responsible for the present concern although its decision did set in motion the re-evaluation of the relationship between religion and public education. In part education has brought the issue to the fore so that a clear and workable definition of the relationship between church and state in the realm of public education can be formed. Many educators who have pushed the question have done so not from a desire for legal clarification but from a deep feeling of uneasiness about the course that our schools are following.

Ten or fifteen years ago, before the Supreme Court decision banning certain forms of religious exercises, there was a common but unvoiced understanding that religion both in the schools and elsewhere was an atrophying force in the nation. In keeping with this feeling, education since Sputnik has dynamically, albeit chaotically, committed itself to the achievement of modern technological egalitarianism, and this commitment, despite glaring failures in civil rights, has led to a new concept of the place and function of education in the nation's dreams of a "great society." The schools all over the country that have been sensitive and responsive to the tenor of the times have abandoned most of the old curricula, philosophies, and organizational structures and have experimented with a host of curriculum revisions and organizational innovations. In most modern schools religion has either disappeared or been so watered down that it is scarcely recognizable.

It seems almost as if the educators who during the last ten or fifteen years have enthusiastically committed American schools to a course of aggressive and dramatic change have now paused to reflect on the long-neglected but basic issue of the place of religion in education, but the schools now are vastly different from what they were even a decade ago. Religion and society too are vastly changed. The posing of the question of the place of religion in the public schools at this point in time raises issues that deeply probe the nature of the dynamic pressures at work in our schools, churches, and the whole society.

The real issue for the public school raised by an assessment of the role of religion in education is not whether to hold a Christmas pageant or a sixty-second silent prayer during a homeroom period but whether a school can achieve any but the most superficial educational goals without some underlying philosophy of life and man's place in the structure of things. The modern school, which has long since effected separation from the church, may present its students with a curriculum purged of the direct and indirect influence of religion and has probably in part freed its pupils from discipline by the Puritan ethic, but this school and the educators that guide it most certainly face a multitude of new difficulties. Once the unifying force of religion, which gave proportion and meaning to the Protestant parochial public school, was lost, forces of disillusion and chaos set in. Many modern heretic schools became imbued with the false absolutes of education for education, of the virtue of further schooling, of the cult of the athlete, and of fellowship for its own sake, none of which by themselves or lumped together provide an interpretation of life and education strong enough to give reality to a school. It is in this atmosphere of heady emancipation but uncertainty that an understanding of the real issues latent in the relationship of religion to public education must be sought.

The Plight of the School

Despite the forward strides that education has made in the last fifty years in the improvement of curriculum, teacher preparation, and plant, chaos and disillusion are rife in American public schools. The many changes that have swept through the schools in the past five decades have not produced either clarification of educational goals or an harmonious, accepted order but have spawned a host of perplexing and as yet unanswered questions. The profound changes in every aspect of our community and family life have driven the schools to search desperately for answers to the technological and social revolution that has shattered the stability and calm of the American way of life. No one and nothing has been spared in the growing upheaval of our society, yet educators find themselves in the challenging position of having to provide meaning and purpose for millions of children caught in the middle of a rapidly expanding, changing world. Religion and traditional philosophy, unable to provide an interpretation of life capable of answering the needs of a world of accelerating change, have generally been abandoned by education, but nothing has risen in their stead to supply a valid and workable interpretation of life in a modern technological society. Students, parents, and educators, despite the obvious improvement in education, are left uncertain and confused by the spreading dictum of change for change's sake.

The emancipated or "swinging" school or school system which has spawned the serious reconsideration of the part religion plays in education can be readily identified by certain increasingly common symptoms revealed by students and teachers. Students in the modern school find that the tasks confronting them are irrelevant to the dynamic thrust of the society in which they live; they are not satisfied with education, and directly and indirectly they question it. Their dissatisfaction with their schooling stems from their feeling that much if not all that they are asked to do and be is not, and probably cannot be, related to a vital philosophy of life. Many students view their academic and extracurricular successes as hollow and false. They believe they have been bribed into competing for senseless prizes by an adult world which values but cannot explain the value of the goals it has set for the young. School societies establish the goals of scholarship, service, leadership, and character and then sanctify them in pseudoreligious ceremonies. But when the students ask, "Scholarship, service, leadership, and character for what?" the only explanation they receive is the ever present one of college admissions. School to an increasing number of students demands discipline, commitment, and loyalty without even attempting to provide a view of life that makes the sacrifices and efforts meaningful. In response to this situation educators have searched desperately for ways to endow the enterprise with validity, and logically they have turned to ask some significant questions of religion.

The Plight of the Teachers

Teachers, baffled and uncertain in the face of the ubiquitous force of change, are confused about their own role, for as the traditional structure of the school gives way, teachers lose sight of the broad and unifying concepts of teaching. They begin to view themselves as isolated and frustrated guardians of a particular subject, who are kept from having a positive impact on the young by the role of policeman which is forced upon them by the school administration; and the administration understands neither the particular academic contribution that they have to make nor the needs of the students. Older teachers hark back to the day when they entered the turmoil of teaching and found peace and purpose at the feet of an elder sage who taught them the ropes and gave them a philosophy of education now at best politely ignored and all too often openly questioned and even attacked by the young teacher. Stirred into the already disquieting situation for teachers are the issues of permissiveness, the value of grades, and the psychological sanctity of the child. A teacher battered and strained by uncertainty is an almost sure sign that a school has responded to the pressure of our age, abandoned the stable verities of the past, and embarked on a course of frenzied change.

The Cult of College Admission

A clear indication that a school has effectively severed its ties with tradition and religion in its pursuit of the as yet elusive absolute is the importance given to admission to college. The old absolutes have vanished, and a new and more monstrous one has risen in their place. The absolute of all absolutes in the apostate school is admission into an Ivy League or Seven Sister university or college. The god and goddess in such schools have become the exclusive academic college and university. For many students in these schools every thought, deed, and action is dedicated to the ritual of entrance. In effect, in the absence of a more profound religion or philosophy, the all-pervasive absolute of college admission tends to permeate every corner of school life. Educators, parents, and students alike slavishly bend themselves to the process of college entrance. Whatever else can be said of this new religion, it produces anxiety and uncertainty in all who labor to serve these fickle gods and goddesses.

Who Is Responsible for the Young?

The issue education faces and is trying to meet in its most recent inquiries into the relationship between religion and the schools is not the simple one of either purging the schoolhouse of the rituals and formal teachings of religion or bringing back into the curriculum a synthesis of the great religious teachings of the past. The issue is much larger than either of these because the whole tradition of primary and secondary education rests upon the belief that the schools bear the major responsibility for the molding of the future citizen. In the past, supported by a community ethic drawn from the basic tenets of Protestantism, the school saw its role as the shaper of Christian men and women. The curriculum was directed to this end, as were the disciplinary systems and activity programs. The strength of the school lay in the unified effort of church, parents, and school to present and make valid the same interpretation of life and of the individual's responsibility to the community and his maker. Clearly no such unified agreement between schools, church, and parent exists in our urban and suburban communities yet even in the heterogeneous city the school is still expected to hold the line and implement the same ethic that found its meaning in the homogeneous Protestant community. The issues for both the schools and religion lie much deeper in the structure of the institution than Bible readings in assemblies or courses in comparative religion.

Bearing directly on the place of religion in the schools is the question of the division of responsibility for rearing the young between school and parent. If the parent gives a deep sigh of relief when his child toddles off to school at age five and turns over to the school the responsibility for deciding what should be studied and what is right and wrong, then, like it or not, the school finds itself determining the ethical and moral beliefs of the child. The reverse situation is found when the parent sends the child off to school for an education and then discovers that an education includes indoctrination in everything from dress to morality and ethics, and not merely training in the basic academic skills. The controversy over haircuts and dress in schools illustrates the struggle between parents and school over who, if anyone, makes the rules for children. It often seems that the old Puritan maxim, "Cleanliness is next to godliness," has been extended to the haircut and the bluejean. The same struggle between parent and school is evident in the issue of what should and what should not be read and the questioning of the extent of the school's responsibility for the action of its students. The present uncertainty about the division of responsibility for the young must be resolved before moral, ethical, and religious education can be either brought into the schools or effectively eliminated from them.

The Religious Issue in a Climate of Change

The raising of the question of religion and education at this moment merely points up the uncertain state of the schools and adds one more element to the confusing wave of change that is sweeping through education. All the components of education are in turmoil, and the uncertainty that has created this situation has already wrenched religion from its traditional place as stabilizer of the establishment. Nothing is sacred in the schools at present. Just as soon as a new math curriculum is established, another rises to challenge it, and so it goes in the other areas of education. Social studies, English, and even foreign languages have been torn from their safe, traditional niches and pummeled by the forces of change. The basic point of all educators' questioning is whether, having been rudely swept out of the establishment, religion can be brought back either as an academic subject or in some new form that will breathe meaning into the uncertain and frenzied attempts of educators to create a workable version of the school. The answer to this question, like the answer to who, parent or school, bears responsibility for deciding how children should be educated, lies in unraveling the educational Gordian knot and discovering the primary and secondary forces that are determining the future of education.

The knot is there, and those in education are acutely aware that who or what will either untie or cut it remains to be seen. Educators' current efforts to find the answer with team teaching, modular scheduling, educational games, non-judgmental guidance, and non-graded schools all represent attempts to bring order out of chaos. These efforts, though, have been almost entirely concerned with either structure or the manipulation of curriculum and not with the very basic issue of the part that schooling plays in forming and shaping students' values and beliefs. It was inevitable that educators would turn partially in hope and partially in despair to religion, for traditionally the church concerned itself with these matters and used the schools to implement its beliefs. Now that the age-old relationship between the two no longer exists, the teacher must not only fill the traditional role but also assume responsibility for shaping the philosophy and ethics of the school, a task that close and demanding contact with the young may make all but impossible. Whether or not religion can or should return and infuse education with meaning remains to be seen; certainly if it does, it will have to be a vastly different force from the one that has vanished with the Christmas pageant and the Easter egg hunt.

There is present throughout education a disquieting sense of the mission of change that our times have placed upon the schools. The burden borne by the schools because of the pressure of change is usually summarized in the statement "If the schools can't do it, then there is no agency or force left in our society that can." The things to be changed range all the way from people's attitudes toward scientific truth to bigotry and discrimination. There is little doubt that education has proved itself a most potent force for change, but if the change is to be anything more than a reaction to the injustices and rigidities of the past, the school must either form or find an interpretation of things to explain not only the changes but also the hopes and goals for the future. Once again, either in action with or in reaction against the schools, religion is inexorably bound to education, for the belief that the schools are a prime agency of social change sets them a task that has traditionally been the province of religion. Whether education can achieve significant and positive change is still problematic, but if it pursues its present tendency to restructure things, it will have abandoned the simple truths of the three R's and plunged into moral, philosophical, and ethical anarchy. It is the awareness of this plunge that has caused educators to pause at this point and raise some long-neglected issues.

New Challenges for Education

That the role of religion in the schools is an issue indicates two things: (1) that the relationship between what are traditionally called religion and education has rapidly deteriorated and almost vanished in recent years, and (2), that secondary schools have set a course for themselves that moves dramatically away from the safe and charted grounds of the three R's and the simpler realms of academic knowledge. Having committed itself or been forced to commit itself to a new role in the shaping of the society of the future, education and the society it serves must face the unpleasant question of whether the schools are prepared for the monumental task confronting them. As it is now constituted, education is having a mighty struggle keeping body and curriculum together without having to assume the complex job of providing direction and soul to a mobile and radically changing society. Much hope is placed in the great teacher who through his wisdom, profoundly influences the lives of the students he comes in contact with, but it is questionable whether in schools wracked by growing pains the great teacher would ever be recognized and given tenure, and, if he proved great and also durable, whether the situation in which he found himself would permit opportunity to press the quality of wisdom on the minds of the young. Caught in the middle of an increasingly bureaucratic educational machine, even the sages of antiquity might not have had the time or energy to find a log, much less sit on it with the young.

Typical of the new responsibilities that education is taking upon itself and that raise such profound questions and doubts in the minds of educators is the task of sex education. The usual tenth-grade biology course no longer suffices. Somehow the schools are taking up the burden — or it is being thrust upon them by a cataclysmically expanding society — of imparting to the young some saving wisdom about the needs and drives of men and women and the implications that they have for the family, the nation, and the world. Philosophy, psychology, sociology, and anthropology may come to the rescue of the harassed teachers who accept this task, with only the most minimal guidance, and make decisions of the most profound and far-reaching nature. At the moment neither religion nor parents seem in a position to relieve the schools of this particular burden. They are, then, for better or worse, beginning to assume the leadership in the crucial areas of morality that once were the sole province of religion, and it is a healthy sign that some educators are pausing long enough to ask the essential questions before they leap into the void.

Although the enlightened school has burned many of its bridges behind it in its abandonment of religion and traditional ethics, the separation in many instances has been a superficial one, for the school is still charged with fostering morality and social responsibility in the young. The present relationship with the verities of the past in even the most modern school is closer to being one of wary distrust than total rejection. Nothing has yet been substituted for the traditional force of religion in the schools, despite the efforts of the Supreme Court and the ravages of the tidal wave of science and technology. The present cautious suspicion of religion by education is part of the climate of the times. A basic issue still to be faced by education is trust, for the disappearance of traditional religion and ethics from the school has signaled the spread of the cancer of distrust.

The schools are shot full of distrust, and if religion ever effectively returns as a force in American education it will be because it finds within itself the power to dispel distrust. Teachers distrust administrators; the psychologically oriented guidance counselor distrusts the teacher; one academic discipline distrusts another; and beneath it all is a growing distrust of the young for any adult. Out of the recent Berkeley riots has come the articulation of the attitude of the young: "Never trust any adult over the age of thirty." The time seems ripe for a new children's crusade, and the young seem desperately ready to follow a Bob Dylan or some other latter-day Nicholas or Stephen. Education is hung between two equally unacceptable solutions to the current climate of distrust: the re-establishment of the inadequate truths and rigidities of the past or surrender to the passionate anarchy of youth.

Neither course is open to education, and this is why educators are now posing the question of the relationship between religion and formal education. Some force must come to the fore to coalesce the elements within the school because the present confusion is making it more and more difficult to maintain a dialogue with the young. Youth has sensed the uncertainty of adults and is daily growing more and more brazen in its gestures of contempt for the adult world, which seems completely unable to articulate a positive view of life. If, indeed, there is no single reasonable view of life that satisfies all of the diverse elements of our population, then there must be at least an honest and courageous confrontation of the eternal and unanswered questions of man's purpose and function because somehow parents, teachers, and students must find a way to create a positive educational conversation capable of generating light as well as heat and of giving meaning to the enterprise of education.

Education must be a growing dialogue between the young and the old. When the process of education fails to be a conversation between the adult and the youth and is a series of lectures, an obstacle course of set and apparently meaningless tasks, or simply a carefully marked road to pragmatic success, disillusion and chaos spread. If public education in this country is to be truly educational, the whole of our society must ponder the questions raised by the educators about the relationship between religion and education, for they represent a desperate plea for a reassessment and articulation of the basic ideals of our nation.

8

The Dangers of Liberty

Theodore Powell

There are fashions in the language of public debate as well as in political vituperation. Words or phrases are discovered or invented to meet a particular purpose, sometimes to gain a special meaning from such use, sometimes to become part of the common language, sometimes to flower only for the duration of the debate and then to pass into history.

A generation ago this nation felt itself threatened by the rise of the vigorous ideologies of fascism in Italy, Naziism in Germany, and communism in the Soviet Union. To characterize these governments by a single term, we coined the label "totalitarianism." For a while it served as a useful description of the antithesis of democracy. With the victory over Mussolini and Hitler, the term disappeared into history. For the purposes of this essay, let it be revived to call more specific attention to a danger that democracy faces both within and without the classrooms of the public school. If we fail to recognize the proper limitations on the reach of democratic government, the principles of a free society will be threatened by the incursions of the totalitarian spirit — incursions that are motivated, ironically, by attempts to advance morality or democracy.

Totalitarianism and Democracy

Lengthy efforts have been made in both popular and scholarly fashion to draw distinctions between fascism and communism. Each such attempt, or any definition of one or the other, always has been subject to challenge or refutation. But one feature is acknowledged as characteristic of both. Under such anti-democratic regimes, the mind and the spirit of the people are not permitted to range freely. Rather, the government seeks to control opinions and beliefs by controlling newspapers, broadcasting, religious institutions, and the schools. There is an official doctrine which has government approval, and the media of communication and education are employed to promote that doctrine and to oppose or suppress all other views.

There is no limit (to risk a tautology) to the reach of a totalitarian government. Not only the actions of men but their beliefs as well are subject to government control. Men may be fined or jailed or otherwise punished, not just for what they do but also for what they say or think. The real anti-democratic government is the one which seeks total control — over man's body, over man's mind, over man's spirit. This is totalitarianism.

Volumes have been written attempting to define democracy. Great and lengthy debate may be devoted to challenging and defending the definitions. But consensus could most certainly be achieved, it seems, on one essential feature of democracy: there are limits to the reach of government. In decrying or condemning totalitarian governments for their attempts to control thoughts, opinions, or beliefs through control of the means of communication and of education for governmental propaganda purposes, the advocate of a free society must declare implicitly, if not explicitly, that such use of government power is precluded in a democracy. This view was expressed forcefully by Justice Jackson: "If there is any fixed star in our constitutional constellation, it is that no official, high or petty, can prescribe what shall be orthodox in politics, nationalism, religion, or other matters of opinion. . . ."

The meaning of the First Amendment, if not the meaning of democracy itself, is that government authority must not invade "the sphere of the intellect and spirit. . . ."

The public school's limits

Public school authorities have persistently and insistently exalted the role of their institution in advancing democracy. But they have given little attention to the limits of their authority over the "sphere of the intellect and spirit." Although the decision proscribing prayer and religious ceremony in the public school seems to have been generally accepted, the question of the use of public school power to advance orthodoxies in other areas of opinion or belief has been given little or no consideration. If the question arises at all, it is likely to be treated in a very superficial fashion. Answers are suggested which show no regard for the complexity of the subject and no respect for the right of the public school child to be protected against government indoctrination. These superficial answers to the not-so-easy question of what the public school should do about beliefs, opinions, values, or ethics are generally based on two portentous assumptions.

First, it is assumed that the public school teacher has the authority — indeed, the duty — so to instruct her pupils as to transmit appreciation of the proper values, the proper ethics, and the proper beliefs. Second, it is assumed that the public school teacher knows, or has access to someone who knows, the proper values, proper ethics, and proper beliefs to be transmitted. These assumptions, if not erroneous on their face, may be dismissed after some examination.

One of the most significant attempts of a state to use its power to imbue children with the true American faith was made by Oregon in 1925. A law was enacted which would have compelled almost all children to attend only public schools. Recognizing such use of governmental power as unconstitutional, the Supreme Court said, "The fundamental theory of liberty upon which all government in this Union reposes excludes any general power of the state to standardize its children . . . the child is not the mere creature of the state" (*Pierce v. Society of Sisters*, 268 U.S. 510 [1925]).

This assertion of the limits on the power of a democratic government has been made on many other occasions before and since, and on many other issues. The basis of the assertion, however, is the major distinction between democratic and totalitarian government. In a democracy a government may control behavior but not belief, may control practices but not preachment, and the public school system in a democracy may educate but must not indoctrinate. The power of government reaches actions but not opinions. A totalitarian government may reach into the classroom as it reaches into the newsroom to mold the minds of the people. In a democracy the mind, the spirit, and the soul are beyond the reach of governors, school boards, or public school teachers. However, not all public school authorities recognize the proper limits of their authority. They commit the error of the second assumption: that someone in the public school system knows the proper values to be transmitted to the children in the public school.

Some curriculum specialists and educational advisers with more temerity than good sense have set forth outlines of what should be done in the public school about the teaching of moral and spiritual values. These treatises are generally filled with warm words and familiar high-sounding phrases. Such public school instruction is proposed from what must be regarded as worthy motivation. And it may seem unkind, if not unduly harsh, to describe the proposals as another expression of the totalitarian spirit. Yet even their advocates would agree that these suggestions are made for the purpose of influencing in quite specific directions the convictions of public school pupils. While the proposals to improve or uplift the morals and patriotism of our children are couched in language which is chosen to express the apparent consensus of the American people, it takes little analysis to discover that they are prescriptions for another kind of orthodoxy, "in politics, nationalism, religion, or other matters of opinion. . . ."

Moral and Ethical Instruction

In the wake of the decisions against public school prayers, educators have been urged to reconsider moral training. (Anyone who views seriously the question of moral and ethical development might well look askance at this prompting. A discussion of moral training growing out of the attitude "We can't have prayers so we'll have to do something else" seems unlikely to produce anything more valuable than the tokens of religion now abandoned.) The urgings have had some effect, or at least some publicity, but the results of efforts to plan programs for instruction in "moral and spiritual values" have been unimpressive.

THE INADEQUACY OF PRESENT COURSES

It is difficult to avoid sarcasm in evaluating or analyzing programs for teaching "moral and spiritual values." In addition to their vacuity, their contradictions, they are so patently designed to be what the designers protest they are not — a new faith, a secular religion. In one sense they are barbaric because they are tribal. They bring to mind the statement of George Bernard Shaw: "He is a barbarian and thinks that the customs of his tribe and island are the laws of nature." In some cases there is no camouflage; the defense of the "godless" public school is made on the basis that teachers are devout and influence their pupils because of their own religious commitment. One educational authority writing of "guidance in social, moral, and spiritual values" explained, "Many teachers are devoutly religious persons and they communicate their spirit of 'reverence for life' and concern for social needs. . . . Almost unconsciously, they guide students 'towards the highest we can know.'" Good words. Warm sentiments. Behind the civilized tone, however, is the spirit of the barbarian and the totalitarian. To whom does the pronoun "we" refer? Who determines what values are "the highest"? Surely, it must be the "devoutly religious" public school teacher, who may be Presbyterian, high-church Episcopalian, Orthodox Jew, or Roman Catholic. It seems plain that the guidance authority feels these different religious commitments are of no great significance in "guidance in social, moral, and spiritual values." Should we ask whether the values of the Presbyterian are the same as those of the Orthodox Jew? Should we ask how the "devoutly religious" public school teacher of any one of these faiths would view the assertion that the doctrines which distinguish his religious commitment from other faiths are unimportant? Can it not be asked how a devoutly religious parent who was high-church Episcopalian would feel about his child's being guided morally and spiritually toward the highest we can know by a public school teacher of Greek Orthodox faith? Above all, must it not be asked, "Who empowered the public school teacher to shape the child's soul?" Thus do the fine words and the warm sentiments dissolve under analysis.

But surely there are values everyone accepts, are there not? Honesty, loyalty, obedience to law, good sportsmanship, equality, democracy. Most of us would say that we honor such values — most of the time. Almost everyone agrees that "Honesty is the best policy" — as a general rule. It is easy enough to agree with the generalities, but even on the generalities a thoughtful parent will hesitate before delegating to the public school teacher authority over the moral and spiritual guidance of his child.

The beliefs of a school child, of any citizen, are not government property — not in a free society. The teaching of values by a government agency or agent, the public school or the public school teacher, assumes that the values of the majority should be accepted and believed by everyone. Suppose you do not share this belief in the dominant values of your community? Suppose you question or reject the values which seem to guide most of your fellow citizens in mid-twentieth-century America? Suppose you hope your children will develop an appreciation for other values? Do you want your child coming home to tell you that his teacher says you are wrong?

We are not made happy but we do not rebel when our fourth-grader reports that his teacher said we were wrong about the homework problem in arithmetic or the geography of Africa. We concede, although we may grumble, that Miss Johnson knows more about the new math, Rhodesia, lasers, and Charles de Gaulle. But what responsible parent will concede that he is wrong and Miss Johnson is right on questions about family relations, the forgiveness of sins, or the literal truth of the Ten Commandments?

MORAL QUESTIONS WITH NO "RIGHT" ANSWERS

The public school, it may be protested, does not deal with that kind of problem in its teaching of "moral and spiritual values." Let us accept the protest (and not be so unkind as to ask how it is possible to teach moral and spiritual values without reference to the Ten Commandments). Let us consider some moral questions that may clearly be expected to arise in the public school classroom, or in the operation of the school system.

Shall we teach the children the story of Antigone? Here is a splendid moral lesson. Antigone would not abide by the unjust law of her uncle and king, Creon. She defied her king and, obedient to her conscience and the laws of the gods, performed the prescribed funeral rites over the body of her brother. We all understand the familiar moral: Defiance of tyranny is obedience to God.

(How many modern parents would encourage their daughters to emulate Antigone? How many would see her as a proud, stubborn, reckless girl who risked her own life and the destruction of the community for no reason at all but a superstition? "What difference does it make whether or not he is buried properly? The boy is dead, isn't he? There's nothing we can·do for him now, and the king must know what he's doing. So forget these foolish ideas and stay in the house.")

Shall we tell the pupils the story of Socrates? A moving drama with a highly moral message. Here is the wise, gentle old stonecutter with the persistent questions that disturbed the Athenian leaders, convicted of corrupting the youth of Athens by endless inquiries about what is good and what is truth. It is never comfortable for those in authority to have a Socrates around. They wanted to get rid of him, and exile would have served their purpose, but the jury brought in the death sentence. No one really wanted to kill this old man, so his friends were able to bring him the news in prison that it was possible to arrange for his escape. Socrates refused. An Athenian all his life, he had accepted and enjoyed the benefit of her laws; by what right could he now make war against the law of his city-state? Merely because it had worked to his disadvantage? Socrates refused the opportunity to save himself. He accepted the unjust conviction and sentence. He obeyed the law and drank the hemlock. The moral? Obedience to law, even to unjust law. But just a minute; what was the moral we taught yesterday when we told the story of Antigone?

(Will anyone guess what percentage of American parents would encourage their son to go on asking questions that disturb the authorities? Will the father of each child in the classroom agree that devotion to the unrelenting search for truth regardless of offense to community sensitivities, regardless of the displeasure of local public authority, that devotion to what is true and what is good even at the risk of your life is a value to be diligently cultivated and developed? And might not some other parents, taking quite another view of the moral of the Socrates story, prefer to teach their children that unjust laws are not to be obeyed? Can the public school teacher find guidance in the school board regulations, the state curriculum bulletin, or the latest publication of the National Education Association on moral and spiritual values?)

Are Socrates and Antigone too far removed from the problems of the American public school? Take a problem familiar to almost any public school teacher. A thirteen-year-old boy in trouble goes to his friend for help and asks the friend to guard his confidence. The friend gives the boy in trouble some money so that he may run away and tells no one, not his teacher or the boy's parents, not even his own parents. He knows that this constitutes disobedience and dishonesty but he holds in higher esteem the values of loyalty and respect for confidence. What guidance will he get from our program for teaching moral and spiritual values?

Lest the memory of what it means to be thirteen and in trouble has dimmed beyond recall, lest the parental burdens loom so large that the problems of adolescents seem trivial, add another factor. The incident described here has occurred in Mississippi or Alabama, and the boy in trouble is Negro. Will the white public school teacher, who belongs to a racially segregated teachers' association, now step forward and recite the passages from the state bulletin on moral and spiritual values concerning honesty and obedience to law?

Change the scene to a playing field next to the public school. Good sportsmanship is certainly a prime value of any American educational program. Obey the rules. Play hard and clean. Accept the umpire's decision. Be a good sport. A boy sliding into second is called out and protests. The teacher reprimands him. You should not argue about the umpire's decision. Three innings later the boy is in another close play sliding home, but this time he is called safe. The catcher protests, but he too is reprimanded. Don't argue about the umpire's decision. Accept it even if you think it is wrong. Be a good sport. After the game, the first boy confides to the teacher with a grin, "You know the umpire was wrong on that play at home. He called me safe, but I was out. I'm sure glad we're not supposed to argue about the umpire's decision." What can the teacher tell us now about honesty and obedience to the rules?

It should not be assumed, of course, that there are any right answers to the moral problems posed here. In fact, the purpose of posing the problems is to illustrate the inadequacy of aphorisms or proverbs or lists of virtues for dealing with any real moral problem. If we have recognized that one minute of daily prayer is no substitute for true religious education, we should also understand that children do not develop character by weekly recitation of the Boy Scout law. The ability to recite without error or hesitation the twelve adjectives from "trustworthy" to "reverent" is no assurance at all that the Scout will behave accordingly. The civilized man and the thoughtful educator know that such precepts are merely labels. Labels provide no solution for a real moral or spiritual problem. The difficult problems of life are not based on the questions, "Shall I be trustworthy?" "Shall I be loyal?" "Shall I be obedient?" They arise out of conflicts of values.

Shall we accept the rule of unjust authority and protect ourselves, our family and friends? Or shall we insist upon justice, heedless of the consequences to those we love?

Shall we tell the truth — and betray a friend? Shall we be tactful to be kind — or is that being hypocritical?

The civilized man, the educated man, knows that these questions cannot be answered in the abstract. He knows that the names for values have little meaning apart from the circumstances in which they must be applied. As William Temple, late Archbishop of York, declared, "There are no general rules about morals which are fit for universal acceptance, unless they are so formed as to include reference to motive or to particular conditions." Such an approach to moral and ethical study in the public school could be both stimulating and fruitful. However, the instruction, when not platitudinous, is likely to be based not so much on the circumstances of the problem as on the location of the school.

COMMUNITY VALUES

The fact is, of course, that the public school is usually a reflection of dominant local public opinion. Despite the restrictions pronounced by the Supreme Court, despite the victory over the totalitarianism of Hitler and Mussolini, probably neither the school board nor the public school teachers are going to be meticulous in avoiding implicit declarations of orthodoxies. Dominant community values (could not one just as well say "community prejudices"?) are likely to permeate the curricula. Indeed, this was explicitly recommended by the National Education Association in a treatise some years ago on "moral and spiritual values." Readers were advised that a curriculum committee adopting any list of values should have due regard for "probable public reaction." This is the spirit of the barbarian, is it not? This is the confusion of tribal custom with the law of nature. It is also the spirit of totalitarianism, which seeks to use a government agency, the public school, to invade "the sphere of the intellect and spirit."

A School for Free Men

A proposal to guard the mind and soul of a child against the intrusions of the public school teacher is susceptible to a number of challenges. These protests may be classified under two categories. The proposal is described as either undesirable or impossible.

OBJECTIVITY AND INDOCTRINATION

The civilized man (who does not confuse the customs of his tribe with the laws of nature) and the democrat (who believes that there must be limits to the power of the state) must respond to such protests. It may be impossible to achieve a school program completely devoid of prescriptive instruction. But if we believe in liberty, surely we must strive to eliminate from the public school program efforts to indoctrinate the pupils in politics, religion, economics, morality, or other areas of opinion, belief, or faith.

The principle being advanced here is the ideal of objectivity and accuracy in instruction, the scholarly detachment that is accepted at the college level but seldom considered for instruction in elementary and secondary schools. This ideal is not always observed, to be sure, in every college classroom, yet it is generally acknowledged.

Why should it be otherwise in the public school classroom? Why should the school board or public school teachers assume they are under some compulsion to shape the curriculum, the lesson plans, the classroom ritual, or the assembly programs so as to imbue the pupils with their concept of "the American way of life" or some other collection of political opinions, religious beliefs, or moral values? Any proposal for such instruction in a college classroom would be immediately recognized as in violation of the student's rights and as outside of the teacher's responsibility. Why is recognition not given also to the rights of the public school student and of his parents? "The child is not the mere creature of the state." Why is it not desirable at the elementary and secondary level, as well as in higher education, that the student be permitted to make his own intellectual or spiritual commitment on such questions as the organization of the state or the nature of God? If the public school child needs guidance in these matters, shall he get it from an omniscient state via the government's agent, the public school teacher, who will tell him what to think and what to believe? Or would we prefer that the privacy of the child's mind and soul be respected and that the teacher refrain from imposing values, guard against upholding or condemning opinions, and never resort to putting the stamp of official approval on any article of faith?

Such limitations on the public school teacher can hardly be described as undesirable if we are to respect the fundamental principle of democracy that there are limits to the reach of government, that state authority must not invade the citadel of the mind and the spirit.

If the desirability of the principles advocated here is acknowledged, a formidable argument still remains. The principles are fine, it may be said, but they are impossible ideals. Textbooks cannot be written, curricula cannot be designed, teachers cannot teach, without dozens, if not thousands, of conscious and unconscious biases that shape the content of the instruction. And since all instruction inevitably is biased, why should it not be biased in the "right" direction?

The difficulty of the task cannot be ignored. It was most aptly described by Justice Jackson in his concurring opinion in the *McCollum* case.

> Music without sacred music, architecture minus the cathedral, or painting without the scriptural themes would be eccentric and incomplete, even from a secular point of view. Yet the inspirational appeal of religion in these guises is often stronger than in forthright sermon. Even such a "science" as biology raises the issue between evolution and creation as an explanation of our presence on this planet. Certainly a course in English literature that

omitted the Bible and other powerful uses of our mother tongue for religious ends would be pretty barren, and I suppose it is a proper, if not an indispensable, part of preparation for a worldly life to know the roles that religion and religions have played in the tragic story of mankind.

To distinguish between instruction which is objective presentation of knowledge and that which is indoctrination or evangelism was, Jackson concluded, "except in the crudest cases, a subtle inquiry." The degree of bias in textbooks has been illustrated in studies by the American Jewish Congress and by George La Noue. If such studies were unnecessary to inform us that schoolbooks are not models of scientific detachment, they do serve to show that inquiry and analysis of textbooks can produce significant information. They give some encouragement that the "subtle inquiry" can be made successfully.

A similar problem must be studied in the area of curriculum revision. Here, also, a careful review will be necessary to produce lesson plans and content designed to educate rather than to indoctrinate.

Finally, and perhaps most importantly, it will be necessary to win the agreement of all of those responsible for public education — teachers, administrators, school boards, and legislators — that the public school is not the instrument for promoting anyone's opinions or beliefs, that its concern should be knowledge and not conscience. To win such agreement will be no easy matter, of course. For too long the public schools have been regarded, even by the professionals (who should know better), as the means for instilling in our children not only American history but patriotism, not merely awareness of religion but love of God. It will not be an easy task for anyone who is foolhardy enough to attempt it to obtain support among educators and public officials for the concept of a public school program that will leave the student free to love God or his country out of his own heart and conscience.

RISKS OF ATTEMPTING NEUTRALITY

It may seem to some that the neutrality proposed here is an invitation to amorality. What will the schools produce in terms of character, in terms of citizenship, if the children are not taught right from wrong? But to decide a question of morality on the basis of what someone else concludes is right or wrong is itself a kind of amorality, is it not? The problem was described most winningly by the pupil of Mrs. Anna Leonowens, the King of Siam. He lamented that when he was a boy

> what was so, was so
> what was not, was not.
> Now I am a man
> world has changed a lot
> some things nearly cold
> some things nearly hot.

This is the essential fact which must be recognized if the public schools are to perform their mission in accordance with the principles of a free society. There are few clear-cut textbook answers to most of the moral decisions or value choices that the student will face in the course of his later life. The moral man, the responsible citizen, should be able to realize how few are the questions that are black or white, hot or cold. He must also recognize that the answers to moral questions have to be in accord with his own mind and spirit. He cannot, he must not, rely on a gauleiter or commissar to tell him what to think, write, speak, or believe.

Our public schools, in short, must be organized and administered in accordance with constitutional limits and the principles of a free society. They are to be dedicated to equality of opportunity, to the dignity and worth of each person, to fair administration of the rules (the schoolroom equivalent of due process), and to freedom of thought and of spirit. If we are to avoid using the techniques of totalitarianism in the hope of teaching democracy, we must keep the hands of government off the soul of the child.

It may seem a dangerous method of education to allow the child to remain free to make up his own mind whether he will worship God, honor his country, or love his fellow man. But our forebears faced that danger time and time again outside of the schoolroom. Out of bitter experience they learned the consequences of letting government exercise authority over the "sphere of the intellect and spirit." The dangers of liberty were preferred to the security of totalitarianism. This, too, is the choice that must be made in any school program, in any classroom.

Let us have the wisdom and the courage to choose the dangers of liberty.

9

Religion and Public Education: The Post-Schempp Years

William B. Ball

As the Ninetieth Congress opened, headlines told the country: "Dirksen Offers School Prayer Amendment." Evidently we are in for more of these Gargantuan labors to achieve at best a symbol. The "very great exertion" of constitutional change, of which John Marshall spoke, will be attempted again in the pursuit of shadow and in flight from substance.

Senator Everett M. Dirksen warns us that "a storm of protest" is once again "gathering in all parts of the nation" over Supreme Court decisions outlawing prayer in the public schools. This is as little to be scorned as it is to be doubted.

When the Court, in 1962, canceled the long-standing option to pray, many people were sincerely aggrieved. But it was the canceling of the option rather than of the prayers which was initially the sharp point of the grievance. The assumed "freedom" to pray was gone — and with it (to many) the very marrow of national tradition. To them the decision also signaled an automatic substitution of secularism in the schools — and probably foreshadowed a pervasive secularism in public life generally. The sincerity of the reaction cannot be gainsaid, nor will its continuance be anything but spurred by crude attempts to label it a Birchite promotion. Five years after *Engel v. Vitale*, and four years after *Schempp*, the wound which these decisions brought still evidently throbs. Perhaps more significant, however, are the questions — legal, educational, and religious — which have been posed in the post-*Schempp* years, not by those who seek to override the decisions but by those who seek to abide by them.

I spoke of "shadow" (to indicate what would be achieved by amendment) and of a flight by the amenders from "substance." By that I meant that the amenders, with their simplistic constitutional answer, seemingly disdain to come to grips with the fact that we are a society plural in outlook and belief, with the fact that for many Americans state sponsorship of even "voluntary" worship is too large an intrusion of government into the domain of conscience, with the fact that to others the permitted prayer is far too slight an infusion of religion in the education of the child. And of great substance, also disregarded by the amenders, is the relationship of religion to secular culture and therefore of school children to both.

The Constitutional Departure Points

Where has the Supreme Court brought us? This is perhaps less well known than the story (no retelling needed) of the litigations that got us here. It has brought us to points from which all our future steps respecting religion in education must be taken. I have called them points of departure because it would seem that the Court has indeed got us to certain points and not to others, set us on certain paths, not others, but has also said, in effect, "From here on, you're on your own!" The Court has given us premises, but we will have to work out the conclusions. To change the metaphor again, the foundation has been laid, but the house set upon it will depend upon our own creativity. It is important to stress these premises and the creativity because there has been no end of mawkish talk of late about the "prescriptions," or "programs," assumedly given us by the Court. In this day of long and multiple opinions, it would be presumptuous to ask the justices to refrain from speculating on where, practically, their logic may take us and hazarding their much-to-be-respected guesses that this program or that (not then before the Court) would seem to fall within (or without) the rule of the instant case. Professor Corwin's puckish reference fifteen years ago to "the Supreme Court as National School Board,"[1] though wide of the mark, is at least a useful reminder to us today that, though we may take dictum as gospel, we do not necessarily take gospel as the law.

The four points to which the Court has brought us concern (1) governmental sponsorship of religion in education, (2) the mode of religious establishment in education, (3) the legal nature of religion, and (4) the church-related school.

1. GOVERNMENTAL SPONSORSHIP OF RELIGION IN EDUCATION

The Court has made it plain that there may be no governmental sponsorship of religion in the public schools. In the *Engel* and *Schempp* decisions the Court, in getting to such conclusion, did not find it necessary to wrestle at length with the assertion that no state compulsion was involved in the religious programs in question. The governmental sponsorship was an establishment of religion and hence forbidden. Professor McCloskey has caught the sense of much scholarly criticism of the decisions in saying that "even if we grant that these [religious program] laws blemish our polity, it is hard to contend that the disfigurement is a very great one." [2] But the refusal of the Court to employ the concept of *de minimis* has far-reaching potential. It may even be true that more things have been wrought by these decisions than the justices ever dreamed of.

Swept away is the hoary principle that establishment, in the school situation, is a matter of degree and that a little establishment — at least where children are concerned — is not a dangerous thing. This, I think, provides the sharpest recognition that the education of children is a very special thing and that religion is a very special thing. Most of all, it says that a breath of state sponsorship of religion, in the situation in which child and state (personalities vastly unequal in power) encounter each other, shall be legally categorized as invasive and forbidden — that is to say, as establishment. In effect, the Court said there is no need to attempt the assay of factors of coercion, with all of their subjective and psychological imponderables. The sponsors, not the children, will be on trial. We will not have to get to any issue of free exercise. Moreover, assertions, in school programs, that the procedures are "voluntary," or even provisions (such as for written requests to be excused) assumedly to make them voluntary, are not to be considered in the determination of constitutionality.

That the education-child-state interrelationship — not the mere fact of government support of religion — is the peculiar basis for this radical determination of establishment is evident from the fact that substantial government support of religion is apparently constitutionally tolerable in other areas. It seems wholly unlikely, for example, that the Court would declare publicly sponsored praying in legislatures an unconstitutional practice.[3] Government supplies substantial financial and administrative promotion to religion in the federal chaplaincies. Yet it is a safe guess that no American appellate court would declare such promotion violative of the First Amendment. Who is affected and in what situation appears to be the key to the question of whether there is establishment. Establishment "in the air" (to borrow the phrase of Holmes about negligence) is of no significance. There is no establishment except in the context of concrete situations. The Court finds establishment in the school situation because it finds children in the school situation.

The first of our departure points, then, is that in the education of children concern for establishment is maximal. Sponsorship itself is imposition. Tolerances allowed in other areas of religion-state relationships are constitutionally unthinkable here. The state need not bother to defend the benign passivity of its role as sponsor. It has no role as sponsor.

2. THE MODE OF RELIGIOUS ESTABLISHMENT IN EDUCATION

The decisions of the Supreme Court tell us that the mode of religious expression in the public schools is constitutionally without significance. The *Engel* and *Schempp* decisions rounded out the statement begun in the *Everson* and *McCollum* cases. The Court's renowned definition of establishment in *Everson* (made in the context of issues of financial aid to religion) stressed establishment principally as support of the church or sect as a religious *body*. The specific holding of the Court, that publicly financed bus transportation could be afforded to children to get them to sectarian schools, appeared in a text[4] which pronounced that government could not, without offense to the First Amendment, "pass laws which aid one religion, aid all religions, or prefer one religion over another." The text also, however, interdicted state support of "religious activities" and coercion "to profess belief or disbelief in any religion," and thus laid groundwork for subsequent decisions which might involve government support of religion other than through support of sects.

In the *McCollum* case support of religious bodies was involved, but the central issue, more broadly, was religious *instruction* in the schools. Although the Court noted compulsive elements in the released-time program, it concluded that the instruction program constituted an establishment of religion. Use of the public schools, even according to a cooperative plan permitting all religious bodies of the community equal opportunity for "dissemination of their doctrines," was declared impermissible.

A third mode of establishment — namely, *worship* — was struck down in the *Engel* and *Schempp* cases.[5] In spite of very broad premises stated in *Everson* and *McCollum*, the belief had persisted that although religious bodies could not be aided or religious instruction carried on in public school classrooms, nevertheless worship could be encouraged. The Court did not agree. From its decisions, it appeared, moreover, that who authored the devotions was of no consequence, but only who sponsored them. That the devotions reflected the inspirations of one sect, all sects, or no sects was not legally significant. Nor was it significant that they were directed to God, rather than to a specific Person of God, or to a saint.[6]

Our second departure point, then, is that the mode of a religious establishment in the schools is constitutionally unimportant. Changing the form of the practice will not free it of an establishmentarian character. One avenue of imagination and resourcefulness is blocked off: attempts to dream up new *modes* of (in particular) indoctrination or worship will prove vain.

3. THE LEGAL NATURE OF RELIGION

It was not inevitable that the legal definition of "religion," as that term is employed (and only once) in the First Amendment, should broaden. The word "religion" could have been kept frozen in Madison's understanding of it as "the duty which we owe to our Creator and the Manner of our discharging it." [7] Rights of non-theists in their beliefs could then have been protected insofar as their practice could be described as a species of speech or press or assemblage, or where governmental action could be said to constitute an unreasonable deprivation of life, liberty (other than uniquely religious), or property, or a denial of equal protection of the laws. Broad though the scope of that protection would be, it would be deficient in three respects. First, it would limit religious freedom. That is to say, it would preclude not only substantial non-theistic religious bodies from being recognized as religions (and thus entitled to all constitutional protections and legal benefits to religions) but even the individual non-theist. Thus bodies whose characteristics fell precisely into categories which characterized theistic religions (e.g., organization and membership, ethical teaching, direction toward some ideal, and perhaps ritual) would be outside the pale of protection to *religion* given in the Constitution merely because the formal object of theistic worship or teaching — i.e., God — was lacking. Not merely constitutional protections but constitutional or statutory benefits (for example, tax exemption) would be denied to these groups.

Second, the definition, viewed merely *as a definition*, partook faintly of an establishmentarian character, giving to theistic religion a constitutional status and prestige denied to the non-theistic cults, beliefs, or practices even though these were considered religious by their adherents.

Lastly, non-theistic religions were exempt from the ban of the disestablishment clause of the First Amendment.

The Supreme Court, over a period of three-quarters of a century, has gradually redefined "religion." The statement in *Torcaso v. Watkins*, in 1961, that the constitutional term includes "Buddhism, Taoism, Ethical Culture, Secular Humanism and others" was only the logical culmination of a long judicial development in that direction.[8] The immense importance of this redefinition of religion is routinely ignored in discussions of *Engel-Schempp* and their practical consequences. We have all heard these decisions criticized as victories for Jews, or for secularists, or atheists, as though to say that the Court had created a special preference for these groups. But that is to do the Court a great injustice, since what the Court has really done is to give recognition to a freedom for *all* from imposition of anything that now is legally "religion." We have heard the decisions attacked as mandating a religion of secularism in the public schools, but that cannot possibly be legally read into them since state sponsorship of any and all religions is now proscribed. Later I shall discuss the difficulties this vast new dimension of disestablishment entails and the responsibilities it involves. Suffice it at this point to say that the Court has now provided the public schools with a rule which — precluding all sponsorship, in any form, of any religion — will cast shadows upon the constitutional validity of many a value prescription which may be sought to be utilized in the public schools.

If from thinking of religion as one of the denominations of our "three faiths" to thinking of it as merely an expression of values seems a breathtaking leap, the fact is that we have not leaped the chasm but bridged it. The bridging process has been gradual. As we have noted, the fact of establishment does not depend upon the fact that a cult is what gets established. No cult was aided by the Regents' prayer; indeed, the only sense in which the prayer could be called cultic was in its expression of the common belief in God of the majority of American religious bodies (which are theistic). Doctrinal religion was bade to depart the public schools with the *McCollum* case, and under the umbrella of that holding, as well as the *Schempp* decision, would appear to come such ethical programs as study of the Ten Commandments.[9] In like manner, worship was ruled out by *Engel* and *Schempp*. So we have long since passed the point at which we might have sponsored religion in the public schools as body, as worship, or as doctrine. It is the last-mentioned classification of religion — namely, doctrine — which calls for particular examination, and examination of the meaning of "doctrine" leads one to speak of "values" as, at least in some sense, identifiable with religion, in the constitutional sense.

The two are closely related. Values, interiorly, are philosophical (including moral) and theological beliefs; their external face is attitude and as such affects or governs conduct, thus having a social dimension. Doctrine means a principle, taught or advocated, or a body or system of teachings relating to a particular subject. There is "doctrine" pertaining to hydraulics, to chess, to marketing, to tennis. There is also doctrine which relates directly to values. The spectrum of value teachings is broad, ranging from the most commonplace of civic virtues to the most complex of theological assertions. Almost universally throughout the history of education the imparting of values has been deemed a prime concern in the schooling of the young.

Our constitutional law, so far as public education is concerned, regards values from both free exercise and establishmentarian points of view. In the second flag-salute case, *West Virginia State Board of Education v. Barnette*, the Supreme Court (per Justice Jackson) declared children who

were members of Jehovah's Witnesses exempt from a flag salute requirement imposed upon public school children. While it has been said that
flag-saluting is generally regarded as a non-religious exercise, the Court
questioned its effects upon the children in question as an exercise of an
"asserted power to force an American citizen to profess any statement
of belief." In coming to its conclusion, it also appeared to identify the
required salute with "matters of opinion and political attitude" and
"ideological discipline." Indicating that the flag salute had a religious
doctrinal dimension, Jackson said prophetically, "Probably no deeper
division of our people could proceed from any provocation than from
finding it necessary to choose what doctrine and whose program public
educational officials shall compel youth to unite in embracing." And he
concluded with his famous statement, "If there is any fixed star in our
constitutional constellation, it is that no official, high or petty, can
prescribe what shall be orthodox in politics, nationalism, religion, or other
matters of opinion, or force citizens to confess by word or act their faith
therein." While the flag-salute program was held to violate the free
exercise of the religion of the Jehovah's Witnesses in the case, it was not
any practice of theirs the freedom of which the Court's action vindicated,
nor in fact any belief of theirs. The case is about something else: the
nature of practices of the *state* and whether these are such that the right
of free exercise may give rise to an exemption from them. The Witnesses
said that the practice of the state was, in effect, to require them to bow
down to a graven image. The Court refused to say that the flag was an
idol but did describe the salute mainly in terms of doctrinal values. It did
not say that these values constituted religion, in the sense of the First
Amendment (though it went some distance in that direction). The whole
thrust of the opinion lies in its emphasis upon *value impositions* as the
feature of the practice which permitted of free exercise objection. From
Barnette it appears clear that, irrespective of considerations of establishment, public school practices calling for affirmations of values deemed in
conflict with one's religion may be asserted as denying free exercise. Although the affirmation called for in *Barnette* was the physical action of
rendering a salute, certainly other sorts of affirmations would appear to
fall within the rule of the case. While in *Barnette* the record showed that
a known sect had an established belief that it would be sinful to engage
in the prescribed practice, it would not appear necessary, in order to
claim exemption, to prove that one's religious objection was based upon
a known religious belief of a known religious body of which one was a
member.

With respect to establishment and the matter of values, it has been
noted that the legal meaning of "religion" in the First Amendment, as now
pronounced by the Court, is broad indeed.[10] The justices themselves may
not yet have perceived how broad their definition is. At the end of

decades of expanding the definition, in the *Torcaso* case the Court gave us
to understand that the term, as used in the First Amendment, embraced
Ethical Culture and "Secular Humanism" (capitalization by the Court).[11]
These are spacious terms, but not without meaning. Ethical Culture is
even an institutional body with members. The value expressions peculiar
to their own orientations are legally religious value expressions. When
sponsored by the state in the schools, a text encouraging the idea that
majorities are the source of right would seem as much an establishment
of religion as one which said that God is.

The meaning of religion broadens further, however, when some contemporary views of religion are encountered. As Professor Stahmer has
well stated, "The term 'religion' as used today might include almost any
kind of ultimate concern with or without an act of personal commitment." [12] He points out, too, that Bonhoeffer, Buber, Bishop Robinson,
and others reject pat distinctions between the "sacred" and the "secular,"
and he quotes Paul Tillich that "the universe is God's sanctuary. . . .
Essentially the religious and the secular are not separated realms." [13] Yet
our constitutional law of religion, as interpreted by the Court, is premised
largely upon the separation of those realms (a separation not merely of
churches from the state) — and a separation which must now take account
of the very great breadth of the religion which is to be separated.

The third of our departure points may admittedly prove troublesome.
I am sure that I have made it more troublesome than the Court thinks it,
but I do not think that to envision the problems encountered by the
Court's definition of religion is a sort of intellectual barratry. The Court
has left the public school with an injunction of "wholesome neutrality";
the test of that neutrality will be found in the nature of the school's
program. Though few value impositions may be challenged, many may
now be challengeable.

4. CHURCH-RELATED SCHOOLS

Church-related schools have constitutional status in the American
system. And the *Pierce* decision upheld the right of the parent to educate
his child in such a school, as a liberty protected under the due process
clause of the Fourteenth Amendment. The Court rejected "any general
power of the state to standardize its children by forcing them to accept
instruction from public teachers only." "The child," said the Court in a
memorable phrase, "is not the mere creature of the state. . . ."

Enrollments in church-related schools (chiefly Catholic) have vastly
increased since 1925 when the *Pierce* decision was handed down. Today,
about one-sixth of all American children are educated in non-public
sectarian schools. This fact has resulted in efforts to acquire governmental
aid to the children in the schools or to the schools themselves (take your
constitutional pick). Government more and more has provided such aid,

with three Supreme Court decisions as its apparent guide: *Cochran* (1930), which recognized that the teaching of secular subjects in church-related schools could amount to the achieving of a public purpose and therefore be governmentally aided; *Everson* (1947), which held, over First Amendment objection, that government may provide bussing for children to get to a church-related school, or more broadly, that government may aid a citizen to obtain his education, even though in a church school (take your constitutional pick); *Schempp*, with its doctrine of "secular legislative purpose" and "primary effect that neither advances nor inhibits religion" — followed by citation to *Everson*.

It is not my purpose here to argue the "parochial school aid" question. That question, however, is germane to issues now pertaining to religion in the public schools and even more germane to the value pluralism of the American society. The Court's denial of a power in the state to "standardize its children" comes to mind, as does the genesis of the case, in the plea of the Imperial Council, A.A.O. Nobles Mystic Shrine, who were the promoters of the Oregon statute, to "mix those with prejudices in the public school melting pot for a few years while their minds are plastic, and finally bring out the finished product — a true American."

The fourth point of departure to which the Supreme Court has brought us is simply the possibility of the alternative of the church school. This is a legal alternative and, under a growing consensual reading of the aforecited doctrine of primary effect, an alternative which may prove viable economically. But whether it is an alternative which will be sought by substantial additional groups of Americans is indeed another question.

Arriving at Policy

Whether concern over religion in public education is universal in the United States today is difficult to assess. It is easy enough for some to conjure up in the imagination Catholic or secularist plots to take over public education. Although that would at least signify a vital concern within these groups, the fact is that neither of them has expressed excited interest in the public schools. In addition, there is no very impressive evidence that we are, as Mr. Justice Douglas once called us, "a religious people" — by whatever definition of religion you choose. We are undoubtedly today a more widely churched and actually heathen people than the "heathen" Americans of the past as described by Littell.

Those of us who do have a concern for the public schools will want the children in them to be afforded values — values which those who care deem wholesome, right, and necessary for the lives of the children and the good of society. Although family responsibility for the implanting of values has not lessened, family life in America is said to be declining (especially in densely populated urban centers) owing to a variety of pressures and circumstances characterizing the post-World War II era. This sorry fact has stimulated three sorts of responses with respect to values in public education. First has been the response that "more and better education" (meaning in secular subjects and skills) is what is mainly needed. This rests upon the idea that if only people know enough and have well enough trained minds and bodies they will be happy individuals and good citizens. Second has been the response that the place for religion and value inculcation is in the home. (Mr. Justice Tom Clark was so impressed by this that, in an address to some Presbyterian laymen a few years ago, he even drew a theological conclusion that private prayers said by children in the home are "much more *effective*" than prayers they recite in public.[14]) The religion-in-the-home view presupposes homes, parents, love, and interest. It also infers that the school is not the place for moral and religious upbringing. This view has gained ground lately because of its plausibility as an argument for getting religion (in the old sense) out of the public schools. It has ancient roots (the confining of the church "to the sacristy"[15]) and an importance going well beyond education.

The third response would assign the public school a role with respect to moral and religious upbringing. There is much discussion concerning what that role should be. The tension between concepts which it reflects is similar to that faced by public education in the nineteenth century. The problem then was how to have the schools Protestant and still non-sectarian. The problem today seems to be how to have the schools non-religious and still imparting values (never forgetting, in this connection, what "religion" has come to mean). Our Protestant forebears solved their problem in crude but effective fashion by permitting (or requiring) a commonly Protestant religious infusion into the public schools and pretending that it was non-sectarian. The old cases, in which this infusion was protested, abound with blithe references by the courts to "non-sectarian religious practices." When the Supreme Court announced its sweeping definition of the "establishment of religion" in the *Everson* case in 1946, Justice Jackson, having stated that the public school "is organized on the premises that secular education can be isolated from all religious training," raised the question of "whether such a disjunction is possible, and if possible, whether it is wise." The earlier attempt of public education to straddle simultaneously Protestantism and non-sectarianism was succeeded by a similar effort to embrace religious neutrality, but "wholesome" neutrality — implying that a *species* of neutrality is the mandate, viz., one that is "conducive to moral or general well-being" (if we may accept a dictionary definition of "wholesome"). Several proposals are made. Each may be thought of as a question.

PROGRAMS FOR MORAL BEHAVIOR?

As we have noted, the Court in *Schempp* went so far as to describe, in general terms, programs in the field of religion which it felt would still be constitutionally viable. Questions are posed by these suggestions not so much with respect to their intrinsic merits as with respect to the fact that they are being taken as though in *substitution* for the prayers and Bible reading. It is suggested, in other words, that moral and spiritual benefits claimed for the old practices need not be lost to the public school child just because the old practices had to go; these benefits can yet be achieved in other ways. It is said that imparting to a child common elements from many religions will increase his religious sensitivity, possibly with good effects upon his behavior. A good summary of this view is contained in a statement circulated as a background paper for the conference on the Role of Religion in Public Education on which this volume is based:

> It has been hoped and often assumed that a consequence of increased religious sensitivity would be the development of moral and ethical behavior on the part of the child. Proponents of this kind of religious instruction have not been content to increase children's knowledge of religious tradition; they have sought a change in the personal and interpersonal *behavior* of their students. Although difficult to "teach" in the usual sense, attempts have been made to influence behavior by holding up standards of conduct derived from religious teachings and historical example.

Other sorts of programs for stimulating desired behavior are also being proposed, some not seeking religious sensitivity as the means. Philosophically they give rise to several questions — and with possible legal consequences:

First, the teacher (or the program) must obviously proceed from some normative reference point in the endeavor to influence the behavior of the pupil. What the teacher (or the people who prepare the program) considers desirable behavior depends upon value judgments resulting from experience, conscience, outlook on life and the world, etc. While we have always allowed for (and cannot escape) the force of any teacher's personal moral example, we are also aware that that example may be insufficient to stimulate desired behavior in the pupil. (For example, the range of situations in which the teacher's moral example is shown may be few; again, the teacher's personal moral example may not consistently be of the sort that he, or the program formulators, would wish followed.) Therefore, resort is to be made to deliberate programming based upon prior value judgments, or what I feel we must call *religious* judgments. These judgments, however benign, are judgments of the state. Do they rest upon a consensus? And will that give them sanction? And if so, may not other consensual judgments be put forward? Although the raising of such questions may be criticized as being all of a piece with the thinking and psychology of the strict separationists, it also must be seen as a corrective to the anti-intellectualism of those who appear not to regard philosophy as important. Recall here that the proposal is a program of morals. It is quite unlike a program of, for example, history, in which the pupil may encounter all manner of men and movements, being inspired by whom he finds inspiring, but only incidentally to the subject matter of the program.

Second, I wonder whether the proposition does not create a sort of denial of "equal protection" to ideas. We may not, in other words, encourage certain moral conduct upon the basis of its presumed identification with the laws of God, but we can (according to the proposition) encourage conduct upon the basis of value judgments not to be identified with the law of God. This may indeed, in a given situation, amount to a religious preference.

Third, the proposition is really one for the teaching *of* religion. I do not think it escapes that fact because the mode of its presentation does not involve "teaching" in the usual sense. If a teacher in a public school were to attempt to influence behavior "by holding up standards of conduct," say, of Christ, the Blessed Virgin, and St. Simeon Stylites, no one, I venture to say, would deny that he had hurdled the well-known Wall. Adding Protestant and Jewish religious martyrs to the list might lessen the sectarianism of the subject matter but not at all the fact that here was a "teaching of."

Looking at such a proposal, we are grateful for its good intentions, and if it were to appear in concrete outline in a given state or school district we should want to examine it with sympathy for what it seeks to do and with comment that is constructive rather than captious. But we dare not write off suddenly all of the teaching so lately provided us by the Court with respect to the impressionableness of the child, the inviolability of the religious personality, the educational process, and the "power and prestige of the state," of which Mr. Justice Black spoke so gravely in *Engel v. Vitale.*

It is easy enough to say that the Court has not banned the teaching of civic virtues in the public schools. Certainly the justices never intended to do so. Certainly public school teachers are going to continue to insist upon traditional virtues of truth-telling and general honesty, for example, and to discourage (indeed, penalize) lying, cheating, and stealing. The life of the classroom, like the life of the larger society, cannot go on otherwise. But precisely because the conduct of life is involved, the bases for conduct are very readily involved. They are obviously involved in the area of sex education, or in efforts to give children some sort of meaningful view of the good society and of what sort of *personal* conduct helps or inhibits making their society "good." All of us feel that the spirit of inquiry is essential in any educational process, and children notoriously raise "whys" in that part of the process which relates to their moral conduct. But may a public school teacher discuss the virtue of justice, for example, in terms of God's will? Equally great difficulties, no doubt, would be imposed in discussing it solely in terms of society's will — with the inevitable train of problems pertaining to majorities, or the state, as sources of moral standards.

BACK TO THE NOBLES MYSTIC?

In connection with the consideration of the role of the public school in the area of morality, we hear more and more insistently that the public school is the chief agent for the creating of cultural and social unity in the United States. Not infrequently this is conjoined with vigorous attacks upon "sectarianism." Professor Ulich speaks of the mission of the public school teacher "to educate free minds who, on the one hand, appreciate the depth of man's religious tradition, but to whom, on the other hand, the old denominational and dualistic conflicts appear secondary, if not inhibitive to, the formation of a unifying world outlook."[16] Again we are brought to inquire about a substitutional role for the public school, the implication here being that the public school will supply unifying values which would otherwise be lacking in our society owing to the existence of sects. In one sense given public schools can perform a unifying function. Depending upon such factors as geographical location and bussing, they can and often do serve as institutions in which children of different races, religions, ancestries, or economic statuses associate. Except with respect to religion, many sectarian schools do too, while the composition of still other public schools is found to reflect a single social group. With the decline of immigration and of the ethnic ghettos in the United States and the great increase in economic and social mobility of people of all groups, the mutual acquaintanceship of people of different faiths and stocks is growing in neighborhoods and other areas of association and will predictably continue to do so. The role of the public school in accustoming different sorts of people to one another through intermixture will probably not become greater.

But where assertions of a "unifying role" go beyond mere intermixture and become doctrinal, we must ask whether it is a proper role for the public school to be a school which promotes cultural unity. I would answer that it is not, and for two reasons. First, I am not sure what is meant by "cultural unity"; second, I do not know to what end, or about what consensus, our children are to be unified.[17] The first reason relates to my concern over an establishment of a religion of cultural unity, freely inculcating in children principles of conduct and world outlook while barring the slightest affirmation of the existence of God, the soul, the

Commandments, sin, or future reward and punishment. *If*, in other words, public education conceives that it is charged with providing a child with a working philosophy of life, if it feels that it must address itself to those ultimate questions of the child which were always deemed religious, I do not think that the answer it gives can constitutionally be one which is agreeable to me as a Christian or agreeable to Mr. Jerome Nathanson as an Ethical Culturist. Public education simply can no longer sponsor religion. Nor does it escape the problem to offer the pupil choices for his selection. The range of choices is very broad; the pupil is a child. Practically, only one choice may be available: to make no choice. His teacher — quite central in his consciousness — cannot affirm; that, too, is a teaching. His teacher may offer religions or religious ideas for comparison — objectively, we hope. The one thing the child is not really able to do is to compare them.

Again, as Professor Ulich's remark reveals, it may well be conceived that the function of the public school teacher is to raise the mind of the child above the warrings of the denominations and bring him to a "unifying world outlook." This presupposes a judgment upon the contentions of the "denominations" (which, to these, are contentions for *truths*) and a judge capable of making the judgment (that is, of arriving at a truth for which he will contend) and then of pronouncing his truth, or a world view, in substitution of older *religious* claims. This in itself is to state a religious claim.

Finally, apart from connotations of state religion, the concept of the public school as a vehicle for unity has direct implications for non-public education. The ghosts of the Nobles Mystic remain with us. Unity, in their terms, meant cultural homogenizing, the single mold. This is wholly contrary to unity in pluralism — contrary in means and contrary in results. The art of life in a religiously plural society consists not in removing differences but in keeping them peaceably. Its matrix is love and the sense of justice. The opportunity before us is in the strengthening of these, not in the encouragement of an ersatz pluralism through a relativizing of the old creeds to make way for new.

Indeed, the very contrary is what the freedom-and-plural character of the American society demand of the public school: that it shall to the extent possible foster the uniqueness and vitality of the religious identification of the children whom it serves. There will be no sense in speaking of the public school as a unifying force if its program of unification finally results in there being little left to unify.

A NEW MC GUFFEY?

A proposal that has made some headway in the United States (again, in seeming substitution for the deposed practices) employs "inspirational" materials for daily classroom use — poems, stories, wise sayings — all brimming with Pealeian optimism, a sort of spiritual Lawrence Welk Show. I have not cited instances of this proposal in my footnotes, realizing at once both its sincere motivation and its lack of meaningful impact. It is McGuffey without his Puritanism, life without its tragic note. It scrupulously avoids theism, in any form, yet it is a program designed to "fill up the void" left by Bible reading and class prayers. It is, of course, religion, but placebo religion to which, it is to be hoped, the courts would apply the doctrine of *de minimis*.

"THE OBJECTIVE STUDY"?

Professor Phenix has correctly discerned the difficulty posed by efforts to substitute one sort of Bible-reading (as a "study" — and especially with exhortations to virtue) for another (as worship).[18] He is wary of the compensatory feature of these efforts, not only on grounds of constitutionality but because of their fostering of religion as a thing isolated and irrelevant. Hence the efforts may prove harmful to religion.

At the same time, he is aware that studies of religion, especially "comparative" studies, may in fact prove to be anti-religious, or to favor a sect, or to create an attitude of relativism toward all religion and hence the view that religion is not relevant to life. Professor Phenix sees two ways in which religious concerns can be expressed in education — "implicit" and "explicit" approaches. In the "implicit" approaches the teacher helps the pupil to see "ultimate" perspectives in many of what are usually considered "secular" matters (e.g., the ultimate perspective of creativity in the making of a work of art). He sees "implicit" religion also in terms of life orientation and ultimate values. While certainly this latter element introduces religion in its constitutional sense, Professor Phenix surprisingly does not so regard it. The program to which he addresses himself is really one involving what he deems "conventional" religion in the public schools. This, he believes, can be presented with objectivity, and he finds constitutional sanction for such "objective study" in the opinions of the justices in *Schempp*.

Phenix is strongly seconded by Niels C. Nielsen, Jr., in his recent *God in Education:* "It is our thesis that specific information about religion has a legitimate place in the public school curriculum. Teaching forms a positive or negative intellectual image of religion. If the school assumes a disinterested or secularist outlook, the child is conditioned accordingly."[19] Both Phenix and Nielsen believe that the "specific information" can be taught objectively. This will mean the fulfilling of certain injunctions: (1) Self-transcendence on the part of the teacher is necessary so that he approaches a religion with sympathy; (2) the "specific information" need not be presented without evidence or without exegesis — in fact, interpretation is desired, provided it is apparent to the child that there are, or may be, several interpretations; (3) indoctrination is to be avoided, not merely because it is a teaching of religion but because it (in Phenix's view) may produce the sort of blind faith commitment which leads to bigotry. The proposal calls for the following of assumed "canons of scholarly objectivity."

Inevitably, the program raises questions. Some are practical, rather than relating to principle, and can conceivably be met. The greatest of the practical questions is obviously the finding and training of the elite of teachers who could fulfill the remarkably exacting assignment cut out for them by the proposal. Questions of principle posed by the proposal are less readily answered. The underlying assumption of the program is that one of the functions of the public school is to teach religion. This assumption is not obviated by the fact that the proposal would present religious *choices* to the pupil. While it may be questioned whether the public school may present any program of choices without, in effect, promoting religion, a more significant difficulty is encountered. A parent, in the exercise of parental and religious rights, may desire to raise his child *to believe that a certain religion is true*. May the *public school* which that child attends compel him to learn that there are many differences with the beliefs his parents or church have taught him, many different ways of interpreting those beliefs, many beliefs that he might entertain instead? Assuming the strictest observance of the strictest canons of objectivity by the most perfect of teachers, the answer can scarcely be in the affirmative.

But if the affirmative answer is given, then the "objective study" proposal (at least as made by Professor Phenix) must face the objection that it is in fact religious.

A related difficulty appears. We cannot demand that any religious group so modify its teachings as to remove all possibility of offense to persons not of that group. Certainly any "objective study" of religion must present (indeed, with sympathy, we are told) the relevant "specific information." If we are to adopt Professor Phenix's proposals, we must be willing to risk offense to the sensibilities of children whose families or churches have provided them with religious identification. Explanation by the teacher may not suffice. This may or may not be a useful or maturing experience for them, but it is questionable whether it is the function of the state to afford it.

RELIGION AS CULTURE?

Close to, but broader than, the idea of "implicit" religion is the study of religion as a part of culture. To some extent such study has always been part of the education of children. But lest extreme readings be given to its decisions on religion in the public schools, the Supreme Court was at pains to say it did not feel that the study of the Bible as literature, for example, ran contrary to the ban it had pronounced upon the Bible as worship or doctrine. By similar dictum it had expressed an equal status for the "objective study" of religion. While constitutional difficulty is posed by some programs of "objective study," similar objections should not be raised with respect to the study of religion as a part of culture.

First, note that the proposal is to study religion *as a part of* given cultural studies and thus subordinate thereto. Absent, therefore, should be the compensatory feature previously mentioned, with all of the undesirable factors which that feature entails. At the same time the uses of the program to teach religion — or to relativize or to downgrade specific belief — are greatly lessened.

Second, at least in the field of the arts, the encounter with religion can be what Paul Freund has described as "an experience which transports to the threshold of religion but does not enter its private precincts, as the shared experience of poetry may carry to the private threshold of grief or ecstasy or intuition."[20] The fastidious secularist may object to such hospitality to religion, especially since much of the "religion" reposing in the arts is conventional religion. But the schools would scarcely perform their secular function properly were not religion as a part of the study of cultural subjects given its full intellectual due.

Third, in such study, "permeation" must be avoided. That is to say, the secular subject should not suffer from a religious distortion; and this spells out a limit to the usefulness of this proposal for religious purposes. As Eric Gill long ago said, "Beauty looks after herself"; she has a nature of her own, and she must not be put to ends which are not hers. Nor can the religiously committed place overly great reliance upon art as a pathway to God. Hitler was immensely fond of good music.

Conclusions

1. THE PUBLIC SCHOOL

The public school may not serve a religious function, even to fill a void supposedly gaping in the lives of the great majority of our young people. We have rejected the more likely means (such as released time) whereby the void might to an extent have been filled. The end result is one which throws the heaviest of burdens upon home and church. Our closest approach to religion in the public schools will have to be the personal example of believing teachers and pupils. This and an atmosphere of hospitality to religion as part of our culture is the most that we can expect from our public schools affirmatively.

For the increase of love, justice, and peace in the community, the public schools will continue to be the common experience of the majority of American children and can, without imposition upon consciences, contribute mightily to intergroup peace.

2. The church-related schools

Church-sponsored schools must be legally and financially available to those whose religious commitments render them the desirable educational milieu for their children. Although a degree of governmental support may properly be entailed, it is wholly unlikely that any exodus from the public schools into non-public schools will take place as a result. The establishing of school systems is a vast undertaking involving far more than money. Few are likely to seek to embark on it. There is little likelihood, too, that any phasing out of parochial schools will occur. Because of American education's effort to run uphill against the demographic avalanche, there will be nothing into which to phase them.

3. Realities and responsibilities

The lawyer's horizon is neither very high nor very broad. If half of the problems of society could be solved by lawyers, the other half have probably been caused by lawyers. My final observation may easily be discounted as the sort of foolishness which lawyers fall into when out of their shallow depth.

For the foreseeable future, public and sectarian education will probably continue in much the same institutional forms as they have today. The one will be permitted to be religious, the other not. The one can fail to live up to its privilege as a religious school by failing to inspire those active concerns in its graduates which all men today should recognize as religious: concerns for peace, for the poor, for the persecuted, the cheated, the ill, the aged — for all that is in the Secular City. While dangers are posed to the religious schools by militant secularism, the greater danger may be posed by the schools' failure to apprehend their radical mission in a world in which, as Erich Fromm recently noted, it is not God that is dead but, quite possibly, man, "transformed into a thing, a producer, a consumer, an idolator of other things."

The religious schools and the public schools may, on the other hand, find themselves engaged in a sort of race for relevance, reflecting the growing desire in religious education for appreciation of the secular and a new desire in public education for appreciation of the religious. To what form of either school this may bring us, or whether to either as we now know them, we cannot predict. But the test for both schools is in reality a test for us, in the community, and for our times. What happens to peace and justice in the next half-century will tell the tale of how faithful to religion and to education we were.

NOTES

1. *Law and Contemporary Problems*, 14:3 (1949).

2. McCloskey, "Principles, Powers, and Values: The Establishment Clause and the Supreme Court," in *Religion and the Public Order* (University of Chicago Press, 1964), p. 109.

3. Professor Freund correctly says, "The opinion of the Court by Justice Clark [in *Schempp*], and the concurring opinions of Justice Brennan and Justice Goldberg, are at pains to point out that the decision is addressed to religious exercises in the public schools and is not to be taken in any doctrinaire way as a barrier to every civil program that in some way involves religion" (Paul A. Freund and Robert Ulich, *Religion and the Public Schools* [Harvard University Press, 1965], p. 17).

4. Mr. Justice Douglas has recently called the pronouncement dictum (William O. Douglas, *The Bible and the Schools* [Little, Brown, 1966], p. 16). Mr. Justice Black, speaking for the Court in 1961, said that it was not dictum (*Torcaso v. Watkins*, 367 U.S. 488, 493–494 [1961]).

5. While in one of the two consolidated cases, *School District of Abington Township v. Schempp*, 374 U.S. 203 (1963), one of the religious practices was Bible-reading, a specific finding of the trial court in that case had been that the reading possessed a "devotional" character (*ibid.*, at 210).

6. Whether any outer manifestation of devotion to country, society, or ideal may be sponsored in the public schools is considered on pp. 152–153.

7. "Memorial and Remonstrance Against Religious Assessments," *Writings of Madison* (edited by Hunt, 1904), Vol. 2, p. 183.

8. The Supreme Court cases marking the development were *Vidal v. Girard's Executors*, 2 How. 205 (1844) (Deism a sect, listed along with Judaism and "any other form of infidelity," giving hint that non-theistic religion might be "religion" in the constitutional sense); *Watson v. Jones*, 13 Wall, 679 (1872) ("The law knows no heresy, and is committed to the support of no dogma, the establishment of no sect," thus inferring that it is more than preference to a sect that is prohibited by the no establishment clause, and that "religion," as intended by that clause, may comprehend dogma — or tenets, beliefs, doctrines, principles); *Reynolds v. United States*, 98 U.S. 145 (1879) (Court speaks, not of the nature of "religion" itself, but of the freedom which a person may enjoy in respect to religion. It notes, however, Madison's and Jefferson's definitions of religion — both describing a relationship with God); *Davis v. Beason*, 133 U.S. 333 (1890) (". . . one's views of his relations to his Creator and to the obligations they impose of reverence for his being and character and obedience to his will." The Court also spoke of "worship" and "religious tenets" as being religion within the meaning of both the no establishment and the free exercise clauses. Why establishment is barred: ". . . the folly of attempting . . . to control the mental operations of persons and to enforce an outward conformity to a prescribed standard"); *Church of Jesus Christ of Latter Day Saints v. United States*, 136 U.S. 1 (1890) (negative definition of religion by asserting that polygamy is not a religious belief. Cf. *Reynolds, supra*, where the Court only held that certain kinds of conduct would not be immune from operation of penal statutes merely because they were expressions of religious belief. The Court in *Latter-Day Saints* said polygamy is merely "pretense" of the same); *United States v. McIntosh*, 293 U.S. 605 (1931) (quotes the definition of religion from *Davis v. Beason*. Chief Justice Hughes, in dissenting opinion, indicates that "cosmic consciousness of belonging to the human family" is a "religious" belief); *Hamilton v. Regents of University of California*, 293 U.S. 245 (1934) (Justice Cardozo raises question of whether requirement of instruction in military science is an establishment of religion, answering in the negative); *West Virginia State Board of Education v. Barnette*, 319 U.S. 624 (1943) (see discussion by Justice Frankfurter, dissenting, and discussion herein,

pp. 149–150); *United States v. Ballard,* 322 U.S. 78 (1944) (religion a part of freedom of thought; subjective test as to what is religion); *Torcaso v. Watkins,* 367 U.S. 488 (1961) (discussed on pp. 150–151).

9. See Anson Phelps Stokes and Leo Pfeffer, *Church and State in the United States* (Harper & Row, 1964), p. 357.

10. See pp. 148–149.

11. *Torcaso v. Watkins,* 367 U.S. 488, 495 (1961).

12. Harold Stahmer, "Defining Religion: Federal Aid and Academic Freedom," in *Religion and the Public Order,* pp. 128–129.

13. Paul Tillich, *Theology of Culture* (Oxford University Press, 1959), p. 41.

14. *New York Times,* September 24, 1962.

15. John Courtney Murray, *The Problem of Religious Freedom* (Newman Press, 1965), p. 37.

16. Freund and Ulich, *op. cit.,* p. 50.

17. See John Courtney Murray, *We Hold These Truths* (Sheed & Ward, 1960), pp. 84, 85; Arthur Gilbert, "Religious Freedom and Social Change in a Pluralistic Society: A Historical View," in *Religion and the Public Order,* p. 118.

18. Philip H. Phenix, *Religious Concerns in Contemporary Education* (Columbia University Press, 1959); *Education and the Worship of God* (1965).

19. Niels C. Nielsen, Jr., *God in Education* (Sheed & Ward, 1966), p. 154.

20. Freund and Ulich, *op. cit.,* pp. 22, 23.

IO

Moral and Religious Education and the Public Schools: A Developmental View

Lawrence Kohlberg

The major impetus for this volume is the recent Supreme Court interpretation of the First Amendment. As the previous essay by William Ball indicates, it is possible to interpret the Court's decision as ruling out any form of moral or ethical, as well as religious, instruction in the school. He points out that the recent Court decisions define religion as embracing any articulated credos or value systems including "Ethical Culture" or "Secular Humanism," credos which essentially consist of the moral principles of Western culture. He concludes that the Supreme Court is in effect prohibiting the public school from engaging in moral education since such education is equivalent to the state propagation of the religion of Ethical Culture or Humanism.

My first reaction to the notion that moral education and religious education are identical in their implications for civil liberties was, like that of most laymen, one of incredulity and shock. This reaction was especially intense because as a psychologist I have attempted to formulate a conception of moral education in the public schools based on research findings, a conception in which a complete separation of moral and religious education is implicit.[1] In this chapter I will try to focus explicitly on both the scientific findings and the philosophical reasoning which leads me to view

164

moral education as completely separable from religion from the point of view of civil liberties.[2]

Justice as the Core of Morality

It appears to me that Ball's interpretation of the Supreme Court's ruling is possible only because of ambiguity and confusion in the Court's definition of ethical values as these relate to public institutions on the one hand and to religion on the other. It is clear that the Constitution and the law of the land compose or imply a "value system" or a body of norms, and it is equally clear that the government's maintenance of the Constitution and the laws does not mean the establishment of a religion. Accordingly, the public school's effort to communicate an understanding of, and intelligent respect for, the law of the land and the underlying conceptions of human rights on which it is based does not constitute the establishment of a religion. The school is no more committed to value neutrality than is the government or the law. The school, like the government, is an institution with a basic function of maintaining and transmitting some, but not all, of the consensual values of society. The most fundamental values of a society are termed moral values, and the major moral values, at least in our society, are the values of justice. According to any interpretation of the Constitution, the rationale for government is the preservation of the rights of individuals, i.e., of justice. The public school is as much committed to the maintenance of justice as is the court. In my opinion, desegregation of the schools is not only a passive recognition of the equal rights of citizens to access to a public facility, like a swimming pool, but an active recognition of the responsibility of the school for "moral education," i.e., for transmission of the values of justice on which our society is founded.

In essence, then, I am arguing that Ball's interpretation of the Supreme Court ruling is possible only if morality or ethics is confused with "value systems" in general, and if it is not recognized that the core of morality is justice.[3] Unless one recognizes the core status of justice, any conscious concern about the school's responsibility for developing the basic values of the society and making citizens as well as scholars will run into difficulties as soon as one tries to define the exact content of these basic values. Obviously the values transmitted by the school should not be the values of an organized minority. Once the school becomes engaged in teaching a particular moral doctrine belonging to a particular group of citizens organized as a religious, political, or ideological body, it may well be accused of the establishment of religion. The principle involved here would be unquestioned if the schools were to impose the moral beliefs of an organized minority upon children, e.g., the doctrine that it is wrong to receive a blood transfusion, or that it is wrong to work on Saturday.

It applies equally, however, if the moral belief happens to be that of an organized majority, e.g., the belief of the majority in some southern states that it is wrong for whites and Negroes to mingle socially or to marry. Neither the government, the law, nor the schools represent a vehicle whereby the values of the majority may be imposed upon the minority. Both prayer in school and segregated education were the will of the majority as determined by the Gallup Poll before the Supreme Court decision, yet the Court had no hesitancy in defending the rights of the minority. The basic values of our society are basic not in the sense of representing majority or even unanimous consensus; they are basic in the sense of representing universal values which either the majority or the minority must appeal to in support of their own beliefs.

The problems as to the legitimacy of moral education in the public schools disappear, then, if the proper content of moral education is recognized to be the values of justice which themselves prohibit the imposition of beliefs of one group upon another. The requirement implied by the Bill of Rights that the school recognize the equal rights of individuals in matters of belief or values does not mean that the schools are not to be "value oriented." Recognition of equal rights does not imply value neutrality, i.e., the view that all value systems are equally sound. Because we respect the individual rights of members of foreign cultures or of members of partciular groups in our society, it is sometimes believed that we must consider their values as valid as our own. Because we must respect the rights of an Eichmann, however, we need not treat his values as having a cogency equal to that of the values of liberty and justice. Public instruction is committed to maintenance of the rights of individuals and to the transmission of the values of respect for individual rights. This respect should include respect for the right to hold moral beliefs differing from those of the majority. It need not include respect for "moral" beliefs predicated on the denial of the rights of others, whether of the majority or of a minority, such as the beliefs of the American Nazis or the Ku Klux Klan.

Formulating Goals in Moral Education

So far, it has been claimed that the schools cannot be "value neutral" but must be engaged in moral education. It has also been claimed that the content of moral education must be defined in terms of justice, rather than in terms of majority consensus, if the civil rights of parents and children are not to be infringed upon by such education. These claims have been made in terms of the political philosophy underlying the school as a public institution.

When we consider the actual workings of the public school, the conclusions become more inescapable. All schools necessarily are involved in moral education. The teacher is constantly and unavoidably moralizing to children, about school rules and values and about his students' behavior toward one another. Since moralizing is unavoidable, it seems logical that it be done in terms of consciously formulated goals of moral development. Liberal teachers do not want to indoctrinate children with their own private moral values. Since the classroom social situation requires moralizing by the teacher, he ordinarily tends to limit his moralizing to the necessities of classroom management, i.e, the immediate and relatively trivial kinds of behavior which are disrupting to him or to the other children. Exposure to the diversity of moral views of teachers is undoubtedly one of the enlightening experiences of growing up, but the present thoughtlessness concerning which of the teacher's moral attitudes or views he communicates to children and which he does not leaves much to be desired. Many teachers would be mortified to know what their students perceive to be their moral concerns. My seven-year-old son told me one day that he was one of the good boys in school but he didn't know whether he really wanted to be. I asked him what the differences between the good and bad boys were and he said the bad boys talked in class and didn't put books away neatly, so they got yelled at. It is highly dubious that his teacher's moralizing was stimulating his or any of the children's moral development, but this type of "moral teaching" is almost inevitable in an educational system in which teachers have no explicit or thought-out conception of the aims and methods of moral education and simply focus upon immediate classroom management in their moralizing.

AMBIGUITIES IN "CHARACTER EDUCATION"

The value problems of moral education, then, do not concern the necessity of engaging in moral education in the school, since this is already being done every day. Value problems arise from the formulation of the aims and content of such education. At an extreme, the formulation of aims suggests a conception of moral education as the imposition of a state-determined set of values, first by the bureaucrats upon the teachers, and then by the teachers upon the children. This is the "character education" employed in Russia, as described by Bronfenbrenner.[4] In Russia the entire classroom process is explicitly defined as "character education" — that is, as making good socialist citizens — and the teacher appears to have a very strong influence upon children's moral standards. This influence rests in part upon the fact that the teacher is perceived as "the priest of society," as the agent of the all-powerful state, and can readily enlist the parents as agents of discipline to enforce school values and demands. In part, however, it rests upon the fact that the teacher systematically uses the peer group as an agent of moral indoctrination and moral sanctions. The classroom is divided into cooperating groups in competition with one another. If a member of one of the groups is guilty of misconduct, the teacher downgrades or penalizes the whole group, and the group in turn punishes the individual miscreant. This is, of course, an extremely effective form of social control if not of moral development.

In contrast to the Russian educators, American educators are not likely to take obedience to, and service to, the state as the ultimate content of moral education. Instead, when they have attempted to formulate some general notions of the content and aims of moral education, they have usually conceived of it as the inculcation of a set of virtues: honesty, responsibility, service, self-control, etc.[5] The implicit rationale for the definition of moral education in terms of virtues or character traits has been that it represents the core of moral agreement in the American community. In fact, however, community consensus on verbal labels like "honesty" conceals a great deal of disagreement about what "honesty" is and when it should be compromised to serve another value or virtue. This is indicated by the results of a recent National Opinion Research Center survey of a representative sample of American adults concerning judgments of right or wrong in situations involving honesty.[6] While in general "dishonest" behavior was said to be wrong, lying, stealing, or cheating was said to be "all right" or not "dishonest" by very sizable proportions of the population in certain specific situations. A majority believe it is right to lie to spare another's feelings, a substantial minority believe it is right to steal to obtain expensive medical treatment for one's wife that is otherwise unobtainable, a considerable minority believe it is all right to take hotel ashtrays and towels, etc. As soon as one leaves vague stereotypical terms like "honesty" and attempts to specify concrete moral actions, then, it becomes very difficult to empirically establish consensus concerning moral values. Does 51 per cent agreement represent moral consensus, does 75 per cent, or does 100 per cent? If the latter, our society has no moral consensus. The problem becomes worse if one considers virtues or character traits other than honesty. The lack of agreement about "moral character" appears when it is recognized that each educator draws up a different list of virtues. Havighurst and Taba[7] include friendliness and moral courage in the list, while Hartshorne and May[8] leave these out and include self-control (persistence). "Religious" virtues (faith, hope, and charity) are hard to distinguish from "civil" virtues. What about "respect for authority" — is that a virtue or not? How about cleanliness — is it next to godliness?

CRITICISM OF PRESENT CONTENT OF MORAL EDUCATION

My criticism of statements of the content of moral education in terms of moral character traits rests on three grounds. First, it is impossible to define the content of moral education in terms of factual majority consensus about good and bad behavior. Though the majority may agree upon the value of cleanliness and proper dress, this does not answer the question of whether it is legitimate "moral education" for a school principal to expel boys whose families allow them to wear long hair. In the second place, even if one were willing to accept a majority opinion as defining moral education, vague character traits or labels do not represent majority consensus, since they conceal a great *lack* of consensus about specific actions and values. A parent will agree with a teacher that "cooperation" is a virtue, but he will not agree that a child's specific failure to obey an "unreasonable" request by the teacher was wrong, even if the teacher calls the act "uncooperative," as teachers are prone to do. In the third place, even if one were willing to ignore the lack of consensus concealed by moral character terms, these terms do not represent objective or observable behavioral outcomes of moral education. Psychologically, there are no such traits as honesty, service, responsibility, etc. Research to date suggests that these words are only varying evaluative labels; they do not stand for separate consistent traits of personality. Insofar as consistencies of personality appear in the moral domain, they are quite different from labels of virtues and vices.[9]

The Development of Moral Judgment

I have so far objected to two conceptions of moral education. The first is the current thoughtless system of moralizing by individual teachers and principals when children deviate from minor administrative regulations or engage in behavior which is personally annoying to the teacher. The second is the effort to inculcate the majority values, particularly as reflected in vague stereotypes about moral character. I shall now present a third conception of moral education. In this conception, the goal of moral education is the stimulation of the "natural" development of the individual child's own moral judgment and of the capacities allowing him to use his own moral judgment to control his behavior. The attractiveness of defining the goal of moral education as the stimulation of development rather than as teaching fixed virtues is that it means aiding the child to take the next step in a direction toward which he is already tending, rather than imposing an alien pattern upon him. Furthermore, I will claim that the stimulation of natural development as the basis of moral education coincides with my earlier statement that the legitimate moral values that the school may transmit are the values of justice.[10]

RESEARCH FINDINGS

This third conception of moral education rests on some recent research findings for its plausibility. These findings suggest that liberty and justice are not the particular values of the American culture but culturally universal moral values which develop regardless of religious membership, education, or belief. This contention is based primarily on my own studies of the development of moral values in hundreds of boys aged nine to twenty-three in various American communities, in a Taiwanese city, in a Malaysian (Atayal) aboriginal village, in a Turkish city and village, in a Mexican city, and in a Mayan Indian village.[11] The boys were interviewed about a variety of standard moral conflict situations and their responses were classified into the system of stages defined in Table 1. Classification was made in terms of placement of each moral idea or judgment of the child in a given stage with regard to one of twenty-five aspects of morality. Table 2 lists these twenty-five aspects, and an example of statements placed in each stage for one of the aspects, "The Basis of Worth of Human Life," is presented in Table 3.

The assertion that the stages of Table 1 are genuine stages implies invariant sequence, i.e., that each individual child must go step by step through each of the kinds of moral judgment outlined. It is, of course, possible for a child to move at varying speeds and to stop (become "fixated") at any level of development, but if he continues to move upward he must move in this stepwise fashion. Although the findings on this issue have not been completely analyzed, a longitudinal study of the same American boys studied at ages ten, thirteen, sixteen, and nineteen suggests that such is the case.

The finding of sequence is extremely important for the assertion that Stages 5 and 6, i.e., stages focusing morality upon principles of justice, are indeed higher stages. In Figure 1 the age trends of the use of each stage of moral judgment for American and Taiwanese boys are presented. In the United States the "higher stages" are still minority stages in the adult American population, even though Stage 5 constitutes the public morality of the Constitution and the Supreme Court. These stages, though they represent the minority, are nonetheless developmentally more advanced because boys in Stage 5 or 6 have gone through the previous stages whereas the boys in the lower stages have not gone through Stage 5 or 6.

The assertion that the stages are culturally universal rests on evidence like that presented in Figure 1. Figure 1 indicates much the same age trends in both the Taiwanese and the American boys. In both groups the first two stages decrease with age, the next two increase until age thirteen and then stabilize, and the last two continue to increase from age thirteen to age sixteen. In general, the cross-cultural studies suggest a similar sequence of development in all cultures, although they suggest that the last two stages of moral thought do not develop clearly in preliterate village or tribal communities.

Questions of the existence of culturally universal moral stages differ somewhat from questions of the dominant public morality of a society. Under certain conditions of social conflict and stress it is possible for the public morality of a society to be formulated by individuals at a lower

TABLE 1

Classification of Moral Judgment into Levels
and Stages of Development

Levels	Basis of Moral Judgment	Stages of Development
I	Moral value resides in external, quasi-physical happenings, in bad acts, or in quasi-physical needs rather than in persons and standards.	*Stage 1:* Obedience and punishment orientation. Egocentric deference to superior power or prestige, or a trouble-avoiding set. Objective responsibility.
		Stage 2: Naïvely egoistic orientation. Right action is that instrumentally satisfying the self's needs and occasionally others'. Awareness of relativism of value to each actor's needs and perspective. Naïve egalitarianism and orientation to exchange and reciprocity.
II	Moral value resides in performing good or right roles, in maintaining the conventional order and the expectancies of others.	*Stage 3:* Good-boy orientation. Orientation to approval and to pleasing and helping others. Conformity to stereotypical images of majority or natural role behavior, and judgment by intentions.
		Stage 4: Authority and social-order maintaining orientation. Orientation to "doing duty" and to showing respect for authority and maintaining the given social order for its own sake. Regard for earned expectations of others.
III	Moral value resides in conformity by the self to shared or shareable standards, rights, or duties.	*Stage 5:* Contractual legalistic orientation. Recognition of an arbitrary element or starting point in rules or expectations for the sake of agreement. Duty defined in terms of contract, general avoidance of violation of the will or rights of others, and majority will and welfare.
		Stage 6: Conscience or principle orientation. Orientation not only to actually ordained social rules but to principles of choice involving appeal to logical universality and consistency. Orientation to conscience as a directing agent and to mutual respect and trust.

TABLE 2

Coded Aspects of Developing Moral Judgment

Code	Description	Aspects
I. *Value*	Locus of value — modes of attributing (moral) value to acts, persons, or events. Modes of assessing value consequences in a situation.	1. Considering motives in judging action. 2. Considering consequences in judging action. 3. Subjectivity vs. objectivity of values assessed. 4. Relation of obligation to wish. 5. Identification with actor or victims in judging the action. 6. Status of actor and victim as changing the moral worth of actions.
II. *Choice*	Mechanisms of resolving or denying awareness of conflicts.	7. Limiting actor's responsibility for consequences by shifting responsibility onto others. 8. Reliance on discussion and compromise, mainly unrealistically. 9. Distorting situation so that conforming behavior is seen as always maximizing the interests of the actor or of others involved.
III. *Sanctions and Motives*	The dominant motives and sanctions for moral or deviant action.	10. Punishment or negative reactions. 11. Disruption of an interpersonal relationship. 12. A concern by actor for welfare, for positive state of the other. 13. Self-condemnation.
IV. *Rules*	The ways in which rules are conceptualized, applied, and generalized. The basis of the validity of a rule.	14. Definition of an act as deviant. (Definition of moral rules and norms.) 15. Generality and consistency of rules. 16. Waiving rules for personal relations (particularism).
V. *Rights and Authority*	Basis and limits of control over persons and property.	17. Non-motivational attributes ascribed to authority (knowledge, etc.). (Motivational attributes considered under *III* above.) 18. Extent or scope of authority's rights. Rights of liberty. 19. Rights of possession or property.

TABLE 2 (CONTINUED)

Code	Description	Aspects
VI. *Positive Justice*	Reciprocity and equality.	20. Exchange and reciprocity as a motive for role conformity. 21. Reciprocity as a motive to deviate (e.g., revenge). 22. Distributive justice. Equality and impartiality. 23. Concepts of maintaining partner's expectations as a motive for conformity. Contract and trust.
VII. *Punitive Justice*	Standards and functions of punishment.	24. Punitive tendencies or expectations. (a) Notions of equating punishment and crime. 25. Functions or purpose of punishment.

level of development than the average, as happened under the Nazis. To indicate this possibility, Table 4 presents a sample of moral statements by Eichmann, almost all scored as Stage 1 and Stage 2 by various raters using a carefully defined rating manual. (Moral statements from Hitler's *Mein Kampf* are different in tone but are also scored mainly as Stage 1 or Stage 2.)

On the whole, however, public morality tends to be expressed or formulated by individuals capable of articulating a more advanced morality than that of the average man. It has been found experimentally[12] that preadolescents will learn or assimilate moral argumentation one level above their own more readily than they will assimilate moral argumentation one level below their own. Furthermore, though they do not learn or assimilate much of moral arguments two or more stages above their own, they choose them as "liked" much more than lower-level arguments. Active members of civil rights movements may often be moved by low-level themes of "black power," but most leaders of the movement, like Martin Luther King, tend to formulate reasons for civil disobedience in Stage 6 terms. It is not surprising, then, that most presidential and Supreme Court utterances are consistent with our definitions of Stage 5 (or Stage 6 in the case of Lincoln and others), even though they are above the majority level of response.

A UNIVERSAL DEFINITION OF MORALITY

Moral development in terms of these stages is a progressive movement toward basing moral judgment on concepts of justice. To base a moral

Table 3

Classification of Statements on One Aspect of Morality ("The Basis of Worth of Human Life") into Stages in the Development of Moral Judgment

Stages	Statements on "The Basis of Worth of Human Life"
Stage 1: The value of a human life is confused with the value of physical objects and is based on the social status or physical attributes of its possessor.	*Tommy, age ten* (Why should the druggist give the drug to the dying woman when her husband couldn't pay for it?): "If someone important is in a plane and is allergic to heights and the stewardess won't give him medicine because she's only got enough for one and she's got a sick one, a friend, in back, they'd probably put the stewardess in a lady's jail because she didn't help the important one." (Is it better to save the life of one important person or a lot of unimportant people?): "All the people that aren't important because one man just has one house, maybe a lot of furniture, but a whole bunch of people have an awful lot of furniture and some of these poor people might have a lot of money and it doesn't look it."
Stage 2: The value of a human life is seen as instrumental to the satisfaction of the needs of its possessor or of other persons.	*Tommy, age thirteen* (Should the doctor "mercy kill" a fatally ill woman requesting death because of her pain?): "Maybe it would be good to put her out of her pain, she'd be better off that way. But the husband wouldn't want it, it's not like an animal. If a pet dies you can get along without it — it isn't something you really need. Well, you can get a new wife, but it's not really the same."

Stage 3: The value of a human life is based on the empathy and affection of family members and others toward its possessor.

Andy, age sixteen (Should the doctor "mercy kill" a fatally ill woman requesting death because of her pain?): "No, he shouldn't. The husband loves her and wants to see her. He wouldn't want her to die sooner, he loves her too much."

Stage 4: Life is conceived as sacred in terms of its place in a categorical moral or religious order of rights and duties.

John, age sixteen (Should the doctor "mercy kill" the woman?): "The doctor wouldn't have the right to take a life, no human has the right. He can't create life, he shouldn't destroy it."

Stage 5: Life is valued both in terms of its relation to community welfare and in terms of being a universal human right.

Bob, age sixteen (Should the captain order the soldier on a suicide mission to save the company?): "If nobody wanted to volunteer, I don't think he has the right to make someone go. I don't know if the army rules give him the right not to go, but as a person in the world I think he has the right not to go. But if it would save so many other lives, he really should go. The captain would have to decide to send him if it's necessary to save all their lives."

Stage 6: Belief in the sacredness of human life as representing a universal human value of respect for the individual.

Steve, age sixteen (Should the husband steal the expensive drug to save his wife?): "By the law of society he was wrong but by the law of nature or of God the druggist was wrong and the husband was justified. Human life is above financial gain. Regardless of who was dying, if it was a total stranger, man has a duty to save him from dying."

duty on a concept of justice is to base it on the right of an individual, and to judge an act wrong is to judge it as violating such a right. The concept of a right implies a legitimate expectancy, a claim which I may expect others to agree I have. Though rights may be grounded on sheer custom or law, there are two general grounds of a right: equality and reciprocity (including exchange, contract, and the reward of merit). At Stages 5 and 6, all the demands of statute or of moral (natural) law are grounded on concepts of justice, i.e., on the agreement, contract, and impartiality of the law and its function in maintaining the rights of individuals. For reasons I have elaborated elsewhere,[13] it is quite reasonable psychologically to expect similar conceptions of justice to develop in every society, whether or not they become the official basis of political morality as they have in the United States.

FIGURE 1

Mean Per Cent of Use of Each of Six Stages of Moral Judgment

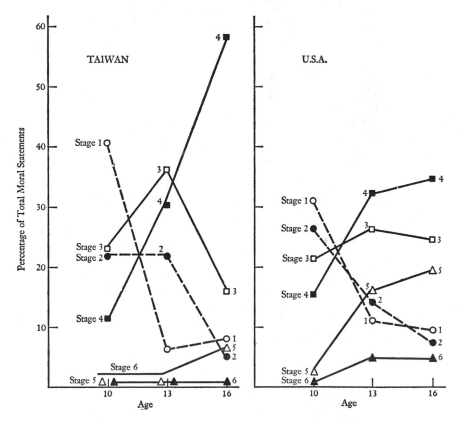

Table 4

Scoring of Moral Judgments of Eichmann
for Developmental Stage

Moral Judgments	Score*
In actual fact, I was merely a little cog in the machinery that carried out the directives of the German Reich.	1/7
I am neither a murderer nor a mass-murderer. I am a man of average character, with good qualities and many faults.	3/1
Yet what is there to "admit"? I carried out my orders. It would be pointless to blame me for the whole Final Solution of the Jewish Problem as to blame the official in charge of the railroads over which the Jewish transports traveled.	1/7
Where would we have been if everyone had thought things out in those days? You can do that today in the "new" German army. But with us an order was an order.	1/15
If I had sabotaged the order of the one-time Führer of the German Reich, Adolf Hitler, I would have been not only a scoundrel but a despicable pig like those who broke their military oath to join the ranks of the anti-Hitler criminals in the conspiracy of July 20, 1944.	1/1 1/1
I would like to stress again, however, that my department never gave a single annihilation order. We were responsible only for deportation.	2/7
My interest was only in the number of transport trains I had to provide. Whether they were bank directors or mental cases, the people who were loaded on these trains meant nothing to me. It was really none of my business.	2/3 2/7
But to sum it all up, I must say that I regret nothing. Adolf Hitler may have been wrong all down the line, but one thing is beyond dispute: the man was able to work his way up from lance corporal in the German army to Führer of a people of almost eighty million. I never met him personally, but his success alone proves to me that I should subordinate myself to this man. He was somehow so supremely capable that the people recognized him. And so with that justification I recognized him joyfully, and I still defend him.	1/6 1/17
I must say truthfully, that if we had killed all the ten million Jews that Himmler's statisticians originally listed in 1933, I would say, "Good, we have destroyed an enemy."	2/21
But here I do not mean wiping them out entirely. That would not be proper — and we carried on a proper war.	1/1

* The first code number in this column refers to Stages 1–6 (see Table 1); the second number refers to the aspect of morality involved (see Table 2).

To a large extent, a conception of moral development in terms of justice coincides with a culturally universal definition of morality. In my view, a culturally universal definition of morality can be arrived at if morality is thought of as the form of moral judgments instead of the content of specific moral beliefs. Although philosophers have been unable to agree upon any single ultimate principle which would define "correct" moral judgments, most philosophers concur on the characteristics which make a judgment a genuine moral judgment.[14]

Moral judgments are judgments about the right and the good of action. Not all judgments of "good" or "right" are moral judgments, however; many are judgments of aesthetic, technological, or prudential goodness or rightness. Unlike judgments of prudence or aesthetics, moral judgments tend to be universal, inclusive, consistent, and to be grounded on objective, impersonal, or ideal grounds. "She's really great! She's beautiful and a good dancer." "The right way to make a Martini is five-to-one." These are statements about the good and right, but they are not moral judgments since they lack the characteristics of the latter. If we say, "Martinis should be made five-to-one," we are making an aesthetic judgment; we are not prepared to say that we want everyone to make them that way, that they are good in terms of some impersonal ideal standard shared by others, and that we and others should make five-to-one Martinis whether we wish to or not.

In similar fashion, when a ten-year-old answers a "moral should" question, "Should Joe tell on his older brother?" in Stage 1 terms of the probabilities of getting beaten up by his father and by his brother, he does not answer with a moral judgment that is universal (applies to all about the situation) or that has any impersonal or ideal grounds. In contrast, Stage 6 statements not only specifically use moral words like "morally right" and "duty" but use them in a moral way: "Regardless of who it was," "By the law of nature or of God," imply universality; "Morally I would do it in spite of fear of punishment" implies impersonality and ideality of obligation, etc. Thus the responses of lower-level subjects to moral judgment matters are not moral responses in somewhat the same sense that the value judgments of high-level subjects about aesthetic or morally neutral matters are not moral. In this sense, we can define a moral judgment as "moral" without considering its content (the action judged) and without considering whether it agrees with our own judgments or standards. It is evident that our stages represent an increasing disentangling or differentiation of moral values and judgments from other types of values and judgments. With regard to the particular aspect, the value of life, defined in Table 2, the moral value of the person at Stage 6 has become progressively disentangled from status and property values (Stage 1), from his instrumental uses to others (Stage 2), from the actual affection of others for him (Stage 3), etc.

A definition of the aim of moral education as the stimulation of natural development appears, then, to be clear-cut in the area of moral judgment, which has considerable regularity of sequence and direction in development in various cultures. Because of this regularity, it is possible to define the maturity of a child's moral judgment without considering its content (the particular action judged) and without considering whether or not it agrees with our own particular moral judgments or values or those of the American middle-class culture as a whole. In fact, the sign of the child's moral maturity is his ability to make moral judgments and formulate moral principles of his own, rather than his ability to conform to moral judgments of the adults around him.

Moral Judgment and Moral Behavior

We have so far talked about the development of moral judgment as an aim of moral education. The sheer capacity to make genuinely moral judgments is only one portion of moral character, however. One must also apply this judgmental capacity to the actual guidance and criticism of action. Thus, in addition to stimulating the development of general moral judgment, a developmental moral education would stimulate the child's application of his own moral judgment (not the teacher's) to his actions. The effort to force a child to agree that an act of cheating is very bad when he does not really believe it will only encourage morally immature tendencies toward expedient outward compliance. In contrast, a more difficult but more valid approach involves getting the child to examine the pros and cons of his conduct in his own terms (as well as introducing more developmentally advanced considerations).

Although we cannot yet be sure that the stimulation of development of moral judgment will result in moral conduct, research indicating considerable correspondence between level of judgment and conduct in children provides some optimism on this score.[15]

Morality and Religion

It is clear that the conception of the words "moral" and "moral education" just advanced distinguishes moral judgment and development from other types of value judgment and development, including religious development. In fact, we find remarkably little use of religion in American children's responses to moral dilemmas, regardless of denomination. In less religiously pluralistic societies, like Turkey, more religious concepts are introduced into moral responses, but mostly at lower levels of development (Stages 1 through 4). Preadolescent Turkish boys typically say that one should not steal because "good Moslems don't steal" and because "God would punish you." They also believe it is worse to steal from a fellow Moslem than from a Christian. As they develop further, they elaborate more intrinsically moral or justice-based reasons for not stealing and use less "religious" reasons. At higher levels, religion may be invoked as the ultimate support for universal human values, but moral action is not justified in terms of conformity to God or to the religious community. Because a morality of justice evolves in every society or religious group, then, a morality of justice cannot be said to represent the beliefs of a religious sect like Humanism or Ethical Culture, or even to represent the "Judeo-Christian tradition."

Our evidence of culturally universal moral stages, then, is also direct evidence against the view that the development of moral ideologies depends upon the teachings of particular religious belief systems. No differences in moral development due to religious belief have yet been found. Protestant, Catholic, Moslem, and Buddhist children go through the same stages at much the same rate when social class and village-urban differences are held constant. With regard to the content of moral beliefs, religious differences exist, e.g., differences in views of birth control, divorce, eating pork, etc. When members of given religious groups attempt to support these beliefs, however, they fall back upon the general forms of moral judgment or moral principles described by the stages discussed above, forms which I said develop regardless of religious affiliation. The same distinctions between specific values and basic moral principles must be made in considering sociological studies of religious differences in values. For instance, values of educational and entre-preneurial achievement have been held to be favored by "the Protestant ethic" or the "Jewish ethic" as opposed to the "Catholic ethic." There is considerable evidence of such differential emphases in various religious traditions, but it should not obscure the common moral ideas and prin-ciples which seem to develop equally in all. All religious and non-religious belief systems distinguish worldly achievement from conformity to moral principles and stress the latter regardless of different notions of the linkage between the two.

Religious persons may readily accept the idea that moral principles develop regardless of religious belief. Since St. Thomas Aquinas, a great deal of theological doctrine has held that moral principles are grounded on natural reason rather than on revelation. It is more difficult, however, for most religious persons to accept the thought that actual behavioral adherence to moral principles is independent of religious belief or commit-ment. They feel that their morality and their religion are closely bound together. In a recent nationwide National Opinion Research Center survey, a large majority of Americans stated that their morality was dependent upon their religious beliefs. Subjectively they may be correct. Objectively, however, empirical studies, from Hartshorne and May[16] on-ward, have found no relation between experimental measures of honesty and type or amount of religious participation or education. Cross-national comparisons suggest the same conclusions as the Hartshorne and May findings. Theft, deceit, and juvenile delinquency are low in some atheistic societies (Soviet Russia, Israeli atheistic kibbutzim) as well as in some Buddhist and Christian societies, while some strongly religious nations have high rates of dishonesty (Islamic Middle Eastern nations, Italy, Mexico, etc.). Although we should not conclude from these and other findings that there is no relation between religious experience and moral character, we can conclude that religion is not a necessary or highly important condition for the development of moral judgment and conduct.[17]

In summarizing findings suggesting the very limited influence of religious education upon moral development, I am not attempting to argue that religious education may not be capable of playing a role in moral development. I am arguing that formal religious education has no specifically important or unique role to play in moral development as opposed to the role of the public school and the family in this area. The primary purpose of religious education in our society is not to develop moral character but rather to develop religious beliefs and sentiments. The teaching of religious beliefs requires a teaching of their moral aspects as well as their theological aspects, since all religions stress an associated moral code. On the whole, however, the mark of success of such teaching is that it helps the child to make his religious and his moral beliefs and sentiments an integrated whole, not that it leads to the formulation of basic moral values not formed elsewhere. Part-time religious education can hardly take as its goal fitting the child for moral citizenship, and is fortunate if it can achieve its primary goal of creating religious meanings in the child's experience.

The Classroom Climate

In contrast to institutions of part-time religious education, the public school is the most important environment of the child outside the home. While the Hartshorne and May findings did not show that specific religious or character education classes had a strong effect on moral conduct, they did demonstrate that the total school or classroom atmosphere had an extremely important influence on such conduct. By and large, basic morality develops "naturally" through a variety of intellectual and social stimulations in the home, the peer group, and the school; it does not require systematic programs of indoctrination. However, recent research suggests that the school may play a positive role in stimulating this development and suggests some lines along which it may be done.[18] Regardless of quantitative findings, the definition of the public school as fitting the child for citizenship and the pervasiveness of moral issues in classroom life and curriculum require explicit educational thought about the moral objectives of education. As an example, recent unpublished work by Grannis at Harvard suggests that teaching comprehension of law in an experimental social studies curriculum for preadolescents entails just the sort of stimulation of upward movement of stages of moral thought one might elaborate if one were concerned with moral education as an explicit school function. It would be unfortunate, then, if the outcome of the recent Supreme Court decision were to inhibit our recognition that an ultimate statement of the social aims and processes of public education must be couched in moral terms.

NOTES

1. L. Kohlberg, "Moral Education in the Schools: A Developmental View," *School Review*, 74:1–30 (1966).

2. My philosophical reasoning as to the relation of the schools to moral education is hardly original. It is largely a restatement of John Dewey (*Moral Principles in Education* [Houghton Mifflin, 1911]) and "The Schools and Religion" in *Character and Events* (Holt, 1929). A recent statement by the philosopher Michael Scriven (*Primary Philosophy* [McGraw-Hill, 1966]) forcefully develops a basically similar position, except that he advocates direct teaching of rational morality whereas I advocate indirect stimulating of its development.

3. I have attempted elsewhere (L. Kohlberg, *Stage and Sequence: The Developmental Approach to Moralization* [in preparation]) to define terms like "morality" and "justice" more explicitly and in a fashion which allows study of these concepts in any culture or society.

4. U. Bronfenbrenner, "Soviet Methods of Character Education: Some Implications for Research," *American Psychologist*, 17:550–565 (1962).

5. H. Hartshorne and M. A. May, *Studies in the Nature of Character:* Vol. I, *Studies in Deceit;* Vol. II, *Studies in Self-Control;* Vol. III, *Studies in the Organization of Character* (Macmillan, 1928–1930). V. Jones, *Character and Citizenship Gaining in the Public School* (University of Chicago Press, 1936). R. J. Havighurst and H. Taba, *Adolescent Character and Personality* (Wiley, 1949).

6. Unpublished data, some reported on an NBC television special in January, 1966.

7. Havighurst and Taba, *op. cit.*

8. Hartshorne and May, *op. cit.*

9. L. Kohlberg, "The Development of Moral Character and Ideology," in M. and L. Hoffman (eds.), *Review of Child Development Research* (Russell Sage, 1964).

10. Justice (respect for the rights of others based on considerations of equality and reciprocity) includes the other cardinal American value of liberty. It also partially includes the second major moral value of benevolence (consideration of the welfare of all other individuals).

11. Kohlberg, "Moral Education in the Schools," and *Stage and Sequence: The Developmental Approach to Moralization.*

12. E. Turiel, "An Experimental Analysis of Developmental Stages in the Child's Moral Judgment," *Journal of Personality and Social Psychology,* 1966.

13. Kohlberg, *Stage and Sequence.*

14. R. M. Hare, *The Language of Morals* (New York: Oxford University Press, 1952) and I. Kant, *Fundamental Principles of the Metaphysics of Morals* (New York: Liberal Arts Press, 1949).

15. Kohlberg, "Moral Education in the Schools."

16. Hartshorne and May, *op. cit.*

17. Relations between conduct and religious experience may be more apparent where the given moral behavior depends largely upon specific religious proscriptions than where it is based upon general secular principles of justice. In contrast to findings on honesty, Kinsey (A. C. Kinsey *et al.*, *Sexual Behavior in the Human Female* [W. B. Saunders, 1953]) indicates that both premarital and extramarital sexual behavior is related to religious devoutness and, to a slighter extent, to religious denomination. The suggestion is also that subjective moral attitudes may be related to moral behavior even if the amount of institutional religious exposure is not. However, we cannot safely draw either of these conclusions because moral attitudes may determine religious ones rather than the reverse. For example, the Kinsey finding may be due to the tendency of young people who fear or condemn sexuality to become religiously devout rather than vice versa.

18. Kohlberg, "Moral Education in the Schools."

II

Education and Community

Fred M. Newmann and Donald W. Oliver

This essay presents a dissenting view of prevailing concepts of education and approaches to educational reform.[1] Reforms currently directed at American schools are grounded in conceptual and institutional frameworks that fail to confront the most fundamental problems of our age. We shall outline the nature of these problems, suggest ways in which education in America both reflects and exacerbates the problems, and finally sketch the outlines of an educational model more appropriate to the challenges of modern America.

Two Interpretations of Modern American Society

We assume that the most fundamental objective of education is the development of individual human dignity, or "self-realization" within community. The broadly stated objective can be specified in many ways, emphasizing either individualism or social association. However one defines dignity or fulfillment, the nature of the society within which it develops is critical. As Kateb points out,

First, the relation between social practices and institutions and the self is not simply one of support or encouragement. To put it that way is to imply that there could be selves without society, that society is at most a device for helping the self to do what it could do alone but only very laboriously, and that eventually the self can outgrow society and be realized in splendid isolation. The plain truth is that without a society there are no selves, that, as Aristotle said, the community is prior to the individual, that the selves to be realized are given their essential qualities by their societies, and that the process of self-realization is a process of continuous involvement with society, as society not only shapes but employs everyone's inner riches. The upshot is that thought about possible styles of life or about the nature of man is necessary to give sense to the idea of individuality. Far from being an oppressive encroachment, social theory (utopian or not) is a basic duty.[2]

Kateb's point applied to education means that educational policy should be based on deliberation and inquiry into needs of the individual within community. Every educator faithful to this premise should be able, therefore, to explicate and clarify the particular conception of society or community upon which he justifies educational recommendations.

Contemporary American civilization can be interpreted with reference to two general concepts: missing community and great society. The former concept embraces the effects of industrialization, urbanization, specialization, and technology that tend to destroy man's sense of relatedness, to disintegrate common bonds, to increase apathy, depersonalization, and loss of identity and meaning in the human career. By way of contrast, the vision of a great society exudes a sturdy optimism in man's progress, a desire to accelerate urbanization, technology, and economic development, on the assumption that such inevitable historical forces can be harnessed to make man freer, more secure and allow him to be more "human" than ever before. Education for the great society involves raising teacher salaries, building more schools, using computers and audio-visual devices to supply training and meet the manpower needs of the "national interest." Seen from a missing-community perspective, however, the major objectives of education involve the creation and nourishment of diverse styles of life which allow for significant choice in the reconstruction of community relationships; formal training and "national interest" are of minor significance. Before delving into the two theories, however, we must examine the concept of community, for its definition lies at the heart of the distinction between the missing-community and the great-society views of America.

REDEFINING COMMUNITY

Nineteenth-century sociologists (and earlier thinkers as well) compared human relationships and groups by reference to a general construct bounded at one end by the concept "community" and at the other by "society." [3] The former signifies a closely knit, generally self-sufficient, rural group in which the extended family serves not only the function of procreation, but also the functions of economic production, education, recreation, religion, care of the sick and aged, safety, and defense. Individuals in such a group know each other well; they share common experiences and traditions; they depend upon each other and assume responsibility for solving group problems. The style of life varies inappreciably from one generation to the next. A sharp contrast to this type of group is mass society, in which large numbers of people, within an urban industrial environment, are influenced by many institutions, each with its separate function: education, religion, economic production, defense, medicine, recreation, care of the aged, legal responsibility, and political control. People shift their places of residence, change their occupations, and follow living styles quite different from those of previous generations. Because of mobility, specialization, and a rapid rate of change, people have less in common with one another, weaker ties to a basic or primary group; their allegiances and loyalties are diffused among many instead of focused on one social unit.

Relationships within community have been described as "organic," and "natural," while societal relationships are seen as "mechanical" and "rational." Community becomes an end in itself, whereas society is a means toward other separate ends. Thus did Tönnies distinguish between *Gemeinschaft* (community) and *Gesellschaft* (society), the former based on shared intimacy and interdependence — the folkways and mores of primary groups; the latter signifying impersonal, logical, formally contractual relationships inherent in commerce, science, and bureaucracy. Tönnies helps to clarify the distinction by asserting that in community human relationships are characterized by acquaintance, sympathy, confidence, and interdependence, whereas in society relationships reveal strangeness, antipathy, mistrust, and independence.

Conventional sociological definitions of community emphasize (1) a set of households concentrated within a limited geographical area; (2) substantial social interaction between residents; (3) a sense of common membership, of belonging together, not based exclusively on kinship ties. The essential criterion seems to be a psychological one: "a sense of common bond," the sharing of an identity, holding things in common esteem.[4] Communities are frequently identified by references to legal-political boundaries (cities, towns, states), ethnic groups (Jewish community or Negro community), occupational classifications (labor or business community), or simply areas of residence (an apartment building or neighborhood block).

We should like to offer a more general definition which should be viewed as a continuum; that is, it is possible to have greater and lesser degrees of community, depending upon the extent to which each of the following criteria are fulfilled. A community is a group of people (1) in which membership is valued as an end in itself, not merely as a means to other ends; (2) that concerns itself with many and significant aspects of the lives of members; (3) that contains competing factions; (4) whose members share commitment to common purpose and to procedures for handling conflict within the group; (5) whose members share responsibility for the actions of the group; and (6) whose members have enduring and extensive personal contact with one another. Using this as a working definition, it should be clear that residence, political units, occupations, etc., may or may not be valid boundaries by which to distinguish one community from another.

As we speak of "missing community," we are constantly reminded how foolish it is to wish for the establishment in the modern world of communities similar to the rural traditional model. We are told that either (1) such communities never did exist; or (2) they may have existed, but they were certainly not very pleasant — on the contrary, human life in the bygone community contained anxieties and problems more tragic than the ones we face today; or (3) they may have existed and were delightful, but inevitable forces have pushed them aside and it is impossible to turn back the clock. If, however, we can conceive of community in terms of our general definition, each of these points immediately becomes irrelevant. The definition makes no historical claims, nor does it implore a return to days of old. Our only claim is that in the modern world, community (as defined above) is missing.

This is not to say that the number of associations and human groups has decreased. On the contrary, we find more organizations than ever before: professional associations, credit unions, churches, corporations, political parties, labor unions, civil rights groups, sportsmen's clubs, and also families. Yet few, if any, of them fulfill our definition of community, mainly because of the relatively special and narrow functions that each serves. The emergence of many institutions, with specialized functions, has created discontinuities, such as the major one described by Nisbet:

> Our present crisis lies in the fact that whereas the small traditional associations, founded upon kinship, faith, or locality, are still expected to communicate to individuals the principal moral ends and psychological gratifications of society, they have manifestly become detached from positions of functional relevance to the larger economic and political decisions of our society.
>
> Family, local community, church, and the whole network of informal interpersonal relationships have ceased to play a determining role in our institutional systems of mutual aid, welfare, education, recreation, and economic production and distribution. Yet despite the loss of these manifest institutional functions, we continue to expect them to perform adequately the implicit psychological or symbolic functions in the life of the individual.[5]

What institutions *do* perform psychological or symbolic functions necessary for viable community? In mass society few can be found, and Nisbet traces the historical developments that account for their disappearance. He sees at the root of the problem the growth of a centralized economic and political system which by concentrating on serving *individual* needs has neglected and eroded community. Objectives of the "great society" are to provide selected products and services: housing, jobs, food, education, medical aid, transportation, recreation for individuals, and centralized bureaucracies now meet many of these particular needs. But the process of centralization and specialization has caused the breakdown of communication among differing groups, the rise of transient, rather than enduring, relationships among people, the disintegration of common bonds, and the reluctance to share collective responsibility. Whether it is possible to create new forms of community appropriate for urban and industrial society should be of great concern in planning for education. The extent to which one takes this problem seriously depends largely upon whether he accepts a *missing community* or *great society* frame of reference. These contrasting ways of construing social issues and educational needs are described below.

THE MISSING COMMUNITY

Modern technological society proceeds at an ever increasing rate toward the breakdown of conditions requisite to human dignity. Neither the contented, "other-directed," "organization man," nor the "American female," nor the "alienated youth" finds genuine integrity or a sense of relatedness to the human community. Experience becomes atomized, fragmented, and humans become "encapsulated," as occupational specialization and social isolation make it difficult for diverse groups to communicate effectively with each other. Human relationships take on mechanistic qualities and become determined, not by tradition, human feeling, or spontaneous desires, but by impersonal machines or bureaucratic flow charts. Career patterns, social roles, and environment change rapidly, producing conflicting demands on the individual, which threatens the establishment of "identity." The size, complexity, and interdependence of political and economic institutions dwarf the significance of the individual. The destiny of community appears to be guided by either elite, inaccessible power blocs or by impersonal forces (such as technology) insensitive to individual protest or opinion. People lack direction and commitment, betraying either a lethargic denial of basic problems, ambiguity and conflict regarding value choices, or outright repudiation of a concern for significant choices.[6]

The first theme prominent in the missing-community view is the *fragmentation* of life. Modern society, it is argued, accelerates specialization, division of labor, and personal isolation, making it difficult for the individual to relate to other human beings outside of a narrow social class or vocational group. The inability to associate or communicate beyond the limits of one's special "place" is destructive to a sense of identity within community, because community demands the ability to perceive (or at least unconsciously assume) relatedness among a variety of people, institutions, stages of life, and events.

Second — and related to isolation or fragmentation — is the theme of *change*. In a way, the essence of American character is a zeal for change, yet the exponential rate of social change in modern society tends to destroy the essential stability required to establish relatedness among people (or between people and the physical environment). Social change aggravates the difficulties of one generation's relating to the next; it thwarts the observing or sensing of continuity within the human career; and it places considerable strain on the human personality by primarily valuing adjustment and flexibility.

Third, critics decry our present state of *ideological and aesthetic bankruptcy*. It is argued that modern society through a reverence for technology cultivates excessive stress on the fulfillment of *instrumental* values, with scant attention being paid to ends or ideals. Mass culture discourages bold or utopian thought. It has slight regard for beauty and contemplation because it directs its major energy toward producing greater quantities of goods with less effort. The quantitative, rather than qualitative, emphasis is most evident in the pursuit of mass materialism, the cult of the consumer. Commitment to conspicuous consumption and techniques or means of social mobility seems to outweigh commitment to what may be considered more vague or visionary ends such as social justice, personal salvation, or the attainment of inner virtue. Total emphasis on the instrumental and the material (it is argued) is harmful because commitment to more intangible ideals is a prime requisite for building a sense of individual worth.

Fourth, and centrally related to all of these themes, is the trend toward *depersonalization* (or impersonalization) of experience, typically noted in "humanist" attacks upon the influence of automation and cybernetics. Delegating to machines a vast number of tasks and activities formerly performed by humans, whether at the factory or in the selection of courtship partners, erodes our ability to discriminate the more subtle, less easily communicated differences among human beings — the differences that make each person unique. Not only automation but a variety of conditions of modern and suburban living (specialization, extreme transiency or mobility, geographic isolation of production and consumption) stifle the development of meaningful interpersonal experience. Outcries against depersonalization — the prospect of man's being governed totally by computer-based, predictable decisions — reveal widespread concern over this problem.

Finally, the missing community is characterized by a feeling of *powerlessness* — the sense that no individual has significant control over his own destiny. Powerlessness becomes a central issue in American culture because of its contradiction of premises of liberal political thought, namely that the destiny of the community is determined by the wishes of individuals, by the consent of the governed, rather than by unresponsive elites, aloof bureaucracies, or impersonal forces. But in the face of such conditions as impersonal bureaucracies, the growing influence of corporate structures both concentrated and diffuse, and extreme social mobility and change, it is difficult for the individual to see how he affects the determination of social policy or the making of decisions that have profound effects on his life.

The consequences of these five themes, leading to internal states of feeling and thought characteristically labeled anomie, alienation, disaffection, identity diffusion, estrangement of man from himself and community, can be viewed from a psychological standpoint; but a psychological interpretation is difficult to establish for two reasons: first, because of problems in accurately assessing inner psychic conditions, and second, because of the possibility that people may believe themselves to be contented when in fact they are unconsciously disillusioned and their community is proceeding to a condition of irretrievable disaster. Thus it is particularly important to examine the various themes not only from the standpoint of reports of "how people feel" but also from more detached and analytic perspectives of changing institutions: roles and functions of family, religion, occupation; procedures for attaining justice in metropolitan and bureaucratic environments; or legal-political arrangements for resolving various kinds of human conflict. In other words, one might see community "missing" in two basic senses: in terms of individuals' feelings about it or in terms of a developing institutional framework inimical to the pursuit of human dignity.

THE GREAT SOCIETY

Opposed to the missing community interpretation is the more optimistic view that conditions in modern America will lead not to the demise but on the contrary to more hopeful forms of "self-realization." Our economic, political, and social institutions offer virtually unlimited promise for the meeting of material needs, the establishment of justice, the cultivation of creativity, and other elements associated with conceptions of the good life. Having reached a level of "high mass consumption," our system may now proceed to stress the development of advanced forms of human service — education, medical care, recreation, psychological counseling, community planning.[7] The accelerated growth of technology offers unprecedented opportunity for solving persistent human problems, whether in the field of meaningful work, extending the life-span, beautifying the countryside, or increasing the motivation of children to learn.[8] The political system, having zealously guarded basic rights and freedoms, continues on a solid basis of consensus, while still encouraging dissent and experimentation with new approaches to public issues.[9]

The great society interpretation has answers for points raised in the missing community view. First we notice a tendency to deny factual claims made in the latter. For example, evidence is gathered to show that most people work in small firms rather than large bureaucracies, performing personal human services rather than manufacturing goods on impersonal assembly lines.[10] Advances in communication and transportation, far from creating divisive fragmentation, have produced unforeseen possibilities for people of widely differing backgrounds to share common experience. Automation has not produced impersonal, mechanistic individuals but has freed individuals to be more genuinely human than ever before.[11] People do in fact have power to determine the destiny of the community through their participation in groups designed specifically for the pursuit of given interests. (Bell mentions some of the thousands of groups which Americans join — evidence both that man is not alone and that his groups give him power to protect his basic interests.[12]) Rather than apologizing for a lack of ideological commitment, one might adduce evidence of fervent commitment to basic and traditional American values such as equality of opportunity, general welfare, etc. The Peace Corps, poverty programs, and civil rights advances attest to this. By reference to figures on the publishing industry and the state of the arts one might also argue that aesthetic appreciation and activity are flourishing more than ever.

The great-society school would accept the existence of many tendencies mentioned in the missing community view: specialization, rapid change, technology, etc. It would argue, however, that their effects are beneficial rather than harmful. For example, specialization and division of labor are said to provide additional alternatives or areas of choice never before open to the individual. A highly differentiated and specialized society offers greater possibilities for meeting specific interests, idiosyncratic skills, and desires. Though change does proceed rapidly, it has the refreshing effect of insuring flexibility, a safeguard against stagnation in fixed styles of living and thinking. Automation and technology also have liberating influences, allowing individuals to pursue interpersonal relationships less constrained by the demands of the environment or material needs. While decisions on important matters may be left in the hands of diffuse bureaucracies or distant "experts," and less directly connected with individual will, bureaucracy and expertise make helpful contributions in the process of decision making and management of human affairs.

The optimism inherent in the great society view does not dampen its fervor in attacking a number of social problems. The National Commission on Technology, Automation and Economic Progress refers to several "social costs and dislocations" caused by technological advance: the rapid migration of rural workers to the city; the decrease in the number of factory production and maintenance jobs; economic distress due to closing of plants; pollution of the water and air; and life below the poverty level for thirty-five million people. Yet the Commission concludes, "Technology has, on balance, surely been a great blessing to mankind — despite the fact that some of the benefits have been offset by costs. There should be no thought of deliberately slowing down the rate of technological advancement. . . ."[13] The Commission's report and others[14] call for bold and inventive new approaches to the solution of serious social problems, but the basic tasks are seen as "unfinished business," or cleanup operations within a general context of unprecedented prosperity and social accomplishment. There is no inclination to debate or question ultimate goals, but only to confront practical problems of putting existing institutions to work, of devising "programs" to fulfill unquestioned objectives (such as full employment, higher teacher salaries, or stability in the Negro family). The solution of problems as construed in the great-society approach does not require changes in the institutional structure of society at large.[15]

Two major reasons are offered by the great society for not questioning current social trends. First, much of what is objected to (urbanization, automation, specialization, rapid change, etc.) arises as part of an inevitable stream of social development that has inevitable social costs. Second, challenging the fundamental premises and organization of the society would result in irrevocable rupture, chaos, destructive revolution, shattering the foundations of modern society rather than improving it. This is what Keniston calls the argument of "psycho-social vise."[16]

Finally, the proponent of the great society "explains away" many of the missing-community criticisms. He claims that critics who embrace the missing-community view cling to an outdated and inappropriate frame of reference, a characteristically Lockean or Jeffersonian idea of society — an agrarian community of yeomen, artisans, and gentlemen-aristocrats living a relatively stable existence, close to nature, with deep-rooted personal relationships and simple social organization whereby individuals exercise power in a way that in fact determines their own destiny. Great society enthusiasts reject the missing-community view by pointing out that the concepts of individuality and community take on entirely new meaning in modern society. For example, consent of the governed should not be grounded in the simpleminded notion that each individual can influence decision makers in government; realistically, influence must be exerted by joining large pressure groups. Or, meaningful work should no longer be judged in terms of obsolete notions of craftsmanship, or pursuing a task from origin to completion; rather, white-collar administrative work within a bureaucracy has important meaning but in a different sense. Modern society cannot be realistically judged through the lenses of what Keniston calls "romantic regression."

CHOOSING BETWEEN INTERPRETATIONS

An adequate evaluation of the merits of each interpretation requires extended investigation, and this paper is only the beginning of our efforts to move the inquiry along. The interpretations presented above are not intended as comprehensive social theories, but as two broadly sketched descriptive statements which contain, on the one hand, clear overtones of protest against current social development and, on the other, a self-assured optimism over the political, economic, and technological character of the "great society." For the moment, we are more persuaded by the missing-community view. We believe that in general the great society orientation is more sensitive to superficial symptoms than to fundamental problems, while the missing-community idea attacks major issues directly.

By way of example, consider the contrasting approaches to the "problem of old age." The great society approach focuses on the attainment of fairly obvious kinds of material needs to reduce direct "burdens" that the aged can impose on the young: guaranteed medical treatment, guaranteed income, physical environments sensitive to the physical capabilities of the aged (fewer stairs to climb, convenient transportation, moderate climate, etc.). The missing-community approach, however, points up the far-reaching impact of programs aimed only at these things. In catering to the specific needs of the aged, we have created entire communities of "senior citizens," segregated and literally fenced off from the rest of society. Their physical isolation helps to reinforce a self-fulfilling mystique about old age which Rosenfelt describes thus:

> Health and vigor, it is assumed, are gone forever. The senses have lost their acuity. The memory is kaput. Education and new learning are out of the question, as one expects to lose his mental faculties with age. Adventure and creativity are for the young and courageous. They are ruled out for the old, who are, *ipso facto*, timid and lacking in moral stamina.
>
> . . . .
>
> While the old person is taking stock of himself, he might as well become resigned to being "behind the times," for it is inconceivable he should have kept abreast of them. As a worker, he has become a liability. His rigidity, his out-of-date training, his proneness to disabling illness, not to mention his irritability, lowered efficiency and arrogant manner, all militate against the likelihood of his being hired or promoted.
>
> . . . .
>
> Nothing is to be expected from the children. They have their own lives to lead. Furthermore, they are leading them, like as not, in distant locations, bridged only by the three-minute phone call on alternate Sundays, if contact is maintained at all. . . . Grandparents make people more nervous than it's worth — easier to get a babysitter, and the youngsters like it better that way.[17]

The aged are not only isolated but clearly discriminated against when it comes to basic decisions in medical services: the life of a young person is generally more highly valued.[18] A missing-community concern with old age focuses on general questions such as the relationship between the quality of aged life and the nature of community — the meaning of "retirement" in an age of constantly changing careers and universal leisure; the challenge of creating integral relationships among generations.

As another illustration, consider two ways of construing the problem of the automobile in America. As Detroit increases its auto production, the great society proposes solutions to relatively specific problems: build more highways, clear the polluted air with special mufflers, and require more effective safety standards. Those viewing the auto from a missing-community framework would focus on such issues as (1) the changes in styles of life caused by the auto (e.g., the fact that we may live, work, and spend weekends in separate geographic areas) and their implications for "community"; (2) the possibility that the auto serves the function of psychological protest against modern society by providing one of the few opportunities for man to enjoy power, freedom, and (for young people) privacy; (3) the changes in our sensitivity to the physical environment (the building of highways, gaudy signs, junkyards, parking lots) that affect aesthetic experience and the conservation of natural resources.

The great society neglects the basic issues of community by focusing instead on relatively immediate individual needs and creating *national* organizations to meet them. The President says, "Our goal is not just a job for every worker. Our goal is to place every worker in a job where he utilizes his full productive potential for his own and for society's benefit."[19] The target is the individual worker, the bureaucracy is the Department of Labor, and, of course, we have an eminent National Commission on Technology, Automation and Economic Progress which, in a far-sighted manner, proclaims that the conditions of work must be "humanized" and we must allow for a flexible life-span of work. Expansive programs are justified and evaluated by reference to the "national interest" (or — above — to "society's benefits").[20] Great-society thinking reveals a huge gap, a vacuum, between the concepts of national interest and the dignity of the individual. That gap is the symptom of missing community. The major issues lie *between* obvious economic needs of individuals and the national interest: in creating complex relationships where humans share common bonds, strengthened not by consensus but by conflict and diversity, where they associate for enduring and important purposes, where national interest is only *one* of many competing ways to justify policy. Whereas the missing-community view gives these issues the highest priority, the great-society approach virtually ignores them.

The great-society view, in its attention to immediate and specific needs, tends to neglect and stifle consideration of basic, long-range issues. The missing-community view, on the other hand, attunes itself to forces and trends that suggest ominous consequences for the human condition. This, we feel, provides the sort of healthy discontent required to construe and deal with major problems. Our sense of missing community, though clearly influenced by conceptions of former social organization (in this country and other cultures), is *not* based on a nostalgic desire to restore types of communities long obsolete and inappropriate for the modern world. Community is "missing" not in the sense that "old-fashioned" communities no longer exist but in the sense that we have not yet devised conceptions of community that deal with particular challenges of the modern environment. To further explore implications of the missing-community view, we shall examine its relevance to trends in American education.

A Re-examination of Some Premises of Contemporary American Education

The acceptance of existing social trends characteristic of the great-society advocate is perhaps one of his more serious limitations. He sees the present as manifesting historically irreversible conceptions of society, e.g., "technology," "urbanization," or "centralization." Desirable outcomes of obvious historical forces are labeled "progress" (e.g., increased leisure), while adverse consequences are called the "price of progress" (e.g., the increasing loss of privacy, or the threat of nuclear war). Applied to education, this perspective postulates that we have a type of education, with us here and now, that is obviously consistent with our equalitarian democratic heritage, and, although it may have problems, we can build on the foundation that history has provided. But from the missing-community point of view, one scrutinizes historical trends as possible *roots* of present problems — roots that may need to be destroyed rather than built upon. The process of evaluating tradition (rather than accepting it as a "foundation") allows one to identify a broad range of alternatives and to question the extent to which they may be applicable to present choices. Honest inquiry leads one to ask whether future actions should be built on prior historical choices, or whether one might reconsider the premises underlying the initial choices themselves.

Because of its apparent inability to re-examine, in either contemporary or historical terms, the major premises underlying its approach to education, the great-society view manifests a narrow construction of what education is and ought to be. It accepts the premises that "education" is (1) formal schooling, operating as (2) a public monopoly, (3) modeled after the organizational structure and utilitarian values of corporate business. Great-society proposals for educational change take these as traditional, inevitable, "given" conditions rather than simply as one peculiar set of options against which a number of alternatives may be continually argued and tested. We shall raise questions with these premises, questions suggesting that it is time, not simply for "reform," but for a radical re-evaluation of our present conception of education and schooling.

EDUCATION AS FORMAL SCHOOLING

To most Americans the term "education" is synonymous with schooling, defined as formal instruction carried on in an institution which has no other purpose. In conventional rhetoric one "gets" an education by going to school. One therefore *improves* education by improving schools. Whether we read progressives,[21] traditionalists,[22] public educational statesmen,[23] prominent professors venturing into curriculum reform,[24] or contemporary analysts of education in America,[25] we find universal agreement that better education requires better schooling.

Federal and foundation monies are channeled into hundreds of projects designed to improve instruction in the schools. New approaches such as team teaching, programmed instruction, non-graded schools, the use of computers, simulation, and educational television are all designed to improve schooling (though they might be adapted to other environments). Millions are spent to prepare the "disadvantaged" for success in school by preschool training programs, to prevent adolescents from dropping out of school, to train teachers to teach in school. In addition to the traditional elementary, secondary, college sequence, we aim to improve education by creating more schools: summer schools, night schools, graduate and professional schools.

The proliferation of schools leads one to ponder whether it might be possible to become educated without going to school, without going through a process of conscious formalized instruction in institutions designed only for that function. Bailyn notes the emergence of formal schools in the Anglo-American colonies as a historical development responding to radical social changes. He boldly suggests that even before formal schools emerged people did acquire most of their effective education through less formal processes.

> The forms of education assumed by the first generation of settlers in America were a direct inheritance from the medieval past. Serving the needs of a homogeneous, slowly changing rural society, they were largely instinctive and traditional, little articulated and little formalized. The most important agency in the transfer of culture was not formal institutions of instruction or public instruments of communication, but the family. . . .
> . . . the family's educational role was not restricted to elementary socialization. Within these kinship groupings, skills that provided at least the first step in vocational training were taught and practiced. In a great many cases, as among the agricultural laboring population and small tradesmen who together comprised the overwhelming majority of the population, all the vocational instruction necessary for mature life was provided by the family. . . .

What the family left undone by way of informal education the local community most often completed. It did so in entirely natural ways, for so elaborate was the architecture of family organization and so deeply founded was it in the soil of stable, slowly changing village and town communities in which intermarriage among the same groups had taken place generation after generation that it was at times difficult for the child to know where the family left off and the greater society began. . . .

More explicit in its educational function than either family or community was the church. . . . It furthered the introduction of the child to society by instructing him in the system of thought and imagery which underlay the culture's values and aims. . . .

Family, community, and church together accounted for the greater part of the mechanism by which English culture transferred itself across the generations. The instruments of deliberate pedagogy, of explicit, literature education, accounted for a smaller, though indispensable, portion of the process. . . . The cultural burdens it bore were relatively slight. . . .[26]

The modern American, however, no longer construes family, church, or other community agencies as vital educational institutions. He is in fact still in the process of distilling from other institutions their normal educative functions and transferring them to the school — e.g., vocational training, auto safety and driver training, rehabilitation of the disadvantaged, early childhood training, homemaking. The consequences of assuming that education necessarily takes place in school, or *should* take place in school, have been profound and far reaching, and require serious re-examination.

The allocation of the educational functions of society to a single separate institution — the school — suggests that such an institution must have a unique responsibility and that the separation must somehow be intrinsically related to the responsibility. This assumption becomes highly suspect when we look at three important aspects of the separation: (1) We conceive of education as necessarily "preparation" and carefully separate "learning" from "acting," "doing," or productive work; (2) we separate the school environment from the "non-instructional" life of the community at large; and (3) we construe *teaching* as a specialized occupation, whose work is isolated from the world of action and decision-making that has no apparent pedagogical function.

Education as Preparation. The establishment of formal schooling is commonly justified on the ground that we need a specialized institution to "prepare" children and youth for life as productive adults. The value of education is seen as instrumental, leading to ends extrinsic from the processes of formal instruction itself. We get an education *now* so that at some *later* time we can earn money, vote intelligently, raise children, serve our country, and the like. The preparatory emphasis implies closure

— education is begun and finished. Graduation or "commencement" signifies the termination of learning and the beginning of real life. Education in America most often consists of formal training through discrete courses and programs. How many institutions have we designed to foster education, not as preparatory activity, but as a legitimate end in itself, insinuated as a continuing integral element throughout one's career?

Preparatory aims of formal schooling are often embedded in a concept of growth. As Bruner remarks, "Instruction is, after all, an effort to assist or to shape growth."[27] To implement such a mandate, schools have isolated children and adolescents from adults and have focused most of the formal training on young people. This procedure, however, betrays a confusion between biological and mental development. Let us assume that the schools should be primarily concerned with mental-emotional development (they can have relatively minor effects on biological growth). First, is it possible to make a useful distinction between people who are "growing" and people who have "matured" with regard to mental-emotional development? One could argue that adulthood, far from being a period of stable maturity, is no more than a continuing process of mental-emotional growth (and biological change) presenting conflicts and problems of adjustment as "stormy" and challenging as growth during childhood and adolescence. Marriage, child-rearing, occupational decision, pursuit of leisure, adaptation to geographic and occupational change, and adjustment to "retirement" and death continually demand "growth" by adults. With the entirety of a human life cycle before us, we would ask, When is mental-emotional maturity reached? If growth, change, and decay continue until death, why confine education to the early years of biological development?

Second, by assuming young people to be dynamic and growing and adults to be static and ripe, one is led to postulate that adults have needs essentially different from those of young people — that conflicts and differences *between* generations are greater than conflicts and differences within a given generation. We would suggest, however, that members of differing generations do have common problems and educational needs, and the needs of members of the same generation may be radically diverse. Compare, for example, an unemployed man of forty with an unemployed teenage dropout, both of whom lack literacy and vocational skills. Could they not share with benefit a common educational experience? Or suppose an oppressed ethnic group is attempting to combat discrimination. Members of that group from all generations face a common problem. Conversely, groups *within* a generation may have quite different educational needs: a thirty-year-old mother on public assistance and a thirty-year-old attorney attempting to establish a law practice, or a teenage girl from a broken lower-class home and a teenage boy from a stable upper-class family.

Our exclusive emphasis on preparation raises another basic question: Is it possible that, in spite of certain commonalities across generations, childhood and adolescence constitute in themselves integral parts of the human career, with certain roles, needs, and behaviors quite unrelated to the demands of a future adulthood? Schools are designed mainly to implant in students knowledge, attitudes, and skills revered by adult scholars and educators, yet we can legitimately ask why it is necessary to stress almost exclusively adult values before children and youth have attained that biological and social status.

We also note a certain pragmatic folly in education as preparation for future adulthood in the modern world. A leading educational innovator comments on "the colossal problem of educating youngsters for jobs which do not exist and for professions which cannot be described."[28] Is it even possible to prepare children to behave fruitfully in a future world, the dimensions and complexities of which educated adults are unable to grasp?

The tendency of formal schooling to isolate children during a period of "preparation" for adulthood has produced a rigid system of age-grading which has as one effect a fractionation of the human career. This tends to hinder the development of meaningful relationships among generations and cultivates a fragmented, rather than continuous, concept of self. The prevailing idea that children can learn only *from*, not with, adults and the forced submission of youth to the rule of adults amplifies the conflict between generations and encourages a posture of dependence, a sense of powerlessness that may carry over from youth to adulthood.

School and the Community at Large. A sizable portion of school training is separated from and has no significant effect on students' behavior outside of school mainly because of the isolation of the school establishment from problems, dilemmas, choices, and phenomena encountered beyond school walls. Teachers readily attest to students' capacity to "tune out," or to memorize but not apply lessons taught in school. There is a sense of unreality inherent in living in two discontinuous worlds, if one is to take both seriously.

The progressives tried to handle this separation by bringing more "real life" activities into the school. They tried to match "work" in school with work in real life, introducing various manual skills and decision-making activities similar to those occurring outside of school. Modern efforts in curriculum reform have pursued the same idea through the development of "simulation" activities — attempts to make school more relevant to non-instructional concerns. But "simulation" still occurs within *instructional* contexts and is, therefore, detached from actual and significant concerns. It may cultivate an attitude that learning or life or both are synonymous with "playing games." The attempt to make school "fun" by exploiting the motivational power of competition or curiosity in children simply avoids the challenge of applying learning to life outside the school. In spite of progressive efforts in the direction of anti-formalism (for example, allowing students more individual freedom, emphasizing play and a variety of arts and crafts), the effect was largely to solidify a conception of education as equivalent to formal schooling. In fact, the most dramatic way for the progressive to demonstrate his ideas was to found a new *school*, which soon become isolated from genuine conflicts and decisions of students' lives beyond school walls.

Teaching as a Specialized Occupation.   Formal schooling provided the basis for a new specialized "profession of education." As Cremin has pointed out, the profession was quick to isolate itself from other professions and fields of knowledge.[29] It also built an educational establishment dedicated to the study, servicing, and expansion of formal schooling as a separate and discrete institution, often accumulating powerful vested interests irrelevant to the real improvement of education.[30] As an alternative to the unquestioned policy of requiring professionally trained teachers in schools, one might argue that in fact students could gain valuable education from each other and from a variety of "untrained" though interesting individuals — blue-collar laborers, politicians, bureaucrats, criminals, priests, athletes, artists, etc. To the extent that schools are staffed by professional educators, learning tends to become isolated from the significant concerns of the community, and the narrower functions and tasks of the "school" come to dominate the broader purposes of education.

EDUCATION AS PUBLIC MONOPOLY

That schooling was eventually expanded as a stable and universal service through governmental compulsion rather than private voluntary associations raises questions regarding the political philosophy underlying the school system. American political thought has traditionally distinguished between society (a collection of various private groupings) and government (the combination of political and legal organs that make up the state). As Tom Paine described the distinction, "Society is produced by our wants and government by our wickedness: the former promotes our happiness positively; the latter negatively, by restraining vices."[31] Lindsay's comments on the distinction illustrate the special value that Americans placed on voluntary associations:

> The English or the American democrat takes it for granted that there should be in society voluntary associations of all kinds, religious, philanthropic, commercial: that these should be independent of the state at least in the sense that the state does not create them. The state may have to control and regulate them. Questions concerning their relations with the state are indeed continually turning up, but it is always taken for granted that men

form these societies and associations for their own purposes; that their loyalty to such associations is direct; that it therefore does not follow that the state will prevail in any conflict between such associations and the state.[32]

The spirit of this laissez-faire philosophy implies that the state exists to facilitate a plurality of diverse interests inherent in men's *voluntary* associations and enterprises. The commitment of a community representing such a plurality of interests was applied to many domains of experience, including religion, where sectarianism flourished, and economic affairs, through the development of overlapping and competing business enterprises. Traditional notions of ordered artisan industries controlled by disciplined guilds, agriculture controlled by the feudal lords, mercantile trading policies encouraged and regulated by a central government, monopolistic industry sanctioned by restrictive state charters — all of these fell before the laissez-faire economics practice in America. It was assumed that the life of the community at large would be infused by the vigor and drive of private enterprise and association, that natural laws of competition and cooperation would prevent any serious conflict between private interests and the public good.

Unlike pluralism in religious institutions and business enterprise, pluralism in the schools was short-lived. The concept of the common school took firm roots in Massachusetts early in the nineteenth century and spread to the other states. The common school was apparently conceived as a deliberate instrument to reduce cultural and religious differences. "The children of all nationalities, religions, creeds, and economic levels would then have an opportunity to mix together in the common schoolroom."[33] Once firmly established, the common school was followed by pressures to establish secondary schools and to open the private academies to all. This was a critical choice point for the school: with the common-school concept accepted, how would the traditional commitment to pluralism be worked out? When children from diverse economic, ethnic, religious, and political backgrounds came together, how would the differences be recognized and handled?

Rapidly increasing immigration from Europe in the latter half of the nineteenth century and the first decade of the twentieth century created in the common school a major test for the pluralistic philosophy. Some Americans viewed the flood of newcomers as an opportunity to renew and invigorate the national and ethnic dimension of American pluralism. In 1915 Horace Kallen sentimentally envisioned

. . . a democracy of nationalities, cooperating voluntarily and autonomously through common institutions in the enterprise of self-realization through the perfection of men according to their kind. The common language of the commonwealth . . . would be English, but each nationality would have for its own emotional and involuntary life its own peculiar dialect or speech, its own individual and inevitable esthetic and intellectual forms. The political and economic life of the commonwealth is a single unit and serves as the foundation and background for the realization of the distinctive individuality of each *nation* that composes it and of the pooling of these in harmony above them all.[34]

But not all Americans had faith in the "distinctive individuality" of national groups. Fearing that continued cultivation of national differences would be disruptive to society, the common schools apparently stressed the need for pooling or assimilating immigrants into a common melting pot.

In addition to tension created by religious sectarianism, free enterprise, and ethnic diversity, the nineteenth century labored under severe strains created by the process of rapid industrialization. Evidently the public school responded to these strains by stressing the common values of routine monotonous work, progress, and the Horatio Alger hope of social mobility.

In the end public schools attained a virtual monopoly on the life of youth between the ages of six and sixteen. This development represents a clear shift in political philosophy. It signifies a blurring, if not total rejection, of the distinction between society and government, formerly so crucial to the American democrat; that is, it indicates a loss of faith in the ability of a pluralistic system of private associations to provide an education that would benefit both the individual and his nation.

Perhaps at this point in history it was necessary and useful for the common school to serve a cohesive and integrating function by emphasizing a common heritage, common aspirations, common learnings, common dress, and a common routine within the school. One could suggest, in fact, that the school simply reflected the needs and requirements of the society by stressing *integrating* elements in the society, rather than the diversity, so blatant and obvious. Granted that the society might have been on the brink of disintegration and in need of cohesive institutions at that time, uniformity and conformity have been continuously characteristic of public education ever since the development of common and secondary schools. Theoretically, even though education is public and compulsory, it can conceivably encourage and reinforce cultural diversity by providing a wide range of alternative types of education. Public education in America, however, has not taken this path. On the contrary, the schools have attempted to file down or erase distinctive cultural traits, denying that important cultural diversity ever existed: the instruction and procedures of the school reflect a mandate to persuade youth that all groups share a common language, common political and economic institutions, and common standards of right and wrong behavior. And although it is somewhat more stylish now to recognize the importance of "individual differences," these are construed in psychological rather than cultural terms. Insofar as the recent effort to educate slum children has forced us to recognize cultural differences, these are still construed largely as cultural "deficiencies."

We are concerned with two general effects of the decision to make education an exclusive compulsory public function.[35] The first relates to the way in which the public monopoly has fundamentally altered the nature of childhood and adolescence in America. Young people spend more than half of their waking hours from the age of six to their early twenties trying to meet the demands of formal schooling. Thus opportunities for random, exploratory work and play outside of a formal educational setting have largely disappeared. One could argue that, psychologically, it is very important for youth (and for that matter all humans) to spend a significant portion of their life in spontaneous, voluntary kinds of activity, as per Erikson's suggestion of a psychosocial moratorium,[36] rather than in regimented, required, planned learning tasks. By denying students basic responsibility and freedom, public schooling prevents the development of a sense of competence in making personal decisions. Though it requires large quantities of work ("industry"), the school's evaluation system generally assumes the work of youth to be inferior to that of adults (teachers). The public institutional milieu of the school discourages the development of intimacy among students, or between students and teachers. Schooling prevents exploratory, experimental activity, it prohibits total involvement in any single interest, it refuses to delegate to students responsibility for seeking their own "education." If public schooling were only one among many major areas of experience for young people, these would be less important criticisms. What makes the criticisms most significant is the fact that schooling has a virtual monopoly on youth's time and energy, possessing the power to suppress the quest for individuation through extraschool activity.

In addition to psychological dangers, the monopoly carries as a second major threat its potential for creating cultural uniformity, destroying diversity in points of view, styles of life, standards of taste, and underlying value commitments. The standard rebuttal for this criticism is to point out that although we do have required public education, it is controlled by local communities — it is not a national system. One can, therefore, have radically diverse types of education, depending upon the unique needs of each community. In theory this seems persuasive, but in fact there are a number of forces at work in modern America — mass media, the publishing industry, national curriculum development programs, and professional educators — which combine (however unintentionally) to produce overall institutional similarity. School curricula of different communities display an incredible likeness. (The apparent differences between schooling in slums and in suburbs cannot be accounted for by assuming that slum dwellers have chosen to have one type of education, suburbanites another.) Although public schooling should not bear all of the responsibility for this cultural uniformity, the fact that it has captive control of youth allows it to accelerate the process of cultural standardization. Our objection to this trend is based on the assumption that the essence of freedom lies in the opportunity for significant choice, and that choice becomes increasingly limited as individual and cultural differences are blurred or erased.

Given the failure of the school to support a vital pluralistic tradition, one might ask why education must be carried on as a publicly controlled compulsory activity. Law and medicine, certainly as "vital" as education for society, have remained largely under the control of the private sector. Communication and transmission of knowledge to the community at large, equally important, is accomplished by powerful but essentially private media industries (books, newspapers, cinema, television). To meet basic subsistence needs, we use a system of production and distribution run mainly by private enterprise. Spiritual-religious activities are exclusively reserved for private associations. Curiously, public schools are required to provide ideological indoctrination (the American creed) of an order comparable to that of religious institutions, yet we have refused public support for "religious" education. In the field of citizenship education, the public schools provide instruction for participation in political process, but in fact that instruction is obstructed by myths and misinformation; the most effective training for political life occurs within various private interest groups, or parties.

EDUCATION MODELED AFTER CORPORATE BUREAUCRACY

Education, having developed into a concept of formal compulsory instruction publicly sponsored, could conceivably have taken many forms. Public schools might have become coordinating agencies which channeled students into a variety of educational experiences provided by existing political, economic, cultural, and religious institutions. Schools might have become supplementary agencies, like libraries, appended to small neighborhood communities. In the long run, however, the institutional structure prevailing in the society at large was adopted for education: the factory was served by an industrial development laboratory and managed according to production-line and bureaucratic principles. Architecturally, the schools came to resemble factories (instruction carried on first in rooms but more recently in large loftlike spaces, with different spaces reserved for different types of instruction) and office buildings (with corridors designed to handle traffic between compartments of uniform size). Conceivably, of course, schools could have been built like private homes, cathedrals, artists' studios, or country villas.

The schools came to be administered like smooth-running production lines. Clear hierarchies of authority were established: student, parent, teacher, principal, superintendent, and school committeeman, each of whom was presumed to know his function and the limits of his authority. Faithful to the principle of the division of labor, activities were organized into special departments: teaching (with its many subdivisions), administration, guidance, custodial services, etc. The process of instruction was seen by the administrator as a method of assembling and coordinating standardized units of production: classes of equal size, instructional periods of equal length; uniform "adopted" books and materials that all students would absorb; standard lessons provided by teachers with standardized training. Departures or interruptions in the routine were (and still are) discouraged because of their potentially disruptive effect on the overall process (e.g., taking a field trip, or showing a film that requires two periods' worth of time, or making special arrangements to meet with students individually). Conceivably, the schools could have been organized on a much less regimented basis, allowing a good deal of exploratory, random, unscheduled activity. However, as Callahan persuasively argues, the corporate bureaucratic model, guided by the "cult of efficiency," exerted a major influence on the organization and program of public education.[37]

In our view the effects of corporate organization in education lead to three major developments, each with important contemporary implications: (1) the "research and development" mentality, which limits its attention to finding or building technology and instrumentation to achieve given specifiable goals, rather than questioning or formulating the goals themselves; (2) the increasingly fragmented school environment, which is sliced according to administrative and subject-matter categories prescribed by educational specialists rather than according to salient concerns of children, youth, or the larger community; and (3) the trend toward centralized, coordinated decision-making for schools by a combination of agencies in government, business, universities, foundations, and "non-profit" research and development institutes.

The Research and Development Mentality. The great society seeks to build a highly educated final product (a graduate) at the lowest possible cost per unit. Armed with such a mandate, policy makers and educators scurry to devise and implement techniques that will achieve visible "pay-offs" in the "terminal behavior" of students. A host of new devices and programs emerge: non-graded schools, advanced placement courses, independent study, programmed instruction, self-administered television and cinema, computer-based instruction. They are lauded and increasingly demanded for their apparent effectiveness in speeding up the educational process by "individualizing" instruction for students. The federal government invests millions of dollars through universities, research and development centers, and private industry to produce more efficient methods. Administrators use the techniques both as yardsticks by which to evaluate and as symbols by which to advertise their schools and build their personal reputation. Policy makers and curriculum advisers beg for definite answers concerning which methods are best. But who seeks reasons for the emphasis on acceleration and efficiency? Why read at age three? Why learn quadratic equations at age ten? Why study American history a year or two earlier? Why try to think like an MIT physicist or an anthropologist at all? The research and development mentality thrives on gadgets, engineering metaphors, and the fever of efficiency but rarely questions the purposes to which its technology is applied.

A new and fashionable manifestation of this general mentality is the current emphasis on "systems." The aim of this approach is to describe in schematic (and often mathematical) detail relationships among all components in a system (i.e., a curriculum, classroom, school, or school district) and to evaluate the extent to which given objectives are being achieved by specific components or the system as a whole at certain points of time. Using diagnostic information provided by intensive testing, the job is to build a related set of components and experiences that will achieve specifiable terminal behavior. The general purpose is to *clarify* and *increase the effectiveness* of the entire process through which a given input is changed into output that meets given criteria or standards of performance. The responsibility of systems development is limited to devising techniques for attaining objectives previously fed into the system; the formulation of ultimate aims is delegated to external sources. (The systems engineer boldly proclaims, "You tell us what you want, and we'll program it.") Though one could build a system that would allow for "flexibility" and even respond to changing objectives, we believe that in essence the systems approach avoids rather than recognizes or deals with the most important problems of education, namely, objectives and substance. The excessive concern with technique, rather than searching examination of ends, results in a tendency to accept as legitimate those objectives that can be translated into operations and products which can be schematically and quantitatively measured.

Despite its "practical" outlooks, the research-and-development mentality constantly runs up against the "relevancy problem": the fact that children and youth do, in fact, see the content of school as bookish and artificial, unrelated to the decisions and actions that lead to important consequences either in school or in the outside world. Both students and teachers attempt to right the disproportionate emphasis on abstract words and thought by stressing instead concrete procedures that provide a context of action and decision — prompt attendance, assignments completed, tests taken — and success. The "progressive" approach to the relevancy problem was to abandon rigid work and grade standards without recognizing that these constraints served the fundamental function of providing structure, definition of task, and consequences of decisions that are palpable and immediate. The new R & D proponent is somewhat more sophisticated: instead of stressing the concrete procedures associated with abstract verbal tasks, he seeks to "simulate" the real tasks of the outside world. Students play at war, peacemaking, monopoly, empire building, showing all the involvement of adult poker and bingo players. Although the R & D specialist sees the conceptual relationship between elements of the simulated activity or game and real-life decisions, does the student? Perhaps the student simply learns that adults get their intellectual kicks out of playing games rather than dealing with real problems in the non-instructional world. At any rate there is some evidence that what students learn from playing games is how to play games, not how to construe more effectively problems faced in out-of-school life.

Unfortunately, the underlying difficulty cannot be corrected by R & D specialists. It is a result of the fact that schooling is divorced from problems and choices of genuine concern to youth and community. Since the kind of learning prescribed is not intrinsically important to students, we contract with engineers and R & D centers to invent trivial tasks and procedures to capture their attention. Significant problems and decisions emanate not from R & D laboratories (questions of basic objectives are beyond their concern) but from strains and dilemmas in the world beyond school walls. In short, educational reform must be construed in more fundamental terms than those of transferring the students' attention from nature study to mealworms.

The Fragmented School Environment. In the spirit of Durkheim's analysis of the effects of division of labor, Thelen comments that one of man's most important inventions was the development of concepts about how to organize human activity. But organization requires division and fragmentation, which can, at times, have undesirable results:

> We have made hard and fast divisions between thinking and doing, creating and applying, planning and acting, preparing and fulfilling. The age of reason, the development of science, the domination of organization, and the simple increase in density of human population have interacted among each other to create these divisions. But these divisions have made modern life purposeless. For as long as we maintain the division we shall never have to find an organizing principle to integrate the parts. The organizing principle we have thus succeeded in avoiding is *purpose*.[38]

The school, faithful to principles of bureaucratic organization and division of labor, has fostered the development of a number of specialized compartments many of which have no apparent relationship to or communication with each other: English, social studies, science, math, physical education, home economics, industrial arts, guidance. Boundaries between the departments often arise from legitimate distinctions among fields of knowledge, but lack of communication among fields can be attributed to parochial interests of human beings who place the highest priority on their own area.

Fragmentation also stems from underlying disagreements over the fundamental purposes of education. In broad terms we might classify differing objectives as: work skills (competences required for successful careers and breadwinning), socialization (values and skills necessary to perform in the role of citizen), psychological guidance (development of mental health), and intellectual excellence (acquisition of knowledge and cultivation of mental abilities). These categories are by no means mutually exclusive, but suggestive of distinguishable factors or values used to support various educational prescriptions. To this list we would add a less commonly stated objective: social reconstruction, that is, the effort to justify schooling as a vehicle for the establishment of a particular social order. Many progressives saw the school as a microcosm of a particular kind of ideal society. Other groups, from Puritans and Amish to Nazis and Communists, have similarly valued schooling as an instrument of social reconstruction.

The corporate educational enterprise tends to minimize conflict among differing objectives and fields of interest; it accommodates a number of philosophies and priorities by establishing isolated compartments, allowing each to pursue its own goals in peaceful coexistence. The "philosophy" of the school is articulated by a simple *listing* of all the differing objectives and course offerings. We have no quarrel with the diversity of objectives and subjects. On the contrary, our commitment to pluralism strongly supports them. We do, however, object to the organizational principle which attempts to minimize conflict by isolating various interests from each other. This has the effect of aggravating fragmentation in community. It discourages attempts to relate various purposes of man in community within comprehensive social theory. It stifles healthy ferment that might arise from tough public discussion of the merits of different specialties and objectives.

New Corporate Coalitions.   Current efforts to construe education as a system of fully articulated components to shape terminal behavior are increasingly evident in mergers among communications, electronics, and publishing industries: Time Inc. owns television stations and a textbook company and has recently become associated with General Electric; Xerox owns University Microfilms, Basic Systems, Inc., and American Education Publications; other mergers include RCA with Random House; IBM with Science Research Associates (a test and text publishing firm); and Raytheon with D. C. Heath and Company. These companies or their subsidiaries, often with the assistance of university research and development centers, are planning programs, financed by federal funds, to "solve" America's educational problems. Similar coalitions of government, industrial complexes, and universities have long cooperated in the development of America's war hardware and space exploration. The federal government raises research and development funds, university and industry supply engineering talent and laboratories, and industry manufactures and distributes the final product. A prototype of this pattern applied to education is the urban Job Corps training center, financed by the federal government, which has contracted with private corporations to recruit staff, refurbish physical facilities, and manage the centers. Industry has now turned to universities to help train personnel and to advise and evaluate the operation. Presumably this type of coalition could expand beyond special groups (such as dropouts, unemployed, preschool disadvantaged, or Peace Corps and VISTA volunteers) and reform all public education in the country at large.

We view with suspicion the emergence of national supercorporations venturing into education production. It signifies most obviously the demise of any hope that education might be rooted in the concerns and pursuits of primary communities. It offers unprecedented possibilities for cultural uniformity, as the large coalitions begin to sketch long-range plans for the production of standardized educational kits or packages to be marketed throughout the nation. The packages will be designed within professionalized and bureaucratized organizations, single-mindedly devoted to educational "projects" as isolated goals. The great society evidently assumes that, since the government-industry-university coalition seems to have solved problems of economic affluence and defense, it should therefore be able to solve educational problems.

It should be clear from our basic criticisms that we seriously question this assumption, and in the next section we shall review the nature and deficiencies of contemporary approaches to educational reform. First, however, let us summarize the three criticisms we direct at the present education enterprise: (1) It fails to accept as legitimate or to support the rich educational potential available in non-instructional contexts; conversely, it conceives of education narrowly as mainly formal instruction occurring in schools. (2) By becoming a compulsory public monopoly it neglects the educational value of diverse public and private associations. (3) It is organized by the model and motivated by the values of corporate industry and bureaucratic civil service.

The Direction of Modern Educational Change

For the most part none of the deficiencies in education discussed above are being challenged by current reforms in American education. On the contrary, what we have attacked as questionable premises and assumptions are being further strengthened in the emerging programs, outlined as follows.

CONVENTIONAL REFORM

Redesign of Content. Stimulated in part by massive federal funds spent to improve courses in the physical sciences and mathematics in the late fifties, educational reformers have now come forward with burgeoning projects in virtually all subjects of the curriculum. The attempt is generally to restructure or rethink the content of existing *courses* or to introduce into the school courses previously taught in the university. These curriculum projects are sometimes heralded as revolutionary because of the great financial resources expended and because of the participation and leadership of university experts outside of the "education establishment." The much trumpeted "structure of the disciplines" has presumably replaced most other considerations as the foundation of curriculum building. While we applaud increased attention given to the substance of school programs, we fail to see any fundamental departures from the past: new programs take the form of conventional "courses of study" designed to fit into or extend the conventional school offering.

Increased Use of New Media. The technological challenge of creating more effective and persuasive educational messages captures much of the effort in educational innovation. Courses of instruction conceived and constructed by content specialists are being embellished through the application of new and glamorous "multi-media" devices: slide-tapes, educational television, programmed instruction, demonstration apparatus, language laboratories, simulation devices, and films. These serve the laudable objective of communicating more fully and more effectively knowledge that the experts consider worth transmitting. We wonder, however, whether the new media are not primarily valued for their mesmeric quality, rather than providing a qualitative change in the students' perception of subject-matter-in-school. The new forms of communication have a significant impact on the organization of schools, scheduling, and possibly on the teacher's role in the classroom, but it is doubtful that they will affect in any profound way the role of the student or the way he perceives his task in school.

Reorganization of School Environment. New approaches to scheduling and grouping of students and teachers have allowed greater sensitivity to individual differences, more efficient use of staff energy, and opportunities for "flexibility." Team teaching, the non-graded school, independent study, large-group instruction, and homogeneous grouping are examples of a general concern for making the school program more responsive to obvious and long-standing inefficiencies. Departures from traditional forms of school organization have been aided by more effective information dissemination systems and architectural innovation (dividing a large classroom into individual study rooms; breaking down partitions to facilitate large-group instruction; installing a central television studio flanked by classrooms with receivers). Such advances, like those in media development, may make schooling more efficient, but do they provide any major breakthrough in the student's ability to explore new learning roles or new relationships with adults?

Use of High-Speed Information Processing. Another salient focus of current reform is the data-processing revolution, making it possible for schools to obtain, store, manipulate, and retrieve vast amounts of information. Taking attendance, constructing schedules, and issuing report cards by computer are only a small beginning. New agencies formed primarily to collect and disseminate information, whether in the form of test scores, research reports, printed text material, or educational films, hold momentous possibilities for more efficient use of diverse resources and information. Schools from different geographic areas will soon be able to share instructional materials, communicate new ideas, and receive "feedback" on them with a minimum of administrative red tape. The more efficient information retrieval becomes, the more options the educational specialist has, but is the student included in the choice-making process? How is this rapidly retrieved information to be related to some concept of the good life in the great society? Can teaching and learning be construed as something besides information processing?

Intensive Recruitment of Talented Personnel. Apart from innovations in content, specific techniques of instruction, and personnel organization, quality education is said to depend primarily on the profession's power to attract more talented people into the field. Higher salaries, financial assistance to students, increasing diversity of specialized roles made possible by developments in the areas mentioned above are seen as transforming education into an unusually challenging and attractive career. Federal legislation, as well as support from private foundations, provides impetus for these changes, and apparently the prestige of the educationist is already on the rise.

Talented specialists will undoubtedly enhance the image of the profession, but will they deliberately disturb the questionable assumptions which underlie the very concept of specialized fields of educational experts? Or, in a less radical vein, will they alter conventional schools and utilize technology in a variety of educational settings to benefit a broader spectrum of the population than those in the six to twenty-two age range? Will they plan types of community education which minimize formal requirements but provide exciting voluntary opportunities running the gamut from literacy training to political action to training in the fine arts? Will they consider encouraging youth to work beside adults in real jobs, and will they allow adults more opportunities for both formal study and play?

We predict that new talent and technology will not be directed toward such innovations because the new breed of specialist has no particular stake in viewing problems broadly. He has more to gain by applying his skills to reform *within* the existing establishment, constrained by a number of vested interests. To name a few, the publishing industry will not promote a "product" unless a profitable market can be shown to exist; the parent, viewing education mainly as a vehicle for economic and social mobility, will withhold support from programs that do not offer such a guarantee; the teacher has a deep emotional investment in traditional bodies of knowledge and conceptions of teaching that would be threatened by radical change.

At first glance, one might applaud recent great society programs for their apparent circumvention of establishment constraints, their presumed departure from the status quo. The Job Corps (as one example), through its relationship with private enterprise, government, and university, might conceivably have developed a fresh approach. Unfortunately, however, its objectives were conservative ones of literacy, hygiene, vocational skill; it adopted the traditional institutional models of college dormitory life and military training; and its instruction is guided by the advice of "experienced" educators. The program as a whole serves the vested interests of business by educating young people to "fit in" to employment in the corporate world.

Orchestration of Modern Techniques. One might argue, of course, that, while all of the various reforms suggested above are less than radical or revolutionary, if they were allowed to converge in a single school it would truly be the "school of the future," supplying education of unprecedented quality. The curriculum would offer the "new math," PSSC physics, advanced placement courses, new approaches in reading, the teaching of "advanced" concepts and skills at younger ages. Wide use would be made of films, slides, tapes, language labs, programmed instruction, overhead projectors, educational television. By way of organizing and grouping, there would be team teaching, non-graded sequence, independent study. The latest contributions in information processing would be employed to take advantage of educational resources beyond the school building. The staff would be composed of talented teachers equipped with the best "liberal arts" education and closely supervised practice teaching experience. The teachers would be constantly evaluating and revising the curriculum in cooperation with professors from nearby universities and media experts working out of a regional educational laboratory. The system would include a "comprehensive" high school catering to the needs of diverse types of students — those with aspirations for business, commerce, and technical occupations as well as those interested in the professions.

We doubt whether a school system like this exists anywhere at present, but from Brown's description the non-graded Melbourne High School in Florida approximates the model.[39] The school environment is designed to respond to individual educational needs (grouping by achievement rather than by age; giving students keys to laboratories and study rooms for use after school hours) and thrives on innovation. Although the school seems to foster a more relaxed attitude toward the student than most (e.g., by less preoccupation with control of each minute in the school day), its program continues to isolate youth from adults, the school from the community; students are not included in significant decisions which might fundamentally alter the role of youth in the school or community. The educational philosophy relies heavily on the judgment that "The primary purpose of education is the development of the intellect." [40] Again we are reminded of a business analogy: allow employees enough personal latitude to increase productivity, but prevent the radical conversation which questions the value of the product itself.

RADICAL REFORM

Utopianism. Reforms which question underlying assumptions of modern education have been carried out largely in isolated schools. Plans and proposals for such schools have often assumed hypothetical or unrealistic conditions of community, or no outside community at all. They resemble the utopian experiments of the nineteenth century or the Walden II of the twentieth. Real examples have usually taken the form of private boarding schools, e.g., Putney and Summerhill. Such schools have attempted to establish a broad, coherent inner community in which education is viewed not as the province of an isolated separate system or as a nine-to-five task. The decision to build a separate educational community is usually occasioned by the fact that the existing community would not approve of or condone aspects of programs that the utopians seek to establish — for example, giving children total freedom to choose the kind of education they want, allowing them to develop their own norms regarding relations between the sexes, or, more generally, delegating to them responsibility for governing their community.

Utopian schools have concentrated heavily on the reduction of adult control over students and have broadened the notion of education to include far more than the completion of traditional or newly thought-out intellectual exercises — for example, by providing more opportunity for artistic expression, craftsmanship, manual labor, experience in child rearing and self-government. Because the activities are rather thoroughly insulated from the pressures of the community beyond, they can explore possibilities for radical innovation that would not be possible otherwise. The catch, of course, comes when the "citizens" of such educational communities find it necessary to return to the larger society. How does the student cope with the re-entry problem, after having been educated within a system of values many of which contradict those of the "real world"? As one college student remarked, "The trouble with girls from Bennington is that they think they've been to Heaven. Where is there to go after that?" Presumably former citizens of utopian educational communities are prepared to have an impact on the great society, one that will move it in the direction of the values and aspirations reflected in the utopian school. Common sense as well as psychological evidence indicates that the "graduate" of a utopian school is more likely to move back into the mainstream of the great society and slough off the effects of an extraneous and temporary educational environment. The major argument for the isolated utopian educational community, that it is the only feasible and realistic way to implement radical reform, is thus vitiated by its negligible long-range consequences. There is little permanent impact either on the students or on the society to which they return. Such schools are more likely to be seen as temporary aberrations of affluent intellectuals than as educational models worthy of emulation.

Reconstruction of the System. As opposed to radical reform through utopian withdrawal, it is still remotely possible that fundamental change might be brought about both in the nature of the institution and in the larger community within which it operates. Some might, in fact, point to progressive education in the first half of this century as evidence that general educational reconstruction is possible. We disagree. On the basis of Cremin's history of "pedagogical pioneers,"[41] we would characterize most of the progressive movement not as an effort to radically change the system but as moderate reform or utopian model building. Though countless changes were made in schooling (creating within the school an "embryonic community," emphasizing creativity and freedom of inquiry, fostering manual as well as symbolic learning, and in many cases involving adults of the community in school programs), the progressives continued to focus on improving the *school* as a means to better education. Whether the school was a utopian community in microcosm or simply a more relevant and humanitarian way of leading youth through verbal mazes, there was no attempt to reconstruct the total context through which the community pursues its educational aims.[42]

As something of an exception to this generalization, Harold Rugg deserves special comment. He saw the school exercising its responsibility as the major agency of education within the community by using the total community as its workshop or laboratory.

> If we should trail one of the new school groups for a week or two and record what they did, we should find that the students spend much of their time outside of their assigned classrooms — for example, in the library, shops, laboratories, studies, auditorium, and offices of the school itself. The scenes of their activity, however, are not only the entire reaches of the new-school plant but also the whole community and the region round about — the government offices, stores, markets, industries, the water supply, the docks, and the like. Pupils survey the layout of the town, collect pictures and old records, and interview old residents, city officials, social welfare secretaries, and a host of others.[43]

As a stopgap measure Rugg suggested that the "nearest approach to a School of Living" is to build the whole educational program of a community around the life of the school itself. While Rugg prescribed a utopian school as an immediate solution, in the long run that school was to insinuate itself into the adult activities of the community, both as a method of study and as a means of social reconstruction.

An impressive modern proposal for radical reform within the context of the broader community is Herbert A. Thelen's *Education and the Human Quest* (1960). Thelen makes a provocative plea for the community to conceive of education as consisting of four basic parts: personal inquiry, group investigation, reflective action, and skill development. The school should be considered only one of a number of possible contexts in which to pursue the development of these areas, and the education for a particular community would be planned by a broadly based "citizens education council." Adult citizens in their regular jobs would assume educational responsibility to each other and to the youth. Youth would participate in "out-of-school" activities such as vocational exploration, recreation, social-political action, religion, etc. This is not simply a proposal for more "field trips" or "projects" but an attempt to create in a more permanent sense whatever institutional arrangements may be required to implement an expanded conception of education. Thelen translates his idea into organizational-financial terms and proposes that a citizens education council present a budget for all the educational efforts in the community (including "adult" education), with the school budget as only one part of the total — that part enabling the school to carry out its particular mandate (probably in the fields of skill development and the guiding of personal and group inquiry).

The spirit of Thelen's work is genuinely radical and strikes at the center of a number of common assumptions behind both conventional and "reformed" schools. He sees education as a function of the total community, not the province of specialized "education" experts. While he has a tendency to view education across generations as a one-way street (adults are constantly helping or guiding young people to learn those things that adults value), at least he is concerned that different generations carry on a dialogue. Unfortunately, like Rugg's futuristic scheme, Thelen's proposals have apparently fallen on sterile soil.

A Proposal for Education in Community

Since we believe that efforts at reform have generally failed to consider the fundamental importance of *contexts* in which education is pursued, we begin by conceptualizing alternative modes of and environments for learning. Imagine a hypothetical community in which learning is pursued in three quite different contexts: the "school" context, the "laboratory-studio-work" context, and the "community seminar" context. Subjects or problems for study, and also the relations between students and teachers, are construed quite differently in each of these contexts.[44]

THE SCHOOL CONTEXT

There is a clear need for systematic instruction in basic literacy skills (reading, writing, mathematics), health and hygiene, driver education, and the like. Learning of this sort is preplanned, programmed, and formalized. The teacher has clear objectives or "terminal behaviors" in mind as the products of instruction. Most of the activity in schools as we now know them falls into this category. This is not to suggest that school-based learning continue to follow traditional subject matter lines, or that instruction be didactic and rote. On the contrary, school learning should be problem-centered and exciting, and should constantly consider reorganizing basic content to make it lead toward more powerful insights and understandings; for example, coordinate and symbol systems used in graphs, charts, and maps might be combined with linguistic analysis and musical notation in teaching a course in "symbolics." Technology has thrust upon us rich possibilities for more effective instruction through (1) greater opportunity for self-instruction, (2) availability of multi-media approaches, and (3) more accurate assessment of student needs and progress. Teaching within a school context may take the many forms of tutorial between teacher and student; student with computer, or programmed instruction; students in small groups; or large groups watching films. The distinguishing feature of the school context is that it concerns itself only with those aspects of education involving systematic, planned instruction. It should be clear from the explanation of the following two contexts that we see this kind of learning as only *one* among three critical types.

THE LABORATORY-STUDIO-WORK CONTEXT

In the laboratory context the major objective is not formal instruction but the completion of a significant task, the solution of problems which the "learner" wants to attack, regardless of educational by-products that dealing with the problem might bring. The physical location of the laboratory context might be a factory, an art studio, a hospital, a library, a science or an industrial laboratory, a political party headquarters, or a government agency. The activity of participants is governed, not by a skill or a product that is programmed for students to learn, but only by the developing nature of the problem-task itself. Such problems would include painting a picture, rebuilding an auto, writing an essay, promoting a concert, organizing a protest demonstration, lobbying for legislation, selling insurance, programming a computer, acting in a play, providing nursing help in a hospital, wood carving, athletic competition, conservation and wildlife management, child care, participation in and planning a church service, radio and television broadcasting, making a dress, printing a newspaper, physical and chemical experiments, serving as a guide at the UN, organizing a raffle to raise money, or even creating instructional materials for use in a school context. Laboratories are contexts for learning in the midst of action; learning occurs not because it is planned, but only as an inevitable by-product of genuine participation in problem- and task-oriented activities. The laboratory is seen not primarily as the site of apprenticeship or vocational training for breadwinning, but rather as a place offering the opportunity to satisfy broader humanistic and aesthetic goals. At present many adults are engaged in pursuits in laboratory contexts — mainly their jobs (these are not recognized or supported for their educational value). Young people are deemed not "ready" to participate until they first spend twelve to sixteen years in "school." We believe the laboratory offers important educational benefits at all ages; it should not be restricted to adults.

THE COMMUNITY SEMINAR CONTEXT

The purpose of the seminar is the reflective exploration of community issues and ultimate meanings in human experience. The seminar provides an opportunity for the gathering of heterogeneous or homogeneous groups, for youth and/or adults, to examine and discuss issues of mutual concern. Seminars might begin by focusing on problems internal to the group (e.g., the meaning of productive work for people dissatisfied with their jobs, unemployed, or retired). Discussion might be stimulated by outside provocateurs who present new ways of viewing economic, ethical, or aesthetic questions. Seminars could have at their service qualified resource staff to gather information (readings, films, television programs) and make arrangements for experiences, such as "field trips" to observe unfamiliar ways of life, technological innovations, social problems in action. In addition to relatively specific problems (What kinds of working conditions are we entitled to?) and general public policy questions (How should the community be zoned?), the seminars would, we hope, concern themselves with the broadest questions raised in planning for education in community. Other possible topics include: understanding various conflicts between youth and adults, the functions of the family in modern society, attitudes toward non-conformity and deviance in the community, prejudice and pluralism among ethnic groups, changing mores in sex and religion, various approaches to child rearing, the use of increased leisure, population control, protection of the consumer, moral implications of advances in biology (e.g., selective breeding), reconstruction of the political and legal system, evaluation of current "programs" sponsored by government and private agencies, creation of new professions and problems of vocational retraining. The major thrust of the seminars is reflection and deliberation, though the questions discussed would be highly relevant to the laboratory context or the world of "action." Learning in the seminar is not preplanned, nor are there specific tasks or problems to solve. Questions are raised, investigated, and discussed; this process, regardless of numerous and unpredictable possible outcomes, is of high educational value. Generally both youth and adults are denied the kind of learning afforded by this context — the time of youth is monopolized by school; that of adults, by jobs, or "laboratories."

POINTS OF CLARIFICATION

The contexts described above are intended to convey the major point that education consists of three important facets: systematic instruction, action, and reflection. The facets are not listed in order of importance, nor chronologically. All three should occur concurrently at all stages of life. A young child learning how to read in a school context can participate in a laboratory project of building a model airplane (using the symbolic skills acquired in "school"); he can also discuss with children and adults in a seminar what to do about noise control for the local airport. An adult interested in politics might study government systematically in school, participate in the "laboratory" of a political campaign, and in the community seminar lead discussions on political organization appropriate for the modern community. While some communities may choose to place most young children in the school context, and allocate much of adult education to the seminar, we see no logical reason for such an arrangement. This scheme allows for various mixtures of the three components to be tailored to the needs of various stages of life or to the unique requirements of different types of communities.

Who would fill the leadership roles in such an educational scheme? If formal school comprises only one-third of the educational program, will professional educators be put out of work? Possibly, but not necessarily. Those most qualified to carry on instruction may well be teachers and educators currently working in schools. Thus many teachers and administrators would stay in schools (although advances in technology suggest radical changes in their roles and jobs even if they do stay there). Since learning in school would occupy only a small portion of the student's day — perhaps three hours — one might expect the school staff to dwindle. If, however, adults also used the school for instruction, the school's student population would increase, even though any given student spent only a small amount of time there. The demand for professional educators would remain high.

Leaders in the laboratory contexts would be experienced persons in the various laboratory areas (engineers, lawyers, mechanics, poets, politicians, athletes, secretaries), who would be given released time to take on educational responsibility for youth and adults interested in laboratory activity. It is possible that professional educationists can be converted into laboratory leaders; for example, an English teacher could take on apprentices in the writing of poetry, but in his laboratory role he would be interested primarily in the creation and analysis of artistic works, not in teaching. The laboratory context would rely mainly upon private enterprise, government, the arts, labor, etc., to provide creative practitioners willing to assume on-the-job educational responsibility. If we are willing to recognize as teachers the vast number of talented practitioners in such fields, we shall approach a dramatic solution to the manpower problem of finding enough intelligent "teachers." By taking advantage of the educational value of the on-the-job activities, we may begin to break the stranglehold by which the education profession has restricted our conception of education to structured activity carried on in school.

Community seminars could be run by professional educators, businessmen, politicians, parents, laborers, policemen, Boy Scouts, gang leaders, criminals, musicians, or journalists. The community seminar, perhaps more than the school or laboratory, raises the issue of incentive. What would induce people to participate in it? The success of such programs depends upon the willingness of various organizations to provide "released time" for leaders and participants. Financial arrangements must insure that the activities do not economically penalize participants. On the contrary, it would be reasonable to give monetary rewards for participation in educational activities. Already, and on a large scale, people are being paid for undergoing training (neighborhood youth corps, jobs corps, scholarships and fellowships, prizes and rewards for high grades, in-training programs of businesses, etc.), and it is quite consistent with the idea of "making an investment" in the development of human resources. We would assume that, given the time and money, the tasks and issues explored in these contexts could be sufficiently exciting to attract wide participation.

A community concerned with implementing some of these general ideas would require coordination of several resources, including private voluntary agencies such as churches, businesses, museums and libraries, political parties, economic and political pressure groups, and social service organizations. It would require flexibility and attention to individual differences; yet, to avoid the problems of fragmentation or specialization, it would have to facilitate participation in common experiences through which members could relate across economic, racial, political, ethnic, or occupational lines.

Implementing a program of this type seems at first glance an administrator's nightmare, involving the coordination of disparate agencies and the cooperation of people with conflicting vested interests. Will colleges recognize the value of laboratory and seminar experience in their admissions policy? Will the education establishment be willing to relinquish much of its control of the learning of youth? Will businesses accept for employment people with varying rather than standardized educational backgrounds? Who will have the power to "accredit" educational programs, and what new criteria will be needed? At the moment, we have no satisfactory answers, and we recognize the difficulty of putting some of these ideas into practice. It is possible that in implementing the three contexts an educational bureaucracy as rigid as the present one would evolve — with tight scheduling and compartmentalization equal to or worse than those in the current system. All we can say at present is that implementation must be guided by serious attention to criteria for building community (such as are mentioned above, p. 187); otherwise the purpose of educational change will be defeated. It thus becomes clear that when we speak of educational change we speak of social and community change — a process for which few people have useful administrative guidelines.

Moreover, we hesitate to suggest specific plans or models, feeling that these should arise from the basic concerns of particular communities. We envision no national model that could be replicated across the land. Instead, there should develop a plurality of structures and programs. Jencks has suggested ways in which private groups could compete with one another and with the public education establishment by offering qualitatively different types of education, sensitive to community needs.[45] In a single community, schools, labs, and seminars might be run by businesses, parent groups, teachers, and churches — all competing for "students." It should be possible to fund competing enterprises without allowing a single centralized bureaucracy to gain total control. In some communities literacy training may be a major problem (e.g., in an urban slum), in others technical retraining (e.g., an area highly concentrated with electronics industry); other areas may have particularly acute problems in human relations, or even in the use of "leisure" time.

Basing education on needs of particular communities does not imply that students (youth and adults) are being trained for life only within that community. On the contrary, with communication and transportation breakthroughs likely to continue, all communities are becoming more dependent on each other, less isolated; their problems are therefore increasingly generalizable. The production of a television program to publicize the plight of migrant workers involves the same considerations as that of a program to plead for better equipment for the local football team. Organizing tenants to protest against landlords and organizing real estate brokers to protest to Congress involve similar processes. Painting a picture of harvest time is in many ways like painting a scene of industrial smokestacks. A discussion of the boring process of cotton picking may be helpful in a later discussion on the meaning of work on an assembly line. We see no reason to be alarmed that a community's education be focused on critical contemporary issues. If "critical," they are, by definition, of relevance to other communities in other times.

Assuming that one could find a community willing to alter its patterns of education along some of the general lines mentioned above, where would it turn for direction? Much of its work would move over uncharted waters. There are, however, a number of educational experiments that could be used as possible illustrations of the broader view. The following examples have come to our attention, but we feel certain that they comprise only a small portion of the total available repertoire. Additional examples should be sought and recorded.

SOME EXAMPLES

In connection with Harvard's Research-Development Center, Belenky, Reed, and Clark have instituted a combination preschool and school study group — an excellent example of a laboratory activity. Four kinds of people are involved: university educationists, mothers, youth, and young children from a "lower-class" ghetto in Boston (consisting of two public housing projects, one white and one Negro). Under the supervision of the educationists and mothers, the youth teach young children in a basement recreation room of the Negro project. At the same time the educationists and mothers take field trips to explore a variety of the more progressive schools in the Greater Boston area and gather information from which to discuss the kind of school experience they would like for their children. There is hope that these discussions will lead to constructive dialogue with the formal school establishment and, if need be, political and social action to bring about a change in the formal schools. One member of the educationist group is from the ghetto itself, an artist skilled also in methods of social action and protest. Rather than viewing this project as an "extra-educational" program to improve formal "education," i.e., the schools, one might consider it a continuing educational program in its own right. Rather than construing this kind of activity as mainly temporary compensatory or rehabilitative (though it may in fact be rehabilitative), why not consider it one of a number of normal educational opportunities that adults and youth might choose to engage in?

A second example is a "radio club" sponsored by an electronics firm in Concord, Massachusetts. Once a week a group of youth come to the main factory and work with engineers and technicians, building ham radio sets, exploring radio theory, and exchanging technical information. At present this club is "extracurricular," piled on top of what for many high school students is an already overburdensome amount of schoolwork. Why not include adult hams as well as young people? Why not construe this as a genuine educational setting and allow the participants to count this time against the school or work responsibilities in their normal schedules?

Some churches are becoming increasingly involved in activities designed to restore community in urban areas. While many of their efforts may be seen as traditional welfare and settlement house services having relatively small influence (e.g., clinics for narcotics or alcoholics, soup lines, employment agencies, family counseling), others reveal a broader concern for the total pathology in community. Church-sponsored projects have combined the buying and renovating of slum housing for low-income people with manpower training and placement of social protests for civil and consumer rights. The Urban Training Center for Christian Mission in Chicago (sponsored by twelve Protestant denominations) takes part in a number of such activities and uses the programs as major portions of a training process for prospective ministers. Trainees live in the slums with the poor (they are given only a few cents for several days) and participate in action projects like the above, as workers for various sponsoring groups. After periods of intensive involvement working in the community, the seminarians withdraw for reflection and deliberation. They are temporarily released from immediate pressures of the day, with time for study and discussion of general issues. The UTC's approach combines the laboratory with the community seminar context and seems to have success in both areas.

Another church-sponsored project illustrates a type of community seminar. Supported by the Presbytery of Detroit, the Episcopal Diocese of Michigan, and the Michigan Conference of the United Church of Christ, the Detroit Industrial Mission (DIM) sends clergymen into industrial plants to initiate contacts with men who organize small discussion groups among the workers. Topics are drawn from concerns of the workers themselves. The mission does not preach any particular point of view but attempts to foster better communication and deeper levels of understanding among all groups in industry. The responsibility of staff members is merely to arrange opportunities for men to say to each other what they think about human and ethical issues that arise in the plant. This illustration has a number of interesting characteristics. (1) It was initiated and carried out by a private voluntary group, not with public funds or public officials. (2) Its purpose was neither vocational training nor "great books" philosophizing, but rather to raise fundamental questions of immediate relevance and importance. (3) The "teachers" operate from a clear ideological base but are not interested in evangelical conversion. (4) The "students" are seen not as preparing for some distant goal but as learning to make better decisions here and now. (5) There are no sharp age or status distinctions; men at different points in their careers talk sincerely with one another.

The Highlander Folk School, in the Cumberland Mountains of Tennessee, began in the depression as a labor school to teach workers in the South how to organize and run unions. Often the center of controversy, it offers another example of an environment of reflection directly related to community action. A non-profit institution supported by private donations and foundation grants, Highlander runs resident adult education programs, teaching adults how to teach others to deal with social problems. The programs consist mainly of "workshops" arranged in response to specific pressing issues. For example, in 1960 the Student Nonviolent Coordinating Committee asked for help in evaluating its own future program. A workshop was held, yielding the decision to concentrate upon voter registration. The school is the scene of many workshops related to civil rights issues and has always been racially integrated. The emphasis is not only on the making of policy decisions but also on leadership training and the dissemination of knowledge gained through the Highlander Programs. Concerned with the most explosive social issues, the school has been attacked legally (the state revoked its charter), investigated for subversive activities, and destroyed by fire. Similar institutions could be developed as "retreat" seminars, not limited to a single community but available as resources to many.

CONCLUSION

The deliberate effort to view education in community from three vantage points and to look for contexts outside of the formal school where people learn is only the first step in any important educational reform — but it is the hardest. After we wrench ourselves loose from the paralyzingly constricted posture that all true education must be programmed, planned, compulsory, and public, and it must all happen in schools, one's imagination trips over a host of exciting places for youth and adults to learn, by themselves and in association with one another. Only after this first long step do really important questions of educational policy arise:

What does the educational system have to do with the system of government, of economics, of politics? It is all very well to say that education is for the purpose of maintaining our nation or developing a world order, but what does that mean? Does it mean that every individual must be made literate, wise, loyal and conforming? . . . Is a school a cultural island, separated from the community mainland by the same kind of thing that separates fantasy from real life? Does the school lead or follow the community or both? We hear a lot about the need to "involve" citizens in school problems. Who, how, why? Is it just to keep them quiet? or to manipulate them into contributing more money? Is school supposed to "induct youth into the community"? What does that mean? . . . Can the school do the job alone? Or is the school only one part of a community-wide educational system which exists in fact whether the school board knows it or not?[46]

Critics of this position tend to ask for specific blueprints and definite answers to such policy questions. They want outlines, schedules, and programs, and wonder: How much time would students spend in school? Would the rest of their time be completely free or planned and supervised in some way? Who would pay for extracurricular activities? How could adults be released from their jobs to take responsibility for community education? How would legal authority be allocated among community agencies? Would state departments of education change their requirements? Would colleges accept students with this sort of education? Would the students perform better on standard tests and attain standards of "excellence" comparable, for example, to European educational standards? Can we demonstrate that education organized around these ideas would have any real payoff in later life?

To answer such questions directly at this point would be inappropriate. Until people in a community have argued about and accepted some of the premises in this paper and are vitally concerned with implementation for their particular situation, it would be foolhardy for armchair professors to prescribe programs. Providing blueprints in the abstract, not tied to a specific situation, would be inconsistent with our premise that education should arise from real needs and issues within community, not from the drawing boards of distant national planners.

We are chastised for evading the issue of "practicality," as critics throw up their hands in despair over our "unrealistic," "unfeasible" ideas. This basic criticism and questions like the above reflect a commitment by critics to the present system, a reluctance to search for fundamental deficiencies in the status quo. The major issue from our point of view is not our inability to give blueprints and specific answers; financial, logistic, and administrative problems of plural educational contexts are relatively minor difficulties with this article. Instead, the major issue is whether we can find people willing to begin serious discussion on premises and ideas rather than only on blueprints and programs. The next step lies, not in a more concrete plan, but in a *search for a group of people*, some "missing community," with the courage and energy to re-examine how education, most broadly conceived as the interaction between reflection and action, can invigorate the lives of all its citizens.

NOTES

1. The authors are indebted to a number of colleagues and students, and to the authors listed herein. We wish to acknowledge, in particular, the work of Robert A. Nisbet, Paul Goodman, and Herbert A. Thelen, and the writings and conversation of our colleague, Joseph C. Grannis. A revised version of this article appears in the *Harvard Educational Review*, Winter, 1967.

2. G. Kateb, "Utopia and the Good Life," *Daedalus*, Spring, 1965, p. 456.

3. Ferdinand Tönnies, *Community and Society*, translated and edited by Charles P. Loomis (Harper, 1963). In the Foreword to this edition P. Sorokin mentions eternal parallels between the work of Tönnies and Confucius, Plato, Aristotle, Cicero, and others. In the Introduction J. C. McKinney and C. P. Loomis discuss analogous concepts in the work of Durkheim, Cooley, Redfield, Becker, Sorokin, Weber, and Parsons.

4. Alex Inkeles, *What Is Sociology? An Introduction to the Discipline and Profession* (Prentice-Hall, 1964), pp. 68–69.

5. Robert A. Nisbet, *Community and Power* (Oxford University Press, 1962), p. 54.

6. These observations relate to a wide range of phenomena, represented in studies of bureaucracy (P. M. Blau, *Bureaucracy in Modern Society* [Random House, 1956]; W. H. Whyte, *The Organization Man* [Simon & Schuster, 1956]); corporate power (A. A. Berle, *The Twentieth Century Capitalist Revolution* [Harcourt, Brace, 1954]); political and legal institutions (C. W. Mills, *The Power Elite* [Oxford University Press, 1956]; H. W. Wheeler, *The Restoration of Politics* [Fund for the Republic, 1965]); ideology (D. Bell, *The End of Ideology: On the Exhaustion of Political Ideas in the Fifties* [Collier, 1962]); youth (E. Z. Friedenberg, *The Vanishing Adolescent* [Dell, 1959] and *Coming of Age in America: Growth and Acquiescence* [Random House, 1963]; Paul Goodman, *Growing Up Absurd* [Vintage, 1960] and *Compulsory Mis-education and The Community of Scholars* [Vintage, 1966]; K. Keniston, *The Uncommitted: Alienated Youth in American Society* [Harcourt, Brace & World, 1965]); education (S. T. Kimball and J. E. McClellan, *Education and the New America* [Random House, 1962]); work and leisure (L. Mumford, *Technics and Civilization* [Harcourt, Brace, 1934]; H. Swados, *A Radical's America* [Little, Brown, 1957]; T. Veblen, *The Theory of the Leisure Class* [Mentor, 1957]); women (Betty Friedan, *The Feminine Mystique* [Dell, 1964]); American character (D. Riesman, N. Glazer, and R. Denney, *The Lonely Crowd: A Study in the Changing American Character* [Anchor, 1953]; G. Gorer, *The American People: A Study in National Character* [Norton, 1964]); voter behavior (B. Berelson, P. F. Lazarsfeld, and W. N. McPhee, *Voting: A Study of Opinion Formulation in a Presidential Campaign* [University of Chicago Press, 1954]); or, more generally, the "human condition" (Hannah Arendt, *The Human Condition* [Anchor, 1958]; J. R. Royce, *The Encapsulated Man* [Van Nostrand, 1965]). The authors of these studies address themselves to a number of questions, only a few of which are explicitly raised in our characterization of the missing community.

7. Victor Fuchs, "The First Service Economy," *Public Interest*, Winter, 1966, pp. 7–17.

8. National Commission on Technology, Automation, and Economic Progress, *Technology and the American Economy*, Vol. 1, February, 1966.

9. See E. E. Schattschneider, *The Semi-sovereign People: A Realist's View of Democracy in America* (Holt, Rinehart & Winston, 1960), and V. O. Key, Jr., *The Responsible Electorate: Rationality in Presidential Voting, 1936–1960* (Harvard University Press, 1966).

10. Fuchs, *op. cit.*

11. N. Wiener, *The Human Use of Human Beings: Cybernetics and Society* (Anchor, 1954).

12. Bell, *op. cit.*

13. *Technology and the American Economy, op. cit.*, p. xiii.

14. E.g., U.S. Department of Labor, *Manpower Report of the President and A Report on Manpower, Requirements, Resources, Utilization, and Training,* March, 1966.

15. Clinton Rossiter, "The Democratic Process," in *Goals for Americans,* the report of the President's Commission on National Goals and chapters submitted for the consideration of the Commission, American Assembly, Columbia University (Prentice-Hall, 1960).

16. Keniston, *op. cit.*, pp. 433 f.

17. Rosalie H. Rosenfelt, "The Elderly Mystique," *Journal of Social Issues,* 21:39–40 (1965).

18. R. A. Kalish, "The Aged and the Dying Process: The Inevitable Decisions," *Journal of Social Issues,* 21:87–96 (1965).

19. *Manpower Report, op. cit.*, p. xii.

20. See, for example, Francis Keppel, *The Necessary Revolution in American Education* (Harper & Row, 1966), chap. IV. He justifies increased federal spending in education almost entirely on the grounds that it will result in more economic use of human resources; that it is, therefore, in the national interest to make a greater investment in education.

21. J. Dewey, *The Child and the Curriculum* (University of Chicago Press, 1902) and *The School and Society* (University of Chicago Press, 1900).

22. H. G. Rickover, *Education and Freedom* (Dutton, 1960).

23. J. B. Conant, *The American High School Today* (McGraw-Hill, 1959).

24. J. Bruner, *The Process of Education* (Vintage, 1960).

25. Kimball and McClellan, *op. cit.*; C. S. Benson, *The Cheerful Prospect: A Statement on the Future of American Education* (Houghton Mifflin, 1965).

26. B. Bailyn, *Education in the Forming of American Society: Needs and Opportunities for Study* (Vintage, 1960), pp. 15–19.

27. J. S. Bruner, *Toward a Theory of Instruction* (Harvard University Press, 1966), p. 1.

28. B. F. Brown, *The Nongraded High School* (Prentice-Hall, 1963), p. 14.

29. L. A. Cremin, *The Transformation of the School: Progressivism in American Education 1876–1957* (Vintage, 1964).

30. See, for example, J. B. Conant, *The Education of American Teachers* (McGraw-Hill, 1963) and *Shaping Educational Policy* (McGraw-Hill, 1964).

31. Quoted in A. D. Lindsay, *The Modern Democratic State* (Oxford University Press [London], 1943), p. 124.

32. *Ibid.*, p. 120.

33. R. F. Butts and L. A. Cremin, *A History of Education in American Culture* (Holt, 1953), p. 194.

34. H. M. Kallen, "Democracy and the Melting Pot," in B. M. Ziegler (ed.), *Immigration, an American Dilemma* (Heath, 1953), pp. 29–30.

35. The fact that state laws allow youth to fulfill educational obligations by attending private as well as public schools does not diminish the influence of the public monopoly. A relatively small proportion of children do attend private schools (approximately 16 per cent at the elementary level and 11 per cent at the secondary level). Moreover, even private schools must conform to publicly established standards.

36. E. H. Erikson, "Youth: Fidelity and Diversity," *Daedalus*, Winter, 1962, pp. 5–27.

37. R. E. Callahan, *Education and the Cult of Efficiency: A Study of the Social Forces That Have Shaped the Administration of the Public Schools* (University of Chicago Press, 1962).

38. H. A. Thelen, *Education and the Human Quest* (Harper, 1960), p. 215.

39. Brown, *op. cit.*

40. *Ibid.*, p. 145.

41. Cremin, *op. cit.*

42. This is not meant to criticize the efforts of "progressives" in general, many of which did focus on problems in the wider community such as revising patterns of political representation, establishing social welfare services, and curbing abuses of monopolistic business. Our point is directed only toward the relatively narrow efforts of professional *educators* known by the progressive label.

43. H. Rugg, *American Life and the School Curriculum* (Ginn, 1936), pp. 340–341.

44. The "three contexts" are discussed in Joseph C. Grannis and Donald W. Oliver, "Walden III" (mimeographed), presented to a seminar at the Harvard Graduate School of Education, 1965. Similar ideas are also contained in an earlier paper by Grannis, "Team Teaching and the Curriculum," in Judson T. Shaplin and Henry F. Olds, Jr. (eds.), *Team Teaching* (Harper & Row, 1964).

45. Christopher Jencks, "Is the Public School Obsolete?" *Public Interest*, Winter, 1966, pp. 18–27.

46. Thelen, *op. cit.*, pp. 13–14.

PART THREE

Secularism, Pluralism, and
Religion in Our Society

12

The New Secularity and the Requirements of Pluralism

Neil G. McCluskey, S.J.

Man has entered the final third of the twentieth century. Its explosive past may be a relatively calm prologue to what lies ahead. One need not don the prophet's mantle to suggest that nowhere will there be more change than in the world of the school. It can be predicted that the public school of the 1970's will differ dramatically from its predecessors, each of which has reflected the constantly changing society of which it is part. It can likewise be predicted that the whole question of the relation of the publicly supported school to religion and religious education, along with the correlative question of the role of the church-related school in the total scheme of things, will be approached in a more sophisticated and socially realistic manner.

Some of the bases for these predictions are immediately evident. There is a growing awareness that an "inner city" with schools that are impoverished, declining, and racially unbalanced has emerged in almost every one of our large metropolitan areas. There is wide concern over the spread of religious illiteracy among American youth and its effect upon public morality. There is an increased acceptance of the reality that no government program to strengthen education can achieve its objective if non-public schools are ignored, and that the contribution of these schools to the common good makes some claim on the understanding and support of society in general. Contemporary ecumenism has increased tolerance, sympathy, and understanding among us, enabling men of divided faiths and of no faith to work together as has not been the case since the pioneer days of the Republic. Perhaps most significant of all is the new understanding and acceptance of the secular nature of certain institutions in society, including the common school in a religiously pluralistic society, with the consequent revision, modification, or abandonment of some of the battle-worn assumptions behind the charges of its "godless" or "irreligious" character.

Catholic Education

"Religious education" is an ambiguous phrase. In a restricted sense religious education is instruction in the beliefs and practices of a systematized or institutionalized religion in order to achieve knowledge and understanding. However, since the sponsoring group usually undertakes religious education because it aims to build commitment among its members, loyalty and service to the ideals of the faith community are also recognized goals of religious education. When the objectives of understanding and commitment are combined, religious education is more properly religious formation. Both of these latter should be distinguished from theology. The science of theology is a strict academic discipline resulting from the schematic application of the principles of philosophy and history to revealed religious truths. Theology has traditionally held a respected place among humanistic studies for the sometimes-lost-sight-of reason that scarcely anything is woven more largely into man's culture than his experience with the divine.

Catholics generally agree that the objectives of religious education are ideally realized in an atmosphere wherein the spiritual and the supernatural are properly ordered in a hierarchy of values. The systematic study of religious doctrine is better achieved in a separate, religiously oriented school, for a person learns religion in somewhat the same way that he learns a language. If he is fortunate enough to be raised in the country where the tongue is spoken, he will almost always have a better grasp of the language than he would through intense self-instruction or private tutoring or enrollment in a special class. The atmosphere of a religiously oriented school definitely reinforces and hastens the learning process. Above all, in a thousand subtle ways that defy definition, this atmosphere strengthens and completes the educational influence of home and church. No one has perfectly analyzed or described it. Exaggerated claims have been made for it. Hostile critics have labeled it brainwashing. And perhaps it is a form of conditioning — but in the same respectable category with the process that results in love of country or family. In such an environment a youngster is more likely to acquire a distinctively "Catholic" attitude or philosophy.

Contrary to a widespread misconception (even among Catholics themselves), Catholic schools do not exist primarily to teach the catechism. Were this the purpose, there would be no need for separate Catholic schools. A moment's reflection bears this point out. One might claim such instruction as the principal task of the school only if there were no way to teach religious doctrine save by means of a separate school. Yet there are many other ways, some long in use by other religious groups as well. Religious instruction can be given by special classes in the church or elsewhere before or after school hours, by parental instruction, by home visits from a teacher, by instruction during Mass, by released-time and dismissed-time programs, etc. It hardly needs stating that any of these substitutes or a combination could suffice as religious education. The teaching of Catholic belief, therefore, cannot be either the exclusive or even the main function of the Catholic school, let alone its reason for existence.

So much for the theory of Catholic education. Upon this theory American Catholics have built 2,500 secondary and in excess of 10,000 elementary schools, serving 5.8 million pupils, or 14 per cent of the nation's total school population on those levels. Yet staggering as this "system" appears to be, it still represents only one-third of the Catholic high-school-age group and one-half of the elementary group. More sobering still from one Catholic viewpoint, simply to maintain the 1962–1963 ratio into 1968–1969 will require places for an additional million students above the 1962–1963 enrollment plus 32,000 teachers and three-quarters of a billion dollars' worth of building.

It can be frankly admitted that the Catholic Church, with some notable exceptions on the local level, has done little for the religious education and formation of the millions of Catholic youngsters in the public schools. Perhaps the reason was the hope of eventually realizing the 1884 goal of the Third Plenary Council of Baltimore: "Every Catholic child in a Catholic school!" With more and more thoughtful Catholics quietly accepting the impracticality (to say nothing of the social undesirability) of a kindergarten-to-graduate-school segregated school system, the question of religion in public education has taken on new relevance for Catholics.

Three Centuries of Education in America

The American school of 1667, 1767, or 1867 operated in a context much more conducive than that which prevails in the school of today to achieving the moral and spiritual aims of education. It is not that "discipline of the moral will, achievement of a genuine sense of personal worth and meaning in existence," as well as "commitment to high purpose," are less needed or less talked about or less aimed at today.[1] It is simply that the traditional role of the public or common school in the transmission of agreed-upon moral and spiritual values has almost totally changed.

When the Massachusetts colonist of the seventeenth century built a school, he could be little concerned over the niceties of church-state relations which today would complicate the question of religion in public education. Schooling was a public concern, and it never occurred to him to worry where religious authority left off and secular authority began. He took it as God's self-evident truth that the common schools were the natural and necessary channel of grace for transmitting the values, attitudes, and ideals of Congregationalist faith and culture. Throughout the nineteenth and even into the twentieth century, Protestant loyalty extended to the public school as a kind of shadowy sacrament of the Protestant Establishment.

The secularization of American society, however, was well under way by the time of the Revolution, powered largely by the liberal philosophies of the Enlightenment. Empiricism challenged tradition, and individualism challenged authority. Of necessity, men had to evolve and test new patterns in social relationships without recourse to precedent or institution. Nor were the people of the New World about to re-create the old authoritarian and sacral order they had left behind. As the established churches of the original colonies lost their privileged status, particular tenets of belief and peculiar organizational emphases in church life began to lose their sharpness among Protestant groups. The community-founded schools, since they were supported by all families of the town, had to adapt to the new situation. A doctrinal common ground had to be found that would satisfy the spectrum of religious affiliations, from liberal Unitarian to rock-ribbed Congregationalist.

In the 1830's Horace Mann, first to hold the position of secretary to the Board of Education of the Commonwealth of Massachusetts, was blamed by religious traditionalists and conservatives for reducing the influence of religion in the common schools. Yet the man who is today honored as the father of the public school insisted that, because nineteenth-century America was a Christian nation, Christianity should have an honored place in the schools. Children should be given, said Mann, "so much religious instruction as is compatible with the rights of others and with the genius of our government." [2] But he argued that it was the responsibility of parents to give children "any special and peculiar instruction with respect both to politics and theology," and "at last, when the children arrive at years of maturity, . . . command them to that inviolable prerogative of private judgment and of self-direction, which in a Protestant and a Republican country, is the acknowledged birthright of every human being." [3]

In other words, religion should have a place in the common schools, but it should not be identifiable with the distinctive beliefs of the Congregational or Methodist or Episcopal churches. Above all, Mann wanted the Bible, the common symbol of Protestant Christianity, to be in the schools. Though "our Public Schools are not Theological Seminaries, is admitted," he wrote in his final report, yet "our system . . . welcomes the religion of the Bible; and, in receiving the Bible, it allows it to do what it is allowed to do in no other system — to speak for itself."[4] Considering the times, almost any other approach but Mann's nonsectarian, Bible-oriented compromise would have meant the probable end of the common school movement.

Historically, the American public school evolved from the Puritan common schools of New England without reference to non-Protestant groups. These schools, for the support of which Catholic citizens paid full taxes, were belligerently Protestant. The texts in general use were loaded with derogatory references to things Catholic. *The New England Primer* is merely a famous case in point. In their joint letter of 1840 the Catholic bishops wrote, "We can scarcely point out a book in general use in the ordinary schools, or even in higher seminaries, wherein covert and insidious efforts are not made to misrepresent our principles, to distort our tenets, to vilify our practices and to bring contempt upon our Church and its members."[5] Catholic citizens sought to alleviate their plight in several ways. They asked that the offensive passages be deleted from the standard textbooks; they asked that their youngsters be excused from the reading of the King James Bible and similar Protestant devotional practices; they asked that a share of their tax money be diverted to support separate Catholic schools. In retrospect, Catholic importuning was probably as much responsible as liberal Protestant theology for bringing about the kind of religiously "neutral" atmosphere which sped up the process of secularizing the public schools.

Along with their protest against vestiges of "established" Protestantism in the public schools, Catholics were among the most reluctant to accept the state's right to educate the child at all. Throughout the last century and into the first two decades of the present one, many people have entertained suspicion and mistrust of the state as principal educator and molder of youth.

No mention of the state's role in education appeared in the series of ten pastoral letters issued by the Catholic bishops between 1829 and 1884, during their periodic meetings in Baltimore. The last and most prestigious of these gatherings, the Third Plenary Council of Baltimore, stated, "The three great educational agencies are the home, the Church and the school," a view which seemed rather eloquently to ignore the state. One Catholic commentator of the time granted that the state had the duty to encourage good education, but "its right to education is but a Masonic invention." [6] The sentiment was even more strongly expressed by the Catholic Bishop of Trenton, who said that "the idea that the State has a right to teach . . . is not a Christian idea. It is a pagan one. . . ." [7]

The reluctance on the part of Catholics (and many others) to regard Caesar as anything but a regrettable substitute for parents delinquent in their duty of educating the child becomes more understandable against the background of the social changes that were remaking the Western mind. Values, sanctions, even institutions in society were perceptibly and imperceptibly shifting from the sacral to the secular order.

One enormous change came about through the state's encroachment upon marriage. From time immemorial, the church had had exclusive custody over the bond of matrimony in Christian lands. Both the marriage contract and the religious sacrament of marriage were considered part of the sacred order. The state's jurisdiction extended merely to regulating the civil aspects of marriage — dowries, inheritances, legitimacy of succession, etc. But during the last quarter of the eighteenth century the secularization of marriage was partially or completely realized in all the principal countries of Europe. The state brushed aside ancient church prerogatives and established the new principle that the secular power alone has competence to regulate the marriage contract, grant annulments, and license divorce. No wonder, then, that men, recalling these changes, feared and opposed the state's encroachment in the field of education.

From "Neutral" to "Secular"

The American people have traditionally regarded the schools as the chief transmitters of the American ethic or of the public philosophy which undergirds our society. It was simply taken for granted that the school had a large responsibility for developing character, for inculcating moral and spiritual values, for the ethical formation of the child. In the pre-Civil War days — in fact throughout the nineteenth century — the social context lent itself to a consensus regarding America's political and religious patrimony. Provided the public school did not favor any one Protestant church or sect, it was free to inculcate the generally agreed-upon moral and religious truths of all reasonable Christians as found in the common Bible.

Even during the more sophisticated postbellum period and into the present century, when it began to be more and more argued that by its nature the school must be completely secular and is without competence to enter the sphere of religious education, this new secularity usually was built upon some interpretation of natural law and the theism of the Hebrew-Christian tradition. In other words, despite sectarian differences, men agreed that moral and spiritual values had their roots in some kind of transcendent value system. It was almost universally accepted that American democracy drew its strength from the general conviction that there was a divine power, the author of the rights of man defined in America's first political documents. "This nation under God" was a more meaningful slogan for more Americans in an earlier day.

What was probably unavoidable in the historic working out of Mann's compromise became, in the twentieth century, inevitable. In an effort to remain "neutral," the educational process in the public schools became completely secular, for the compromise approach bore the seeds of its own dissolution. The area of agreed-upon beliefs shrank inexorably, leaving no group really happy with things. The attrition worked to the advantage of those holding the minimum of positive doctrine or none at all. Belief in "the God of our Fathers," the Bible, and the annual baccalaureate sermon by the local Protestant reverend were about all that universally survived this process of disintegration into the post-World War II world. However, even where the substance of religious schooling had long since disappeared, uneasy parents for a while could know that the sacral character of education was secure because some symbols of church and faith remained in the public schools: the Bible was read daily, prayers were recited, Christian religious holidays were observed, church groups actively collaborated, etc.

But "neutralism" was not destined to endure. The final factor in converting the school from neutral to secular was the ascendance of the new philosophies of secularism — scientific humanism, social psychologism, ethical culturism, pragmatism, instrumentalism. These philosophies departed radically from the traditional religions of the West, rejecting the idea of the supernatural and limiting reality to the purely natural order. Man's origin and destiny and relation to a transcendent deity could no longer be the starting point and the basis of a child's educational formation insofar as the humanist was concerned and for his child in the *common* public school. Given the courts' modern sensitivity to alleged or real violations of the rights of conscience, it required very little to ease "the God of the Pilgrim Fathers," the Bible, and the local reverend out of today's public school. The compromise idea begun in the 1840's had at last become bankrupt. America's public schools were no longer either Protestant or Christian. They were no longer religiously oriented. They were now from a judicial point of view "neutral" but from a social point of view "secular."

The courts have imposed a theoretical neutrality upon the public school. The prevailing interpretation by the courts of the no establishment and religious freedom clauses of the First Amendment has forced the public school to assume a neutral posture between those who believe in the God of the Judeo-Christian tradition — or, for that matter any transcendent personal deity — and those who do not. Yet the neutrality could only be apparent since, of necessity, the public school has had to find another starting point and basis: a kind of naturalist religion of democracy. Civic or political virtue has had to be the almost exclusive objective of public school education in the moral order. In other words, public schools can now exist only to train up the good citizen. Even more significant is the fact that responsibility for educating the child has passed from the family to the state.[8]

A Review of Recent Supreme Court Decisions

The social pressures and conflicts which brought secularity to the public schools are themselves reflected in the series of decisions regarding religion and the state schools handed down by the U.S. Supreme Court over the past twenty years. In fact, some of these decisions have accelerated the secularization process itself.

The *Everson* (1947) decision declared that the establishment of religion clause of the First Amendment means that neither a state nor the federal government "can pass laws which aid one religion, aid all religions, or prefer one religion against another."[9] More sweeping still was the interdiction in *Everson* on the use of public monies and cooperation between the state and religious communities: "No tax, in any amount, large or small, can be levied to support any religious activities or institutions, whatever they may be called, or whatever form they may adopt to teach or practice religion."[10] These words, seemingly in sharp contrast to a tradition of more than 150 years, were followed by an even more astonishing statement: "Neither a State nor the Federal Government can, openly or secretly, participate in the affairs of any religious organizations or groups, and vice versa."[11]

Here, indeed, was thrown up a legal wall which, had it been taken literally, would have gone far beyond the most extreme *laïcisme* of nineteenth-century France. It would have demanded that church and state live together as if neither knew of the other's existence. Moreover, it would have demanded the unraveling of hundreds of cooperative undertakings between philanthropic societies with church relationship and the federal and state governments. It would have demanded an end to chaplaincies in the armed forces and public institutions, to invocations by ministers or priests at official dedications and functions, to draft deferment for clergy and clerical students, to exemption of church property from many direct taxes, etc.

The *McCollum* decision, the following year, outlawed the released-time program, a cooperative venture which had been providing religious instruction on public school premises.[12] The case in question arose in the Champaign (Illinois) public schools. Pupils were admitted to the thirty-minute weekly classes held inside the public school buildings only on the written request of the parents. All instructional expenses were borne by the fifty sponsoring church groups in the classrooms made available by the school district.

With the 1952 *Zorach* decision, the U.S. Supreme Court swung back closer to what many observers judged its "traditional" position. It sustained the legality of the New York program for religious instruction, the pivotal difference appearing to be that in New York the instruction took place off public school property, whereas in Illinois it was on public school property. The 6–3 majority opinion written by Justice William O. Douglas took pains to explain that the separation of the state from religion must not result in a relationship that is "hostile, suspicious and . . . unfriendly." The decision affirmed that "when the State encouraged religious instruction . . . it follows the best of our traditions." The state may "encourage" religion, though it cannot aid it; the government should "sponsor an attitude" that lets each religious group flourish.[13]

Some caustic commentators suggested that *Zorach* had forgotten with improper haste what *Everson* had said: "Neither a State nor the Federal Government can, openly or secretly, participate in the affairs of any religious organizations or groups, and *vice versa*."[14]

A decade later the pendulum swung in the reverse direction, when the court reviewed the *Engel* case.[15] The issue revolved around the optional recitation of a brief prayer composed by the New York State Board of Regents for classroom use. The Supreme Court ruled this a step toward an establishment of religion and, consequently, a violation of the First Amendment. In its action the U.S. Supreme Court reversed rulings on three levels by New York State courts which had upheld the provision.

During its 1962–63 sitting the Supreme Court passed on three other cases involving religious practices in the public schools.[16] The *Schempp* and *Murray* cases were ruled on in a single set of opinions, while the *Chamberlin* case was remanded to the Florida Supreme Court for reconsideration in the light of opinions covering the Pennsylvania (*Schempp*) and the Maryland (*Murray*) cases. The issue common to all three was the required reading of some passages of the Bible without comment, and, in the Maryland and Florida cases, the opening of the school day with a non-sectarian prayer. The court declared these practices unconstitutional.

As far as religion and public education goes, in this series of decisions over the past twenty years the Court has simply underscored the practical impossibility of having an officially (and necessarily) "neutral" state school *itself* provide what millions of American families consider an essential dimension of education. It is impossible in the practical order because by definition the school is "common" and must yield to all reasonable community compromises. The American people continue to charge the public school with a large responsibility for character education but have no consensus on what constitutes the ethical side of education and the best means of accomplishing it. The perennial frustration is the fundamental limitation inherent in the idea of a single *common* school, established to serve a religiously fragmented society.

Most Americans would readily agree that the public school is a civic and not a religious institution, and that, in the nature of things, it cannot be turned into a community of worship. However, what is a concern to very many Americans today is that the alleged neutrality, often described in lofty language by the U.S. Supreme Court, does not leave the public school truly neutral but establishes conditions which allow cooperation with the school exclusively to a-religious, non-religious, and anti-religious groups in society. In his dissent in the Bible-reading and prayer cases, Justice Potter Stewart underscored the point. A refusal to permit these minimal exercises on a voluntary basis is seen, he said, "not as the realization of state neutrality, but rather as the establishment of a religion of secularism, or at least, as government support of the beliefs of those who think that religious exercises should be conducted only in private."[17]

Neutrality and the Value System

Though the *Torcaso* decision in 1961 dealt with a public oath required of officeholders by the state of Maryland, the Court's explanation of neutrality in religious versus non-religious issues is relevant to the school question. In this decision the court ruled, "Neither a State nor the Federal Government can constitutionally pass laws nor impose requirements which aid all religions as against non-believers, and neither can aid those religions based on a belief in the existence of God as against those religions founded on different beliefs."[18]

One commentator has made a sharp riposte, arguing that if neutralism in religion means anything at all the Court's proposition is reversible: "The State cannot pass laws or impose requirements that aid non-believers as against religion or which aid religions that are *not* based on a belief in God as against those that are."[19]

The dilemma of "neutrality" becomes worse when transferred to public education because of the Court's premise that it is the state, not the community, that is the educator in the public schools. *L'école, c'est moi!* Because the state is secular, it must be above conflicting and differing religious philosophies and, in fact, neutral between religious believers and non-believers. This must be granted. But can the state as educator follow the same line of neutrality in the schools?

To borrow from the same authority:

What the State cannot do, according to the court, the school cannot do either, because the school is the State in action. The State has no religion. The school, therefore, not only has no religion, but cannot make a place for religion in its curriculum. It cannot do this even for those who want it, and even when private persons rather than public school teachers are allowed to use public school classrooms for religious instruction on a voluntary basis.[20]

Is it time for a hard new look at the premise? Should education in a public school be exclusively an activity of the state? Or is education an activity with a dimension that extends beyond the competence of the state and, therefore, better achieved by actively enlisting the cooperation of other agencies whose qualification in this respect is larger than the state's? Given its present structure, one may grant, the public school by itself is incapable of providing religious instruction. But this is not to grant the necessity or desirability of barring the cooperation of agencies in society that are competent here.

At this point it is usually urged that religious education should take place in the church or home, leaving the public school properly busy with the business of secular education. This solution has the beauty of simplicity but it just cannot work. The new complicating factor is the greatly enlarged place that the modern school occupies in the life of a youngster. In view of the conditions of family living in our industrialized and urbanized society, what other major educational influences on the life of the child are left? Is it an exaggeration to say that the modern school, particularly for the twelve- to eighteen-year age group, consumes the majority of waking hours? What with school-sponsored activities, socials, athletics, etc., the youngsters' interests and friendships center around the school. Such was not always the case. In earlier times, philosophers of education could truly talk of dividing the time of the pupil, and their efforts at reaching compromise on the religion-in-education question were based on some theoretical division. Columbia's respected historian of education, Lawrence A. Cremin, has observed: "Jefferson was a great believer in schooling, but it never occurred to him that schooling would be the chief educational influence on the young."[21] It is only with John Dewey and his time that "public education has become coexistensive with the education of the public."[22]

Moreover, there are defenders of the "neutral-secular" public school who seem not to understand that culture rises out of a value system, and that every value system has its roots in religion — at least in the broad sense of the word. To convey a culture minus its religious dimension is to substantially alter and thereby falsify the culture. If the public school makes no provision to insure a role for outside agencies here, is it to be wondered at that only secularist ideals and values come to govern the lives of many graduates of public schools? Study of sacred books or codes along with a gradual introduction to religious rites, traditions, and ceremonies are the normal means of initiating a new generation into a faith community. These are woven closely into a total culture, and formal schooling is its ideal means of transmission. We repeat: the coexistence within a society of faith groups holding different religious philosophies makes it impossible for one common public school itself to give religious education and formation. Indeed, this can be done only in a society in which there exists a unity of religious faith. Historically, it was attempted in the first American public schools.

Because of the religious and spiritual diversity in our society, there is a narrowing basis for any general agreement on values and none at all relating to their sanctions. At one time Protestant and Catholic alike could talk of a Christian ethic built on the Old World legacy of Greco-Roman natural law and the central religious concepts of the Judeo-Christian tradition. But no longer, despite the overwhelming consensus favoring such an ethic, can it directly figure in any public school program of moral and spiritual values, for the U.S. Supreme Court has decided that even the traditional theistic bias in the state schools conflicts with the constitutional rights of non-believers. Nor can the point of law be simply dismissed with an impatient shake of the head. Conscientious public school administrators and boards of education have long agonized over this point: To what extent should the children of Jehovah's Witnesses, Orthodox Jews, Zen Buddhists, Ethical Culturists, Christian Scientists, Asian Moslems, atheists, and agnostics — all equally citizens with Protestants, Jews, and Catholics — be made to conform to a religious tradition that is alien to them? Before condemning the Court, a person would do well to reflect what his own reaction would be, were his child required to follow even nominal religious observances in a public school in Pakistan, Israel, or Japan.

Even without legal restrictions, the public school *as such* is in no position to appropriately teach distinctive or general religious beliefs for either understanding or commitment. This point should no longer be the subject of debate. But what about general prayer formulas and the reading of the Bible? A counter question can be fairly raised. Other than their traditional and symbolic values, just how much religious formative influence is actually exerted by a symbolic prayer or by the reading of ten verses from the Bible without comment? In many communities it might have been better to continue such practices, but since now they have become subjects of litigation and dissension, one wonders whether the struggle to maintain them brings anything but bitterness in its wake.

As far back as 1840 Catholic opinion was divided on the practical value of Bible reading in the schools. In their joint pastoral letter of that year the Catholic bishops voiced their desire "that at an early period, children should be instructed in the Sacred History . . . and be judiciously led by proper selections, under discreet and pious guides, to the right use of this rich treasure." [23] However, they at once added, "We are disposed to doubt seriously whether the introduction of this sacred volume as an ordinary class book into schools is beneficial to religion." Their reasons were that thereby the Bible is exposed "to that irreverent familiarity, which is calculated to produce more contempt than veneration"; that the sacred book would be placed "side by side with mere human productions, with the fables of mythology and the speculations of a vain philosophy," finally making the Bible "the subject of a vulgar jest" and sinking it "to the level of task-books." [24]

"Secularization" and "Secular"

For good or for ill, the character of the public school has moved by stages from non-denominational Protestant to ever broadening neutral to unabashedly secular. But is everything lost? Is the secular nature of the modern public school a completely bad thing? Has the process of secularization been a total loss for America? Not if several points are kept in mind. The first is the distinction between "secularization" and "secular." Few have argued the point so lucidly as Harvey Cox: "Secularization implies a historical process, almost certainly irreversible, in which society and culture are delivered from tutelage to religious control and closed metaphysical world-views. . . . Secularism, on the other hand, is the name for an ideology, a new closed world-view which functions very much like a religion." [25]

It is perhaps surprising to learn that in 1884 the same Third Plenary Council of Baltimore which symbolizes rigorous Catholic commitment to the parochial school discussed the necessarily secular nature of the public school: "The friends of Catholic education do not condemn the State for not imparting religious instruction in the public schools as they are now organized: because they well know it does not lie within the province of the State to teach religion." [26] A decade later John Lancaster Spalding, the scholarly Bishop of Peoria, wrote even more to the point: "I am willing to assume and to accept as a fact that our theological differences make it impossible to introduce the teaching of any religious creed into the public school. I take the system as it is — that is, as a system of secular education. . . ." [27]

The sixth of the Fourteen Propositions presented to the American hierarchy by Archbishop Francis Satolli, sent by Pope Leo XIII in 1892 to settle the "School Question," states that the Church "holds for herself the right of teaching the truths of faith and the law of morals in order to bring up youth in the habits of a Christian life," and then adds, "Hence,

absolutely and universally speaking, there is no repugnance in their learning the first elements and the higher branches of arts and the natural sciences in public schools, controlled by the State. . . ." [28]

The Shadow of Bigotry

The separate parochial school in America as a system to provide for
the total schooling of Catholic children was born of desperate necessity.
It might never have come about — at least on the scale it did — had the
mood of nineteenth-century America been different. The voices of
moderates willing to discuss adaptation and compromise were drowned
out by the bigots and extremists — at times on the Catholic side as well.
The 1830's saw the burning of the Charleston convent and the *Awful
Disclosures* of Maria Monk. The 1850's saw the Philadelphia riots, the
anti-papal demonstrations which greeted the Pope's representative, Archbishop Bedini, the tarring and feathering of the Jesuit John Bapst, the
Massachusetts law for the inspection of convents, and the riots of Louis-
ville's "Bloody Monday." The Civil War broke the political power of
the Know-Nothing movement, but the forces of nativism banded together
again in the 1880's to form the American Protective Association.

The 1928 presidential campaign disclosed that the virus of nativism
was still active in the American body politic. Anyone who has followed
the post-World War II history of federal aid to the schools is aware of
how close to the surface are the nerve endings, how deep the fears, how
bitter the debate when proposals are made to assist Catholic institutions
in any way.

Religion and the Culture

Does acceptance of the secular character of the contemporary American public school then mean that it should be altogether excluded from
the area of religious education? Directly, and in its capacity as an
extension of the state, the answer has to be "Yes." Indirectly and functioning as an extension of the community, the answer is "No." Nor by
religious education is meant here the study of religious events or religiously based literary pieces in the accepted curriculum, which must
have place in proportion to their relevance to the larger fields of history
and literature. If the schools cannot talk about the Crusades, the breakup
of Christian unity, or the Cromwellian period with honesty and sensitivity,
perhaps they should be closed.

The American Association of School Administrators in a recent national policy statement says,

A curriculum which ignored religion would itself have serious religious
implications. It would seem to proclaim that religion has not been as real in

men's lives as health or politics or economics. . . . Whatever else the Supreme Court decisions may or may not have done, they have stimulated the public schools to a search for appropriate means to deal effectively with religion as one of the great influences in man's history.[29]

I doubt that there is either the personnel, the audience, or the genuine need to promote a course in "Comparative Religions" or "Great Systems of Religious Thought" at the sixth- or ninth-grade level, as is urged in some quarters. However, at the eleventh- or twelfth-grade level, a chapter or two in "American Civics" or in "Modern Social Problems" discussing these areas would have much to recommend it. Ignorance (to say nothing of distortion) of what one's neighbor believes can lead to misunderstanding and mistrust. It should be an obviously normal preparation for full membership in our pluralistic society to have learned as part of social studies the background and rudimentary content of the value systems of the people of America. The failure may be laid mainly to the teacher training institutions and religious educators, and theirs is the challenge. Some steps have been taken to repair the situation; it is to be hoped that its urgency will bring about others.

Cooperation of Church and School

What practically can the American public school do? As has long since been done in many other equally modern and democratic nations, it might put certain of its facilities at the disposal of church or religious groups for biweekly religious instruction, at an hour and in a way that by no stretch of the imagination would honestly infringe on the constitutional rights of anyone. The school administration could also cooperate with these groups in a variety of dismissed-time and shared-time programs. Too long have imagination and initiative been stifled by the fear of some alleged breaching in the wall of separation between church and state. American churches and church-related institutions have flourished because of the atmosphere of benevolent neutrality on the part of the state and should be counted among the first defenders of the authentic doctrine of separation.

If religious educators today are willing to accept the state-supported school system as an institution of the secular order, the state schools must be willing to take positive steps to enlist the services and resources of other agencies which share concern for the education and formation of the child. In effect, this means the quiet burial of the "no communication" philosophy expressed in the *Everson* case.

In its turn, the Catholic school must move away from another kind of "no communication" philosophy expressed in Canon 1374 of the Church's *Code of Canon Law:* "Catholic children may not attend non-Catholic, neutral or mixed schools, that is, those which are open also to non-Catholics. It is for the local bishop to decide, in accordance with the instructions of the Holy See, under what circumstances and with what precautions against the danger of perversion, attendance at such schools may be allowed." [30]

The eighth of the Propositions of Archbishop Satolli frankly avowed that the Catholic schools had to be established in the United States because the public schools of 1892 were generally "a proximate danger to faith and morals." This danger, the Proposition detailed, lay in the total exclusion of religious teaching, indiscriminate selection of teachers from every sect, and coeducation. The same Proposition goes on to indicate, however, that when these dangers to faith and morals disappear, "then it is lawful for Catholic parents to send their children to these schools, to acquire the elements of letters and arts, provided the parents themselves do not neglect their most serious duty, and the pastors of souls put forth every effort to instruct the children and train them in all that pertains to Catholic worship and life." [31]

Satolli's first problem would be eliminated if the general European pattern of cooperation between the state schools and the church groups were adopted, or any variation of the shared- or dismissed-time programs. The second difficulty is scarcely recognizable today. Our modern public school teachers are as much drawn from the Catholic community as from any group, and the official policy of neutrality leaves small opportunity to proselytize for anyone inclined to missionary indiscretions. The Archbishop's third point, again, has become less significant in a more sophisticated age, which has grown accustomed to the mingling of the sexes in education and in recreation.

The separate religiously oriented school will continue to play a key role for a significant portion of the school population, Catholic and (to a lesser extent) Protestant. Perhaps at no time in history has America had greater need for the distinctive witness of this type of school. However, more and more Catholic youngsters will receive all or part of their formal schooling in the secular public school. Catholic educators will have to devise new ways and improve existing ones of providing something of a Catholic *education* for them. But the responsibility is not a Catholic one only. The clear and calmer atmosphere of 1967 allows all of us concerned with America and the schools to discuss these issues in a constructive way. Quite obviously, there is no uniform pattern that can be sewn to fit local and regional problems from coast to coast. There is, nonetheless, a single attitude that does fit — a willingness to look to the future with fresh eyes and firm heart, seeking the best for America's greatest treasure: her young people.

NOTES

1. Preliminary Report of Task Force on Education, prepared for the White House Conference, "To Fulfll These Rights," Washington, D.C., April 21, 1966, p. 1.

2. *Life and Works,* II, 289–290.

3. *Ibid.*

4. *Twelfth Annual Report,* facsimile edition, pp. 116–117. Quoted in Neil G. McCluskey, *Public Schools and Moral Education* (Columbia University Press, 1958), p. 91. This book contains a several-chapter discussion of the specific problem.

5. Peter Guilday (ed.), *The National Pastorals of the American Hierarchy, 1732–1919* (National Catholic Welfare Council, 1923), pp. 124–125.

6. P. Bayma, "The Liberalistic View of the Public School Question," *American Quarterly Review,* 2:17 (1877).

7. Quoted in Daniel F. Reilly, *The School Controversy* (1891–1893) (Catholic University of America Press, 1943), p. 107. Bishop Bernard McQuaid of Rochester, N.Y., who argued that a Catholic's conscience "informs him that the state is an incompetent agent to fulfill his parental duties," could quote in his favor the authority of the British philosopher Herbert Spencer: "In the same way that our definition of state duty forbids the State to administer religion or charity, so likewise does it forbid the state to administer education" (*The Public School Question* [Duffy, 1876], p. 7).

8. Merle Curti has pointed out that, up to the time of the struggle by the Catholic community of New York in the 1840's for tax support of parochial schools, "Catholics and non-Catholics had been in essential agreement regarding parental responsibility for the education of children." But because of the factors discussed here, "the older idea that education was a parental responsibility gave way to the belief that it was an enterprise of the State" (*The Social Ideas of American Educators* [Pageant Books, 1959], p. 349).

9. *Everson v. Board of Education,* 330 U.S. 1 (1947).

10. *Ibid.*

11. *Ibid.*

12. *McCollum v. Board of Education,* 333 U.S. 212 (1948).

13. *Zorach v. Clauson,* 343 U.S. 306 (1952).

14. Emphasis added.

15. *Engel v. Vitale,* 370 U.S. 421 (1962).

16. *Abington School District v. Schempp,* 374 U.S. 203, 225 (1963); *Murray v. Curlett* (June 17, 1963), Part V; *Chamberlin v. Dade County,* 143 So. 2d 21 (1962).

17. *Abington v. Schempp.*

18. *Torcaso v. Watkins,* 376 U.S. 488 (1961).

19. Francis Canavan, "Implications of the School Prayer and Bible Reading Decisions: The Welfare State," *Journal of Public Law* (Atlanta, Ga., Emory University Law School), 13:443 (1965). Emphasis added.

20. *Ibid.*

21. *The Genius of American Education* (Random House, 1966), p. 6.

22. *Ibid.*

23. See Neil G. McCluskey, *Catholic Education in America: A Documentary History* (Teachers College, Bureau of Publications, 1964), p. 6.

24. *Ibid.*

25. *The Secular City* (Macmillan, 1965), pp. 20–21.

26. McCluskey, *Public Schools and Moral Education*, p. 92.

27. *Means and Ends of Education* (McClurg, 1895), pp. 140–150. No Catholic leader of the last century commanded the respect or wielded the influence of Bishop Spalding of Peoria (1840–1916). He had an appreciation of the function of public education not shared by all his brethren in the hierarchy. In 1913 Archbishop John L. Glennon of St. Louis described him as "the one Catholic who has best understood the American mind."

28. McCluskey, *Public Schools and Moral Education*, p. 154.

29. AASA, *Religion in the Public Schools* (The Association, 1964), p. 55.

30. Translated from the Latin in McCluskey, *Public Schools and Moral Education*, p. 176.

31. *Ibid.*, pp. 155–156.

13

The Nature of American Pluralism

Talcott Parsons

Many other members of the Conference on the Role of Religion in Public Education are better qualified than I to discuss detailed problems of the place of religion in relation to the public schools in this country. I believe that I can contribute best by discussing two problem areas and then drawing a few inferences for the concerns of the Conference from each area. The first area covers certain broad aspects of the religious constitution of American society, understanding the term "constitution" in more than a legal sense. The second area concerns the bearing of certain features of our system of higher education on problems of the public school system. I approach this area on the theory that there must be some "strain to consistency" in education and that, if so, higher education will in important respects set the tone for the educational system as a whole.

The Growth of Religious Toleration

At the time of the adoption of the First Amendment, very few Europeans would have thought that the new American system of separation of church and state and of the resultant denominational pluralism constituted the "wave of the future." There is no doubt, however, that the historic European system of established churches has been greatly weakened in the intervening period. With few exceptions outside the Communist countries where organized religion is severely repressed, a pattern of religious toleration prevails — even Spain has moved a little in this direction.

There are of course differing opinions about the consequences of the latter development. An important school of thought holds that disestablishment and toleration have been phases of a general "decline of religion" in the Western world, of a process of secularization in the purely negative sense. However, many observers, including de Tocqueville, have felt, on the contrary, that religion has been particularly strong in the United States — and not long ago we heard a good deal about a religious revival.

My own interpretation is strongly with the more favorable view.[1] I also think it is possible to fit that view into a more inclusive sociological analysis of the trends of development of Western society generally, concerning especially some respects in which American society has taken important leads.[2] The critical process of development has involved differentiation in the structure of the society, which in turn has been accompanied by a major restructuring of the societal community as a whole. One prime aspect of this restructuring has been the inclusion, in the status of full informal "citizenship," of elements not previously accorded that position.[3]

The process I have in mind has been under way a long time, recently reaching a culmination very important for the present context: the relatively full inclusion in the national community of major non-Protestant and non-Anglo-Saxon elements, especially those of the "New Immigration" which arrived in great numbers after 1890. These elements have been mainly Roman Catholic and Jewish, religiously, but their ethnic differences from the older majority groups of the population should not be overlooked, including their internal ethnic diversity.[4] Despite their common Catholicism, the Irish, Italians, Poles, and French Canadians are by no means ethnically identical; nor is the Jewish contingent ethnically homogeneous. The American Negro presents special problems, which have their religious aspects. Yet we can now say that American society, as Herberg[5] first clearly showed, has become an ecumenical "Judeo-Christian" society; it is no longer a Protestant society in the sense which applied down through the first part of the present century. It has moved from largely negative toleration of non-Protestants to their inclusion in a denominationally pluralistic community, the pluralism of which comprises *all* the most important religious groups of Western history.

A symbolic seal was placed on the more difficult of the two inclusions, that of the Roman Catholic, by the career of John F. Kennedy, first by his election as the first Roman Catholic (indeed, the first non-Protestant) to the Presidency of the United States and then by the tremendous public emotional response to the tragedy of his assassination. If there had been any lingering doubts that *this* President was truly the nation's "First Citizen," they were dispelled in the tragedy, except perhaps for a tiny die-hard minority.

THE ECUMENICAL MOVEMENT

It is also of major significance that this development in the American religious situation has been closely linked with the ecumenical movement in the whole Christian world. The latter, of course, has included Christianity's relations with Judaism and, rather more remotely, with other religious traditions altogether outside the historic Western orbit: Islam, Buddhism, and Hinduism. Indeed, in a very important way, the "political religion" of Marxism-Leninism has been involved. The most salient development on this front has been the change in view of the Catholic Church as a whole, symbolized above all by the brief Papacy of John XXIII and by the Vatican Council which he first called. It is not possible here to explore the undoubtedly important connections between American developments and these changes in the outlook of Catholicism generally. However, the coincidence in time, for example, of the Kennedy story and that of Pope John is of cardinal significance.

INDIVIDUALIZATION OF RELIGIOUS AFFILIATION

With this most recent phase in the development of its religious constitution, America has carried the differentiation of the specifically religious components from the main secular social structures farther than any previous society. This means that religious collectivities become, not only in the eyes of the law but even in more informal senses, *voluntary associations*. Historic origins in traditions of national background, as in the case of Irish or Italian elements, or of ethnic history, as in the Jewish case, need not be abandoned by individuals or groups. Yet one born of Irish Catholic parents is not under compulsion to remain a Catholic, nor is one born of ethnically Jewish parents under compulsion to be a religious Jew. Parallel reasoning of course applies to Protestant origins. In this sense of voluntarism, religious affiliation has become "privatized"; what it shall be, or whether one shall have any at all, is the private affair of the individual.

There is an important parallel here to the family. Our society has very fully privatized the matter of choosing a marriage partner, including the decision whether or not to marry at all. To be sure, neither parents nor children can evade the implications of the relation of biological parenthood and its social concomitants, but the consequences of having been brought up in a particular religious atmosphere cannot be evaded either

— no one brought up as a Protestant can ever be exactly the same kind of Catholic or Jew as a person born into one of these faiths. In neither case, however, does the early experience ascriptively determine adult affiliation or conduct; what it does is "condition" it.

The religious aspect of the consequences of this differentiation has an obverse in the "secular" sphere. In matters touching the basic structure of the societal community there should be minimal discrimination on the basis of the specifics of religious preference and affiliation. The application of this proposition may require much subtlety. In the specifically private sphere, there can be no obligation for an individual to make uncongenial choices. Thus, to pressure anyone to marry someone belonging to a religious group different from his own would be as unacceptable as forbidding him to marry outside his own group or attaching especially onerous conditions to such a marriage.

AREAS OF PUBLIC CONCERN

The critical problem concerns the definitions of what is "specifically private" and what is in some sense a *public* matter. It should not be expected that concretely the line can remain unchanged for long in a society which is undergoing such important processes of structural change as ours. Nevertheless, one can give a rough account of where in principle the line should be drawn. The public concern for the basic rights of the individual and of legitimate groups is directed to religious freedom to "worship God in one's own way" and in the company of those who share that way, so long as the rights of others are not infringed. However, it is also extended to access to the opportunities both to gratify private wishes and needs and to succeed in the competitive aspects of securing status and the related possibilities for socially valued achievement.

Recent developments in constitutional law have been clarifying some of the main points here. In a highly monetized economy, access to consumers' income falls in this category of essential opportunities. For units in the market system, therefore, some universalistic principles must be upheld both in that specific levels of income must be maintained and in that limitations of access to particular markets are not admissible. Thus, although no law prescribes who an individual may or may not invite as a guest to his home, he is forbidden to discriminate in certain ways if he runs a restaurant, hotel, or motel. A second basic context is that of employment. Access to opportunity for employment, as far as it is controlled by particular employing organizations, cannot be treated simply as the employer's right to hire whom he pleases; in many ways the employer must give equal opportunity over a range of criteria to prospective employees. It has now been clearly established that discrimination in terms of race alone — and the same surely applies to religion — is not acceptable.

The corresponding principles in the political field are familiar. The "common man's" stake in the political power system, i.e., his franchise, may not be infringed on the basis of race, creed, or color, or place of residence. The same applies to the openness of opportunity in the influence aspect of the political process insured through freedom of speech, of the press, and, in some respects, of association, at the level both of parties and of interest groups. Finally, there has to be a universalization of freedoms in the field of specific morally grounded commitments. This is the crucial field for our purposes and requires elucidation.

If we trace sufficiently far back in cultural history, we find that the deeper religious commitments have very generally had highly specific moral corollaries. Thus, a good Catholic (or Protestant) in pre-Revolutionary France (or England) was morally obligated to accept the political authority of the duly established monarch and not to claim a right to a voice in the choice of the nation's political leadership. Similarly, in the days of fully established churches, a man was morally obligated by his religious commitment, not only to maintain orthodoxy himself, but also to cooperate in combating heresy anywhere in the societal community to the point of the political suppression of all religiously dissident opinion. The implication of religious pluralization, however, is that the moral commitment is to toleration of religious differences and to treatment of the members of all the included religious groups without discrimination in matters of *public* concern. This moral commitment can be solid in religious terms only if the religion itself accepts the ecumenical principle that there is no "one true religion" which adherents have a moral right to force upon non-adherents. The level of moral consensus is more general than that of the morality of a particular denomination.

IMPLICATION OF RELIGIOUS PLURALISM

The pluralization of which we have spoken has a double implication. One aspect concerns the restraint imposed on historic religious particularism by the principles of toleration and pluralism. No one group has the right to *impose* its preferences on the others, which means on the community.[6]

The other aspect is that the community itself must be grounded in a moral consensus. Groups within the community who differ on the explicit religious level not only are to be "permitted" to go their varying ways but must be held to have a *moral right* to do so — the difference is crucial for our argument. Unless there is genuine consensus on this point, the integrative basis of the societal community must remain shaky, a matter of unstable "compromises."[7] Clearly the "fundamentalist" elements in all three principal religious groups in American society tend to reject the consensus on these terms, though the great amount of ambivalence should not be overlooked, for groups who repudiate it in one context often "go along" in another. Further, it should be recognized that there are "secularist" fundamentalists as well as the "religious" variety. The compulsive atheist who denies any legitimacy to believers in historic religions is one of these. He is just as difficult to fit into the American type of ecumenical pluralistic system as the fundamentalist of religious orthodoxy.

The Rise of Higher (Private) Education

As the American public school system began to develop, especially in the 1840's, the First Amendment precluded its being under direct control of any denominational group. For example, it was impossible to follow the pattern long obtaining in the province of Quebec, where public funds have been used to support both Catholic and Protestant schools and parents have been permitted to choose their children's schools. However, the understanding that public schools had to be in a broad sense secular left unsolved many problems of just how the lines should be drawn. I do not propose to enter into the intricacies of this complex field but wish to suggest its bearing on another line of development in American education.

Although Americans showed a strong concern for education from early colonial days, anything like a university system of the type which then existed in Europe did not begin to develop until after the middle of the nineteenth century, the period of the Land Grant Act of 1863 and the beginning of the state universities. Yet, it is probably correct to say that on the whole the main lead in the first generation of the development of full-fledged universities was taken by the private institutions. Except for certain new ones which were established during that period, they had *all* originally been religious foundations.

The "takeoff" into full university status in these cases broadly coincided with a process of secularization in much the same sense in which we have used that term for the society as a whole. It is symbolic that President Eliot of Harvard, one of the great leaders of the movement, was the first Harvard president who was not a Protestant clergyman. Before corresponding developments took place at Oxford and Cambridge, religious tests for teaching on the faculties and for admission as students were abolished. The general expansion of the curriculum, especially with the liberating effects of the elective system, immensely increased the range of essentially secular, as well as non-classical, subjects that were taught. Particularly noteworthy was the growth first of the natural sciences and later of the social disciplines. It is crucial that this was the period of controversy over Darwinism, and that the emerging universities became increasingly committed to the new scientific points of view, even where they were bitterly opposed by conservative religious opinion.

Decidedly important was the development of the new graduate schools of arts and sciences. In certain respects the model for them was borrowed from the German universities, where many in that academic generation had gone for their advanced study.[8] However, there were major innovations both in the character of the work done and in the way it was fitted into the rest of the university structure. In the first place, the graduate school did not merely upgrade, and definitely did not replace, the undergraduate college. Rather, it took its place in addition to the college — none of the most important universities became graduate universities alone.

ACADEMIC PROFESSIONALISM

In addition, it seems that, compared to the German model, predominantly that of the Philosophical Faculty, the American graduate schools were upgraded. They became the loci of a rapidly professionalizing academic group, whereas the great majority of students in the German Philosophical Faculties had been training to become secondary school teachers, with only a small elite group aiming for a fully academic career. The American academic profession gradually came to be drawn from a much wider base in social origins than any in Europe. Hence, it was much more dissociated from anchorage in elite groups, which in the European cases were more "high bourgeois" than aristocratic in the narrower sense. The American academics became increasingly professionalized[9] in a number of respects. One was diversity of social origin — here the drawing of large proportions from the smaller colleges of the Midwest was an important fact, as was the later inclusion of sizable contingents of Jews. This tended to involve an increasing dependence on the part of academics on their occupational status; they usually had less independent wealth, fewer independent bases of prestige, and the like. It is probably not fortuitous that early in the present century the organization of the American Association of University Professors compiled the first formalized demand for full institutionalization of a set of principles of academic freedom and tenure.

Graduate students then came to be the focus of the professional aspirations of the system. For their teachers, this meant adopting a somewhat different focus of pedagogic concern from that of the older type of college teacher, who taught only undergraduates and knew that no more than a minority of these would become teachers themselves. Probably the biggest change, however, was the stimulus given by the organizational changes to the professionalization of the research function. Although the older type of college teacher was often also a "scholar," his scholarship was for the most part on an amateur basis. Criteria for appointment and advancement in the colleges were not nearly so likely as later they became in the universities heavily to involve research accomplishment and promise. Indeed, it can be said that, at the core of the higher reaches of the system, the graduate faculties (usually not separate in personnel from the college faculties of the same universities) of the most prestigious universities, contribution to the advancement of knowledge is now probably the most important single governing standard for appointment and promotion.

SECULARIZATION AT THE UNIVERSITY LEVEL

It is crucial for the present argument that the new focus of the enormously developed academic system lay in the *secular* intellectual disciplines. The typical professor was no longer the "divine" who had scholarly interests on the side, but a professional expert in a secular field of learning. In a very important sense, the German conception of *Wissenschaft* came to provide the central norm of intellectual endeavor. It included the narrower meaning of the English term "science," but also objective scholarship in all fields, particularly including humanistic fields. We might say that the dominant academic value pattern has become "cognitive rationality." This is by no means unrelated to religious background and legitimation, but it is not a *direct* basis for the implementation of religious commitments. It is in this sense that one can speak of the *secular* intellectual disciplines.

Along with the general changes in the status of the clergy in the society as a whole, this development has removed religion from its former place as the primary cultural focus of the university system. Despite the variety of complex problems in this area, it is sufficient for our purposes to say, first, that general education at the undergraduate level in the private institutions has become greatly secularized in that socialization at the higher cultural levels into a specifically denominational religious orientation system has ceased to be dominant. Secondly, the new graduate schools now concentrate, in both research and teaching, specifically on the secular intellectual disciplines. They are, moreover, the apex of the American university system, which in turn is clearly the apex of the academic system as a whole, i.e., the system of higher education and research in the broad sense.

This development has a special implication for the status of the so-called professional faculties. In the German system, essentially, all faculties were equal; that is, the Philosophical Faculty was the Faculty of Education in a much more specific sense than is our Faculty of Arts and Sciences, which in most major universities is differentiated from a Faculty of Education. Above all, the Faculty of Arts and Sciences is no longer on the same level as the faculties of Law, Medicine, and most important for our purposes, Theology, or, to use the American Protestant term, Divinity. The fact that the Faculty of Theology has become a "professional school" faculty is the crucial index of the secularization of the American university. Since the cultural focus of the university as a whole is in the secular intellectual disciplines, the *university* function of theology, as well as law, medicine, and education, has come to be training in the "application" of the knowledge developed in and by these disciplines.

Clearly, modern university structure is quite incompatible with higher education's remaining under denominational auspices in the older traditional sense. There have been many stages in the working out of the major institutional changes, but their main direction is evident, especially in the context of the more general American religious constitution as sketched above.

Specifically religious practices and institutions in the setting of the university have presented a whole series of problems. For example, when I was an undergraduate in a not-too-conservative liberal arts college, Amherst, compulsory chapel attendance was a bitterly fought issue. The solution in my time was, as so often, a compromise; but it was inevitable that the battle to maintain it would be lost *if* Amherst was to remain in the mainstream of the American academic system rather than becoming a religiously "fundamentalist" college.

A second case, farther along the line of development, was the controversy at Harvard in 1958 over the status of the College Church. Here, no less a figure than the president of the university took the position that it was a consecrated Protestant church and thus not available for services of Jewish religious significance. It is of the first importance to the present argument that President Pusey was overruled by the Corporation, which declared the church to be what we might call an "ecumenical" facility, open to Jewish, Catholic, and, indeed, "secular" ceremonial occasions, such as funerals and weddings, independent of Harvard's historic Protestant commitments.

Particularly interesting in this context is the situation of the massive Roman Catholic system of higher education. The main trend of change in this system is certainly toward full inclusion in the more general American system upon the same basic organizational patterns. Thus, not only are Catholic universities open on a very considerable scale, without pressure to conversion, to non-Catholic students and increasingly to faculty members, but non-Catholics now hold high-level administrative positions (e.g., the new dean of the Faculty of Education at Fordham is a Jew) and even positions of trusteeship.

Secularization in a Pluralistic Society

In the light of the current controversies over the justification of the recent Supreme Court decisions with respect to religious observances in the public schools, it is easy to assume that only (or mainly) a formal matter of legal status is at issue. However, the foregoing discussion has shown that trends in the American educational system which have not in any simple sense been legally prescribed are relevant to this problem. I do not doubt that the value orientations which underlay the policy of the separation of state and church also underlay the later emergence of a predominantly secular system of higher education in the private as well as the public sector, but the secularization of the private sector of higher education was clearly not legally required. Nor, to my mind, has the desire to become eligible for federal financial aid been playing more than a secondary role in the secularizing trend which is proceeding in the Catholic institutions. These trends are deeply grounded in the general structure of American society, including certain of the positive implications of its religious tradition.

The essential point, then, is that the strong trend to secularization — in the sense that religious concerns have become newly differentiated from secular concerns in a number of specific fields, thereby rendering religion increasingly "privatized" — is one primary aspect of the development of a highly differentiated, pluralistic society. It is a cardinal fact about any such society, however, that its very pluralistic diversity is possible only because it has institutionalized a firmly patterned system of normative order, incorporated in its legal system but extending beyond the realm of the legally enforceable, especially in the direction of moral commitments.

"FREEDOM OF RELIGION"

The general process of differentiation involved in secularization always has both restrictive and liberating aspects. What we call "religion" has been a matrix from which many series of cultural elements and subsystems that we call "secular" have differentiated in the course of long and complicated operations. Specifically relevant here are the secular intellectual disciplines, in which previous areas of the "freedom of religion" have been restricted. For example, religious authority may no longer exercise the final judgment on whether man as biological organism is or is not the product of an evolutionary process; this is now treated as a question for empirical science. Of course, the obverse restriction should also apply, namely, natural scientists are not, qua scientists, the ultimate authorities on what have come to be defined in the differentiated sense as religious questions. In addition to restriction, however, a major advance in differentiation has a concurrent liberating effect. It creates a new freedom for *both* of the differentiated subsystems, because they are no longer constrained by their earlier structural fusion and because new resources and opportunities are open to them.

This is easily seen for the newly differentiated sector. Thus it is relatively obvious that a university system organized around the secular intellectual disciplines has certain freedoms not enjoyed by traditional religiously controlled systems of higher education. For the residual matrix, however, it is more difficult to see. Has not "religion," in losing control of higher education, simply become less important than it was? The answer to this question depends on many assumptions, but surely the view is tenable that "the worship of God" can be freer if its specific forms are not linked to specific responsibilities for decisions over a whole range of fields of empirical learning, e.g., with respect to the biological origins of men. This is not to say that, when two such previously fused realms of culture are differentiated from each other, they simply become dissociated in the sense of losing all mutual relevance. The philosophical and theological problems of the religious significance of organic evolution remain; they may be crucial both to science and to religion in different ways. It is the old dilemma, whether the origin of man is a matter of divine creation or of organic evolution, that has ceased to be meaningful.

As Professor Freund brings out with such clarity in his Burton Lecture of 1965,[10] the authors of the First Amendment wrote these two aspects of a differentiation between the religious system and the government into the amendment itself. There is mention of both the prohibition, to the federal government, of the establishment of religion and the guarantee of the "free exercise" of religion. Professor Freund makes clear that from the legal point of view the two requirements occasionally come into conflict but that both are essential to our religious constitution and independent of each other. It is in accord with the present argument to claim that the prohibition of a religious establishment has in fact been an essential condition of a great enhancement in the free exercise of religion.

GROWTH OF GOVERNMENT

The topic of the Conference of which this book is an outcome is the relation of religion to public education. It is particularly important that the same process of differentiation in the structure of the society which produced the First Amendment also restricted the powers, not only of "religious establishment," but of government more generally. Seen in the light of the whole history of Western political organization, the American Constitution was a notable advance in the differentiation of the functions of government from various other components of the society. Religion was one of the crucial contexts of this differentiation, but various more secular liberties, of the individual and of private collectivities, have been equally important.

In the present century, American society has continued to undergo a remarkable process of structural development and change. One of its primary aspects is the growth in the size and power of government, not alone but particularly at the federal level — the change which so distresses our older-style "individualists." There is no question whatever that the role of government has increased substantially not only in making national commitments of great magnitude in the foreign field but also over a wide range of domestic concerns, such as health and welfare, urban development, and education.

The growth of government has been accompanied by differentiation, however. One reason why the growth in the federal government has attracted so much attention is that the more diffuse involvements of government with other interests at the local and state levels have been progressively undermined by this differentiation process. Since the American system has tended to restrict government most at the federal level, its extension there has aroused opposition. Perhaps the most conspicuous illustration of my point is the recent massive federal restriction of the rights of state and local governments to enforce policies of racial segregation and discrimination even where these policies are desired by majorities of white or, indeed, all voters in the localities.

The development of the legal system, of which the recent decisions of the Supreme Court on the religious issue form a part, is related to this broad process of differentiation. In field after field the courts — and to some extent the legislatures — have been strengthening the protection of rights of individuals and private collectivities against governmental intervention. The whole civil rights field has been involved, but there are other prominent cases, for example, the rights of persons accused of crimes to have counsel and the like, and the rights of voters to gain equal voice in the selection of their leaders through reform of unequal apportionment systems. From this point of view, the legal system is the boundary structure between government and the private sector of the structure of the society, of cultural interests, and of the personal freedoms of the individual.

DIFFERENTIATION IN PUBLIC EDUCATION

I would like to suggest, therefore, that the problem of religion in the public schools presents a case of the intricate interweaving of two interdependent, but partly independent, aspects and levels of the ongoing process of differentiation in American society. The more fundamental one is that illustrated by the secularization of the system of higher education in the private sector. Quite apart from the First Amendment, for Columbia, the University of Chicago, and Harvard to be denominational religious establishments in the older sense would be completely anomalous in contemporary society — for a really drastic contrast, compare them with Bob Jones University in North Carolina, where "muscular Christianity" is specifically required of both students and faculty.

The other element has specific reference to the role of government. Just as, with respect to the first element, private education has been fully as important as public education, if not more important, so, with respect to the role of government, interests other than the religious have been at least as important as the religious, if not more so. Public education constitutes the principal point of intersection of these two essential processes of change.

There is no inherent reason why the specific current position of the Supreme Court on religion in the public schools should be definitive. However, I strongly support Professor Freund's position — especially since, as he puts it, the children in the public schools constitute a "captive audience" in so definite a sense.[11] The main justification for this position is, from my special point of view as a student of American society, a conviction that the line between governmental and private spheres of concern is inherently delicate in general, but particularly so in the present phase of the development of our society. A rigorous position on the "establishment of religion" seems to me to constitute one of the most important safeguards of our general liberties.

NOTES

1. Talcott Parsons, "Some Comments on the Pattern of Religious Organization in the United States," in *Structure and Process in Modern Society* (Free Press, 1960).

2. Talcott Parsons, "Christianity," in the forthcoming *International Encyclopedia of the Social Sciences*.

3. Talcott Parsons, "Full Citizenship for the Negro American? A Sociological Problem," *Daedalus*, Fall, 1965.

4. *Ibid.*

5. Will Herberg, *Protestant, Catholic, Jew* (Doubleday, 2nd ed., 1960).

6. A historic shift seems to have taken place in the position of at least a very important part of the American Catholic hierarchy in the matter of public policy toward birth control. This was expressed in the recent hearings in the Massachusetts legislature on repeal of the well-known restrictive law. Cardinal Cushing issued a statement that, though his church does not accept the views of certain other religious groups on the matter of birth control, it has no moral right to attempt to impose its way of thinking by law on non-Catholics. This is a fundamental change from the position of his predecessor, the late Cardinal O'Connell, who held that the prohibition of all "artificial" control of conception was "God's Law" and that it was the moral obligation of the church to promote its enforcement by every available means, including the coercing of Protestants and Jews to conformity with the Catholic position, if it was legally and politically possible. If my memory is correct, Cardinal O'Connell was quite explicit on this point.

7. Jan J. Loubser, "The Development of Religious Liberty in Massachusetts," doctoral thesis, Harvard University, 1964.

8. Joseph Ben-David, *Science and Society* (Prentice-Hall, forthcoming).

9. Talcott Parsons, "Professions," in *International Encyclopedia of the Social Sciences*.

10. Paul A. Freund, "The Legal Issue," and Robert Ulich, "The Educational Issue," in Paul Freund and Robert Ulich, *Religion and the Public Schools* (Harvard University Press, 1965).

11. *Ibid.*

PART FOUR

Theological Perspectives
on Public Education

14

Judaism and the Secular State

Eugene B. Borowitz

The logic of religious utterance is admittedly odd, but the range of constructs which can simultaneously be contained within the legal mind is equally unexpected. First the United States Supreme Court prohibited the practice or teaching of religion in American public schools. That decision, climaxing years of litigation, carried such an air of finality about it that the proponents of school prayer abandoned further court action and sought legislative redress instead. With the failure of the Becker amendment, it seemed, an era ended. Yet at the same time as it uttered its definitive "No," the Court, or rather several of its justices, took the occasion to indicate that they did not by their prohibition intend to oppose teaching "about" religion in state schools. To the contrary, the justices specifically commended such instruction and suggested that competent school personnel look into certain specified subject areas for newly authorized offerings.[1] Thus, while locking and barring one door more firmly than many a separationist had dared expect, the justices simultaneously provided another entry for religion into the public school system which opens farther than the eye can see at present. So indeed a new era begins.

What should be done with this new-found public pedagogic freedom? This question comes with particular poignancy to the believing American Jew. His tradition has long emphasized the great virtue of education and he has had a magnificent experience pursuing it in the American public school. What he found there was not merely economic access to the social order from which he had so long been barred. Because of the unique American separation of church and state, religion had no place in the public school and, thus, the school was the place where the American Jew first found effective social and human equality. That is why he viewed, generally with great satisfaction, the progress made in recent years to eliminate the remnants of religious practice and indoctrination which still persisted in the public school.[2] Now he must face up to the possibility of schools that will consciously seek to teach about religion. If there is anxiety in the Jewish heart at this development, it is because such instruction will have all the power and prestige of the state behind it.

The Power of the State

The might of the state is critical to this discussion. The issue is obviously not whether private schools may teach about religion. The right to private education has long been established as consistent with American democracy. The issue is precisely centered on the public school, and it is hardly a volitional institution. Once a parent does not choose to make private provision for the education of his child, the law in all its majestic power — no less great for not being blatantly brandished — takes over. Public educators do not like to think of themselves as agents of the state in the full coercive potential of a role more commonly associated with the police or tax collectors. Yet the full executive power of the government stands behind them. Without it they would be compelled radically to revise their programs.[3] Indeed, what has largely concerned the Supreme Court, as the essays in this volume by Ball and La Noue *inter alia* make abundantly clear, is what the government through its educational officials may impose on the child. Let us not dodge the reality: legal compulsion is the foundation of American public education.

Now that governmental power and prestige may be placed behind programs of instruction about religion, what guidance might the believing Jew offer to officials who are considering implementing this new understanding of American democratic procedure? More specifically, what light can Jewish theology (with all the methodological difficulties involved in this formulation) throw upon the proper relation of the state to educating about religion?[4] Three questions seem logically to require answers: (1) Since the authority of the state is the critical factor in this program, what attitude did traditional Judaism take to human governments, Jewish and non-Jewish? (2) How did it view their responsibility for education? (3) How might these views guide a modern believing Jew as he seeks a responsible answer to the problem of teaching about religion in the public school?

Judaism's View of Government

The traditional Jewish attitude toward states is inevitably dialectical. It cannot be categorically propositional, for biblical Judaism affirms fundamentally both that God is the undisputed Sovereign of all creation and that He fulfills His sovereignty in human history through individual men and social institutions (without thereby infringing on man's freedom). The first belief sets limits to the authority of human governments; the second authorizes them.

THE SOVEREIGNTY OF GOD

The universality of God's sovereignty in early Israelite belief is still a matter of debate among students of the Bible. Minimalist estimates concede only that He was already in the days of the Judges the exclusive God of the Hebrew people; others now argue that Hebrew monotheism originates with the Patriarchs.[5] More important is the dimensional question. This God, apparently from the earliest days, transcends nature and may not be identified with anything in it. That is in many ways His most characteristic attribute. It gives rise to the unrelenting fight against idolatry which some consider central to the biblical experience.[6] It is equally the source of that other unprecedented biblical passion, that human kings are themselves fully subject to God's law. They may not, as in other nations, seek to identify themselves with God Himself, nor insist that what they do is necessarily His will. The seer-prophet who authenticates Hebrew monarchy and in increasing glory, until its disastrous end, stands over against it in judgment and rebuke is the incarnation of God's claim to undivided ultimate loyalty.[7]

No wonder then that when the Hebrews request a king, God is heard to say, "They have rejected Me from being King over them" (1 Sam. 8:7). God alone should be the Hebrews' immediate ruler as He was in the wilderness or in the period of early settlement when He raised up occasional leaders to serve His purposes in times of crisis. To impose a lasting human government between the ruling, transcendent God and His people seemed blasphemy. That sense of limit to man's self-government is surely at the heart of this classic chapter. It is so much a continuing reality in Jewish religious thought that centuries later, after the Exile, it reappears in Ezra's validation of Jewish existence without political autonomy as already evidenced in the changes made in Zechariah's proclamation to Zerubbabel.[8] There, too, the ideal Israelite king, the Messiah, is not an autonomous *Übermensch*, but a man who rules in God's name to effect God's law. God alone is truly King, Sovereign, Governor.

Yet the other side of the covenantal understanding of religion is also affirmed. Though God is transcendent, He is not normally withdrawn from His creation. He cares for it and participates in it. He guides it in revelation, redirects it in justice, and preserves it in love, awaiting with infinite patience and understanding its ultimate free acceptance of His rule and, thus, the full establishment of His Kingdom. He is, therefore, intimately involved with marriages and inheritance, with slavery and the stranger, with priests and seers, and thus ultimately with kings. They are the very stuff of history in which His sovereignty must be made manifest. The author of 1 Samuel attributes the Israelite call for a human king to the people's baseness, in itself a human historical reality not to be ignored. The modern mind cannot help noting that a crisis had arisen which made the inherited social structure unworkable. In the face of Philistine military organization and technology, a divided Israel could not long survive. If Israel now insisted on maintaining forms of social co-operation suited to a previous period, when foes were few and temporary, it would die at the hand of a persistent, powerful Philistine people. But — for God's sake — Israel must survive! It exists not for itself or for the moment, but as God's instrument for the transformation of all human history! It must wait and work in history until the Messiah comes. To withdraw from history by suicide or social paralysis would be to deny its covenant root and branch. Thus Samuel learned what later Jewish sages institutionalized, that in the face of social change God will teach Israel how it may find the new forms which will enable it to continue to serve Him amidst the realities of history. In this case He unexpectedly permits a king, providing, to be sure, that this new social structure not be construed as any diminishment of His real if ultimate sovereignty over this people. In succeeding centuries His Torah tradition, progressively developed by the rabbis, will be the continuing medium of reconciling the simultaneous demands of His rule and Israel's need to serve Him in history.[9] Thus, in a word, governments are authorized, but only conditionally.

ESTABLISHMENT OF A JEWISH MONARCHY

The Jewish tradition views the account of 1 Samuel as the adumbration of the Mosaic commandment to appoint a king (Deut. 17:14–15). The interpretation accorded these authoritative verses by the classic rabbinic texts illustrates well the fundamental dialectic being described here. Because the Deuteronomic wording exhibits the ambiguity typical of much biblical formulation, the Tannaitic commentators (pre-200 of the Common Era) divide as to whether the appointment of a king over Israel was obligatory or optional. Their positions, theologically, are but another form of the biblical dialectic.[10] These differences were already reflected in the Hellenistic Jewish thinkers of the first century. Philo, reflecting the Greek philosophic concern for proper political organization, apparently believed monarchy a Mosaic mandate.[11] Josephus, whose background was aristocratic and Boethusian/Sadducean, follows the latter's predilection for a priestly, theocratic rule and therefore considers the text only permission, not a religious requirement.[12] To all these Jewish thinkers, the question posed live, political options. When two Judean revolutions failed and time passed, it became increasingly hypothetical. When no normal historical ruler seemed imminent for the Jewish people, Jewish politics became almost completely eschatological. That, it seems to me, explains why the monarchists gained the ascendancy, since all discussions of a Jewish king were now conducted in the context of waiting for the promised Son of David.

Thus almost all medieval Jewish comment on this question is to the effect that the establishment of a Jewish monarchy is obligatory. Maimonides lists it as one of the 248 positive commandments[13] and the *Sefer Hachinuch* specifies it as one of the duties incumbent upon the Jewish people.[14] Such major intellectual and legal figures of the thirteenth and fourteenth centuries as Nachmanides, Moses of Coucy, Gersonides, and Bachya ben Asher may be mentioned as sharing this position.[15] By contrast, only two dissenting authorities can be cited.

Abraham Ibn Ezra, commenting on the Deuteronomic provision, regards it as an option, but we are unable to tell whether his comment has more than grammatical significance. Only Isaac Abravanel presents a major argument against having a Jewish king.[16] His position almost certainly derives from his experience as a statesman and practicing politician and is focused upon immediate historic reality. Having served under several monarchs (always with tragic result) and having been influenced by the Christian and humanist political thought of his day (unlike his Jewish philosophical predecessors), Abravanel revives the anti-monarchic arguments of the Book of Samuel. He is too much a realist to believe that men in sinful history can actually be ruled by God directly. Rather, he considers monarchy an inferior form of government to what might be called a democracy of the elite.[17] That is the best hope of doing God's will until the Messiah comes, for he alone can be a king pleasing in God's sight.

ATTITUDES TOWARD NON-JEWISH GOVERNMENTS

Abravanel, commenting on the law of the Torah for Jewish states, is undoubtedly thinking of what it may teach non-Jewish governments. Yet Deuteronomic law is not addressed to the nations of the world, but only to Israel. Does the inner tension it knows between the divine and

Jewish kings extend to non-Jewish kings ruling over a non-Jewish state? Though there is little generalized opinion available on this topic, the answer may be ventured with some confidence that the same basic dialectic holds true.[18] It may most conveniently be exposed by a consideration of the attitudes clustering around the concepts *dina d'malchuta dina*[19] and *galut*.

The Amoraic master Samuel enunciated the principle *dina d'malchuta dina*, "the law of the (non-Jewish ruler of the) land is the law (for Jews)," early in the third century in Parthia (Babylonia), and it became an accepted legal norm for succeeding Jewish law and thought.[20] Samuel was referring only to non-Jewish legal procedures, such as witnesses and documents, but the sense of his pronouncement must be seen as far more inclusive. By the third century Jewish life in the Land of Israel was in serious decline both as to numbers and in communal vitality. The spiritual strength of Judaism was to be found in communities widely scattered through the Roman and — more influentially — the Parthian empires. If Israel was to survive amidst the realities of human affairs as God's witness, it had to find a social pattern other than independent national existence on its own land to make that service of endurance possible. And it had to be as authentic to Israel's messianic purpose in history as it was useful to its survival.

All this was implied in Samuel's dictum. The Jew could bind himself to the civil law of the land in which he found himself, as part of his Covenant with God. He therefore could be loyal to his non-Jewish king even as he remained loyal to God in his special relationship to Him. Though no Talmudic references are made to it, the modern mind sees here the recapitulation of the message Jeremiah sent centuries earlier to that same Babylonian Jewry: "Seek the welfare of the city where I have sent you into exile, and pray to the Lord on its behalf, for in its welfare you will find your welfare" (Jer. 29:7). This passage may be called the charter of authenticity for Diaspora forms of Covenantal existence.

"The King's Law" and "The Law of the Kingdom."   Samuel's principle, affirming the religious legitimacy of non-Jewish governments and their rights, is not without limits in its development in later Jewish law. Two qualifications are relevant to the question of the general Jewish attitude toward non-Jewish states. If the king acts in an arbitrary and capricious fashion, such as taxing one group of citizens or one province in a way incommensurate with what he has demanded of others, then his decrees are not considered binding by Jewish law; they are *dina d'malka*, "the king's law," rather than *dina d'malchuta*, "the law of the kingdom." The other case is more obvious. The authority of the non-Jewish king does not extend to more strictly "religious" matters such as what is ritually clean or unclean, permitted or forbidden. What Judaism

seeks in non-Jewish governments is obviously God's righteousness fulfilled. According to Jewish law the sons of Noah (that is, all men) are
commanded by God to be just to one another. Thus the non-Jewish
king is obligated to establish justice and authorized when he does so.
Therefore, the Jew has a religious basis for his civil responsibility to such
a non-Jewish king. The fuller obedience to God would, of course, be
for Israel to live as a community whose life was structured by God's
Torah. The non-Jewish world is not commanded by and does not observe that fuller law. Hence life for the Jew in the midst of a non-ob-
servant people can never have the same quality of sanctity that independent life on its own land might have. That is the source of the negative
religious attitudes toward non-Jewish states and they may best be analyzed in terms of the concept *galut*.

Galut. *Galut* may be translated "exile," but the political and geographic connotations of that English term are misleading.

Since the biblical God is the God of history, politics and geography
can be religious matters to Judaism. God grants a land to His people as
part of their Covenant and He makes their continued happy existence
on that land contingent upon their observance of His commandments.
God authorizes a king for them as noted, but he and they are expected
to be no less observant of God's behests because of it; when they are,
God's prophets warn both king and people that God will exile them in
punishment for their sins. Thus *galut* is fundamentally a theological category.[21] It testifies to Israel's past infidelity and her present punishment,
for that is what life under a non-Jewish government is when compared
to full Covenantal existence on one's promised land under the divine law.
And as centuries went by and the experience of cruel and oppressive
monarchs multiplied, the sense of *galut* deepened and messianic expectation grew more fervent. How soon this concept was applied to God
Himself, that God has become an alien in creation, is difficult to say, but
early in the Common Era Israel's political-geographic-religious situation
was seen as a symbol of God's own alienation, and the hope of Israel's
restoration to its land under its messianic king became inextricably identified with the return of God's presence to the world and the full establishment of His Kingdom. (That is why the religious Jew will still be able
to say, much to the consternation of the Israeli nationalist, that the State
of Israel itself is *galut*. Zionist theoreticians in their thoroughgoing political
secularization of traditional Jewish religious concepts transvalued *galut*
into simple geographic exile. For them, therefore, to return to the Land
of Israel and live as part of the State of Israel is the end of exile.[22] What
a warning this should sound in the ears of those who are eager to give
secular, particularly political, interpretations of traditional religious concepts! For the present State of Israel in this Zionist system becomes the

answer to centuries of Jewish prayer for the end of exile and the resolution of the mysteries of the people of Israel's millennial service. The religious Jew, however, knows that the real *galut* is metaphysical and so cannot end until God manifests His Kingdom. For him the State of Israel is at best, as the mystics put it, *atchalta d'g'ula*, "the beginning of redemption," and, as we shall see below, he is therefore preserved from jingoism and uncritical nationalism. Rather he must judge that state as he judges other states, by the prophetic criterion of its fulfillment of God's law.[23])

JUDAISM AND THE MODERN DEMOCRATIC STATE

The dialectical "Yes"/"No" of Judaism toward non-Jewish kings took a radical shift in the direction of an almost unqualified "Yes" with the rise of modern democracy and the secular state. Where there had been for centuries only Zoroastrian, Moslem, or Christian governments, now there was to be a government which was not directly concerned with religion. Political loyalty was one thing, religious commitment another. The state cared only about good citizenship; religion was in effect a private decision removed from the public domain. Because the non-Jewish state no longer held a religion antagonistic to Judaism, because it had no religion at all but was secular, the Jew could be a part of it, and equal in its midst.[24] Indeed, for the first time it became his state as much as anyone else's.

No wonder the Jews hailed Napoleon with messianic fervor and gladly rushed from their enforced segregation to share a new life.[25] Much of the history of nineteenth- and twentieth-century European and American Jewry may be read as one continuing fight to find ways to win in practice the opportunities promised in this emancipation. In some countries democracy was largely fraudulent, and Jewish rights never became widely meaningful. In others it provided a measure of opportunity rarely equaled in the history of the Jewish dispersion. The newness of the gift of freedom and the continuing effort to expand and safeguard it still set the dominant tone of Jewish life and thought in the United States. This may be somewhat more sophisticated today than in the days of mass immigration and frenzied acculturation, but with the overwhelming number of American Jews only three generations away from the degradation of the *shtetl*, equality is still too fresh to be taken for granted by most American Jews.

That mood of euphoric acceptance and wholehearted commitment lies behind the virtual absence of *galut* concepts from the religious thought of Jews in democratic countries in the past century or so.[26] By comparison to the oppression of religious governments, the tolerance created by secular governments seemed in effect an end to *galut*. Nothing made Zionist theoreticians (largely East Europeans) of the late nineteenth and early twentieth centuries more unpopular with their Western brothers than their assertion that Jews would never fully be accepted in modern democracies and needed a country of their own. Nor did the Jewish masses of Europe accept the argument, for they directed their migration in overwhelming numbers to the United States, and only the later immigration laws and Hitlerian conquests made the Land of Israel their personal goal. Metaphysical conception of *galut* similarly had little meaning for them when contrasted with a country whose streets, rumor said, were paved with gold and whose social and economic opportunities proved realistically far greater than any Jewish immigrant to these shores could have anticipated. Compared to the grim poverty and human misery of life in eastern Europe, America seemed too much like the answer to a prayer to be considered exile. The Jew has had a rapturous love affair with America, and it has made him almost unable to say "No" to her.

THE THREAT OF STATE POWER

Yet the time has clearly come to reassert the negative side of the dialectical Jewish view of states. In part this is motivated by the profound general sense of personal alienation which marks so much of the criticism of contemporary society. For the believing Jew it is the duty deriving from his affirmation of the Covenant. To take God and His demands seriously provides a perspective in which even the best of secular, democratic, welfare states is not nearly good enough. To wait and work for the Kingdom of God requires a renewed commitment to the concept of *galut* in all its theopolitical depth.

This is a matter of particular urgency because the contemporary nation-state is the closest thing to an effective absolute modern man knows. The totalitarian states are only a dramatic example of what seems to be happening wherever governments organize and, in the name of efficiency, centralize. Let the needs of the state become paramount, as in a war, and the almost unqualified nature of its power and the absence of any significant right greater than its self-preservation are made abundantly clear. No wonder Orwell could predict that the normal political situation in 1984 would be continual war. So, too, where states agree to join in international parliament, their sovereignty in internal affairs must be guaranteed them, with some countries even being granted a veto over the will of the entire body.

As the democratic state has effectively made its rights increasingly paramount, so it has moved to neutralize or control all potential rivals for social power. It does this not as in the days of tyranny by proscription or persecution, but more dangerously by paternalism and patronage. Who then can stand up to so beneficent a federal government? States' rights mean little in the face of necessary federal aid; independent capitalism is a fantasy exploded by non-legislated economic guidelines and luscious defense contracts; academic autonomy walks a cliff-edge, lured below by research grants and building loans; now artists of every variety are to benefit from government largesse. The next step, one may be certain, will be fellowships to stimulate protests and dissent. Economic determinism aside, when one's mouth is full of gravy, it is difficult to cry out.

The threat of government without significant opposition will hardly be affected by American politics or secular morality. Since World War II Americans have shown themselves substantially unwilling to commit themselves to any large-scale political ideology that might make radical criticism of government a necessity. Perhaps no more than a minority of Americans ever was active politically, but there was always hope that the creative few might change social policy. Hot politics, except for some few specific face-to-face issues, is out of place in a world seeking to play it cool. Passionate conviction is even less evident as an effective offset to governmental self-aggrandizement. Affluence has had its dulling effect on individuals as on institutions. Most Americans could define the immediate good as being left alone by the government to enjoy what they have, or perhaps as being given a little more. The morality of private-ism may make for better families and friendships, but its foundation is withdrawal from responsibility for politics and history.

The issue becomes more painfully difficult as the state takes on what must be termed a new and broader ethical responsibility. Today it seeks to fulfill many of the injunctions the Bible taught that God demanded of His people. Moreover, it does its work of righteousness in a technically competent, full-scale outreach whereas the religions operated, at best, with great spirit but also in a piecemeal, frequently ineffectual fashion. By finding work for the poor, teaching the illiterate, housing the dispossessed, healing the sick, dignifying the elderly (throughout the world!), the American government may claim a certain religious merit. How easy then for the state to excuse its other failings by the goodness it does. How soon a little righteousness becomes a general justification, and like the bad Pharisees and impious Christians of every generation, even what little was good now becomes an instrument of self-delusion and thus moral perversion. Niebuhr's burden concerning immoral societies joined to Acton's confession of the teleology of power should at this late date free us sufficiently from our illusions to see that the very good the state does demands more than the religious "Yes"; it demands religion's watchful and chastening "No."

TEMPTATIONS AND DUTIES FACED BY RELIGIOUS GROUPS

Join to these harsh realities the special temptations confronting American religious groups. Protestantism is not only a minority faith; it no longer dominates the American ethos. Could it not somehow use governmental control of children to complement its lagging evangelical outreach? Catholicism is no longer an outsider to the American consensus.

Can it not somehow utilize the lessened hostility to parochial education to garner aid for its non-religious aspects while seeing that the government schools provide some useful information to that increasing number of children who cannot or do not wish to attend church-sponsored schools? And the Jews are no longer an oppressed minority. They have arrived, but only so recently that they worry about the permanence of their situation. Would it not be possible, therefore, to utilize the government's new openness to religion by teaching everyone about Judaism, thereby not only checking such prejudice as arises from ignorance but, more significantly, placing the prestige of the state behind the acceptance of Judaism as one of America's three great religious groups?

These decades-old temptations have not been ended by the firmness of the Supreme Court decisions against teaching religion or conducting religious observances. Like all self-seeking they reappear as soon as a new pretext is available. In this case, the eager ego need not create an imagined opportunity. The several justices immediately and objectively provided it in authorizing teaching "about" religion. The old hopes may have been thwarted. They merely reassert themselves in a different guise, this time with full legal sanction. Why should not the religious groups take the fullest possible advantage of the new openings, delimited though they be, that the government has now provided?

The answer from my Jewish religious perspective (intertwined with a social-political analysis as is always required of a religion of history) is that religion is the major remaining social body that has hope, as long as it maintains its loyalty to a transcendent God, of standing over against the government and its idolatrous self-seeking, and that every alliance with or dependence upon the government weakens the possibility of its fulfilling that role. To put it less socially and more theologically, as it serves God religion must criticize government, particularly where the state seeks to supplant or ignore Him, and the more a religion relies on government, the less it will be able to remain faithful to its primary tasks, to serve Him before all else.

Israel's prophets may serve as the classic example of this truth.[27] As long as they were hirelings — royal seers and diviners — the men of God could in only rare instances, as Samuel, Nathan, and Elijah did, rise to the heights of later prophecy. Perhaps of that latter group Isaiah was part of the Establishment. If so, he is an even greater genius than men have thought. For it is only when the herdsman is taken from the sheep, almost against his will, and the unknown Amos confronts the professional visionary Amaziah in the royal sanctuary, that prophecy reaches classic proportions. The vicissitudes of Israel's prophets, loners almost to a man, are proof of the stand one must be ready to take and the cost one must be ready to pay to bring God's judgment to bear on society even when one stands in the midst of a people covenanted to Him. How much the more is this the case in the secular state. This is not to argue that the sole function of religion in modern America is prophetic criticism. There is ample room for the appreciation of what the state has and can continue to do, for the religious "Yes." Yet that is the easy word in a day of politics by consensus and social manipulation by human-relations techniques. Religion will be most true to itself today as the home of all those alienated ultimately from any government but the Kingdom of God, and therefore uniquely valuable to American democracy as the institutionalization of the principle and practice of social judgment and dissent.

Judaism's View of State Responsibility for Education

In view of the attitude toward the state and its powers, set forth above, which I derive from my Jewish religious tradition, what may be said about the Jewish conception of the state as educator? The biblical tradition, though its instruction concerning educational responsibility is quite specific, does not consider education a matter for the state. Every father is commanded to teach God's word to his child. This duty is of such importance that it follows shortly after the *Shema Yisrael* ("Hear, O Israel") and is the first explicit obligation given the man who loves God with all his heart, soul, and might. Such community obligation for education as exists in the Bible is directed essentially to adults.[28] In Ezra's reading of the Torah on New Year's Day to the whole Judean community, Jewish tradition saw the beginning of the custom to read scripture to the people each Monday, Thursday, and Sabbath, a practice, it should be noted, which precedes the establishment of a formal, communal liturgy for worship outside the Temple. Since God's law is not primarily intended for children, Jewish education as a religious duty has always aimed at the adult. By the time of the rabbis the public reading and explication of Torah and Prophets to adults had become a significant religious practice. It was not until 64 C.E. that the community as such became involved in the education of children. Joshua ben Gamala (Gamaliel), the High Priest, is reported to have established elementary schools for children in every sector of Judea. These schools did not usurp the responsibility of parents with regard to education, for the well-to-do still had their children privately tutored. They did, however, make it possible for the children of the poor also to receive an education and so made the education of Jewish children in effect universal. This pattern of public assistance to those who could not fulfill a private obligation continued unbroken down to the modern period. Of special note is the fact that while rabbinic law also required the parent to teach his child an occupation, there is no record of a Jewish community's considering it so important a communal obligation that it established vocational schools, though the many and advanced religious academies with quasi-communal support are among the proudest accomplishments of Jewish history.

From these religious positions it should be clear that the non-Jewish state, even the democratic one, has no competence from the Jewish religious point of view to teach Jewish children Judaism and should not teach Jewish children Christianity. That is why Jewish religious and organizational authorities have with almost complete unanimity welcomed the Supreme Court decisions barring the practice or teaching of religion in the public school system. Indeed, for a notoriously quarrelsome folk, American Jewry has had an unprecedented singleness of mind over the years in support of a strict interpretation of the separation of church and state as applied to the schools. Now "separation," in the constitutional sense, is no longer the issue. Our concern is teaching "about" religion, and that has been legally authorized, or nearly so. The response must be given in religious, not legal, terms; that is why I have spent the major part of this analysis clarifying my Jewish understanding of religion's — that is, Judaism's — role vis-à-vis the state in general and its educational competence in particular.

Since I believe that in contemporary America the most authentic and useful thing Judaism can do is to reassert its distance from the state so that it may remain an effective prophetic critic, my attitude toward teaching "about" religion is essentially negative. Intrinsically, I consider it of limited value where it is not reductive and therefore damaging to religion. Symbolically and socially, since it creates a tentative alliance between religion and government, it is a most undesirable breach of what should be the theological wall of separation between church and state.

Issues Involved in Teaching About Religion

NEGATIVE PERSPECTIVE

Let me begin my practical analysis and recommendations with several negative theses.

1. The public school will merit greater confidence if it first acknowledges that it has limited aims in the education of our children. As is typical of government activities, there is a strong temptation, considering how many children one has under one's expert control, to utilize the school to correct every major social problem.

It was hardly a surprise, therefore, when a psychiatrist recently suggested that schools should educate to prevent alcoholism, and since this was best done by practicing beneficial drinking patterns early, he suggested mild drinking as part of elementary school training.[29] Somewhat similarly, teaching "about" religion has meant for some the possibility of educating for those ultimate commitments about being which are the foundation of a healthy and integrated personality. Yet even before one reaches this existential level, it seems reasonably clear that the single factor which effectively prevents most Americans from making mature commitments is their emotional maladjustments. Before teaching "about" religion in this way, the schools might better spend their time doing psychotherapy (which is obviously not "guidance") so that the child might be free enough to make responsible religious decisions! It should be obvious that the school is not set up to deal with every social problem, and the more intimate and personal the problems are, the better they are left to others, such as home or church or social agency, to handle, and that specifically applies to religion as the ultimate ground of personality structure.

Some enthusiastic supporters of teaching about religion have argued for it on the ground that its omission from the school program is one effective way of indicating to children that religion is not really important. Religion, objectively taught, needs to be part of the school program so that the child will know that it is a significant part of life as far as the majority of our society is concerned. Such truth as is contained in this argument seems to me to be satisfied by far less radical curricular revision than is generally suggested by its proponents. Ending the silence about religion in the public school to allow for a proper appreciation of its social significance is one thing; full-scale teaching about religion is another. The school is not the mirror of life. Every child knows (though graduate students must keep reminding themselves) that the school is always an artificial creation and not reality itself. Children know that the most important things of life are not found in school. Why must administrators seek to bring everything, like love, faith, psychic wholeness, and other ultimate realities, under their programmatic sway?

The public school cannot long continue to take on every teaching function that parents once held, and then wonder why parents do not take an active interest in their child's education. Castration rarely begets gratitude. The home and synagogue may be educationally delinquent, but the school will not strengthen them in their proper tasks, or win them as the allies it requires in its legitimate tasks, by taking *in loco parentis* as a justification of its own omnicompetence.

2. The objectivity which lies at the heart of teaching "about" religion is badly in need of demythologization. The customary argument about objectivity is the unavailability of adequately trained or properly oriented personnel. That is a real and valid argument against the practicality of the new proposals. It needs no reiteration here. But the matter must be seen in its full theoretical difficulty as well. Philosophically, I must insist,

there is no such thing as objectivity; there are only varieties of subjectivity held in check by certain contrivances whose subjective foundations are masked by the academic mystique called methodology. Perhaps an exaggeration will help: In most undergraduate instruction in the humanities, as students quickly discover, "objectivity" means learning the instructor's lingo for structuring phenomena and repeating it to him on examinations as if it were one's own. A liberal approach includes studying opposing views and learning the instructor's refutation of them. Objectivity is generally a species of brainwashing, at least to what constitutes proper objectivity!

The matter is of special importance here because in the field of religion objectivity can never hope to mean the same sort of impersonal public testing and agreement that it attains in the natural sciences, or even in the social sciences, some of whose aspects are quantifiable. The best it can hope to be is a delimited subjectivity which gives heavy weight to documents, chronology, and the community of scholars. As anyone knows who has participated in the field, that still allows for an extraordinary range of subjectivity. The use of the magic term "objectivity" should not be allowed to conjure away the serious problems involved in defining the material to be included in teaching "about" religion.

These complications become insupportable on the instructional level. Nothing, for example, could be more deadly than to try to teach social studies or great literature as objective data. Knowing Salinger's biography or the plot outline of *The Catcher in the Rye* is no substitute for arguing, even deciding, whether people are as phony as he describes them. If you wish to change behavior you must drive your argument to the existential level. Merely giving pupils the facts about smoking or reckless driving is useless. To the contrary, the first rule of decent pedagogy is to show the relevance of the material under study to the student's own life, to involve him personally and not just verbally in the issue. Thus if the teaching "about" religion is to be meaningful, it must involve opening up the student to the truth of the religion under discussion and having him confront its relevance. That is hardly what proponents of teaching "objectively" would seem to be advocating; yet it is the logical parallel to what is being done to teach the social studies and literature effectively.

3. Nor can religion be satisfied to have the aesthetic experience once again substituted for the holy. Genesis was not written so people could worry about the appropriate form of the short story. Had its authors been aware that people would be more concerned with their style than their God, they would have considered it blasphemous. Though we are far more distant from the Holy One than they, we should not seek to increase the distance by reading the good book for the wrong reasons. By abetting such typical secularization of the religious we foster that

substitution of the pretty for the sacred which impedes every effort at genuine liturgical revival. The bridal party needs marching time to be ogled properly; that is why the rabbi should "keep it short."

Reading the Bible as literature rather than as revelation is worse than not reading it at all. In the latter case, at least, the word waits for us without a superimposed secular construction. Yet to read it as literature but really hope it is heard as revelation, which is probably the hidden agenda of most religionists advocating this practice, is as immoral in its deception as it is illegal in its substance.

4. And I do not see how with the best of good will I can approve of having Jewish children study the New Testament under non-Jewish, almost certainly Christian, auspices.[30] The matter is sensitive, but it is not to be avoided. From my Jewish religious perspective the New Testament is inevitably a polemical document. Its very name, the "New" Testament, implies that the people of Israel's Covenant (Testament) with God is archaic, if not obsolete. The Gospels are replete with references to Jesus as the fulfillment of Jewish prophecy; thus they always make a claim upon the Jewish reader, and his situation in a government-sponsored, Christian-dominated classroom is quite uncomfortable. To accept the Gospel claim is to reject Judaism, from the Jewish point of view. To reject it is, from the Christian side, at best odd, perhaps willful, at worst sinful. The Epistles deepen the predicament. Though they affirm God's continuing love for Israel, they seem to a Jew radically to reject the saving power of the "old" dispensation. For a believing Jew to study these books must therefore inevitably mean involvement in apologetics and polemics. They need not today arouse fanaticism or lead to violence as they have in the past. Yet if the fundamental challenge of the New Testament is not openly met with counterchallenge and argument, they are not being read fairly, from a Jewish point of view. Such controversy is inappropriate to the public school as it is outside the competence of even most well-trained non-Jews to handle satisfactorily from the Jewish standpoint. (These strictures apply with lesser effect to study about Islam and are largely inapplicable to Far Eastern religions.)

Positive perspective

My positive recommendations should be seen within the foregoing perspective. They must, however, be prefaced with a plea for full-scale attention to the still barely met challenge of teaching ethical values in the public schools. Concern for the new possibilities the Supreme Court has opened up should not blind us to the fact that we have not yet done much to create imaginative means of arousing ethical concern and genuine human understanding in our youngsters. The effective teaching of moral and spiritual values in schools would be of far greater significance to Judaism and to America than the new efforts to teach "about" religion.

1. The most useful thing the Supreme Court has done for us is to remove the sense of anxiety that gripped so many conscientious teachers when it became impossible for them to avoid mentioning religion, religious institutions, or religious concepts. The negativism involved in that sense of absolute separation communicated itself to students. Surely teachers ought to feel free to mention religion and religious institutions where these legitimately come up in the course of their teaching. Lifting that barrier of silence has conferred upon religion the dignity of equal mention, if not time and value, with James Bond and the National Football League. Recognizing the existence of religion and religious institutions as an integral element of American life and the history of man is long overdue and would end the curious hiatus in the study of man which has made religion seem somehow unimportant today.

2. There are some places in the current curriculum, such as in the study of history or literature, where an understanding of religious backgrounds would provide greater insight into events or ideas. It would seem reasonable in these circumstances to spend some time clarifying the underlying religious context. Here the discussion about religion might hope to retain substantial objectivity since it would be a tangential issue, not the central matter under discussion. Nor should one minimize the effect of introducing such learning along the way rather than by units of their own. The indirect and unexpected materials are often the ones which make the process of education most interesting and are therefore the best retained.

3. Rather than try to teach religious data it would be far more helpful to encourage those universal human experiences which, though germane to general education, in our present understanding seem to be the basis of a religious outlook. In this way the school could make the possibility of religion real to children while leaving its development and interpretation to the home and religious institutions. Two such experiences seem widely significant: One is the sense of awe, the other the sense of unity which underlies all multiplicity. Too much of our education these days seems designed to empty the child of wonder and transfer him into another efficient switching point in the giant communications-production complex we call society. Instruction in the arts is supposedly oriented in this direction, but even the arts are often technique rather than experience oriented, and everyone knows most art is elective where math and science are required! Without lapsing into "see how the miracles of nature prove the existence of God," one could make the study of nature less technical and more personal. Together with indoctrination in methodology, quantification, and classification, the child should learn a basic surprise that there is anything present at all and continuing astonishment that the human mind can find ways to cope with these multiple experiences.

The sense of unity offers a similar opportunity and one which is missed because it is simply taken for granted. Yet though the world about us is incredibly diverse and multifaceted, the most astonishing interrelationships appear when one insists on seeing it in its unity. That sense alone makes possible the concept of development basic to the social sciences and the concept of the integrity of universes which is the foundation of all mathematics. To foster these experiences in the public school curriculum would allow students to have personal sense about religion that no amount of dispassionate data could ever provide.

4. If Martin Buber is right, an even more important form of teaching about religion would be that sort of instruction — better, that sort of student-teacher relationship — which would help students know what it means truly to be a person.[31] Buber insists that the heart of all religion is the experience of genuine encounter between persons. In an age so obviously bereft of opportunity for being and meeting a real person, that is something our schools might well dedicate themselves to. By helping students find themselves as selves, the school would not only develop them in the deepest personal sense and teach them critical communal values but simultaneously help them know that basic human sense of reality which Buber says lies at the heart of all religion.

5. The discussions of possible curricular changes based on the Supreme Court suggestions have thus far paid little attention to the appropriate age for such instruction. If, as I believe, the questions of objectivity and polemical materials are not to be underestimated, a partial solution to dealing with them would be to reserve the instruction for an appropriate level of maturity. The older student is grown up insofar as he has learned to think in an ever more autonomous fashion. So, too, the instruction he receives becomes more nearly "objective" as he becomes older. One simply cannot compare the style of instruction in even a good twelfth-grade class with that of most universities but one year and probably two years later. Although perhaps it is more social change than psychological maturation, still most children do not arrive at reasonable intellectual independence until they have spent some time at a university — and too many not even then. College age would seem the most reasonable age level on which to experiment with direct teaching "about" religion. Such courses would normally be elective and thus have the advantage of not coming with the compulsion of the state behind them while yet being made available to large and increasing numbers of students. Since state universities have experimented in this direction, now may be the time to move forward with new and different offerings in the field of religion.

Nevertheless, my essential negative orientation returns. If religion is to maintain a prophetic stance on the American scene, the final word must be one of caution. Anything that would encourage or seem to involve religious alliance with or reliance upon the state should be steadfastly avoided. The religious groups should therefore exercise the greatest possible self-discipline in their expectations of such new school programs as are begun and should be as tentative as is responsible in advancing or cooperating with any suggestions for teaching "about" religion under government auspices.

NOTES

1. The critical cases are *McCollum v. Board of Education* and *Abington v. Schempp*, with the remarks of Jackson to the former and of Clark, Brennan, and Goldberg (concurred in by Harlan) to the latter the basis of the understanding. Fuller documentation is provided in the legal discussions in this volume.

2. Though several groups in the Jewish community dissented for the first time from the strict separationist position on the issue of federal aid to private schools in non-religious areas of instruction, the only one to have deplored the ruling barring prayers in the public school was the leader of the Lubavitcher group of Hasidic Jews. On the former topic see Milton Himmelfarb, "Church and State — How High a Wall?" *Commentary*, July, 1966.

3. In the several years I served as national Director of Education for Reform Judaism I often noted the difficult problem of adjustment many competent public school administrators had when they sought to lead synagogue schools, because the latter were fully voluntary institutions.

4. The problem of whether there is, or can be, Jewish theology is rather less heated today than it was some years ago, probably because American Jewry today largely considers itself a religious community. As it asks with increasing seriousness, "What do Jews believe?" the answers are Jewish theology. Today the discussion seems more to turn on proper method than on the feasibility or virtue of the enterprise. For the earlier level of discussion see my "The Jewish Need for Theology," *Commentary*, August, 1962, and the resulting correspondence, February, 1963. A good picture of the methodological argument may be seen in the *Yearbooks of the Central Conference of American Rabbis* for 1962, 1963, and 1964 in the papers on theology.

5. So Theodore Robinson can write, ". . . such doctrines as those of Amos and Isaiah must lead *in the long run* to a pure monotheism . . ." (*A History of Israel* [Oxford University Press, 1932], Vol. I, p. 407, emphasis added). The discussion by Gerhard von Rad is far more tempered but essentially skeptical of early monotheism (*Old Testament Theology* [Harper, 1962], pp. 210 ff.). E. A. Speiser's revisionism gives vigor to the more traditional position (*The Anchor Bible*, Genesis [Doubleday, 1964], pp. xlv ff.).

6. "The dominant tenet of Hebrew thought is the absolute transcendence of God. Yahweh is not in nature." This, by contrast to Mesopotamian and Egyptian thought, is the summary of H. and H. A. Frankfort (*Before Philosophy* [Pelican, 1946], p. 241). Walther Eichrodt links this emphasis on transcendence with the sense of His immanence, though that is a different thing from being "in nature" (*Theology of the Old Testament* [Westminster, 1961], p. 205). The centrality of anti-idolatry to biblical Judaism is itself the dominant motif of Ezekiel Kaufmann's *Toldot Haemunah Hayisraelit*. See the very first sentence of Vol. 1, Part 1, p. 1, Dvir, 1937.

7. The inner experience is clarified by R. B. Y. Scott, *The Relevance of the Prophets* (Macmillan, 1944), pp. 52 f. and 106 ff. On the king's role and Israelite law see Roland de Vaux, *Ancient Israel* (McGraw-Hill, 1961), pp. 144 ff., especially section 5 on the king's legislative and judicial powers.

8. Robert H. Pfeiffer, *Introduction to the Old Testament* (Harper, 1941), pp. 605 f., is more graphic but less detailed than Otto Eissefeldt, *The Old Testament* (Harper & Row, 1965), pp. 430–432.

9. The early statement of R. Travers Herford in *The Pharisees* (Macmillan, 1924), pp. 69 ff., on tradition supplementing the written Torah remains basically correct. Succeeding scholarship has only extended this insight that law is an adaptive instrument which allows change to enter Judaism without the loss of Judaism's essential character.

10. The same material is given in three places with some variation, none of special conceptual note: *Sifre* Dt. par. 156, p. 105a; *Midrash Tannaim* to Dt. 17:14, pp. 103–104; *Sanhedrin* 20b. In the former text, R. Judah, who considers the Deuteronomic injunction mandatory, gives this explanation for what then seems the surprising rebuke of 1 Sam. 8, viz., they asked for the king at too early a date. The dichotomy of views continues into later rabbinic literature. Positively, one should recite a blessing upon seeing a Jewish king (Ber. 58a); impudence to him is like impudence to God (Gen. Rab. 94); when the people obey their rulers God does what they decide (Dt. Rab. 1); for even the smallest of appointees has great status, some say he acts with God's authority (R. H. 25b and B. B. 91b); and even the Roman government might be called "good" for it established justice (Gen. Rab. 9.13). Negatively, many a remark approaching the cynical is recorded with respect to the action of Jewish community officials, much less non-Jewish governors. (See P. A. 1.10, Pes. 87b, Tan. Mish. 2, *Midrash Hagadol*, ed. Schechter, p. 412, and Yoma 22b, which notes that Saul's kingdom ended because it was not dishonest!)

11. *De Specialibus Legibus*, IV, 30, 157, read with Harry Austryn Wolfson, *Philo* (Harvard University Press, 1947), Vol. II, p. 329.

12. *Contra Apion*, 2.16; *Antiquities*, IV, 8, 17, 223. The interpretation of his Boethusian background is taken from *The Rise and Fall of the Judaean State*, vol. II, by Solomon Zeitlin, which will shortly be published by the Jewish Publication Society of America. Simon Federbush contends, however (*Mishpat Hameluchah Beyisrael* [Mosad Harav Kuk, 1952], pp. 26 f.), that Josephus' position on theocracy has been misunderstood and that only later generations ever thought it meant hierocracy, the rule of priests. Jewish faith demands equality for all religions and peoples. Hence religious and political powers were always separated in Israel. The exceptions, the Hasmonean rulers, were derogated by rabbinic Judaism. His proof, aside from a rather general statement in the Jerusalem Talmud, is a citation from the thirteenth-century Nachmanides. The ideological intent behind this reconstruction is discussed in note 17 below.

13. *Sefer Hamitzvot*, positive commandment 173, and note the implicit assumption that the king is expected to follow the Torah to be worthy of pre-eminence. Monarchy is given a generally Aristotelian justification in *The Guide of the Perplexed*, II, 40. The legal prescriptions are given in *M. T. Hilchot Melachim*, and note that the messianic laws are part of this discussion of Jewish kings (chs. 11 and 12). See the discussion in Leo Strauss, "Abravanel's Political Theory," in *Isaac Abravanel*, ed. Trend and Loewe (Cambridge University Press, 1937), pp. 106 ff.

14. *Sefer Hachinuch*, par. 497.

15. So Strauss, *op. cit.*, p. 119, referring to the biblical commentaries to Dt. 17:14 f. of the former two. An instructive parallel to the Moslem position is drawn by S. D. Gotein in his "Attitudes Toward Government in Islam and Judaism," in *Studies in Islamic History and Institutions* (Brill, 1966). Since the Koran contains no references to political regimes, some authorities could argue that the Caliphate was not religiously required and no form of political organization is preferable to another. While such arguments were heard when the Caliphate made its appearance, they gradually disappeared in the face of the reality. The matter apparently caused no intellectual concern to later generations for the topic of monarchy is not dealt with in the later Moslem codes or classic philosophies.

16. Strauss, *op. cit.*, is particularly helpful for his study of the context of contemporary political theory in which Abravanel's departure from past theory is best to be understood. A somewhat more detailed discussion of Abravanel's ideas in their development is found in Ben Zion Netanyahu, *Don Isaac Abravanel* (Jewish Publication Society, 1953), pp. 183 ff. His rejection of the influence of contemporary political thought on Abravanel is not convincing to me after Strauss's demonstration.

17. Simon Federbush seizes upon this position as a means of arguing that traditional Jewish law does not require a monarchy and hence the establishment of a democracy in the contemporary State of Israel is fully halachic! His treatment of the prevailing, opposing view may be seen in his comment, "But from the simple meaning of the Torah text it is clear that it is not commanded; and the phrase 'like all the nations' is a clear implication of derogation, which is also clear from the simple meaning of Samuel's reply to those seeking a king" (*op. cit.*, p. 39). He further points out that since there is no prophet or Sanhedrin today to induct and ratify the king, a monarchy is a practical impossibility. The conclusion is, however, made "*lefi ruach hatorah*," "according to the spirit of the Torah," a phrase and concept he would roundly condemn when utilized by non-Orthodox interpreters for similar treatments of traditional law to allow for more modern social arrangements (*op. cit.*, p. 40).

18. The dialectic developed by Joseph Baer Soloveitchik regarding the two kinds of peoplehood, the one biological and compulsory, the other an especially human response because free, is of a different order. Soloveitchik operates here, characteristically, with a typology which he uses to understand history but which is not fully reflected in any historical phenomenon. His contrast is not so much the rule of God versus the rule of men in actual institutions, but the two modes of Jewish existence as a people, biological and theological, not separate but intertwined. This makes possible the positive acceptance of the current secular State of Israel but demands an effort to help it live up to its full Jewish character ("*Kol Dodi Dofek*," *Torah Umeluchah*, ed. Simon Federbush [Mosad Harav Kuk, 1961], pp. 11–44).

19. An alternate possibility for these positive attitudes may be found in the prohibition against rebellion, the laws of *mored bemalchut*. These are, however, less central to Jewish law, and the attitudes around them seem to have developed most clearly at a much later period. See the somewhat abstract discussion by Simon Federbush, *op. cit.*, pp. 84 ff. For a brief description of the legal tradition see J. D. Eisenstein's *Otzar Dinim Uminhagim*, art. "*Mored Bemalchut*" (Hebrew Publishing Co., 1917), p. 211. I know of no English discussion of this theme. A brief list of *aggadic* passages calling for reverence to kings is given in *The Jewish Encyclopedia*, art. "King," section "In rabbinical literature," vol. VII, p. 502. A more realistic picture of what the average man expects of a king is given in the imaginative contrasts between the immorality of earthly kings as contrasted with the righteousness of the King of Kings. See the index entry "Earthly Kings" in *A Rabbinic Anthology*, ed. Montefiore and Loewe (Macmillan, 1938), p. 791.

20. See the full discussion of this principle, noteworthy for its full citation of later and occasionally diverging authorities, in the *Talmudic Encyclopedia* (Hebrew), Jerusalem, 1956, art. "*Dina Demalchuta Dina*," vol. VII, columns 295–308. However, Salo Baron cautions that this principle was never given definitive limits or fully clarified (*The Jewish Community* [Jewish Publication Society, 1942], vol, II, pp. 216 ff.; *A Social and Religious History of the Jews* [Jewish Publication Society, 2nd ed., 1957], vol. V, pp. 75 ff.).

21. The major study of this concept to date is Yitzchak B. Baer, *Galut* (Schocken, 1947), the English translation of a German text published in the early thirties. Baer's nationalistic and rationalistic concerns seem to me to constrict his treatment of what he recognizes as the essentially religious origins and connotations of the concept. Thus there is no discussion of the biblical concept of *galut*, only a short discussion of the *aggadic* notion of the Exile of God's Indwelling Presence, and but brief mention of medieval mysticism. Hence Baer's study cannot be relied upon for a rounded understanding of this doctrine, particularly from the standpoint of its meaning and place within the structure of Jewish faith.

22. For an excellent introduction to Zionist ideology see Arthur Hertzberg, *The Zionist Idea* (Doubleday, 1959). Of particular interest are the Introduction, which carefully distinguishes between Jewish religious tradition and modern secular thought, and the selections in Parts 4, 5, and 6. Note that a separate section, and only one at that, is given to religious Zionism (including, quite properly, Martin Buber). David Ben-Gurion's secular messianism is a particularly interesting effort to blend the two streams from the secular side.

23. A sensitive discussion of this problem is to be found in Ernst Simon, "Are We Israelis Still Jews?" *Commentary*, April, 1953. See also my brief, popular statement, "Who Is Israel?" *Jewish Heritage*, Fall, 1961.

24. See the convincing analysis of Arthur Hertzberg, "Church, State and the Jews," *Commentary*, April, 1963.

25. The story of the period is engagingly narrated by Howard M. Sachar, *The Course of Modern Jewish History* (World Publishing Co., 1958), particularly chap. III but *passim*. Napoleon was quite harsh to French Jewry, yet they bore his rigors patiently and then exalted him as the founder of their freedom. The latter was what they found surprising. See the perceptive remarks of Zosa Szajkowski, "Judaica-Napoleonica," *Studies in Jewish Bibliography and Folklore*, June, 1956, p. 108.

26. It is typical of the mood of the times that *The Jewish Encyclopedia* of 1904 treats "Exile" with a brief linguistic note and then refers its readers to articles which deal essentially with the biblical experience of "Banishment" or "Captivity" (in Babylon) but treats Jews off the land of Israel by the neutral term "Diaspora."

27. Note the comment by Harry Orlinsky on the possibilities of Israel's prophets' taking pay ("The Seer in Ancient Israel," *Oriens Antiquus*, vol. IV, fasc. II, 1965, p. 154). Bear in mind too that the entire burden of this study is the uniqueness of Israel's prophets (as contrasted with her seers) from so-called prophets seen elsewhere in Near Eastern literature. From a quite different perspective there is the still relevant preachment of Martin Buber in "False Prophets," *Israel and the World* (Schocken, 1948), pp. 113 ff.

28. A good brief description of the history of Jewish education and its institutional forms is given by Julius Maller, "The Role of Education in Jewish History," and Simon Greenberg, "Jewish Educational Institutions," chaps. 21 and 22 of *The Jews*, ed. Louis Finkelstein (Jewish Publication Society, 1949).

29. As reported in the *New York Times*, January 12, 1966, and *Time*, January 21, 1966.

30. Steven S. Schwarzschild argues that for a Jew to read even the "Old" Testament means to utilize the rabbinic understanding of what the biblical text says, thus effectively preventing reading even that text jointly ("Judaism, Scriptures and Ecumenism," in *Scripture and Ecumenism*, ed. Leonard J. Swidler [Duquesne University Press, 1965]).

31. The working out of the educational implications of *I and Thou* is most clearly given in the essays "Education" and "The Education of Character," reproduced in *Between Man and Man* (Macmillan, 1948). Cf. the interpretation given by Maurice Friedman, *Martin Buber: The Life of Dialogue* (Harper Torchbook, 1960), chap. XX.

15

Protestant Echoes of the Constantinian Era

Max L. Stackhouse

The Issues

From the standpoint of theological ethics and theology of culture, it appears that at least three fundamental relational problems pervade most discussions of religion and the public schools: What is the relationship of the divine and the human, what is the relationship of the one and the many, and what is the relationship of continuity and change? Although the terms and accents shift, one concerned with cultural matters from a theological perspective cannot scratch the surface of any of the literature about the practical, legal, or moral issues involved without confronting these problems.

When we look, for example, at the legal statements trying to define that fine line, sometimes called a wall, between church and state, we find that the public schools are an instrument of the state and thus have no power to inculcate particular ideas of the divine or require any prescribed worship. When we ask about teaching "moral and spiritual values" and courses on Western ethics or *"about* religion," we find significant sections of the academic and religious communities, those charged with professional concern for such matters, convinced that the integral relation between faith and reason makes any instruction based on reason alone incapable of sustaining interest. Some even claim that instruction of this type is, frankly, dishonest in that rational efforts are premised on the prior faith commitment that the world is essentially rational. Still further, it is quite clear that many advocating these courses are interested in exposing the corruptions and distortions of faith and thereby rooting out the residual, "sacred" superstition that they see as characteristic of religious "mythology" while others are trying to find a captive audience to teach their own disguised version of piety as a way to "save America" from its decline into secularity.

The three questions arise when we think of how we would go about building a course about religion into the curriculum of a good educational system. Shall we teach that Buddhists believe this and Shintoists that, Christians thus and Jews so, with no attempt to introduce any critical principles? Does it make no difference to education what one believes and what the statuses of various truth claims are? Shall we show the ways in which peoples in different sociological situations throughout the world developed different versions of the divine, suggesting by our very course structure that the sacred is a variable product of the secular? Shall we perhaps describe how different psychological bents find solace in various types of religious ideology and experience, thereby making the divine a therapeutic need fulfiller par excellence? Or shall we adopt a more literary approach and show how divine symbols are expressive of the dramas of human action, but perhaps neglecting the ways in which religion over the ages has shaped the setting wherein the action occurs? Is the sacred found in the secular? How do we prevent an institutionalized baptism and sacramentalization of the status quo? Is it not true that the sacred or divine is distinguishable from, and indeed stands over against, the secular and human? Then how do we prevent a fundamental dualism of life and thought?

No treatment of the many problems of religion and the public schools can be finally satisfying from a theological ethical point of view until it grapples explicitly with the relationship of the divine and the human.

Perhaps, however, we should look at the issues from another perspective. Clearly, political problems are involved. Not only do educators, at the level of the local community, have to try to accommodate the particular unified program of the school system to the diverse groups in the community and the many individual talents, limitations, and commitments of the students, but the schools have become the instrument of national integration, the way by which the diverse youth of the country are socialized into a sufficiently common pattern so that the country is not torn asunder in each generation. At a deeper level still, there is little doubt that many pressing for the teaching of or teaching about religion are convinced of the necessary theological and moral foundations of cultural and political integration and see such efforts as providing a more profound, more deeply rooted national identity than prevails at present.

There has been, of course, more constitutional and *de facto* recognition of the rights of private religious belief in the last few decades than in any previous period in our history, reflecting and allowing a diversity of religious commitment perhaps unparalleled on so vast a scale. At the same time, the development of councils of churches, the mergers between Protestant denominations, the ecumenical movement, the election of a Catholic President, and the increased frequency of the term "Judeo-Christian tradition" indicate an overcoming of some divisive aspects of the American religious tradition. It is not clear whether such accents on what is common among the various groups are a defensive maneuver of organized religion in its death throes, a compensating accent on unity in the midst of proliferating diversity at other levels, or an attempt to construct a new social cement for a nation no longer sure of its destiny. In any case, the problem of the relationship of the one and the many is part of the unarticulated agenda of many discussions of religion and public education that will find no resolution or direction until it is made articulate.

If we look at the discussions of religion and public education in another way, we notice a widespread feeling that the issues confronting us at the moment are new problems. The situation of modern man in a technological culture that can show fantastic capabilities of control over his environment is so different from previous conditions that every provisional solution of the past regarding separation of church and state and the relationship of the person and of groups to the whole of society is deemed irrelevant and a hindrance to our successful dealing with the present. We are, indeed, at a juncture where the drama of change obscures the latent continuities. But we should not be seduced into too rapid abandonment of our past lest we lose the tools to deal creatively with the moment of change. The notion that modern culture has no relationship to previous ages, expressed several times in the conference on the Role of Religion in Public Education from which these essays have been drawn, is utterly without foundation and frequently reflects only a romantic willingness to sound exciting at the expense of careful analysis.

While romantics bewail the loss of mystery, of meaning, and of organic *Mitsein*, in a way that overlooks the awe, the significance, and the increased interdependence of modern life, they are matched by the celebrants of the discontinuity. Among people concerned with cultural and theological ethics today, the widespread accent on discontinuity often requires us to begin each task *de novo* with new freedom. Their call, which has sometimes been my own, has some legitimacy, for ethical reconstruction, exorcism, and creativity are perennially necessary. But unmitigated, such a perspective distorts the human condition as greatly as does that of the nostalgic romantics. It represents, we suggest, the adolescence of American theological ethics, in spite of continual use of the terms "maturity" and "world come of age," for it changes the legit-imate thesis "because our fathers did it thus and so, it is not necessarily right," to "because our fathers did it thus and so, it is necessarily wrong for today." Historical and cultural problems, like the ones we confront in pressing the questions of religion and the public schools, are ever prob-lems that involve discontinuity *and* continuity, novelty *and* analogy, difference *and* similarity, change *and* stability. And no solutions to con-temporary problems will stand the test of history that do not take history into account.

Because other essays in this series deal with the differences between our age and previous ones, I shall attempt to point out certain historical continuities that still obtain. By tracing, in rather broad, generalized terms, the development of Christian perspectives on these three funda-mental problems, I shall try to allow some of the great spokesmen for the theological tradition and some of the traditional formulations themselves to speak to the present situation. At each point, it is my intent to find common bases of understanding for Catholics, Jews, and Protestants, with-out obscuring the differences.

It might be suggested, of course, that, at one highly abstract level these three problems *are* among the half-dozen central problems of man seen from a philosophical standpoint, but that they are always the problems of human institutions. We cannot expect to resolve issues which the greatest philosophers have stumbled over before we deal with the problems at hand, or we never will do anything. But the suggestion need not be heeded too seriously on several grounds. First, if these are indeed funda-mental problems, we are intellectually dishonest if we avoid them, for every generation has to pose some tentative answer, consciously or uncon-sciously. Second, various provisional solutions to these problems lead to quite different effects. The ways Christians set forth their solutions in patristic times have had effects to the present day, as will be evident shortly. And, knowing this, we are irresponsible if we do not attempt to take potential consequences into account in our answers — a task that requires some conceptual abstraction. Third, every pragmatic solution is grounded in some, if unexpressed, interpretive model of what an appro-priate solution might be, and we need to know what that is. If one calls for a pragmatic solution, we need to know what it is that the pragmatist wants to work. Is it national integration? Personal integrity? The social system? Western culture? And finally, although most important, the fact of the universal recurrence of these problems does not tell us anything about the particular forms in which they present themselves to us. Although every culture does seem to have some definition, for example, of what is divine and what is human, it is by no means universal that cultural forms, the state, or educational processes, or even aspects of these, should be deemed secular. Indeed, throughout most of world history quite the contrary has been the case. The three problems identified here, however, have taken their present form because of a deeply rooted religious tradition that has shaped them.

Perspectives

Modern American culture has been shaped by many, many forces. But one force, perhaps, more than any of the others, has been crucial in defining the problems in their present form. That force is Christianity — and predominantly a Christianity in Calvinistic forms. One need only think of the covenantal-federal structure of the Constitution, the work ethic, the this-worldly activism given saintly status, and the role of the Protestant church in founding schools under the control of and paid for by the public (and becoming a bulwark for the preservation of the "wall" when Catholics wanted their share of the action). But, in spite of the Protestant propensity to see everything of significance growing out of the sixteenth century, Calvinists drew on resources that were there before them. If, then, we want to deal with the issues in a way that relates these fundamental influences to the present from the perspective of Protestant theological ethics, we might well engage in a constructive reinterpretation of the forces that shaped the religious, political, and cultural problems into their present form.

Christian theological ethics, at its best, is ever sensitive to at least three dimensions of concern: (1) the fundamental structures of existence that serve as a stage whereon every man and society walk, (2) the dramatic peculiarities of a given history, its events, its patterns, its ethos, and (3) several essential motifs or models by which it interprets that history and defines that ethos. It is concerned with history not only because the Bible is primarily an interpretation of events and patterns of events but because it sees the significance of both human life and life's divine foundation to be revealed in history, in events, and in the patterns of meaning that arise from them. But Christianity also recognizes that the meanings of history are not altogether self-evident; they cannot be read off at a glance. An interpretive model is required. Indeed, one of the ways in which history is differentiated from natural phenomena, upon which it is partly based, is precisely in the fact that history is history only when it is interpreted; and history is valid only when the model is a good one. Some apt metaphor, some conceptual framework, some set of adequate terms is indispensable in order for the reality to be perceived.

There is, of course, no single model in Christianity, but there are three metaphors or interpretive models that are not only necessarily related in Christian thought but nearly universal in their acceptance within the Christian community and integral to the problems at hand. Still further, these models in both explicit and implicit form have so influenced the shape of Western thought and institutional life that their influence is impossible to avoid. The precise character of the models and the relations between their terms remain crucial centers of controversy, not only explicitly in the theological schools, but implicitly in the courts, in political rhetoric, and in educational circles, for differences in values, accents, and parameters in the interpretation of these models make tremendous differences when the models are used to interpret the whole ebb and flow of human life, as they frequently are.

The three fundamental motifs are as follows: The sovereign God is one God; His Son, Jesus Christ, was fully God and fully man; and the one God is triune in nature — Father, Son, and Holy Spirit. These three conflicting, highly formal theological motifs or models — monotheistic, dualistic, and trinitarian respectively — may well provide the tools whereby we can offer guidance in approaching the crucial problems.

The first model suggests that all of life has a single coherence in the final analysis. While we may not know or see the ultimate coherence, the model demands a quest for the singularity of truth that is involved. One cannot presume to be preaching or teaching or politicking if he does not attempt to adjudicate between conflicting opinions and to work out a coherent understanding of truth. The second model points out that in crucial historical events the divine and the human are integrally related without losing their analytical autonomy and distinctiveness. Thus, church and state, faith and reason, religion and culture are not irrelevant to each other, even if they are analytically distinct. And the third indicates that constancies such as those involved in the first two models are made alive only when differentiated and when linked to charismatic movement, showing the necessity for dynamic personal and group freedom. But we must look at the historical origins and influences of these models if we wish to claim their historical relevance.

The three models of Christian theological ethics that pertain to the problems at hand were shaped at every point by the biblical tradition, but they did not find their abstract and institutional definition in the biblical period. It is primarily to the debates of the fourth century that we must turn if we wish to see most clearly some of the basic motifs that, with differing accents in each period, provided the conceptual framework for subsequent patterns of church, state, and education. It was then that the crucial interpretive models, common in many respects to Catholics and Protestants and having strong analogues in the Jewish community, were hammered out.

The Establishment of the Model[1]

BACKGROUND

In the fourth century, the sectarian Jewish movement called Christianity with a fresh definition of the divine *had* to come to explicit terms with the institutions and structures of the secular world. To be sure, this movement, premised on the shocking absurdity that an obscure man of an obscure people in an obscure province of the known world was the Lord of Life and the Son of God, from its beginning drew on social, political, and cultural resources and had social, political, and cultural implications. By modifying patterns present in previous Jewish and Hellenistic groups, the primitive church developed forms of internal organization and discipline that became a model for social organization at large. The church very early had a theory of historical periodization and an expectation of eschatological transformation that relativized all existing institutions and suggested that change had positive possibilities in the final analysis. As Amos Wilder has shown, the common use of natural metaphors in the Gospels and Epistles illustrated an assumed, if uncritical, natural law theory.[2] And the church required such an intensity of involvement in and commitment to a new, more universal, center of loyalty that it undercut previous familial, clan, ethnic, and national egocentricities. But the movement was, by and large, so inconsequential that it did not *have* to spell out the implications of these notions except on an *ad hoc* basis for quite a long time.

As we approach the fourth century, however, we find that more explicit formulation was required. Not only was it necessary for Christianity to defend itself against the persecutions, and not only was it necessary to develop an intellectual apology in a Greco-Roman world if it was to get a hearing in many quarters, but in fact some of the fundamental cultural assumptions upon which the empire had been founded were proving to be inadequate. Already, a number of Greek intellectuals had abandoned the polytheism of their forebears and assumed a unified philosophical understanding of the world through various kinds of Logos, monotheistic or philosophical monistic speculation, even though pagan rituals remained a part of public political life[3] and deeply established in education.[4] But neither the philosophical assertions of unity nor the recurrent upsurges of pagan polytheism that philosophy could never quite control were sufficient interpretive frameworks for the dynamics of the history of the moment. R. G. Collingwood portrays the situation clearly:

> Christian writers in the time of the Roman Empire asserted, and no historian today will deny, that in their time the science and civilization of the Greco-Roman world were moribund. . . . The Patristic diagnosis of the

decay of Greco-Roman civilization ascribes that event to a metaphysical disease. The Greco-Roman world, we are told, was moribund from internal causes, specifically because it had accepted as an article of faith . . . a metaphysical analysis of its own absolute presuppositions which was at certain points erroneous.[5]

The debates leading to the fourth century that produced a restructuring of the interpretive model of man and his place in the world were at first largely centered on the character of the one God, problematic in Greek metaphysical thought at least since Aristotle's polemical use of a line from the *Iliad:* "The rule of many is not good; one ruler let there be," [6] and indigenous to Jewish and therefore Christian thought. But these debates were by no means "purely" theological, for they informed, were informed by, and were at each point related to, political, cultural, and educational issues.

The conceptions of monotheistic unity from Philo through the Apologists to the Council of Nicea took numerous forms but had several common themes. The discussion centered around the term "Logos," a term that bridged divisive intellectual currents because it was common in the philosophy of the day and was identified in Christian sources with the "Word Incarnate." Philo, speaking philosophically, tended to see in the Logos both "God's agent in creation and the medium by which the human mind gets in touch with him," [7] and thus the Logos is equated with "archetypes in God's mind which are expressed by his acts of creation and providence." [8] What was at stake at this point was a monotheism that sees all the world as a "great chain of being," to use Arthur Lovejoy's fortunate phrase, at the apex of which is the one God. Culturally, this vision provided a pattern for comprehending in hierarchical fashion various dimensions of diversity on a vast scale, claiming for the diversities a common rationality, and integrating the various cultural loyalties by preserving the monotheistic sentiments common to partially Hellenized Judaism, Christianity, and the intellectual world in general. It was a vision developed in the academic centers of the age and in that setting it provided a set of conceptual tools for education by which man could rationally approach and arrange all phenomena. Erik Peterson, for example, states quite flatly that the Logos monarchism was developed for its pedagogical and culturally unifying functions.[9] But politically, which seems also a direct concern of both Philo and the early Christians, since their position was frequently imperiled by the political powers, such a view links all present power with the single cosmic structure as it had been linked in the pagan world. Not only, therefore, could it provide an apologetic against accusations of subversive teaching and activity, but it suggested a proper obedience to authority for all under the Logos. We have an organically integrated vision in which "the powerful is that which constitutes the efficacy and end of things, and it appears as the holy, as that which *has* power or excellence. . . ." [10] Indeed, Peterson, after surveying Philo and the literature of the early Christian apologists and showing how they again and again drew upon Greek and Roman literature to reinforce their monotheistic tendencies, states quite clearly that the monarchical concept was a politically laden theological concept that was used for politically significant theological purposes.[11]

Clement and Origen, not to mention a whole series of more extreme authors, were even more significant thinkers who deeply influenced the fourth-century debates. Not only did they adopt certain Neo-Platonic modes of thought, but they more than the others attempted to face the whole of Greek culture directly. As Werner Jaeger points out, "They try to see Christianity in the light of the supreme concept of what the Greeks had contributed to higher life of the human race. They do not deny the value of that tradition, but they claim that their faith fulfills this paideutic mission of mankind to a higher degree than had been achieved before." [12]

While Clement, in an attempt to combat a residual Gnostic movement, sometimes conceived of this teaching in Gnostic terms, Origen, who reflected more Platonic and Stoic influences, saw Christianity primarily in terms of "the greatest educational power in history and was in essential agreement with Plato and philosophy." [13] For these men, and for many of the period, there was a series of hierarchical mediators between God and man, and they saw both these mediators and that which was most real about man himself as a universal quality that was manifest in the particular. Hence the elaboration of the universal encompassed each particular and provided the principle of educational and cultural formation. Werner Jaeger partially summarizes voluminous research in this area when he says:

> Considering the importance of this overarching idea . . . for the evolution of a unified culture in the Greek intellectual world, this step in the discussion between Christianity and the Hellenistic tradition marks the beginning of a decisive development in the aspiration of the Christians toward the goal of a Christian civilization.[14]

Yet, throughout this period, a problem confronted the fathers that recurs again in the fourth century and throughout subsequent theological history. If the unity of the one God or universal principle as the creator and orderer of all is asserted, how is it that those who most earnestly confess the single sovereignty are persecuted by the one political order that He must maintain but which denies Him? The theological idea of one monarch has obvious analogies to a political monarchy, but one denies the other.

The question of the viability of a Christian civilization was not long in posing itself existentially, for Constantine came to power in the early part of the fourth century. Constantine's sympathy for the Christian God as an assurance for victory and his (at first) toleration and (later) desire to use Christianity to bind together a scattered empire provided an occasion when a Christian empire might be a possibility.

The educational and politically informed theological definitions of the one God were hotly resisted by some. On the one hand, there was a clear recognition of the validity of monotheism. It was recognized that there is one ultimate truth and order and not a multiplicity of "truths" and "orders" which have validity according to where one lives and what race one belongs to. Each particular set of "truths" and "orders" can be brought under more universal and usually rational criticism. On the other hand, Christianity was asserted by several defenders to be superior to the truth and order of philosophy and political power respectively, and not merely contiguous with them in a hierarchy of validity. Philosophy presupposes education, and not all are educated. Education is always premised on ability, but truth is not. Thus, the efficacy of the educational treatment of Christianity is qualified.[15] Further, it was asserted that the power of Christ defeated the power of the political order when crucifixion and suppression by political authority did not once and for all seal him in a tomb. Thus the validity of a purely political-theological definition was also qualified. Again, there was the continuing subdominant eschatological theme that resisted such interpretations. Tertullian in the West and Nepos and Methodius in the East, for example — accenting the eschatological New Jerusalem, the millennial Kingdom, and resurrection — preserved the crucial distinction between innocence and perfection, creation and salvation, what the present in reality is and what life will in fact be when transformed. Thus they always claimed a religious tension between even the best political and educational orders and the religious one, for the former are subject to transformation in the future. In contrast, the spiritualization of eschatology by Origen, which regarded the Kingdom, eternal life, etc., as merely higher ranks in the chain of cosmic being, made him at least partially heretical. It was recognized, accordingly, that monotheistic statements based primarily on a Logos doctrine allow no tension, but only continuity between present rulers and the divine ruler. Indeed, as George Williams has brilliantly shown, many of the fathers of the church under the influence of the Origenistic mode of thought were at first betrayed into an uncritical acceptance of political and educational monotheism on theological grounds once a sympathetic ruler came to the fore, and nearly a century of debate had to occur before the church had developed the tools to stand against the emperor when necessary, even though it ever recognized its responsibility to political authority as well.[16]

Just as important, Logos monotheism temporarily obscured major strands of the Judeo-Christian biblical heritage that had to be rehabilitated later. The Jewish concept of monotheism was a radical one which Christianity shared. And "radical monotheism," to use H. R. Niebuhr's term, fashioned out of Israel's social, political, and theological conflict with earlier polytheism, drew a sharp distinction between creator and created, between the divine and that which was not. Indeed, the distinction is accented by the concept of the Fall, which makes the breach more radical. One cannot know creation by reciting the names of the gods. They are no longer of the same mold. God is set over and against creation and its powers, an understanding of reality which not only leads to a more differentiated pattern of conceptualization but gives the world some integrity in its own right (in spite of the possible temptation to interpret, under Gnostic influence, salvation as liberation from the world). This division becomes particularly important at the institutional levels that represent the two realms in human affairs. The division implied by radical monotheism raises the issues of whether there is a "sacred language" that is different from ordinary language in symbolic institutions and whether the bishops are independent of the political powers at the societal level.

Many Christian thinkers (Peterson included) wrongly see the exhaustion of Judaism at this point, for they perceive the undifferentiated, if radical, monotheism of Judaism as one leading inevitably to the conflict that confronted early Christianity: a right recognition of the separation but an inability to accept God's offer of new relationship. They see Christianity as responding by accenting Christological formulations in a way that Judaism cannot do. In fact, however, we must on the one hand see that Jewish ingredients are those which again and again preserved Christianity from its own temptations to Gnosticism on one side and Christocentric monotheism on the other. We must, on the other hand, see that the affirmation of the distinction between creator and created was dealt with in both forms of radical monotheism. In Christian thought it led to a provisional dualism that could be overcome only by a "two-natures Christology" affirming the relevance of both "Jesus" and "Christ," of which we shall shortly speak. Within the Jewish community it led to an analogous dualism resolved in structurally similar fashion in terms of the two sides of the concept "Chosen People." The difference is that, at this juncture in history where the fundamental motifs for subsequent development were worked out on Gentile grounds, the Christian way of resolving the necessary dualism to which it was forced had more universal implications and at the same time more personal overtones while the Jewish integration of chosenness and peoplehood found its primary validity on this question within a specific community. This historical observation, further, does not compromise the universality implied in the Jewish concept of radical monotheism. On such grounds as these, Christian theological ethics may well be inclined to agree with the conclusions reached by Krister Stendahl on exegetical grounds, that the Jews are the

Chosen People of God's Covenant, that Jesus Christ is how Gentiles become related to it, and that dialogue with the Jews is necessary for Christianity to understand and preserve itself.[17] But we digress; we are concerned with Christian responses in the fourth century. The theoretical point of this digression, however, is that radical monotheism, any singular view of truth or validity, leads to duality, for it demands the recognition of that which is not God, true and valid.[18] Institutionally, the church and the state are not the same thing. Nevertheless, some affirmative relation between the poles must be worked out. Otherwise, all of ordinary life becomes religiously suspect or religion becomes culturally suspect.

After it became powerful under Constantine's protective supervision, Christianity had to deal with three modes of thought that grew out of the cultural, political, educational, and theological pressures briefly rehearsed above. The debates were often abstract, but, as Seeberg says in a subtle undercutting of Harnack, the great anti-dogmatic church historian of the early twentieth century, "We shall utterly fail to understand the conflicts of the period before us if we shall interpret them as merely a result of the metaphysical tendency of Grecian thought. On the contrary, beneath these controversies lay most thoroughly practical and religious motives." [19] Four possibilities were at hand that have lived in the West since these debates. A radical dualism that saw a negative relation between the two realms of the creator and the created, a sustained Logos or organic monotheism that had its roots in Clement and Origen, and two major varieties of modified dualism (that saw either the church exerting a hegemony over the state "for its own good" or the state using the church as a political and cultural cement) were the chief options. None of the options proved viable and a new alternative finally emerged. At each juncture, two of the fundamental questions with which we started were involved: What is the relationship of the one and the many, and what is the relationship of the divine and the human? The form of the debates had to do with the location (between creator and created) and nature of the Logos (or Son, or Christ), the mediating principle.

CHRISTOLOGY

The Donatists,[19a] members of a North African schismatic movement, exemplify the option of radical dualism. The Donatists identified the divine with the present spiritual body of Christ, the church in North Africa. There, they attempted to keep themselves interiorly pure from the corrupting influence of creation, for they had become a part of the order of the creator's redemption. Such a theology is hardly likely to become the basis for a new civilization. Yet they represent a position in which the supreme authority and loyalty are invested in the "pure church," which possesses the true spirit of Christ, a church that is superior to politics. Externality was so suspect that the structures and offices of the church were seen as of not determinative importance and by some even as necessary evils, and the authenticity of the sacraments was guaranteed only by the purity of those administering them. Not only do the Donatists represent a perennial, fundamental, withdrawing sectarian drive in much Christianity, but they illustrate the long-term frailty of such movements and, indeed, their parasitic relation to society, in spite of their charismatic power. Even this radical group felt called upon to appeal to the benevolence of the ruler for financial support. It was denied, undoubtedly confirming the anti-worldly dualism.

More significant in view of the power that this group exercised under the Constantinians and in view of the fact that the crisis came out of a politically and educationally understood Logos (or, as we have called it, organic monotheism) were Eusebius and his party. Sometimes called semi-Arian or Arianizing, they held that the Logos was a rational principle emanating from the mind of God and serving as a cosmological mediator between the supreme God and the created world of men, which itself was a more distant emanation of the same God's divine potencies.[20] Christ is seen as a manifestation of this Logos, as were all great powers and principles. Indeed, great rulers are such a manifestation also, and it was a short jump to comparing Constantine with Christ. As George Williams shows, the ruler of the churches and the political ruler were regarded

> . . . as alike instruments . . . of the one Eternal Logos, the former to preach monotheism, to exorcise demons, and to proclaim God's Kingdom; the latter to establish monotheism and, by routing the lesser gods around which the demonic forces of nationalism and dissension centered, to usher in the long promised forces of the messianic age. In thus enthusiastically comparing Caesar and Christ it was indeed hard for Eusebius not to leave the impression that the work of a Christian Caesar was of more importance than the work of Christ.[21]

The result of this view was that Constantine, particularly, but others also who naturally favored the same view, became authoritative on church and doctrinal matters, for it became very difficult to argue religious matters with one who embodied the supreme Logos. The position of Eusebius has always seemed a dangerous one to much of the church, for obvious reasons; but it has also found its advocates in countries where religion is a department of state, where there is direct collaboration between the established church and the government, or where there is much celebration of "God and country." In short, the organic view of Logos monotheism, based on educational and political motifs, was, from a theological and practical standpoint, as much in danger of subverting the freedom of the church as the culturally irresponsible radical dualists were in danger of losing their prophetic witness by failing to shape the social and political forces toward justice and righteousness.

The crucial battles, however, took place between the Arians and the Athanasians. Both of these groups recognized the sovereignty of one God that overcomes all lesser loyalties and the attendant pluralism of polytheism. Both of these groups recognized the necessity of a distinction between God and man, creator and created, sacred and secular. But how these things were spelled out is quite different. In general one can say that the dualistic sectarians tended to be on the side of the Athanasians, although they were usually so disengaged it is difficult to tell, while the Eusebians lined up with the Arians. The splits were such, however, that the alliances could not be long sustained.

There was, between these two parties, a common recognition of monotheism. But the Arians saw God the Father as sole and undifferentiated unity that is radically different from creation. The Logos for them was the principle that was to overcome the dualism produced by radical monotheism, or the division of higher and lower in organic monotheism. But the Logos was not a part of the reality of God. It was something other, something created by God. Speaking of the Logos or Christ, the watchword became "There was when he was not."[22] Hence the structure that unites the sacred and divine with the created and human is created also. There was nothing capable of overcoming the dualism to which the radical monotheism led. Educationally, they saw the Logos, sometimes translated by them as sophia (wisdom), as part of creation and hence subject to rationality. At the same time, they asserted that the Logos is mutable, and thus a kind of dynamic rationalism was involved. But politically, they considered the unity of the created Logos with the created man Jesus superior to men and hence they introduced, in the midst of their modified dualism, a hierarchical conception that has analogues to, and evoked sympathy from, the Eusebians. The picture is further complicated by their denying that Jesus had a human soul. Thus they denied both the full divinity and the full humanity of the mediating concept. But such a strange assertion makes sense if one perceives that they were really structuring a series of hierarchical beings independent of God except that they were all created. This led to a view of Constantine and the rulers that made them beings of superior status to man, and indeed to the church, for they, too, were unities of the created Logos and created men. Jesus and Caesar as abstract men find their common form in the fact that they were adopted by God through His created Logos and gain thereby an autonomous state subordinate to God but superior to men. The next step, as one might suspect, was the creation of demigods, a whole series of cultural "Goods" that religiously bound society together and that were unassailable from man's side. Since man was inferior to these powers and since there was nothing that had in fact overcome the duality of creator and created so that man had access to anything above the demigods to shatter their pretensions, cultural and political powers were beyond religious criticism. We must recognize here a dynamic and differentiated view of the centers of human loyalty and rationality that theoretically avoids the schizophrenia of the radical dualists and the monolithic totalitarian conceptions of the organic monotheists. But there is no critical center, only a series of distinct levels, and no way of harmonizing. Further, the split between the divine and the human remains in spite of the proliferation of intervening categories.

The Arians were opposed and finally defeated by the Athanasians and the subsequent "Catholics," a fact that must be troubling to those who see all disputes as determined by power relations, since the Arians and the Arianizing Eusebians had much imperial sympathy on their side most of the time. The Athanasians saw that the two sides of the duality were always related, always distinct, always pressing for resolution of the tension, and always resisting premature identification and unity in any way except by Christ and the Spirit.

The Athanasian view of the one God was a radical one too, in that it made a clear distinction between creator and created. But the one God was viewed in a more differentiated fashion. There was the creation, where God's Fatherhood is seen, yet Fatherhood does not exhaust the modes of divine operation as the Arians thought. There was also the Sonhood, the merger of that which is fully of God with that which is of the created world to overcome the alienation. And there is the Spirit, which was to be the subject of debate later in the century.

The Athanasians were concerned with the relation of the divine and the human. And they articulated what much of the church has thought was the proper biblical understanding — namely, that the dualism of creation and creator to which radical monotheism leads can be overcome only by a principle involving both. Hence, following the option laid down by Athanasius, the Council of Chalcedon, meeting long after Athanasius' death, defined Jesus Christ explicitly as fully God and fully man. Thus was a crucial theological principle established. Precisely what this statement means is still hotly debated. R. G. Collingwood,[23] Werner Jaeger,[24] and Erik Peterson[25] (although from another perspective) all see the Athanasian motifs as clarified by Chalcedon as providing a positive metaphysics that shapes subsequent history, and Peterson even suggests that this formula has positive dogmatic import for subsequent faith. Paul Tillich[26] is probably more nearly right when he suggests that these articulations must be understood as negative formulation in the sense that it is impossible to write off or undercut either of the two sides. Nevertheless, from present perspectives, we are inclined to see a variety of positive content, even if it is not metaphysical in the Greek sense that

Collingwood and Jaeger want to articulate. We now see an affirmation that the divine and human split is overcome primarily in particular historical events, a conclusion that the dualists with their contempt for the world, the Eusebians with their organic monotheism, and the Arians with their dynamic rationality and "demigods" could not quite accept.

For the Athanasians and "Catholics," even if not always for Athanasius himself, the dualism is overcome by the incarnation, which is quite distinct from creation. At certain points in history, new unities of those realms that are quite distinct create new positive centers of loyalty superior to either the old distinctions or particular powers on the creation side. To be sure, during this period, the leading churchmen were more deferential toward the imperial power than the theory suggests, and they saw it a Christian duty to pray for and support the power of even relatively just rulers. But standing behind their credentials of Christ, they succeeded in declaring a degree of separation of church and state that is the theological basis of all subsequent efforts.

The trinity

The creedal articulation of the doctrine of the two natures of Christ provisionally solved the problem of the relation of the divine and the human, although more than another century of sometimes vicious debate was required to establish a stable agreement as to the meaning of the formula. At least it focused the issues in such a way that some answers were clearly excluded on theological and practical grounds, even if it provided no positive prescription for all times. It further suggested the terms by which subsequent battles can best be fought. But it had not solved the other two questions with which we started this paper and with which the fourth century dealt. What is the relation of the one and the many, and what is the relationship of continuity and change?

The terms for solving the first of these, the one and the many, were, however, already at hand. As a subdominant theme throughout the Christological debates, the Holy Spirit is treated as subtle counterpoint. If the Donatists spoke of the pure body of Christ, so also of the pure Spirit. If the Arians saw the Logos as a middle-level existent, so also the Spirit. If the Eusebians treated Christ as an emanation of the Logos that fitted into the hierarchical chain of being, so also the Spirit. If the Athanasians saw Jesus Christ as of two natures, so also the Spirit had two aspects. At least, there was the theoretical parallel. Very soon, however, three slight shifts of accent altered the victorious Athanasian model considerably. The Spirit was identified with, or placed within, the church, which comes from the Father through the Son, somewhat limiting its freedom to blow "where it listeth." The Christological aspect of the debate became specified in terms of the identity of the true apostolate and

thus the sanction for the authority of the vicars of Christ. The Christological reference thus became a personal symbol of ecclesiastical authority
while the Spirit derived from it became a more collective one. But since
the collective model was incapable of engaging creatively the more static
material and political powers of the day, a genuine "two aspects"
pneumatology that would be a full correlate of the Christological debate
never was established. The divine-human split that had been overcome
in Christology is re-established as a secular-sacred split on the pneuma-
tological basis. One set of institutions is seen as based on reason and
another on belief. A two-level social universe ensues, a natural and
spiritual morality, a *Civitas Mundi* and a *Civitas Dei*. Such a development meant, since the spiritual was deemed superior to the material, that
the major structures of authority and the major expressions of culture
were under the tutelage of the church. We have, it is true, come to see
that the Middle Ages were not nearly so dark as our grandfathers thought,
and that the church did, in large measure, keep the political and the
educational dynamic alive. But the church feared independent dynamic
(spiritual) movements also, and prevented these from developing outside
of the authority of Christ, for the "Christian civilization" was only precariously covering a deeply rooted paganism. The chief protectorate and
bearer of that civilization could not let any movements which drove
toward collective novelty in theological, political, or educational ways
and claimed spiritual sanction directly from the Father without the Son,
break its fragile grip and unleash either the polytheisms of tribal and
national loyalties that it had only so recently subdued, the rationalisms
that drove toward unity but denied its mystery, or the schismatic effects
of fresh outbreaks of religious enthusiasm.

The notion of any real independence of the Spirit from the Son is not
a part of the modified dualism of the fourth century's explicit formulations. Although Gregory of Nazianzus comes quite close at times, the
notion did not gain any clear articulation until the Joachite movement
several centuries later, begun by Joachim of Floris and now seen by
Marxist and some Protestant scholars as a chief forerunner of the Reformation. Yet it was implied in several widespread phenomena, not the least
of which was the frequent recognition of "spirituality" that existed in
some academic centers and the spiritual dynamic of the education processes that were not under the control of Christ's vicars. (Indeed, under
Julian, Christians were severely restricted from teaching, but the legitimacy of the educational process even under pagan auspices was not
seriously challenged.) Had the Christians denied the spiritual legitimacy
of this "independent" enterprise, they would also have had to challenge
the spiritual authority of Plato, Aristotle, the Stoics, and many other upon
whom they too depended. Instead, they frequently spoke of these figures

as the Moseses of the Greeks, whose spiritual authority derived from the Father, and only very indirectly from the Son. Many subsequent debates on church-state relations are theologically based on this development.[27]

Nevertheless, the Athanasians and their successors, the Cappadocians and other "Catholics," had by their treatment of Christology already set the stage for coping theologically with the problem of the one and the many. God Himself was differentiated into Father, Son, and Holy Spirit without compromising His unity. Singular truth can have — indeed, demands — complexities of expression that enrich its significance and provide relationships to other factors without compromising the fact of simplicity. We need not rehearse the details of this debate as it progressed, but rather to point out that the intense struggle which eventuated in the victory on the Christology question brought a correlative victory for fresh perspectives on the problem of the one and the many. Using the economic model of Trinity in such a way that monarchistic unity or duality could not result, permitted the fundamental possibility of diversity within unity and unity with diversity to be affirmed.

The concept of the Spirit, which became as important as the concepts of Father and Son with the affirmation of the Trinity, preserved, it must also be acknowledged, the possibility of change that had been somewhat compromised by the defeat of Arianism's "dynamic rationalism." The Spirit, if we see the way the concept functioned with regard to education, for example, rather than relying only on the formalized confessions, provides a theological model of the fact that new charismatic powers and centers of loyalty may be found sporadically either on the basis of created order and rationality or on the prototypical and redemptive historical basis of Jesus Christ and the church — although even in the former case it must be tested by the Son as the Son is to be tested by the Spirit. It also left open what was to be a possible later development, that some "spiritual" movements claiming legitimacy directly from the Father can stand against perversions of the religious community that grow out of loyalty to the Son, and vice versa.

We must recognize in the concept of the Spirit a latent anti-rational, anti-Establishment sentiment. The church was not terribly secure in its new role. The empire was the Establishment, and the church, through the concept of Spirit, was implicitly providing an alternative center of loyalty. Further — a sentiment that had educational significance — some aspects of human experience that are valid are ultimately non-predictable. Frequently linked to the experiential or cultic in religion, the prophetic or reformist in political affairs, and the artistic and creative genius in educational matters, but not limited to these, is the recognition of factors that are not subject to explicit religious, educational, and political rationalization.

Thus, the period of the Constantinians proves to be an age that established a conceptual model for subsequent Christian interpretations about fundamental problems of Christianity in its relation to culture. It involved the complex juxtaposition of the unity of truth, the duality of the divine and the human finding resolution in particular historical moments of revelation, and a trinity that both offered a portrait of differentiated but not fractured reality and introduced a dynamic element that suggested novelty, enthusiasm, and change related to continuity and constancy.[28]

A further word about the Spirit is necessary before we leave this section, however, for another movement not yet touched upon is relevant to the fully articulated model.

As with the semi-independence of the Spirit from the Son, the second problem of theories about the Spirit, which we have defined as its two-aspects structure, was only a subdominant theme in the fourth century. The two-aspects structure was implied as much in some of the church institutional and historical developments as it was in the articulated model itself, indicating that at some points the theological ethical conversation between the dramatic events of history and the interpretive model may not have been sufficiently maintained. Athanasius himself was responsible for the introduction of monasticism in the West following the lead of Pachomius in Egypt — Pachomius was the founder of institutionalized monasticism that involved a "rule," economic production, and literacy as an admissions requirement. In the subsequent rise of monasticism many orthodox theologians who saw themselves in the Athanasian camp insisted that what the church and the culture at large was to recognize as spiritually legitimate had to take on some organizational embodiment. The proto-monastic movement had attempted to accent radical and pure spirituality by encouraging a hermetic, ascetic life in the wilderness, eschewing all contacts with and dependence upon creations of the human spirit such as culture and civilization. The heirs of Athanasius were much concerned to bring that spirituality into an organized institution, under a group discipline, and into a responsible relationship with the surrounding community by performing certain services to the community, by engaging in economic production, by advancing scholarship, or at least by providing an institutional haven for the spiritually elite outcasts of conventional culture. The concern of these theologians can be seen at least in part as an attempt to affirm a two-aspects understanding of the Spirit — although it was still a "modified dualism" understanding — that never really became theologically built into the dominant model.

From a Protestant perspective, the Reformation is seen as the time when the Spirit was unleashed from the encumbrances of its modified dualism and began to relate — to incarnate in historically significant and transforming ways — the Spirit that proceeds from the Father to the most mundane enterprises that occupy the human spirit in a vitally creative way.

The perennial Catholic criticism that the Reformation leads to a post-Christian civilization, whatever the intentions of the Reformers, thus may well be judged an accurate appraisal of Protestantism's effects, for the Catholics (and some "Christendom" Protestants) tend to see all Spirit as continuously proceeding "through the Son." But the Protestant who asserts the necessity of partial independence and two aspects of the Spirit regards such developments as having theological legitimacy.

The Model's Value

What is fundamental about these traditional formulations is their connection with contemporary issues in which church and state are involved that prevent our ignoring the fourth century in this area of inquiry as other contemporary debates require investigation of other periods.[29]

Most obviously, there is an analogy between the problems of the Constantinian period and the present that even the radical differences do not obscure. The sectarian, Eusebian, Arian, and Athanasian points of view have present-day correlates on similar theological grounds. We see then and now a series of divergent religious groups moving toward consolidation and working to find common ground at the levels of theological formulation, ecclesiological polity, and cultural-political responsibility. The most exciting reports emanating from the World Council of Churches, the National Council of Churches, Vatican II, and such efforts as recent as the conversations on church unity of the major American denominations are centering precisely on these issues. Further, both the age of Christological debates and the present century are periods of comparatively rapid social change in which the usual radical separation of church and state is being called into question, to the joy of some and the chagrin of others. Local community and local church and local ethnic authority patterns are being challenged as their parochialism and incapacity force higher-level assumption of responsibility and the implementation of more universal values and programs. Finally, there is an analogy between then and now in that predominantly non-Christian forms of thought, at least on the conscious and explicit level, demand the construction of a Christian apologetic that can prove its efficacy and power. The situation at that time, as Jaeger has described it, obtains today: "Christians had to show the formative power of their spirit in works of superior intellectual and artistic caliber and to carry the contemporary mind along in their enthusiasm," if they were to be heard at all.[30]

But there is more than analogy between then and now. There is also a theological continuity. Not only does Christian periodization of history see the time between the coming of Christ and the eschaton as one time span with common elements, but in fact theologians and churchmen who deal with questions of the one and the many, the divine and the human, and change and continuity, use consciously or implicitly the terms from this period, even if they put accents in different places or argue against the traditional formulations. Protestant "holiness sects," for example, are very suspicious of rationalized forms of education and are usually disengaged from institutional problems that call for specification of the relationship of religion and culture or church and state. Withdrawing sects also dualistically accent the pure law of Christ against the laws of the world and attempt to establish interior purity on the Donatist model. (Note the problems of the local school boards with the Amish throughout the country.)[30a] A national civic religion of an organic monotheistic variety is clearly a part of American political life, as Robert Bellah has recently shown in a very helpful paper.[31] And this should not be confused with the "God, Constitutional Government and the Middle Class" or "God, States' Rights, and the White Southerner" forms of Arian faith that prevail in sections of all churches.[32] The Athanasian resolution of the problems, deeply informed by the failure to develop a two-aspects doctrine of the Spirit, became the rationale for Lutheran and Catholic parochial education in this country and for modern Catholic education, for example, in Europe and South America. Jewish, Unitarian, and liberal Calvinist theologians (United Church of Christ, American Baptists to a degree, and some Presbyterians) tend to accent the sovereignty of the one God in radical monotheism and see the church as quite distinct from the state. Thus, they endorse the Supreme Court decisions taking cultic practice out of public domain. At the same time, they are skeptical about the "teaching of moral and spiritual values," for they fear surrogate forms of proselytism, innocuous forms of piety, and "God and country" baptized patriotism; but they frequently favor public education as a matter of principle, support rational and "objective" teaching *about* religion in public education if it can be done well,[33] and implicitly press in their social concerns (civil rights, for example) for a new two-aspects understanding of the Spirit.[34]

The historical and theological underpinnings of this last option can be found in the Calvinist and aggressive sectarian branches of the Reformation, especially as worked out in theories of the "Covenant." The failure to develop a two-aspects understanding of the Spirit led in Catholicism and Lutheranism to a split between "spiritual" and "material," "gospel" and "law," "revelation" and "reason" that was overcome only in the sacramental forms of the church for the Catholics and only in the hearts of individuals through the work of Christ for the Lutherans. Thus they could not see non-sacramental transforming political or economic reform as really spiritual and did not consider it the task of the "spiritual" church. It is true that they recognized the created validity of the natural, but their recognition involved sacramentalizing it and thus again they asserted the superiority of the spiritual. The consequent reassertion of the creature, of the materialistic, of created potency against the spiritual in Catholic or Lutheran forms by Feuerbach, Nietzsche, Marx, and Freud was an inevitable reaction to a false view of life and history presented by the theological model.[35] But we must introduce a word of caution about drawing lines. Twentieth-century Scandinavian Lutheranism and Vatican II suggest that revision of this typology may be necessary, for the correctives seem to have been taken seriously. Pope John XXIII correctly stated the issue when he spoke of the Vatican Council in terms of the Holy Spirit and referred to it as *aggiornamento,* a shaking up by "opening the windows to the world."

The Calvinist part of the Reformation, and the sectarian movement that followed on its heels, became the basis of the American denominations and shaped American concepts of the relation of church, state, and education.[36] This tradition accepted the basic Athanasian formula and much of Lutheranism, but it pressed vigorously for a more independent communitarism, more "incarnated" understanding of the Spirit in a variety of ways.[37] It saw political-economic action as a legitimate part of one's spiritual calling.[38] It saw legal reconstruction as a part of the Christian vocation.[39] It saw natural reason as a corollary to revelation,[40] it defined the saint as the citizen establishing a righteous new order in the civil community,[41] and it saw new community formation on a voluntary associational basis as a function of the spiritual vocation of the company of true believers.[42]

Further, its concept of the radical sovereignty of God, so acute as to demand an impracticable theocracy in Geneva, the Cromwellian revolution, and Puritan New England, nevertheless gave a center to the drive toward unity of truth that allowed a partial synthesis with the rationalistic universalism of the Enlightenment,[43] a well-known development which shaped the destiny of American education in a direct way. Yet this radical sovereignty, controlled by a theological legitimation of diversity and differentiation (or pluralism as we usually call it less precisely) through a continued trinitarian insistence, never succumbed to the drive toward a monolithic structure that was the result of the French Revolution.

Of course, a whole series of influences that separate us from our predecessors are here omitted: conflicting definitions of law, conflicting lusts for power by heirs of Caesar and Christ alike, cultural crosscurrents and population migrations, the rise of science and technology, to mention a few. But in spite of radical change on these fronts, we are bound to the theological-cultural-political debates of the fourth century in significant ways. There are continuities of thought, analogies of problems, and direct historical influences that shape our problem of religion and the public schools today in the midst of rapid change.

Implications of a Trinitarian Model Today

We see, then, that motifs deriving from the age of Constantine have echoes in the underlying structures of the problems facing America today with regard to religion and public education. Whether we fully agree with this influence and the trinitarian conceptual framework that is entailed or not, we can now begin to specify, looking to the present and future rather than the past, what the implications of these views might well be. Indeed, future efforts to devise viable institutional arrangements concerning religion and state-supported education will only be satisfactory from the standpoint of contemporary Protestant theology, now undergoing considerable reconstruction, if certain ingredients are included. Let us look at the various elements of the interacting models as they are pertinent today beyond the ones already suggested in the preceding sections.

MONOTHEISM

Educationally, monotheism involves the affirmation that there is a singularity of truth and that, politically, "We are a religious people whose institutions presuppose a Supreme Being." [44] Such an affirmation, on either count, is a matter of faith, although reasons can be given to show that it is a necessary assertion to make life, education, and politics — not to mention religion — valid and valuable. It is not the purpose of this essay to spell out the ways in which the assertion is deemed "necessary," but it is a fact that when someone, at some time, has full access to truth, we expect not to be confronted with paradox and contradiction. Some things are true or partly so and some are false or partly so. Politically, we are bound to affirm universal goals and we concede judgment when we accent only particularisms in national or local policy. There is, thus, in educational and political life alike, a drive toward the universal that both opens new horizons and judges our narrow preferences.

Such an affirmation suggests further that all areas of human endeavor, including religion, can legitimately come under rational critique and can be taught among the disciplines supported by public institutions if the following conditions are met: it is recognized that teaching which is a genuine quest for the unity of truth may shatter the parochialism of the institution that supports it as well as point up its valid aspects; there is developed a trained, professional group with explicit standards to define the boundaries of the discipline and the basic structure of the material; there is established a precedent of freedom of the lectern for those professionally seeking that unity, comparable to the traditions of freedom of the pulpit in some denominations and academic freedom in the universities.

DUALISM

There is one truth, but man is separated from it. There is a crucial difference between creator and created. No one person, no one group, nor several groups cumulatively have the final answer. We have only provisional models, subject to correction, that point in a better or worse fashion toward it. There is no place for indoctrination with a sacramentalized "the Truth" in genuine education, and all public monies must be kept separated from groups that make such claims, implicitly or explicitly. If private and church groups wish to participate in the *quest* for truth under professionally defined, universalistic criteria, and gain the support of the public in this effort, they should subject their curriculum to the same conditions mentioned in the preceding paragraph.

TWO-NATURES CHRISTOLOGY

The perfect joining of divine-human distinction that grows from dualism occurs in particular historical events. In the Jewish community and the Christian church there is the memory, celebration, and anticipation of such integrating events. There are also the prophetic and eschatological concerns that militate against premature wedding, sacramentalized joining of these realms in events or institutions that fail to relate the unities completely with the universal truth and with the full integrity of the natural and human in their universal dimensions. Thus, these traditions entail a prophetic suspicion of nationalistic religion, which is the constant temptation of state-supported teaching about religion.[45] Nevertheless, it is recognized that unity of the divine and the human has occurred and that it will recur on even grander scales. The identification of these unities, however, is not the work of the state. Nor can Jews and most Protestants recognize an organic, hierarchical, non-historical position which attempts by its cultic or thought life to produce them as theologically legitimate. Therefore, they oppose both varieties of "modified dualism."

The two-natures Christology, by the way, also puts the church on its mettle by demanding that its memory, its celebration, and its anticipation both recognize the fully human element in theologically significant events and bring its past, present, and future under "natural" human criticism by apologetics in the community of faith as well as vis-à-vis the non-believers.

Still further, there is here the affirmation that salvation does not singularly depend on education, even education concentrating on "moral and spiritual values." Salvation, for persons, is related to identity and obedience to God's will, trust, and hope, through participation in historically significant events and movements. Such participation is not confined within the institutions of the state.

THE SPIRIT

The one truth manifests itself in more ways than through universality, and through particularity of identity, obedience, trust, and hope that overcomes the divine-human split. There are many varieties of movements and moments of personal or social ecstasy, some proceeding from the very power of creation and some from the community that remembers, celebrates, and anticipates, even if they do not acknowledge their sources, which are valid and revelatory. Education at large and education about religion in particular must not only provide openings as a part of the total educational process in which students are exposed to charismatic figures and movements but recognize the power of such movements as a genuinely religious force in all human affairs.

The clear preference of this paper for a two-aspects doctrine of the Spirit sees as legitimate, and in some cases demands, formation and support of voluntary associations dedicated to universalistic values to speak out and act on national and international affairs with, for example, humanists, Marxists, and beatniks, not to mention artists, poets, musicians, and others who may be non-believers but who nevertheless act according to the Spirit incarnate. Here again we must acknowledge the importance of the Jews, whose spirit often leads them to the forefront of intellectual, artistic, and social creativity, disproportionate to their numbers. The Christian, while affirming the validity of their efforts, however, also affirms that these groups and actions must be tested according to their ability to establish personal identity and to relate the divine and the human aspects of existence. They must, theologically speaking, be tested against Christology to gain Christian certification.

While it remains the primary purpose of education to bring such movements under rational criticism and exegesis, education itself will never be capable of character formation and socialization of our young in an adequate way if it is divorced from these movements. And it is always a question whether religion, politics, or education will allow itself to be revised by institutionalizing new charismatic movements.

THE TRINITY

Such diversity of interests and concerns as itemized under the various headings above is not the fracturing of truth or education or state or religion. Rather, these matters represent a fundamental conceptual model that allows the divine legitimacy of pluralism, differentiation, and diversity. This does *not* mean that anything goes; whatever I believe is true for me. Some varieties of difference — for example, personal identity, membership in voluntary associations, ways of being related to the total system — are here seen as crucial and positive whereas other varieties are seen as negligible or negative. Separations between men and groups based on tribal or ethnic divisions, nationalistic loyalties, and educational or economic levels are of the negative type from theological perspectives; where they exist they must be overcome in order that valid forms of differentiation may emerge. Such a model would clearly seem to legitimate economically and racially integrated schools, increased accent on individual research, guided studies, give-and-take between teacher and student in the classroom (a relatively new phenomenon in the history of modern education), and the right of students to a view contrary to that of the teacher if it is adequately defended, all within a unified structure.

These elements, juxtaposed, present a complex interpretive model that underlies many of the debates even where it is not recognized. And it clearly has been informative on Protestant views of the substantive problems that confront the whole discussion of religion and public education: the one and the many, the human and the divine, and change and continuity.

A Theological Coda

Four observations should be made in conclusion.

First, theological ethics cannot specify what courses ought to be taught, how they ought to be taught, and who ought to teach them. But it can provide basic conceptual tools to help professional public school administrators, professional teachers, and consultants on religion decide what resources are available and what kinds of issues are significant. In general, that has been one of the concerns of this paper.

Second, it is my conviction that the self-conscious structure of this paper suggests a major option in theological ethical method. One begins by an analysis of the contemporary setting, moves to find the underlying historical and conceptual structures that have informed and distorted the present, and, by reconstruction of the derived interpretive model in view of contemporary developments, points toward the future and the next steps that may be involved — without presuming to produce a blueprint.

But that brings us to the third point, which is really a question. Is reconstruction of the trinitarian model necessary and possible? I have tried to show that it is. In fact, the discussion of a two-aspects pneumatology involved considerable model reconstruction although it was primarily a spelling out of elements already present in the tradition according to the historical requirements, and from a particular perspective. A more systematic treatment of the problem would be very helpful in sorting out some theological issues that were beyond the boundaries of this paper. I know of none now available.

More difficult, finally, is a problem that Tillich pointed to.[46] Is the Trinity historical or eternal? That is, are its significance and richness found in the fact that it corresponds to the metaphysical structure of being? Did it exist before creation and will it continue beyond history?

The fathers thought so. Or is this a humanly and historically developed conceptual framework that has had a deep influence and that continues to be somewhat powerful when people see how it functions? I have treated it as the latter, for such a model as this seems to point directly toward the dilemmas and conflicts of history as much as to the metaphysical, and I have assumed that the most viable theology today is a "historical theology of history." Indeed, at some points I have argued that important developments (such as the monastic movement and the post-Calvinistic sectarian movement) were carried by historical institutions in a way that outstripped the metaphysics of the day and the theological interpretive model itself. The power of any model is found in its ability to change and adapt without collapsing under the pressure of new historical data while claiming continued and normative interpretive relevance due to its articulation of perennial issues that recur in ever new forms. What gives a model continuing significance is not the beauty of its internal logic but the sustained pertinence that transcends its own history and even the concerns of those who devised it.

NOTES

1. I am deeply indebted throughout this section to the work of several noted scholars: George H. Williams, especially his "Christology and Church-State Relations in the Fourth Century," *Church History*, Vol. XX, No. 3, pp. 3–33, and Vol. XX, No. 4, pp. 3–26; Erik Peterson, *Der Monotheismus als Politisches Problem* (Jacob Hegner, 1935); Werner Jaeger, *Early Christianity and Greek Paideia* (Belknap Press, 1961); Talcott Parsons, especially "Christianity and Modern Industrial Society," in *Sociological Theory Values and Socio-Cultural Change*, ed. Edward A. Tiryakian (Free Press, 1963); and Paul Lehmann, *Ethics in a Christian Context* (Harper, 1963), especially "The Trinitarian Basis of Christian Ethics" in Chapter 4, pp. 102–123.

2. Amos Wilder, *Eschatology and Ethics in the Teaching of Jesus* (Harper, 1950).

3. Charles M. Cocrane, *Christianity and Classical Culture* (Oxford University Press, rev. ed., 1944), pp. 223–224.

4. H. I. Marrou, "Christianity and Classical Education," Chapter IX of *A History of Education in Antiquity* (Sheed & Ward, 1956).

5. R. G. Collingwood, *Essay on Metaphysics* (Oxford University Press, 1940), pp. 223–224.

6. *Metaphysics*, Book XII, chap. 10., last line.

7. Gerard S. Sloyan, *The Three Persons in One God* (Prentice-Hall, 1964), p. 13.

8. *Ibid.*, p. 14.

9. Peterson, *op. cit.*, p. 27.

10. Charles Fox, "Theology and Secularization," paper delivered at Albion College, Mich., in March, 1966.

11. Peterson, *op. cit.*, pp. 36–37.

12. Jaeger, *op. cit.*, p. 60. Compare Henry Chadwick, *Early Christian Thought and the Classical Tradition* (Oxford University Press, 1966).

13. Jaeger, *op. cit.*, p. 65.

14. *Ibid.*, p. 61.

15. I am dependent here on Tillich's lectures on "History of Christian Thought" delivered at Union Theological Seminary in 1953, as recorded by Peter H. John.

16. Williams, *op. cit.*, No. 3, pp. 6 ff. Compare also Reinhold Seeberg, *The History of Doctrines* (Baker Book House, 1956), especially pp. 185–187.

17. Krister Stendahl, "Judaism and Christianity, Then and Now," *Harvard Divinity Bulletin*, October, 1963, pp. 1–9.

18. Kenneth Burke, *The Rhetoric of Religion* (Beacon, 1961), reaches similar conclusions; cf. pp. 23 and 174–176.

19. Seeberg, *op. cit.*, p. 201. The import of the term "practical" should not be overlooked. Contrast this statement and the statements referred to in note 1, above, with the view of A. H. M. Jones, *Were Ancient Heresies Disguised Social Movements?* (Fortress Press, 1961). Jones obviously does not know what he is arguing against and claims far too much for his vaguely anti-Marxist polemic.

19a. I choose the Donatists as the best example of the withdrawing sectarian type because of the importance of Augustine's arguments against them in shaping medieval institutions and because the legal restrictions against them were utilized against the Anabaptists during the Reformation. Both Catholic and Protestant attitudes bear the indirect marks of this group. Other sects of the same general type were as significant in purely theological terms, but did not evoke comparably deep institutional responses.

20. Williams, *op. cit.*, pp. 3, 16 ff.

21. *Ibid.*, p. 17.

22. Seeberg, *op. cit.*, p. 203.

23. *Op. cit.*, p. 217.

24. *Op. cit.*, pp. 60 ff.

25. *Op. cit.*, pp. 49 ff.

26. *Op. cit.*

27. Cf., for example, the new collection of documents of the church-state struggles edited by Brian Tierney, *The Crisis of Church and State* (Prentice-Hall, 1964).

28. This formulation should be compared to Collingwood's more metaphysical and scientific interest and Parsons' more sociological reading:

"By believing in the Father they [the fathers of the church] meant (always with reference solely to the procedure of natural science) absolutely presupposing that there is a world of nature which is always and indivisibly one world. By believing in the Son they meant absolutely presupposing that this one natural world is nevertheless a multiplicity of natural realms. By believing in the Holy Ghost they meant . . . that the world of nature, throughout its entire fabric, is not merely a world of things but of events and movements" (Collingwood, *op. cit.*, p. 224).

"The theological significance of the Christ figure as the mediator between God and man is central as defining the nature of man's relation to God, in and through the church of Christ. . . . It constituted the differentiation of Christianity as a religious system (a cultural system) from the conception of a "people" as a social system . . . further, the development of the conception of the Trinity . . . implied, correlative with the differentiation of the church from secular society, a differentiation within the religious system itself. . . . Action decisions in particular cases had to be left to the conscience of believers and could not be prescribed by a comprehensive religious law. . . . This differentiation occurred, however, within a genuine unity" (Parsons, *op. cit.*, pp. 40–41).

29. Cf., for example, my "Toward a Theology for a New Social Gospel," *New Theology No. 4*, ed. M. Marty and D. Peerman (Macmillan, 1967), pp. 220–242.

30. Jaeger, *op. cit.*, p. 73.

30a. Franklin Littell, in *The Origins of Sectarian Protestantism* (Macmillan, 1964) documents the way in which sectarian Protestantism derives much of its view of culture and politics from a myth about the fall of the church during the Constantinian era. He also shows that recent publications continue this interpretation. Cf. especially p. 56 ff.

31. Robert Bellah, "Civil Religion in America," *Daedelus*, Vol. 96, No. 1 (Winter, 1967), pp. 1–21.

32. While I was writing this article, a copy of *Christian Economics* (Vol. XVIII, No. 12) came across my desk. Not only does one of the major articles begin with an analysis of the responses of the church to Constantine in 311, but the entire issue shows that there are a series of demigods represented as that which is essentially Christian in good Arian fashion. The free market, individual initiative, local authority — these are only some of the "dynamic rationalistic" principles that stand over man and under God without relating them.

33. Cf., for example, Niels C. Nielsen, Jr., *God in Education* (Sheed and Ward, 1966).

34. Thus, involvement in such activities as civil rights by these groups is quite legitimate. Two papers in the present book deal quite directly with fresh suggestions as to how education might open up new efforts in this direction. Cf. the constructive parts of the papers by Fred M. Newmann and Donald W. Oliver from the educational side and by Harvey G. Cox from the theological side.

35. Ernst Troeltsch, *The Social Teaching of the Christian Churches*, Vol. II, translated by Olive Wyon (Harper, 1960), is still valuable on the comparison of Catholic and Lutheran positions.

36. C. C. Wright, in an address, "Church and State: An Unconventional View" (*Crane Review*, Spring, 1967) presents convincing evidence of the Puritan concern for a non-established church in New England but a correlative concern for religion's fulfilling several important social functions. Parallels and distinctions between religion and education are also drawn. Cf. also Franklin Littell, *From State Church to Pluralism* (Doubleday, 1962).

37. I discussed this somewhat in my "Toward a Theology for a New Social Gospel," *op. cit.*, p. 38.

38. Relevant here are the discussions proceeding from Max Weber's *The Protestant Ethic and the Spirit of Capitalism* (1904–1905, tr. 1931).

39. David Little, "The Logic of Order," unpublished Th.D. dissertation, Harvard, 1963.

40. E. Harris Harbison, *The Christian Scholar in the Age of the Reformation* (Scribner, 1956), especially pp. 144–164.

41. Michael Walzer, *The Revolution of the Saints* (Harvard University Press, 1965). Parts of this material must be contrasted with the Weber thesis, *op. cit.*, and is in conflict with the work of David Little, *op. cit.* Cf. also A. S. P. Woodhouse, *Puritanism and Liberty* (University of Chicago Press, 1951).

42. James Luther Adams, "A Critique of Max Weber," a paper delivered at the 1966 Annual Meeting of the Society for the Scientific Study of Religion.

43. Wright, *op. cit.*

44. Justice Douglas, opinion on the *Zorach* case, 1952.

45. Cf. Eugene Borowitz' fascinating paper in this book.

46. *Op. cit.*

16

An Experiment in Vocabulary

William F. Lynch, S.J.

In this essay I will address myself in an initial way to an exploration of the long task of constructing a *vocabulary* that might help to reduce the polarities, the distances, the great gaps our thoughts and sensibilities are commonly subject to when we think of the relation between religion and secularity in the serious area of the public schools. Vocabulary can be a constructive or a destructive thing. It can create problems. It can reduce or solve them. My hope is that continuous exploration over the course of years will lessen our difficulties. At any rate, nothing ventured, nothing gained.

A particular vocabulary is sometimes quite successful in dealing with one problem but may do nothing but distort the reality of related problems. Thus, when we are trying to work out important features of the relationships between church and state, we properly tend to insist on certain radical divisions between the forms of the sacred and the forms of the secular. To be able to achieve the structural situations we want and to avoid others we do not want in the political order, we declare that the sacred is not the secular, meaning especially, in this case, that the ecclesiastical is not the political. Or again, if we are trying to explicate the idea of sacraments and sacramentality, we find ourselves proposing radical and decisive divisions between things that are holy and those that are not, those that have been set aside for the service of God and those that have not. But, as will become apparent, in other matters the altogether clear distinction is not helpful.

For good purpose after good purpose we have found it necessary to declare for difference and distance between the religious and the secular, the sacred and the world. If we allow ourselves to draw the picture in rough, broad strokes, we could say that we had been recurrently faced with the need of defending the holy as holy or the secular as secular. And whatever the case and whatever the issue, it frequently demanded an act of isolation for the holy as holy or the secular as secular.

About this kind of dialectic and vocabulary two things can be said: (1) It has indeed served many a good purpose; (2) but its persistence as rigid dialectic and vocabulary is the partial root of a number of new crises and will not adequately serve the purpose of our present discussion of religion in the public schools. Are there, then, more fruitful ways of talking about the same thing? Let me say more about these two propositions.

Achievement of a Distinction Between the Sacred and the Secular

The distinction between the sacred and the secular, between religion and the world, between the holy and the non-holy, was originally a difficult and painful achievement. At our point in time the idea of a completely secular world, of completely religionless public schools, is causing considerable anguish to many people, but this is only a new crossroad on the path of a remarkable achievement. The goal, if not the achievement, was nothing less than the destruction of all the idols of the world, all the images man has formed of the secular as holy. The secular at long last was being allowed to drop the burden of being the holy and was being allowed to be itself, while the holy was emerging as holy, at the price of confession and martyrdom. This was the problem and this was sometimes the price. The vocabulary was historical, actual, and essential. It is impossible in a short space to describe how many reality problems were being faced and solved by the achieved separation of the holy and the secular. Now many of us protest against it, and lampoon it, but only because we are now confronted with any number of satirical forms of this original achievement, forms which mock it and parody it and rightly drive us into rebellion against it.

THE SATIRICAL SITUATION

What are some of the satirical forms of this great achievement? What are some of the broken forms of the great distinction?

They are the forms of the great dialectic of the sacred and the secular which now throw us into an understandable concern and which make us thrash about after a new vocabulary. The mocking forms began to tell us, in various vulgar ways, that the secular is not holy and the holy is not secular. The new forms of the distinction began to be distressing. The public schools are one site of the new debate. But we would misunderstand *their* crisis if we did not see the range of the present vulgarization of the old achievement. The problem of the public schools will be more comfortably handled if it is seen as only one instance of a new and general crisis.

I believe, then, that we can deal better with the crisis in the public schools if, first of all, we generalize the problem. Let us look for more forms and shapes of the same concern over the breakdown of an honorable vocabulary.

It is only necessary to give a brief reminder of the broadest form of what I will call the satirical situation — the situation, that is, that parodies the great achievement. Like the achievement, the parody also has two pieces. On the one hand there is an irrelevant religion that has been pushed into a corner. It does not sit there in majesty, the majesty characteristic of many forms of isolation. From its very beginnings in the history of American development and expansion it has occupied a lesser position than that. In the history of the growing West, for example, the preacher is indeed isolated and the church is the collection of the respectable people and the good guys. In American language this was and is a fate worse than death.

On the other hand there are preachers in the wider sense of the word, preachers with imagination who went to school in the right secular places and could hand back to the secular world as much as they might receive in the order of satire. Themselves fallen from their sacred thrones, they have been able to do a reasonably good job of dragging the secular from *its* mighty throne and revealing how cheap an imitation of itself it too could be. However right or wrong, T. S. Eliot and his many followers created a language which is only beginning to be protested, a language that characterized the secular as the non-sacred, as a world without depth, a wasteland, a loveless, arid desert, a secularity that is an unreal city in which live Apeneck Sweeney, Mrs. Porter, Mr. Eugenides, a J. Alfred Prufrock who is "almost, at times, the Fool."

So much for the back and forth of satire between the sacred and the secular. More recently we are engaged, it seems to me, in what might be called a back and forth of *parody*, in another obfuscation of the original vocabulary of sacred and secular. The holy had tried often enough to reduce the political order to a purely mechanical or administrative role while, hypothetically, it would proceed itself to the care and preservation of the moral order as part of the sacred. But historically, as we all know, things simply refused to work out with that kind of arrangement and precision of terms. And was it not fortunate that the political order declared itself, in several crises, to be a moral order? Where the order of religion again and again failed to act, it was the Supreme Court that assumed the moral role in its famous and unanimous vote on desegregation in the *Brown* case in 1954. And a few years later it was John F. Kennedy who called the religious leaders of the nation to the White House to tell them in even more definite terms that this was indeed a moral question and that he expected their support. Thus the secular refused to remain secular in some rigid and superficial sense of the word. In its own way it had taken hold of the task the holy had thought of as its own.

The reaction of the holy to these and other compelling events has been an intense, dedicated, and disturbed invasion of the secular order. I say *disturbed* because the religious conscience is still deeply troubled by memories of superficiality and irrelevance to a secular order vast areas of which had been left unoccupied. A great theological debate has now begun. Its importance is too readily discounted by some — I do not count myself among them — but it centers a great deal on the place, the locus, the situs of the holy. There are new and powerful wishes not only to place it in the midst of the secular but to go a step farther and to secularize it. There are passionate statements from many theologians that the only place where the sacred can be found is in the secular order. Such statements and feelings move religion and the sacred increasingly into the social and political order.

At this point let me repeat what I am doing. I am saying that the original sharp distinction of a particular kind between the sacred and the secular represented a magnificent intellectual and spiritual achievement, of which as a matter of fact the great classical religions of Greece and Rome had not been capable. In witness of how great their failure was, Fustel de Coulanges has outlined for us the degree to which, both in Greece and Rome, the lines of many natural things in the structure of the family and the structure of the state were weakened or dissolved by the imposition of the forms of religion. The desacralization of the secular order of which Harvey Cox has given so fine a description in the early chapters of *The Secular City* could never be quite managed by Greece and Rome but was the achievement of the Hebraic-Christian culture. What I am proposing now, however, is that this achieved separation and dichotomy was able to perform yeoman service for a long time in several fields, but its overly sharp forms are now breaking down in the face of other problems (the possibility and feasibility of religion in the public schools is one of them!) and it is passing through a clouded period of transition. The secular refuses to accept a mechanical definition of itself and insists on taking over many of the moral functions of the sacred; the sacred on its part has never more firmly refused to be desecularized than at the present moment.

THE NEED FOR A TIME OF CONFUSION

I think that this confusion will turn out to be in many ways a very good thing and that much of the confusion will later remain as virtue and permanent acquisition. For one thing it will, in our present discussion, relieve us even more from the burden of a completely mechanical notion of secularity in the public schools, a secularity that absolutely forbids the invasion of some of the qualities of the moral, the religious, the sacred. We need a period of confusion.

I grant that at certain points the confusion has become confusion indeed, especially at the point where the sacred is so anxious to be secular that it is willing to cede its own identity, as though this were a necessary price to be paid for a new life. If this price is paid, the day will come very fast, I think, when the secular order will welcome the order of the sacred into the world but on the terms of purely secular competence, no better and no worse than anyone else. And there may be the strange irony that the sacred will never be welcomed in the public schools in any form if it does not also keep its own identity in the very process of secularizing itself.

It seems to me that we need a vocabulary that will relate the moral, the religious, the sacred, to the secular order in a substantial, continuing, and natural way, at the same time that it preserves the absolute differences. We need a vocabulary that may some day make possible a taken-for-granted relationship between the ideals of religion and the ideals of the public schools, at the same time that it threatens no part of the identity crisis of either.

The following exploration of vocabulary is an experiment in that direction. It is one of a hundred such explorations by other people.

New Definitions of the Sacred and the Secular

Can we find definitions for the sacred and the secular which keep the thoughts, the action, and the sensibilities of both on a continuous line, if I may use that simple image, at the same time that the continuum does not destroy identity? Let us have a try at it.

By "secular" I mean a spirit of thought and a state of things which permits or even compels things and orders of things to emerge in their own forms, their own identities, their own native and inward lines. Let us, therefore, not choose to describe it in negative terms as the non-sacred or as that which has been desacralized. The word "secular" has, as a matter of fact, had many meanings, and out of all this ambiguity I choose this neutral and, I hope, creative meaning: the spirit which drives things and orders of things toward their own actuality.

Certainly not to exhaust the endless ramifications of religion — and the sacred — but only to seize it at one of its most difficult points of identity, I describe it as that which in God has the most absolute identity, autonomy, inwardness (according to the whole achievement, for example, of the language of the Old Testament), and as that, therefore, which is the absolute paradigm for, and generator of, the spirit of true secularity.

THE MEANING OF SECULARITY

Such an understanding of secularity, once it is chosen as a definition and a pivot of discussion, has nothing of the recondite about it and contains considerable immediate clarity. In fact that will turn out to be an occasional difficulty, that it may have too much clarity about it. Holding this in mind as a temptation and danger, however, let us look at some of the implications of the principle of emergence in different fields, and then let us return to its meaning for religion itself.

Secularity means the emergence of the political order as such, in all its fullness and possibilities. It means the same for the order of economics. But already we must watch what we are saying and guard the secular from too much clarity. I feel safe in saying that there are no eternal *laws* or *forms* of politics or economics save the forms and the needs and the wishes of man himself. If we decide, for example, that we had best begin at all costs to think of the feasibility of world government, we do so not because it is an "eternal law of politics" but because the historical crisis of man at a particular moment begins to project this political idea. Facts, therefore, can emerge with great pain and confusion, and not merely with form, structure, clarity, and law. Part of what I am or will be trying to say about secularity is summed up in the thought of Eliot that the highest or severest test of a culture is its sense of fact.

The meaning of secularity also has reference to the work of the literary imagination. We will understand the latter in the sense of secularity if we understand that it is free to imagine new things, new stories, new images that have never been imagined before, if we understand that it is free to push its own exploration of the human as a completely open idea as well as a rather fixed one. The only thing we ask of it is that it always come out with something human! But it cannot be bound by either a philosophy or a theology or an aesthetic which in substance holds that all truth already exists as a set of norms and that the only function of the literary imagination is to supply a mere rhetoric of stories, rhythms, and images that will illustrate these norms or make them interesting. Rather, the creative imagination is itself and secular when it is allowed to become itself, on its own — that is, when it creates or imagines the really new. There is a considerable fear on the part of many imaginations and many artists that any relation to any concept of the Absolute or to religion will necessarily block this newness and freedom which is their special way of being secular. (Is this not still another cousin to fears and threats we feel in the air when we think of the relation of religion to the public schools?) And the fear is quite understandable because this is one of the images we have often constructed and communicated about the Absolute and about religion: that the latter has foreordained all things and has left no possibility for the truly new or for the truly secular. My own thought, on the contrary, is that Homer was on his own when he imagined the *Odyssey*, and Hemingway was on his own when he imagined *For Whom the Bell Tolls*, and both extended the idea of man into fresh fields and images.

I draw my next illustration for the meaning of secularity from the group of studies, research, and practice summed up as the new mental sciences (though here again we will have to take account of an interesting development of relationships between the secular on the one hand and the sacred, in a broad sense, on the other). The inner life of man has usually been the ground most pre-empted by the order of religion, but the new mental sciences, especially the history of psychoanalytic thinking and practice, have revealed the depth, number, and strength of the psychic forms and dynamisms in man which define his inward life independently of any moral or religious forms. They have defined that actuality and secularity in man which emerge as the fact to be dealt with by morality and religion. No forms constructed or imagined by the latter would any longer think of trying to negate them out of existence. There they are, defining a great deal of the very psychic substance of man. They might be called the psychic secularity of man.

There were all kinds of early quarrels between religion and these new sciences of the mind, so many that it is impossible to try to summarize them. It is doubtful, however, that the most traditional quarrel was really the most important for religion. I am thinking of the frontal attack (by the early psychoanalytic writers) on religion as neurosis and as projection, and as therefore unreal; this was equivalent to a form of secularity insisting on occupying the whole ground and telling the sacred, being irrelevant, to go drop dead. By far the more difficult problem for religion, I think, was the intrusion of an alien force into the area of human interiority — that is to say, for all practical purposes, into the area of the sacred. Add to this the fact that the new psychology was not really willing to remain psychological. Ernest Jones, one of the first great psychoanalytic handful and the biographer of Freud, tells us that the greatest achievement of the latter was not the exploration of the subconscious but the construction of the great dualism of the primary processes and the secondary processes, the dualism of the pleasure principle and the reality principle. Let us, therefore, not think for a moment that again the secular is not asserting itself to be moral, and more moral in the bargain than the sacred. Many a man has passed since through all those stages of analyses which lead him to curse the moralist Freud as the awful imposer of reality.

(Once again, in the very midst of our attempt to define the secular, we run into another form of our earlier question: What do we mean by a purely secular version of man's world? Are not the secular and the various forms of the sacred everywhere more intermingled in our day than we think? What "pure version" of the secular should possibly hope to be permanently established in the public schools?)

It would be possible to continue in an open-ended way with illustrations of secularity as I have chosen to work with the word in this essay. But that is not necessary. Even though there will always be argument in particular instances, the meaning is clear enough, I hope. Let secularity mean the emergence of nature and areas of nature according to their own forms, dynamisms, and history. Let it mean identity. Let it mean a sense of fact. I cannot help thinking that it is, among other things, a wider and more phenomenological translation of an older and more pious language, a language that had spoken of salvation but that had often restricted itself to an unhistorical world of the salvation of souls. Now we are enlarging this concept, as religion itself is in process of doing, and are extending the notions of identity, emergence, and salvation to all the forms of history and society within which the soul must breathe to become itself.

THE MEANING OF SACRED

If I turn at this point to the idea and the reality of God, to the point, that is, at which the idea and the reality of the sacred and religion come to their sharpest definition and focus, we will not, in such a transition, have to depart in the least from the dialectic chosen to define secularity and all its values. If I may rather take the New Testament for granted, surely one of the great motifs of the Old Testament is that, in relation to the mind and sensibility of man, God must be given His own identity. He is nothing other than Himself, and nothing else is like Him. Who is like unto God? The Jewish people are separated out from all other peoples in order that their God may also be separated out from all other gods. This God of the universe, who is not the universe, has His own absolute interiority, autonomy, and freedom. He will not tolerate losing His identity or being confused with anyone or anything else. Though He is certainly in everything else and participates in their struggle, He is also completely set aside as that intensity of self-possession which has no equal. It is the depth of this intensity of inner life, identity, and self-possession which is one of the great marks of the sacred, as it is the origin both of all fights against idols and of the worship and cult of the one, true God. All worship has its roots in the pre-eminence (but not in the isolation) of God's self-identity.

It should be easy to conclude, therefore, that the sacred, when so defined, is that supreme and universal principle in the universe which insists on secularity as the only thing in history and society which bodies forth its own nature. It is the generating force for all true secularity. It prevents the latter from being an ad hoc, a transient decision of a culture or of the universe, a decision which might be changed tomorrow. Secularity is the permanent reality of the whole universe. The sacred is its supreme and generating instance and ground.

According to this way of looking at things, the sacred is truly that which is set apart, in the most classical religious sense. But, and here is the source of the continuum between the two, so is the secular, in all its forms, that which is set apart. I suggest, therefore, that we no longer define the sacred merely as that which is set apart from the secular (and therefore worshiped) but as that which is pre-eminently set apart as the forms of the secular must also come to be set apart.

The spirit which would be most opposed to this common dialectic of the sacred and the secular is the spirit of reductionism. I may be talking of a common logic of the sacred and the secular, but it happens to be a logic which forbids reductionism. It forbids that the sacred ever be reduced to the secular; it forbids that any form of the secular ever be reduced to any other form of the secular. The values are the same in all orders, but not the identities. If we accept reductionism anywhere, we will equivalently be accepting it everywhere.

The Myth of Pure Secularity

Although I might and actually do believe that the case is so, I have no wish to prove in this paper that such a principle of secularity as has been described cannot survive without such a principle of religion and the sacred. There are those who will feel, affirmatively or negatively, for good or for bad, that this is the only question that matters in any discussion of religion in the public schools. My own central thought has been that there is important spadework to be done first in the construction and appraisal of vocabulary, ideas, and attitudes. Is it not important first to discover that possibly we are talking about the same things and about the same world when we talk about the secular and the sacred — that the latter, when it is most purely itself, is neither invader nor outsider in the values of a human world or of a set of public schools?

Not for political purposes or for accommodation but because the sacred is what it is, it must welcome and help to create a truly democratic society. It must be the enemy of every form of mechanical organization and collectivist society. Over against every concept of a mass society it must always wish to construct a true people, one whose ideal is that all its members are emergent, responsible, and self-actuating, not blown around and influenced, like reeds, by every wind from the outside, or subject to every demagogue and every fascination. Everyone in its membership should be able to say no as often as yes.

If true secularity, on the other hand, were looking for an ethos, a code of action, to insure its own steady construction, it would be difficult for it to invent anything better than the Ten Commandments. But it has done marvelous work over the centuries in concretizing so fundamental a code of action, and as filling in its interstices: in the great codes and systems of law, in the Magna Carta, the Bill of Rights, the documentation of human freedoms by the United Nations, the codes of customs, behavior, and honor of so many nations and cultures, and how many other endless forms of the implementation of the idea of the good.

I would like to say again that I strongly distrust the possibility or the advisability of a completely secular situation, in the public schools or anywhere else. The idea of the secular as a world which has been desacralized has served, and will continue to serve, several important dialectical purposes. But when pushed to its limits, when understood as a mechanically neutral area which must remain free of anything remotely approaching the sacred concepts of value, morality, religion, *this* secular world is a pure abstraction, rising twenty-four hours a day on its own hind feet to protest such an indignity, such a dehumanizing process. Is *this* concept of the secular (or of the public schools) an unreality, as irrelevant to any actual situation as religion or the preacher in the wild West, on the other hand, ever feared *themselves* to be?

This may very well be so true for the public schools that, ironically, the one thing that will bring its general moral and religious instincts to a slower and a slower movement in the next generation might be all the formal raisings of the issue toward which many of us are now tempted. Perhaps what we need is the giving of a more general assurance that the whole idea of a dehumanized secular order of any kind is a farce and that it is more than all right for a thousand natural human forces to exist or come into existence in our public schools.

Is it possible, therefore, that we will not in the foreseeable future have formal courses in religious instruction in the public schools? May it not turn out to be much more important that we come to see that the idea of a purely secular order is a myth and that every teacher is responsible in some part, in a thousand and different ways, for the moral life of his students?

PART FIVE

The Concept of the
Religiously Neutral School

17

Public and Private Values and Religious Educational Content

Paul H. Hirst

To anyone who cares about religious freedom and toleration, the American public school is a magnificent attempt at maintaining the strictest religious neutrality by the state while providing the best possible education for all. Yet, as the essays in this volume show, the system today faces harsh criticism from many sides. There are those who think its basic concept of neutrality spurious. There are those who think its educational intentions confused and mutually incompatible. There are those who think the theory fine but quite unworkable in important respects. But for all the criticisms, no clear alternative system has been produced which begins to maintain the neutrality of the state half so successfully while guarding the rights of minorities and protecting children from an education impregnated with religious or non-religious forms of indoctrination. What is perhaps most needed at present, then, is first a clarification and reformulation of the concept of common school education so that it is as coherent as possible and more genuinely neutral. And next, successful ways of embodying this clearer concept in the institutional working of the school need to be devised. It is with the first task that this paper is concerned, for the real significance of this conference would seem to lie in its contribution along these lines. Taking leads from other

essays in the volume, I shall first seek to clarify certain principles that necessarily underlie any coherent concept of religiously neutral education in
a common school, then comment on the kind of religious content that
can consistently figure in an education based on these principles.

Commitment to Common Values

In considering the principles underlying the common school, one simple
yet quite fundamental point must be maintained throughout. Whether
we like it or not, the whole enterprise of education is, from top to bottom,
value-ridden. It is surely just nonsense to think otherwise. The very
selection of what is to be taught involves major judgments of value. To
teach the chosen content involves attention to standards of value of many
kinds. Schools are institutions which involve complex human relationships
where not only moral ideas but also patterns of moral conduct are being
shaped. There must be rules and principles governing the functioning
of the institution if it is to be a civilized community at all, let alone an
educational one.

It follows directly that even if the common school is religiously neutral,
it cannot be neutral in morals, aesthetics, and other matters. If it were, it
would simply cease to be an educational institution. The whole notion
of the common school therefore presupposes an area of agreed moral and
other values that are compatible with the widest possible divergence in
religious and non-religious beliefs. If there is to be a common school at
all, there must be commitment to such a body of values, acceptable to
all irrespective of any particular religious or non-religious claims. The
schools cannot be morally neutral, but fortunately moral neutrality is not
entailed by religious neutrality, nor does moral commitment necessarily
presuppose any particular religious or non-religious commitment. What
matters, then, for the common school is that there be an appropriate area
of agreement on moral and other issues in spite of the religious differences
existing in the society. The forms of justification that are recognized for
these values may be diverse, but agreement on any particular form of
justification is not, in the first instance, necessary to the concept of the
common school. Disagreements about the forms of justification do have
important educational implications but they do not threaten the notion
of the common school itself, as is sometimes assumed.

PUBLIC AND PRIVATE BELIEFS

But can there be, in a multi-belief society, a body of common values
sufficient for the conduct of education? Even if we for the moment ignore
questions of justification, can we find an adequate consensus? The very
existence of a society with a common way of life and viable legal and
social institutions is a strong indication that a fair range of values is widely
shared. Yet religious and non-religious groups are extremely diverse in

their beliefs and consequently many seem to hold values that are not acceptable to others. In some areas, at any rate, the range of agreement would appear to be strictly limited. There is, however, some awareness, and a growing awareness, that a distinction can and must be drawn between what might be called the public and the private areas of values and beliefs. It is in terms of the public area of values that we can conceive the function of our public institutions, including the common school. Dr. Talcott Parsons in his essay in this symposium explores the distinction in some detail, rightly stressing that no once-for-all line of demarcation between the two domains can possibly be drawn. Nevertheless, there are grounds which make certain beliefs and values indisputably part of the public world — for instance, the domain of scientific knowledge. And certain conditions make other beliefs very strong candidates for the private area — for example, the domain of religious beliefs, which have no generally acceptable public tests of validity. If the distinction is made simply in terms of public agreement, then the boundary is certainly a changing one and the mandate for the public school will, at least to some extent, be variable.

What is particularly important here is the public acceptance of the principle that religious beliefs belong to the private domain. And with it goes the recognition that the values which necessarily rest on particular religious beliefs must also be regarded as private. The same thing is true of the beliefs and values associated with any non-religious or anti-religious *Weltanschauung* or philosophy of life. Within the common framework of what is publicly agreed, the individual is free to live a pattern of life, and also of course to have an education, that is consistent with his private beliefs. Indeed, it is one of the fundamental principles of the public domain in Western societies that he shall be free to do just that. Public institutions, however, must not involve themselves in any matters that turn on merely private values and this stricture applies to the public school.

PARTIAL EDUCATION

But the question remains: Is there an area of public values which permits the school to do a significant educational job? If not, then the notion of the religiously neutral school is a theoretical dream. What is quite certain is that, if the notion is practicable at all, the common school cannot be considered a place for the total education of children. Precisely because the area of public values is not in general the total area of values for any individual, and because questions about the justification of values are frequently outside its competence, there are aspects of education which it cannot appropriately undertake. That public schools necessarily have a limited scope is a simple point that needs much greater recognition than it normally gets. If the common school is to remain neutral vis-à-vis private beliefs and among different religions, its education must be partial education.[1]

The problem then is whether the notion of a partial education is in itself an idea offensive to some. There are certainly two ways in which it might be. In the first place, the education might be given so as to imply, in a subtle if not an obvious way, that no other elements of education are important. In that case it might be argued that certain non-religious beliefs are being favored at the expense of other beliefs. However, it is surely not true that a partial education need be given with such emphasis. This aberration can be guarded against in many ways; teachers can be made much more aware of their responsibilities in this respect, and the schools can publicly and repeatedly stress the limited nature of their work.

In the second place, partial education in a common school could be held to be offensive because the very separation of certain elements from the rest might be thought to distort all that is done. It is sometimes maintained that every element of education when adequately conducted depends as much on private as on public values. The two areas are indeed thought to interpenetrate inextricably in educational problems. Certain Christian thinkers in particular have strongly asserted this view. But is it in fact defensible when one examines the details of education? Can one not teach science and mathematics — and art, literature, and history too — without prejudging matters that are "private" in character? To maintain that one cannot is either to make claims about private values implicit in educational processes or to deny that there is a separable content of education that is fully public in nature. As to the former, it is by no means clear how private beliefs and values do enter, for instance, the teaching of science. Are there Christian methods of teaching Boyle's law that differ from atheistic methods? Provided we strictly consider any agreed content and the methods appropriate to communicating it, refusing to be sidetracked into discussing the presentation of other non-agreed issues, it is difficult to understand how methods could be distinguished on "private" grounds. It is not disputed that teachers can for "private" purposes use methods that involve "private" values. What is being contested is that if one is talking about the teaching of an agreed public content, the methods used *must* involve such values. That this is the case has not been demonstrated as far as I am aware.

To deny that there is any separable content of education that is fully public is to go against the principles that lie at the foundation of modern knowledge. The development of knowledge as distinct from opinion, both in arts subjects and in the sciences, has depended on the progressive establishment of public and objective canons of scholarship which are in principle universal and which are not dependent on private religious or non-religious beliefs. The existence of such canons is now recognized as a necessary condition for any valid claim to knowledge. We are surely at last clear that the problems of literary criticism and history are no more religious questions than the problems of the sciences. And this being so, education in these areas no longer reflects particular religious or non-religious commitments but is dependent solely on the canons appropriate to the domains. Where religious elements arise within these areas, their validity is not at stake, and full unprejudiced recognition of the diversity of private beliefs must be given in the interests of the objectivity demanded within the domains.

Of course what is often taught under the labels, say, of science and history can, and often does, involve considerations that are not strictly scientific or historical. One can under the teaching of science discuss the religious bearing of evolutionary theory, for example. One can in a history period go into the religious questions that arose during the Reformation. But to teach religion is not to teach science or history. What is being argued is that one can dissociate the teaching of science or history from questions of the truth of private beliefs and values. This is possible, though, only if one sticks to scientific questions. If one insists on trying to pass on matters in the area of private beliefs, then of course the limits of public agreement will be exceeded. But such offense is not at all necessary in a limited and partial education. The autonomy of the various domains of human knowledge is surely a fundamental guarantee that they can have their place within a genuinely religiously neutral education.[2] I conclude that there can be neutral public education, at any rate in established areas of knowledge.

Education and the Giving of Reasons

It has been maintained thus far that the common school, if it is to be religiously neutral, must confine itself to education that can be carried out within a framework of agreed public values. There is, however, a further guarantee of the strict neutrality of what is done, insofar as the school confines itself in all areas to the activities of education and teaching in their strictest senses. The sciences, for example, do not consist of a body of beliefs which have been merely agreed upon and passed on to the next generation; they constitute an area of human knowledge whose truths have survived public tests of observation and experiment. Public agreement on scientific truths is thus not a mere consensus of opinions but an agreement that is rationally compelled because the propositions can be seen by all prepared to examine the case, to be justified according to the relevant criteria. There is thus an objective warrant for what is taught in the sciences. Moreover, one could not be said to teach science in any strict sense if the foundations of its claims to truth were not being passed on. For a pupil to understand science as science demands that he appreciate that its claims must satisfy the public tests of observation and experiment. The teacher of science is therefore introducing him to a public world of discourse with its own criteria of validity. To fail to present the public foundation of scientific claims is to fail to educate in science. This introduction of pupils, not simply to a public domain of concepts and beliefs, but also to the public criteria for what is asserted, lies at the heart of all education, not just in the sciences, where the public tests are in principle so easy to recognize. The teacher, if he is educating, is concerned that pupils shall, as far as possible, grasp the validity and justification of the knowledge and beliefs he is passing on. His commitment is not directly to achieving the acceptance by pupils of certain statements or judgments. It is to their rationally understanding what he is presenting, to their discovering "the reason why" of things and therefore to their accepting them or not on the relevant grounds. What is demanded is that the teacher present matters according to their logical status. Claims that should satisfy public tests are recognized as standing or falling by these. Claims that are matters of debate are seen as such and those of pure conjecture are presented as just that. Thus in all things the teacher will be governed by the objective canons of the public world of reason, not by his own private beliefs and values.

We may have to recognize that much that goes on in the common school at present is not governed by such principles. What is frequently thought to be the teaching of history may often be the passing on of prejudice as if it were justifiable historical judgment. The critical canons appropriate to the subject may be too often ignored. Indoctrination may be being substituted for education. Nevertheless, the teaching of history in an objective manner is neither logically nor practically impossible. And further, it is above all by strict adherence to the canons of historical scholarship that religious neutrality in teaching in this area can be achieved.

Education in Agreed Beliefs and Values

But if the common school can legitimately hope to provide strictly neutral education in the areas of its activity where there are acceptable rational foundations, what is its province in other spheres? What is its function in moral matters? At its lowest, the school cannot in fact evade a minimum amount of moral training, if only to enable it to get on with the teaching of science, history, etc. But we need to get clear about the limits of the task it can consistently undertake in moral education. It is in this area that the school tends to be thrown back onto building on a mere consensus of values. There is wide agreement on many moral values in Western societies, even if equally clear agreement on the way these values can be justified is lacking, the school would therefore seem to have some right to instruct pupils in the accepted principles and their application, and to insist on practical adherence to these. But from what has been said previously, if the school is to educate in this area and not merely to train or even perhaps to indoctrinate, the question of the justification of the values cannot be simply ignored. Objectivity would seem to demand, in this situation, first the full recognition that there is in fact agreement on these values, and that the school is not being arbitrary in the moral principles it adopts, and second, as indicated above, the recognition that very diverse forms of justification are given in the society for the values — justifications frequently based on "private" beliefs. How far it is legitimate for the school to concern itself with the different justifications will be briefly commented on in due course. Obviously, moral education in these terms is incomplete both in the range of values with which it is concerned and in its approach to them. Nevertheless there is once more nothing here which need offend the adherents of any particular *Weltanschauung* or religion.

Yet it must not be too readily assumed that agreement on the justification of moral principles is unattainable.[3] There are indications of a growing awareness even among religious believers that at least some fundamental moral principles may be autonomous vis-à-vis religious beliefs and that independently of "private" appeals some form of public rational justification might be given for them. Indeed we frequently engage in straight rational argument with children on matters of stealing, respect for persons, and other basic moral principles. Insofar as such forms of justification can be established, a much more satisfactory form of moral education becomes possible in the public school. As in other areas, instruction in the critical foundations of moral principles is then permissible. Just such a rational approach to moral questions is beginning to be developed in some English schools.

The possibility of the rational justification of a body of moral principles, besides opening up a new approach to moral education, might equally well provide a much more satisfactory basis for the whole concept of the public school itself. The distinction between the public and private areas of belief and values has here been drawn in terms of simple agreement and disagreement in the society. Yet within the sphere of agreement it has been pointed out that some agreement is mere consensus of opinion whereas some is rationally compelled on the basis of public criterion. In public education we are at present committed to working on moral values for which there is only general consensus. If the rationally compelled agreement could be extended to include these moral values too, then the distinction between the public and the private domains could be made not in terms of mere agreement and disagreement but in terms of the justifiable in public rational terms and the dependent on private beliefs. In that case the concept of the public school would no longer hinge on mere agreement on beliefs and values. It would rest simply on the existence of a body of rationally justifiable beliefs and values. Its neutrality toward private beliefs and values would then be maintained by its provision of education in the strictest sense within that rational framework. At the moment such a concept is hardly viable, and the schools must educate on a foundation which contains a hard core of rational knowledge and belief and a penumbra of merely agreed beliefs and values. The hope is that the area of the hard core will progressively increase and the dependence on mere agreement become progressively less.

Education in Private Beliefs and Values

Whatever developments there may be in these directions, the education the public school can offer will necessarily remain partial in its scope as long as a domain of private beliefs and values exists. There will remain too the question of the function of the public school in relation to private beliefs. What teaching, then, of or about religious and other private beliefs is consistent with the concept of the public school as here considered? To reply "None" is of course absurd, for such beliefs have played an extremely important part in human affairs and no adequate education in, for example, history or literature can possibly ignore this fact. We are faced not only with no generally acceptable rational foundation for the beliefs but with no agreement about the beliefs themselves. How are we to remain within the agreed values that provide the school's framework? Surely the principle that will again maintain neutrality is the school's educational commitment, to teach everything strictly according to its rational status. Private beliefs must then be presented as private beliefs about which men are disagreed. But it must also be communicated that there is disagreement as to how one would ever know which beliefs are to be accepted. People differ in the evidence they think it appropriate to consider and how it should be understood. The area is thus a radically controversial one, in which people come to very different conclusions. It is again important that the school emphasize the limitations of its legitimate task so that no false inferences are drawn about the significance in human life of private beliefs. That there is radical disagreement on these issues is no indication that the issues are unimportant. What is more, a person must take up some position on the issues and that position will have significant consequences in his life. In dealing with these beliefs, then, the school must be true to their character, distorting neither their status nor their implications.

What must be, and is, universally rejected is instruction in private beliefs as if they were part of the domain for which there are publicly agreed rational criteria. Nor must they be presented as if the beliefs themselves were accepted even though there is dispute about the grounds of belief. But to reject these approaches is to reject forms of indoctrination, not to reject religious education. Provided that in this area, as in all others, the school accepts the canons of rational objectivity as governing all that is said, it is hard to see why any matters of private belief cannot be properly dealt with. In particular the teacher can perfectly well discuss the different forms of "private" justification for the generally accepted moral values of our society. In this way at least some forms of backing for our values will be presented to pupils, even if it is appreciated that people differ in their estimates of these. The teacher must of course remain firm on the private character of beliefs of this kind and refrain entirely from any suggestion that there are established public criteria for dealing with the claims in these areas.

Questions of Objectivity

The public school's function in religious matters is now customarily described as that of teaching about religion rather than teaching of religion. This supposedly indicates the objective nature of what can be legitimately undertaken. The phrase "teaching about religion" is, however, open to misunderstanding. It has sometimes been taken to imply that the school must not concern itself with religious beliefs in themselves as distinctive claims but only with the history or sociology of religious beliefs, or with their historical or literary bearing. Certainly, in such studies the objectivity of the treatment can be carefully guarded, for questions about the truth or falsity of the beliefs are irrelevant. That the beliefs are or were held is all that is important. But it is surely a mistake to think that one can seriously study the history of religion or the significance of certain beliefs in literature without a clear understanding of religious claims, their implications, and the kind of justification they are thought to have. One cannot discuss the history of science or the influence of scientific theories on literature without a very good grasp of science, its implications, and the kind of justification it demands. In just the same way, to take seriously the history of the Christian faith or the significance of Christian beliefs in the writings of T. S. Eliot one must be able to pick out Christian beliefs as such and grasp their basic character and significance, and that involves appreciating the kind of claims they make as claims to truth.

To teach about religion in these senses, then, the teacher must either presuppose an understanding of religious claims for what they are in their own right or pursue such an understanding as the literary or historical study develops. It is surely just a confusion to think that these approaches can be adequately followed without considering religious beliefs as making distinctive claims. But this is not to say that the treatment of the beliefs need be anything but an objective one in which fundamental disagreement on their acceptability and justification is recognized. In an adequate treatment one must seek to present religious concepts and propositions so that pupils can enter into their meaning without any prejudging of questions of truth. It certainly involves showing the kind of claim to truth that is made, however. It demands enabling pupils to see how believers look at the world and human experience, in an imaginative grasp of what makes the believer tick. It means getting a glimpse of the world "through religious glasses," a procedure which must surely come before looking at religion "through secular glasses."[4] After all, religions are claimed to be ways of seeing things, and not just cultural objects to be observed, say, historically. But there are alternative sets of religious glasses, each giving a different view, and it is not the function of the public school to determine in any way which, if any, its pupils shall wear. To imaginatively appreciate beliefs for what they are is one thing; to accept them is another. Appreciation can surely be within the purview of the school even if matters of commitment are not.

Although religious education in these terms may be consistent with the principles that underlie the common school, the practical provision of it might well prove extremely difficult. Many teachers are at present quite incapable of this objective teaching of religion. What is more, it is far from certain when, in the general educational development of children, they may appropriately be introduced to any systematic treatment of such important yet controversial issues. Faced with the alarming evidence of current practices contained in Rabbi Gilbert's chapter, one cannot but agree with his conclusion that there should be much careful experiment and investigation in this area rather than hasty attempts at radical change. It must also be recognized, as Dr. Olafson has pointed out in his chapter, that religious education in these terms is likely to have little or none of the direct moral effect that many would like to see. Yet there is here a vast task of promoting religious understanding, which I have maintained is thoroughly within the province of the religiously neutral public school. It may be a difficult task and one not to be undertaken lightly. But if it could be agreed on and seriously taken up, it would be an educational achievement of no small importance. I have sought in these pages to shed some light on the matters of principle that must lie behind any such enterprise in the common school. My only hope is that the light that is within me is not darkness, and that this outsider has not totally misread the American situation.

NOTES

1. The distinction here being drawn between the public and private domains is in some respects coincident with the distinction between the domains of church and state emphasized by Rabbi Borowitz in Chapter 14 of this volume. There is, however, at least this difference, that for Rabbi Borowitz, matters of religion cannot by the nature of the case ever be the legitimate concern of the modern democratic state; they must therefore remain part of the private domain, no matter what public agreement there might come to be about them.

2. I am in complete agreement with Dr. Wolterstorff (see Chapter 1 in this volume) that the only possible form of neutrality the public school can hope to achieve is his "affirmative impartiality," in which "Nothing that the public school says or does shall have as its purpose, or as an avoidable feature or effect of its manner of achieving its purpose, the manifesting of approval or disapproval of some citizen's religion or irreligion." What I have here tried to argue is that there is no good reason for thinking that a partial education cannot be given within this principle.

3. For a discussion of this whole problem and its educational significance, see R. S. Peters, *Ethics and Education* (Allen and Unwin, 1966).

4. See Chapter 4, by Frederick A. Olafson, in this volume.

Selected Bibliography

prepared by
PAUL E. CAWEIN
Harvard Graduate School of Education

Theology and Philosophy

*Bayles, Ernest E. *Pragmatism in Education.* New York: Harper & Row, 1966.

*Buber, Martin. *Between Man and Man.* New York: Macmillan, 1965.

*————. *I and Thou.* New York: Scribner's, 1958.

Butler, Richard, O.P. *God on the Secular Campus.* New York: Doubleday, 1963.

*Christ, Frank L., and Gerard E. Sherry, eds. *American Catholicism and the Intellectual Ideal.* New York: Appleton-Century-Crofts, 1961.

*Cox, Harvey. *The Secular City.* New York: Macmillan, 1965.

*Dawson, Christopher. *The Crisis of Western Education.* New York: Sheed & Ward, 1961 (Doubleday Image).

*Eiseley, Loren. *The Firmament of Time.* New York: Atheneum, 1960.

Finkelstein, Louis, ed. *The Jews: Their History, Culture, and Religion,* 3rd ed. New York: Harper, 1960.

Friedman, Maurice S. *Martin Buber: The Life of Dialogue.* New York: Harper, 1960.

*Frye, Northrop. *Fables of Identity.* New York: Harcourt, Brace, & World, 1963.

*Fuller, Edmond, ed. *The Christian Idea of Education.* New Haven: Yale University Press, 1957.

*————. *Schools and Scholarship: The Christian Idea of Education, Part Two.* New Haven: Yale University Press, 1962.

Jaspers, Karl. *The Idea of the University.* Boston: Beacon, 1959.

Lynch, William F., S.J. *The Integrating Mind.* New York: Sheed & Ward, 1962.

Lynn, Robert. *Protestant Strategies in Education.* New York: Association Press, 1964.

* Titles preceded by asterisks here and on the following pages are available in paperback. In cases in which the original publisher differs from the paperback publisher, the latter is listed in parenthesis.

*McCluskey, Neil G., S.J. *Catholic Viewpoint on Education.* New York: Doubleday, 1959.

*————. *Public Schools and Moral Education.* New York: Columbia University Press, 1958.

————. *Religion and the Schools.* New York: Columbia University Press, 1964.

*Maritain, Jacques. *The Aims of Education.* New Haven: Yale University Press, 1964.

*Morris, Van Cleve. *Existentialism in Education: What it Means.* New York: Harper & Row, 1966.

*Niebuhr, Richard. *The Kingdom of God in America.* New York: Harper, 1959.

Nielson, Niels C. *God in Education.* New York: Sheed & Ward, 1966.

*Polanyi, Michael. *Personal Knowledge.* Chicago: Chicago University Press, 1958 (New York, Harper).

Taylor, Marvin, ed. *An Introduction to Christian Education.* Nashville: Abingdon, 1966.

Thelen, Herbert A. *Education and the Human Quest.* New York: Harper & Row, 1960.

*Tillich, Paul. *Theology of Culture.* New York: Oxford University Press, 1959.

Trilling, Lionel. *Beyond Culture.* New York: Viking, 1965.

Ulich, Robert, ed. *Education and the Idea of Mankind.* New York: Harcourt, Brace & World, 1964.

————. *The Human Career, A Philosophy of Self Transcendence.* New York: Harper, 1955.

Vorspan, Albert, and Eugene Lipman. *Justice and Judaism.* New York: Union of American Hebrew Colleges, 1959.

Behavioral and Social Sciences

Benson, Purnell H. *Religion in Contemporary Culture: A Study of Religion Through Social Science.* New York: Harper, 1960.

*Brameld, Theodore. *Education as Power.* New York: Holt, Rinehart & Winston, 1965.

*————. *The Use of Explosive Ideas in Education.* Pittsburgh: University of Pittsburgh Press, 1965.

————, and Stanley Elam, eds. *Values in American Education. Phi Delta Kappan* Symposium Report, 1964.

Bruner, Jerome S. *Toward a Theory of Instruction.* Cambridge: Harvard University Press, 1966.

*Cogley, John, ed. *Religion in America.* New York: Meridian, 1958.

*Cremin, Lawrence S. *The Transformation of the School.* New York: Knopf, 1962 (Vintage, 1961).

DeVries, Egbert, ed. *Man in Community*. New York: Association Press, 1966.

Dunn, William Kailer. *What Happened to Religious Education?* Baltimore: Johns Hopkins University Press, 1958.

*Erikson, Erik H. *Childhood and Society*, 2nd ed. New York: Norton, 1963.

*———. *Identity and the Life Cycle*. New York: International University Press (*Psychological Issues*, Vol. I, No. 1), 1959.

*Fichter, Joseph H., S.J. *Parochial School: A Sociological Study*. South Bend, Ind.: University of Notre Dame Press, 1958 (Doubleday Anchor).

Goldman, Ronald. *Religious Thinking from Childhood to Adolescence*. London: Routledge & Kegan Paul, 1964.

*Goodman, Paul. *Compulsory Mis-Education and the Community of Scholars*. New York: Horizon, 1964 (Vintage).

Greeley, Andrew M. *Religion and Career*. New York: Sheed & Ward, 1963.

———, and Peter H. Rossi. *The Education of American Catholics*. Chicago: Aldine, 1966.

*Henry, Jules. *Culture Against Man*. New York: Random House, 1963.

Keniston, Kenneth. *The Uncommitted: Alienated Youth in American Society*. New York: Harcourt, Brace & World, 1965.

*Kimball, Solon T., and James E. McClellan. *Education and the New America*. New York: Random House, 1962.

Kolesnik, Walter B., and Edward J. Power, eds. *Catholic Education: A Book of Readings*. New York: McGraw-Hill, 1965.

*Loukes, Harold. *Readiness for Religion*. Wallingford, Pa.: Pendle Hill Pamphlets, 1963.

———. *New Ground in Christian Education*. London: S.C.M., 1965.

Neuwien, Reginald A., ed. *Catholic Schools in Action*. South Bend, Ind.: University of Notre Dame Press, 1966.

Niblett, W. R. *Christian Education in a Secular Society*. London: Oxford University Press, 1960.

———. *Moral Education in a Changing Society*. London: Farber & Fischer, 1963.

*Oliver, Donald W., and James P. Shaver. *Teaching Public Issues in the High School*. Boston: Houghton Mifflin, 1966.

Parsons, Talcott. *Social Structure and Personality*. New York: Free Press, 1964.

*Peck, Robert F., and Robert J. Havighurst. *The Psychology of Character Development*. New York: Wiley, 1960.

Peters, Richard S. *Authority, Responsibility and Education*. New York: Hill and Wang, 1960 (New York, Atherton, 1966).

Phenix, Philip H. *Religious Concerns in Contemporary Education*. New York: Columbia University Press, 1959.

*Piaget, Jean. *The Moral Judgment of the Child*. New York: Free Press, 1965.

Royce, Joseph R. *The Encapsulated Man*. New York: Van Nostrand, 1965.

Sebaly, A. L., ed. *Teacher Education and Religion.* Oneonta, N. Y.: American Association of Colleges for Teacher Education, 1959.

Sherif, Muzafer, and Carolyn Sherif. *Reference Groups: Exploration into Conformity and Deviation of Adolescents.* New York: Harper & Row, 1964.

Smith, James W., and A. Leland Jamison, eds. *Religious Perspectives in American Culture.* Princeton: Princeton University Press, 1961.

Sweet, William W. *Story of Religion in America.* New York: Harper, 1950.

*Toynbee, Arnold. *Christianity Among the Religions of the World.* New York: Scribner's, 1957.

*Weiner, Norbert. *God and Golem, Inc.: A Comment on Certain Points Where Cybernetics Impinges on Religion.* Cambridge: M.I.T. Press, 1966.

Law and Political Science

Bennett, John C. *Christians and the State.* New York: Scribner's, 1958.

Blanshard, Paul. *Religion and the Schools: The Great Controversy.* Boston: Beacon, 1963.

Blum, Virgil C., S.J. *Freedom in Education: Federal Aid for All Children.* Garden City, N.Y.: Doubleday, 1965.

*Boles, Donald E. *The Bible, Religion and the Public Schools,* 3rd ed. Ames, Ia.: Iowa State University Press, 1965 (Crowell-Collier).

Brickman, William W., and Stanley Lehrer, eds. *Religion, Government, and Education.* New York: Society for the Advancement of Education, 1961.

Dierenfield, R. B. *Religion in American Public Schools.* New York: Public Affairs Press, 1962.

Douglas, William O. *The Bible and the Schools.* Boston: Little, Brown, 1966.

Drinan, Robert F., S.J. *Religion, the Courts and Public Policy.* New York: McGraw-Hill, 1963.

Drouin, Edmond G., F.I.C. *The School Question: A Bibliography on Church-State Relations in American Education, 1949–1960.* Washington: Catholic University Press, 1963.

*Duker, Sam. *The Public Schools and Religion: The Legal Context.* New York: Harper & Row, 1966.

Freund, Paul A., and Robert Ulich. *Religion and the Public Schools.* Cambridge: Harvard University Press, 1965.

*Gordis, Robert, *et al. Religion and the Schools.* New York: Fund for the Republic, 1959.

Healey, Robert M. *Jefferson on Religion in Public Education.* New Haven: Yale University Press, 1962.

Howe, Mark deWolfe. *The Garden and the Wilderness: Religion and Government in American Constitutional History.* Chicago: Chicago University Press, 1965.

Katz, Wilber G. *Religion and American Constitutions.* Evanston, Ill., Northwestern University Press, 1964.

LaNoue, George R. *Public Funds for Parochial Schools.* New York: National Council of Churches of Christ in the U.S.A., 1963.

*Loder, James E. *Religion and the Public Schools.* New York: Association Press, 1965.

Powell, Theodore. *The School Bus Law,* Middletown, Conn.: Wesleyan University Press, 1960.

Stokes, Anson Phelps, and Leo Pfeffer. *Church and State in the United States.* New York: Harper & Row, 1965.

*Walter, Erich A., ed. *Religion and the State University.* Ann Arbor: University of Michigan Press, 1958.

List of Participants

Allen, Mr. Yorke, Jr., Rockefeller Brothers Fund, New York, New York

Ball, Mr. William B., General Counsel, Pennsylvania Catholic Conference, Harrisburg, Pennsylvania

Barth, Mr. Roland S., Assistant to the Dean, Harvard Graduate School of Education, Cambridge, Massachusetts

Benignus, Miss Emma Lou, Associate Professor of Education, Episcopal Theological School, Cambridge, Massachusetts

Borowitz, Rabbi Eugene B., Professor of Education and Jewish Religious Thought, Hebrew Union College, Jewish Institute of Religion, New York, New York

Brickman, Prof. William W., Professor of Comparative Education, School of Education, University of Pennsylvania, Philadelphia, Pennsylvania

Brown, Dr. Charles E., Superintendent of Schools, Newton Public Schools, Newton, Massachusetts

Brown, Dr. Sterling W., President, National Conference of Christians and Jews, New York, New York

Buchner, The Rev. Frederick, School Minister and Chairman, Department of Religion, Exeter Academy, Exeter, New Hampshire

Cawein, Mr. Paul, Harvard Graduate School of Education, Cambridge, Massachusetts

Cleveland, The Rev. Thomas, Chaplain and Chairman, Department of Religion, Milton Academy, Milton, Massachusetts

Cooney, Mr. John, Director, Interreligious Programming, National Conference of Christians and Jews, New York, New York

Cox, Dr. Harvey G., Jr., Associate Professor of Church and Society, Harvard Divinity School, Cambridge, Massachusetts

Crocker, The Rev. John, Headmaster Emeritus, Groton School, Groton, Massachusetts

Deneen, Rev. James, Superintendent of Diocesan Schools, Evansville, Indiana

Dillenberger, Dr. John, Dean, Graduate Theological Union, Berkeley, California

Dowell, Mr. Chris, Harvard Graduate School of Education, Cambridge, Massachusetts

Drachler, Dr. Norman, Associate Superintendent of Schools, Detroit, Michigan

Dreibelbis, Mr. Paul, Associate Director, Instruction for Social Studies, Pittsburgh Public Schools, Pittsburgh, Pennsylvania

347

Drinan, Rev. Robert F., S.J., Dean, Boston College School of Law, Boston, Massachusetts

Eisenstein, Rabbi Ira, Editor, *The Reconstructionist*, New York, New York
Elder, Mr. John, Assistant to the Dean, Harvard Divinity School, Cambridge, Massachusetts

Fister, Mr. J. Blaine, Director, Religion and Public Education, National Council of Churches, New York, New York

Geer, Mr. William D., Jr., Principal, Newton South High School, Newton Centre, Massachusetts
Gilbert, Rabbi Arthur, Director, National Department of Religious Curriculum Research, Anti-Defamation League of B'nai B'rith, New York, New York
Graubard, Mr. Stephen, Editor, *Daedalus*, American Academy of Arts and Sciences, Brookline, Massachusetts
Guy, The Rev. William, Bethesda Baptist Church, Port Chester, New York

Hirst, Mr. Paul H., Professor of Education, King's College, University of London, London, England
Horchler, Mr. Richard, Director, National Program Development, National Conference of Christians and Jews, New York, New York
Hornback, Dr. Jack, Superintendent of Schools, South Huntington, Long Island, New York
Hunt, Dr. Herold C., Charles William Eliot Professor of Education, Harvard Graduate School of Education, Cambridge, Massachusetts
Hunter, Dr. Carmen, Chairman, Department of Education, Episcopal National Executive Council, New York, New York

Jarrett, Dr. James L., Associate Dean and Professor of Education, University of California, Berkeley, California

Katz, Prof. Wilbur, University of Wisconsin Law School, Madison, Wisconsin
Kircher, Dr. Everett, Professor of Philosophy of Education, Ohio State University, Columbus, Ohio
Kohlberg, Prof. Lawrence, Associate Professor of Psychology and Human Development, University of Chicago, Chicago, Illinois
Kuhn, Dr. Harold, Visiting Scholar, Harvard Divinity School, Cambridge, Massachusetts
LaNoue, Dr. George R., Assistant Professor of Government and Education, Teachers College, Columbia University, New York, New York
Letson, Dr. John W., Superintendent of Schools, Atlanta, Georgia
Lipp, The Rev. Frederick, First Unitarian Church, Beverly, Massachusetts
Little, Dr. Lawrence C., Chairman, Department of Religious Education, School of Education, University of Pittsburgh, Pittsburgh, Pennsylvania
Long, Dr. Herbert, Dean of Students, Harvard Divinity School, Cambridge, Massachusetts
Lynch, Rev. William, S.J., Department of Religion, St. Peter's College, Jersey City, New Jersey

McCarren, The Rt. Rev. Monsignor Edgar P., Superintendent of Diocesan Schools, Rockville Center, New York

McCluskey, Rev. Neil G., S.J., Department of Religious Education, University of Notre Dame, Notre Dame, Indiana

MacDonald, Mr. William D., Education Editor, College Department, Houghton Mifflin Company, Boston, Massachusetts

Martin, Mr. David, Teacher, Underwood School, Newton, Massachusetts

Martin, Dr. Jane, Lecturer and Research Associate in Education, Harvard Graduate School of Education, Cambridge, Massachusetts

Martin, Dr. John Henry, Superintendent of Schools, Mount Vernon, New York

Michaelsen, Dr. Robert, Chairman of Religious Studies, University of California, Santa Barbara, California

Miller, Dr. Samuel H., Dean and John Lord O'Brian Professor of Divinity, Harvard Divinity School, Cambridge, Massachusetts

Morris, Dr. Van Cleve, Professor of Philosophy and Education, University of Illinois at Chicago Circle, Chicago, Illinois

Nash, Dr. Paul, Associate Professor of Philosophy and Education, Boston University, Boston, Massachusetts

Newmann, Dr. Fred M., Assistant Professor of Education, Harvard Graduate School of Education, Cambridge, Massachusetts

Ober, Mr. Nathaniel, Assistant Superintendent of Schools, Minneapolis, Minnesota

Olafson, Dr. Frederick A., Professor of Education and Philosophy, Harvard Graduate School of Education, Cambridge, Massachusetts

Oliver, Dr. Donald W., Professor of Education, Harvard Graduate School of Education, Cambridge, Massachusetts

O'Neil, Rev. Michael, St. Peter's Church, Cambridge, Massachusetts, and Doctoral Candidate, Harvard Graduate School of Education

Parsons, Dr. Talcott, Professor of Sociology, Harvard University, Cambridge, Massachusetts

Peterson, Dr. Walfred H., Director, Research Services, Baptist Joint Committee on Public Affairs, Washington, D.C.

Pfeffer, Dr. Leo, Professor of Constitutional Law, Long Island University, and Consultant, American Jewish Congress, New York, New York

Plantinga, Dr. Alvin, Chairman, Department of Philosophy, Calvin College, Grand Rapids, Michigan

Plotch, Mr. Walter, Educational Director, Anti-Defamation League of B'nai B'rith, New England Regional Office, Boston, Massachusetts

Powell, Dr. Theodore, Executive Officer, Connecticut State Board for Regional Community Colleges, Hartford, Connecticut

Price, The Rev. Charles, Preacher to the University, Harvard University, Cambridge, Massachusetts

Scheffler, Dr. Israel, Victor S. Thomas Professor of Education and Philosophy, Harvard Graduate School of Education, Cambridge, Massachusetts

Shedd, Dr. Mark, Superintendent of Schools, Englewood, New Jersey

Sizer, Dr. Theodore R., Dean of the Faculty of Education, Harvard Graduate School of Education, Cambridge, Massachusetts

Sobol, Mr. Thomas, Chairman, Department of English, Fox Lane School, Bedford, New York

Spivey, Dr. Robert, Chairman, Department of Religion, Florida State University, Tallahassee, Florida

Stackhouse, Dr. Max L., Assistant Professor of Christian Ethics, Andover Newton Theological School, Newton Centre, Massachusetts

Stager, Mr. Jay, Teacher of Mathematics, Manchester High School, Manchester, Connecticut

Stahmer, Dr. Harold, Associate Professor of Religion, Barnard College, New York, New York

Starr, Prof. Isadore, Queens College, New York, New York, and Chairman, National Council of Social Studies

Stendahl, Dr. Krister, Frothingham Professor of Biblical Studies, Harvard Divinity School, Cambridge, Massachusetts

Warshaw, Mr. Thayer, Teacher of English, Newton High School, Newton, Massachusetts

Watts, Mr. W. Glenn, Harvard Graduate School of Education, Cambridge, Massachusetts

Whittaker, Miss Grace, Chairman, Department of English, Dorchester High School, Boston, Massachusetts

Wicks, Mr. Robert, Chairman, Department of Religion, Lawrenceville School, Lawrenceville, New Jersey

Wolterstorff, Dr. Nicholas, Professor of Philosophy, Calvin College, Grand Rapids, Michigan

Index

351